# History of Computing

**Founding Editor**
Martin Campbell-Kelly

**Series Editor**
Gerard Alberts, Institute for Mathematics, University of Amsterdam,
Amsterdam, The Netherlands

**Advisory Editors**
Gerardo Con Diaz, University of California, Davis, CA, USA
Jack Copeland, University of Canterbury, Christchurch, New Zealand
Ulf Hashagen, Deutsches Museum, München, Germany
Valérie Schafer, ISCC, CNRS, Paris, France
John V. Tucker, Department of Computer Science, Swansea University,
Swansea, UK

The *History of Computing* series publishes high-quality books which address the history of computing, with an emphasis on the 'externalist' view of this history, more accessible to a wider audience. The series examines content and history from four main quadrants: the history of relevant technologies, the history of the core science, the history of relevant business and economic developments, and the history of computing as it pertains to social history and societal developments.

Titles can span a variety of product types, including but not exclusively, themed volumes, biographies, 'profile' books (with brief biographies of a number of key people), expansions of workshop proceedings, general readers, scholarly expositions, titles used as ancillary textbooks, revivals and new editions of previous worthy titles.

These books will appeal, varyingly, to academics and students in computer science, history, mathematics, business and technology studies. Some titles will also directly appeal to professionals and practitioners of different backgrounds.

John F. Dooley

# The Gambler and the Scholars

Herbert Yardley, William & Elizebeth Friedman, and the Birth of Modern American Cryptology

 Springer

John F. Dooley
William and Marilyn Ingersoll Professor Emeritus
of Computer Science
Knox College
Galesburg, IL, USA

ISSN 2190-6831          ISSN 2190-684X   (electronic)
History of Computing
ISBN 978-3-031-28320-8          ISBN 978-3-031-28318-5   (eBook)
https://doi.org/10.1007/978-3-031-28318-5

This Springer imprint is published by the registered company Springer Nature Switzerland AG
The registered company address is: Gewerbestrasse 11, 6330 Cham, Switzerland

*For Diane, Patrick, and for David Kahn*

# Preface

These days pretty much everyone has heard of the various cryptologic agencies of the US Government. The National Security Agency (NSA) comes to mind first, but there are also cryptologic groups in the FBI, CIA, State Department, Secret Service, and other departments of the government. These organizations are arguably the most sophisticated—and secretive—on the planet. It was not always like this. While the major European and Asian powers have had permanent, professional code and cipher bureaus for several hundred years, the United States did not have a permanent code and cipher organization until after World War I.

This book is the story of how that permanent organization came to be. More specifically, it is the story of the two men and one woman who were there at the beginning and were instrumental in the creation of modern American cryptology and our modern code and cipher organizations.

For the first one hundred fifty years of its existence, the United States depended on ad hoc intelligence organizations that would come into being in the Army and Navy during wartime and just as quickly disappear as soon as peace was finalized. As late as March 1917, just as America was getting ready to enter World War I, the entire military intelligence organization of the US Army consisted of a single officer stationed in Washington, DC. That officer, Major Ralph van Deman, however, was the right person in the right place at the right time. Van Deman was determined to create a professional military intelligence section for the United States and hopefully have it continue in existence after the war. Van Deman did two things in the spring of 1917 that made his dream come true. First, he worked out an arrangement with a private research laboratory in Illinois to decrypt secret messages for the Army while the new Army intelligence operation was being set up. Second, he went looking for ambitious government employees who were interested in intelligence. These two acts brought to the Army's attention three individuals, Herbert Yardley, William Friedman, and Elizebeth Smith Friedman.

We will explore their origins and examine how they came to learn the arcane science of cryptology. We will look at how they came to cryptology because of happenstance and then the entry of the United States into World War I and the efforts they made to make sure the United States had the best code and cipher experts in the world. In 1917, Herbert Osborn Yardley, a young telegrapher from Indiana, was a code clerk in the U.S. State Department who had become interested in codes and ciphers. Interested enough that he had broken the State Department's own systems. After the Americans entered the Great War, Yardley was referred to van Deman and talked himself into a job heading up a fledgling cryptanalytic bureau in the US Army. At the same time, William Fredrick Friedman, a Russian immigrant of Jewish descent, and his wife, Elizebeth Smith Friedman, a mid-Western Quaker, were working on the Illinois prairie for an eccentric millionaire in a private research laboratory and trying to decode cryptograms that may have been found in the plays of William Shakespeare. Just as Yardley was convincing the Army to set up a cryptanalytic organization, the Friedmans were volunteered by their boss and approved by van Deman to set up a group to decrypt messages sent to them by the Army, Justice, and Treasury departments. For all three of these people, this was the beginning of life-long careers in code and cipher creation and breaking that would transform the American intelligence community.

All three of our subjects have had biographies written about them. William was first, with an unfortunately flawed biography commissioned by Elizebeth Friedman and written by Ronald Clark within a decade of his death in 1969. Yardley's excellent biography was written by the cryptologic historian David Kahn in 2004, 46 years after Yardley's death in 1958. Elizebeth was last, with her first—and excellent—biography appearing in 2017, 37 years after her own death. What none of these biographies have done, however, is to deeply examine the relationships between these three remarkable people, their competition, friendship, and later animosity, and how their paths continued to cross over the course of 40 years. That is what the current book hopes to do. The book draws on resources from the Library of Congress, the National Archives, the National Security Agency's Archives, the collections of the National Cryptologic Museum Library, where David Kahn's and the Yardley's papers are housed, the Research Library at the George Marshall Foundation, where William and Elizebeth Friedman's papers are held, and the papers of a number of other people who were instrumental in the creation of the American intelligence community and which are held in a number of other collections. As much as possible, I have tried to take materials, stories, and quotes directly from the words and writings of Yardley and the two Friedmans.

Galesburg, IL, USA                                                                         John F. Dooley
26 January 2023

# Acknowledgments

This book is the result of over a decade of work, so there are many people to thank. I would like to thank the library staff at Knox College for their patient and professional help in finding copies of many of the articles and books referenced here. The Faculty Development office at Knox College provided me with travel and research funds for several years so I could work on various projects, including this one. My colleagues in the Computer Science department at Knox were always supportive and encouraging of my research. I would also like to thank the staff of the National Archives and Records Administration (NARA) in College Park, MD, Librarians René Stein and Rob Simpson in the Research Library at the National Cryptologic Museum in Ft. Meade, MD, and Paul Barron, Jeffrey Kozak, and Melissa Davis of the George C. Marshall Foundation Research Library in Lexington, VA for their excellent help. Thanks also to Wayne Wheeler and his excellent team at Springer Nature. They are always a pleasure to work with. As always, the World Wide Web allows a writer in the middle of the American prairie to access libraries and archives around the country and the world, for which I am very grateful. Thanks to an anonymous reviewer of the first draft of the manuscript who did herculean work and made a large number of very helpful suggestions that have improved the text greatly. Thanks also to our furry feline roommates Arlo and Janis for walking on the keyboard at all the right moments. And, of course, special thanks to my wife, Diane, who inspires me, encourages, me, and—above the call of duty—reads and edits everything I write (except for the equations and cryptograms, which she skips right over).

# Contents

# About the Author

John F. Dooley is the William and Marilyn Ingersoll Professor Emeritus of Computer Science at Knox College in Galesburg, Illinois. After more than 16 years in industry and 22 years teaching undergraduate computer science, he retired in 2017 but continues to do research and writing, particularly in the history of cryptology. He has written more than two-dozen refereed articles and numerous book reviews published in journals and in computer science and cryptologic history conference proceedings. He has published six previous books, *Software Development and Professional Practice* (Apress 2011), *A Brief History of Cryptology and Cryptographic Algorithms* (Springer 2013), *Codes, Ciphers, and Spies* (Springer 2016), *Software Development and Design* (Apress 2017), *Codes, Villains, and Mystery* (CreateSpace 2017), and *History of Cryptography and Cryptanalysis* (Springer 2018). Since 2004, his main research interest has been in the history of American cryptology, particularly in the period from the beginning of the twentieth century through World War II. His web page is at https://www.johnfdooley.com.

# Chapter 1
# Introduction

In all of the wars and insurrections in which the United States was involved from 1776 through 1916, the Army had never had a permanent code and cipher organization. Whenever the United States would enter into a war—the Revolution, 1812, the Civil War, the Spanish-American War—the Army, usually at the encouragement of a single officer, would create an intelligence service that would mostly be involved in what is known as positive intelligence, that is, gathering intelligence about the enemy usually through the use of human resources. This organization would also have a technical body—the cryptographers who would create and use codes and ciphers to hide the contents of Army communications from enemy spies and whose members would attempt to decrypt intercepted enemy communications. There would also be a negative or counterintelligence branch whose job was to prevent enemies from using espionage or sabotage against American resources or intelligence services; they would try to catch enemy spies. Intelligence operations were generally seen as necessary but somehow not gentlemanly or fair. It was the type of service for which very few officers would volunteer. As soon as the current conflict was concluded, the intelligence service would be disbanded, and all its knowledge and experience would be lost. When this knowledge was needed again for the next war, it would need to be created from scratch. This cycle of creation and dissolution of intelligence services continued primarily because the American military "did not feel threatened by enemies on its borders and thus saw no need for an early warning mechanism."[1]

The State Department recognized the need for diplomatic codes and ciphers to protect diplomatic correspondence, so they would periodically create new code systems and replace existing ones at embassies and consulates. However, they never felt the need for having an organization designed to break other nations' codes. It

---

[1] James L. Gilbert, *World War I and the Origins of U.S. Military Intelligence* (Lanham, MD: Rowman & Littlefield Publishing Group, Ltd., 2015), https://rowman.com/ISBN/9780810884601/World-War-I-and-the-Origins-of-U.S.-Military-Intelligence, 1.

© The Author(s), under exclusive license to Springer Nature Switzerland AG 2023
J. F. Dooley, *The Gambler and the Scholars*, History of Computing, https://doi.org/10.1007/978-3-031-28318-5_1

was only during wartime that the United States government saw the need to attempt to break enemy codes and ciphers. This was in stark contrast to most of the European powers that had had secret departments known as Black Chambers that were used to intercept and break diplomatic correspondence since the late 1500s. All European armed forces also had their own cryptologic staff that continued in existence even between conflicts.

Once again, at the entry of the United States into World War I in April 1917, a formal military intelligence organization was created. And once again, it was likely to be disbanded at the end of that war. However, that is not what happened. Finally, in 1919, the War, Navy, and State Departments were convinced of the utility of a continuing organization dedicated to creating codes and ciphers for the government and for breaking the codes and ciphers of other countries—friend and foe alike. This change in attitude was largely because, first, with the easy victory over Spain in the Spanish-American War, and second, in coming to the aid of the faltering Allied powers during World War I, the Americans had finally realized that their country was a world power on par with the Europeans and as such needed to not only protect itself but also project power around the globe. America couldn't do either of those things without being able to gather and assess intelligence about friends and potential foes in a timely fashion and communicate securely with its own far-flung forces. Codes and ciphers were key elements of that intelligence organization.

It turned out that in 1919 there were two men in the country who were uniquely positioned to take on the challenge of creating the cryptographic and cryptanalytic organizations that would provide the type of intelligence America would need in peacetime and would prepare the armed forces for assuming that task in wartime. Born 2 years apart at the end of the nineteenth century, they had both served in the Army during the war, performing exactly the tasks that would be needed in the new permanent cryptologic organizations. Both were self-taught in cryptology, having read and digested nearly all the available cryptologic texts available in English in the United States just before America's entry into the war. Both were ambitious, driven by curiosity, service to country, and a deep, abiding need to succeed.

At the time that the United States entered World War I on 6 April 1917, there were just about a dozen people in the US Army and Navy who knew anything at all about cryptography and cryptanalysis. Half of them never got to practice their skills with codes and ciphers because the Army and Navy needed them elsewhere. The other half were generally assigned to the newly forming signals intelligence units in the American Expeditionary Force (AEF) and the Office of Naval Intelligence. Resources were thin, and the Army was scrambling to put together its General Staff organizations for the entire Army and the AEF. Anybody with any skills in codes and ciphers was being recruited as quickly as possible.

Herbert Osborn Yardley was a code clerk in the State Department where he had worked since 1912. Yardley, bored on overnight shifts in the State Department code room, had set himself the task of seeing if he could break the State Departments' own codes. It turned out he could. This appalled him, and he wrote a report on his midnight adventures and gave it to his boss, who did not quite believe him but who made a change in a State Department code anyway. Yardley broke that one as well, just in time to be recruited by the Army, commissioned an officer, and told to create a cryptanalytic section within Military Intelligence. His section, originally called the Cable and Telegraph Section and later the Code and Cipher Section, was the eighth in Military Intelligence, MI-8. Yardley immediately began recruiting cryptanalysts. But this was not an easy task because the skill set was rare, and he was competing with every other section in the Army for personnel.

William Frederick Friedman was a Russian immigrant who had come to the United States at the age of two. A graduate of Cornell University in genetics, at the American entry into the war he was working for an eccentric millionaire at a private research laboratory in Illinois, outside Chicago. Friedman was also an amateur photographer, and his boss, George Fabyan, roped him into taking pictures of pages from a First Folio of Shakespeare for another project at the laboratory, proving that Sir Francis Bacon had written all of the Bard's plays and had hidden coded messages in the plays that proved his authorship. The coded messages were allegedly written in a cipher of Bacon's own devising that used differences in the shapes of typefaces to disguise different letters of the alphabet. Enlarging the pages from the First Folio was thus essential to finding the typeface differences, hence the need for Friedman's photographic skills. Friedman became fascinated with the cipher and proceeded to teach himself cryptology. He was eventually dragooned into the Bacon-Shakespeare project, a prospect he anticipated eagerly mostly because in addition to the cipher, Friedman was interested in one of the project assistants, Elizebeth Smith.

While the Army was busy forming Yardley's MI-8 section, it still needed to create codes and break German Army and diplomatic cipher messages. With Yardley having no one in his section early on, the Army turned to Fabyan and his Baconian researchers to help decrypt intercepted messages. So, in the summer of 1917, William Friedman, the now Elizebeth Smith Friedman, and several others at Fabyan's Riverbank Laboratories began a side project working to decipher messages delivered from various US government departments.

Over the course of the 20 months that the United States would fight in World War I, these two men, Friedman and Yardley, would become the nucleus of that new permanent US government cryptologic organization. Yardley grew his MI-8 section from two people, himself and a clerk, into an organization with half a dozen subsections and more than 165 personnel by the end of the war. Friedman, after spending 9 months training cryptanalysts for the Army and breaking codes and ciphers on the Illinois prairie, would join the Army himself, be assigned to Military Intelligence, and end up as the head of the Code Solution Section of the AEF in France. The two men would meet for the first time in France in December 1918. It was an interesting and cautious meeting. They knew of each other by reputation. Friedman was rapidly gaining status within the Army as a brilliant cryptanalyst; he soaked up new cryptologic ideas like a sponge and generated new ideas almost as quickly. Yardley had shown he had the organizational skills to quickly grow a large, efficient bureau; he was an excellent manager and a terrific salesman, and he had already convinced his boss of the need for a permanent cryptanalytic bureau after the war, with him at the head.

This was their beginning.

# Chapter 2
# Beginnings: Herbert Yardley

Herbert Osborn Yardley was born on 13 April 1889 in Worthington, Indiana, which at that time had a population of 1,448. Herbert was the second of four children of Robert Kirkbride and Mary Emma Osborn Yardley. His father was a railroad station manager and telegrapher, and his mother was a housewife. Herbert's mother died of a sudden heart attack in February 1903 when he was 13, and his father's parenting skills were tested in the years after that. In high school, Yardley was not tall, just five-feet-five-inches, but he was good looking, intelligent, personable, and a terrific storyteller. He edited the high school paper, was elected class president, and captained the football team. He was also a voracious reader and an excellent poker player, having picked up the game early and starting at sixteen was a regular at games in the back room of one of Worthington's seven saloons. Herbert graduated from high school in Michigan because he'd been expelled from the Worthington high school for a senior prank in 1907.[1] He attended the University of Chicago for a year studying English but then quit. He spent two summers in 1906 and 1907 traveling the rails around the American West with a high school friend working odd jobs and playing poker before ending up back in Worthington, working in 1908 and 1909 as a railroad telegrapher like his father. However, Worthington, indeed no small town in the American Midwest, was big enough or exciting enough for Herbert, and his ambition drove him to the big city. He ended up in Washington, DC, in the second half of 1912 at the age of 23 after having taken the Civil Service exam for telegrapher and receiving the highest score. On December 23rd of that year after swearing an oath to "support and defend the Constitution of the United States against all enemies, foreign and domestic," Yardley started work as a $900 per year code clerk at the State Department in an office in the State, War, and Navy Department Building (now the Eisenhower Executive Office Building (EEOB)) immediately to the west of the White House on Pennsylvania Avenue (Fig. 2.1).

---

[1] David Kahn, *The Codebreakers: The Story of Secret Writing* (New York: Macmillan, 1967), 5.

© The Author(s), under exclusive license to Springer Nature
Switzerland AG 2023
J. F. Dooley, *The Gambler and the Scholars*, History of Computing,
https://doi.org/10.1007/978-3-031-28318-5_2

**Fig. 2.1** Herbert Yardley.
(US Army photo)

Young, living in a big city for the first time, and employed at the center of Woodrow Wilson's new government, Yardley had a great time. The State Department and its code room fascinated him.

> This spacious room with its high ceiling overlooked the southern White House grounds. By lifting my eyes from my work I could see a tennis game in progress where a few years earlier President [Theodore] Roosevelt and his tennis Cabinet had played each day.
>
> Along one side of the room ran a long oak telegraph table with its stuttering resonators and sounders; cabinets containing copies of current telegrams almost blocked the entrance. In the center sprawled two enormous flat-topped desks shoved together, about which a few code clerks thumbed code books and scribbled rapidly, pausing now and then to light cigarettes. The pounding of typewriters specially constructed to make fifteen copies of a telegram mingled with the muted click of the telegraph instruments. The walls were covered with old-fashioned closed cupboards filled with bound copies of telegrams from and to consular and diplomatic posts throughout the world. In the corner stood a huge safe, its thick doors slightly ajar.
>
> There was an air of good-fellowship in the room and I was soon at home.[2]

Yardley's time at the State Department was interesting but eventually boring. The code clerks handled all the telegraphic and cable communications for the State Department, and the office was full of diplomats of all levels coming and going even

---

[2] Herbert O. Yardley, *The American Black Chamber* (Indianapolis: Bobbs-Merrill, 1931), 17–18.

into the late evening. Yardley was not that impressed with the Ivy League diplomats but was certainly interested in their power, influence, aplomb, and finesse.[3] His career progressed at a nice clip, and he was given a raise to $1000 a year in April 1914, enough money for a small family to live on.

When Herbert left Worthington, he also left behind the girl next door, Hazel Milam. Hazel's family was well off for Worthington, and her father was a big player in local Republican politics. Hazel, five weeks older than Herbert, was in the same classes as he all through elementary and high school. They had dated on and off and finally became engaged on 12 May 1914. Hazel immediately got on a train and followed Herbert to Washington. Herbert Yardley and Hazel Milam were married in Washington, DC, on the day she arrived, 20 May 1914, both of them just twenty-five. They moved into the small apartment that Yardley was renting in northwest Washington. Over the next couple of years, they visited Worthington a few times, and their younger brothers, Pat Milam and Dick Yardley, came out to Washington in 1915. Hazel escaped the Washington heat and humidity and spent the summer of 1916 at her parent's home in Worthington. In 1917 Hazel got a job as a typist with the Quartermaster's Corps at $1000 per year. Nearly doubling their income allowed them to move into a row house at 542 Shepherd Street NW.

Yardley was intensely interested in the code and cipher messages that passed through the State Department Code Room. They were a challenge to his inquisitive mind. Ambitious as he was, Yardley figured that learning more about those codes and ciphers would help his career. "As I asked myself this question I knew that I had the answer to my eager young mind which was searching for a purpose in life," he wrote. "I would devote my life to cryptography. Perhaps I too, like the foreign cryptographer, could open the secrets of the capitals of the world. I now began a methodical plan to prepare myself."[4]

Starting in early 1915 he proceeded to learn as much as he could about the mysterious field of cryptology. He explored libraries, including the Library of Congress, for books on cryptography, only to be very disappointed. It turned out that in 1915, there were precious few books in English on cryptography and even fewer in the libraries around Washington. He read fiction, finding the classic story of codebreaking in Edgar Allan Poe's *The Gold Bug*, and relishing it. But he was ultimately disappointed in Poe and his declarations of expertise in cryptanalysis. "I searched Edgar Allan Poe's letters for a glimpse of the scientific treatment of cryptography. These were full of vague boasts of his skill - nothing more... I know that Poe merely floundered around in the dark and did not understand the great underlying principles."[5] One slim, 105-page book he found at the Library of Congress and

[3] Yardley, *ABC*, 18.

[4] Yardley, *ABC*, 20.

[5] Yardley, *ABC*, 20–21.

devoured was the then new US Army *Manual for the Solution of Military Ciphers* by Captain Parker Hitt, which was published early in 1916 (Fig. 2.2).[6]

Hitt's book was an excellent place to start. It reads like an introductory course in cryptography and cryptanalysis. It covers language characteristics, transposition ciphers, substitution ciphers—both monoalphabetic and polyalphabetic, and polygraphic ciphers such as Playfair, which was the standard English Army cipher at the time. It also discusses methods of analyzing encrypted messages to determine their type and examines errors that encipherers make. Yardley ate it up. The book provided his real foundation of cryptologic knowledge and his first introduction into breaking enciphered messages. As we will see, Hitt's book was also the introductory text that William and Elizebeth Friedman used to learn elementary cryptanalysis and was their initial textbook when they taught cryptanalysis to Army officers at the Riverbank Laboratories in 1917.

Unfortunately, Hitt's book contains nothing about codes, only ciphers. However, one thing Yardley knew was that many messages in code were also enciphered

**Fig. 2.2** Parker Hitt during World War I. (US National Archives)

---

[6] Parker Hitt, *Manual for the Solution of Military Ciphers*, SRH-004 (Fort Leavenworth, KS: Press of the Army Service Schools, 1916).

before they were dispatched. This is called superencipherment. So, in order to break an encoded message, the first thing to do was to remove this superencipherment to reveal the underlying code words. For homework, Yardley would make copies of select State Department coded messages and try to break them. He also convinced a friend or two at the telegraph companies in Washington to slip him the occasional coded telegrams of foreign embassies.[7]

Yardley was shocked by what he found. The American State Department codes were distressingly easy to break. In 1915, the State Department was using three different codes to transmit messages between Washington and embassies and consulates around the world. The Red Code, released in 1876 and named for the color of its cover, was a 1200-page book that listed nearly ten thousand plaintext equivalents, codewords, and associated numeric codewords. The codewords were real English words designed to make it easier for telegraphers to send messages and recover from mistakes. The Blue Code, released in February 1899, added 300 pages to the Red Code, for a total of 1500. Finally, the Green Code was a 1418-page book that was released in 1910 and was the current code used for messages between Washington and most embassies abroad when Herbert Yardley started work in the State Department code room in 1912.[8] The biggest change in the Green Code was the replacement of plain English codewords with five-letter random codewords. All three of these codes also contained a separate sixteen-page addendum with the wishful title *Holocryptic Code, An Appendix to the Cipher of the Department of State.* In the spirit of the inconsistency of cryptographic nomenclature, the *Holocryptic Code* describes a cipher and the *State Department Cipher* was a code. The Holocryptic Code contained fifty (later seventy-five) rules on how to increase the security of the three Department codes, including rules on how to add a superenciperment to code messages.

All three codes were *one-part codes*, which consisted of a single table with the plaintext words and their alphabetic and numeric codeword equivalents listed in ascending order. This type of code was easy to use for encryption, slightly more difficult for decryption (because for the code numbers, one had to find the right number in the right-hand column) and, unfortunately, fairly easy for an experienced cryptanalyst to crack. One-part codes are easier to solve because the cryptanalyst needs to uncover just a few words and their equivalent codewords before they can start to guess the meanings of plaintext around nearby alphabetic or numeric codewords. When Yardley was working in the State Department Code Room, many European powers were able to read all three of the American codes (Fig. 2.3).

Yardley's most interesting piece of "homework" was a 500-word enciphered message sent in the spring of 1915 after a peace-making trip that President Wilson's confidante Colonel Edward House took to Europe and written in a cipher system devised by House and used between the two men. This message presented Yardley

---

[7] Yardley, *ABC*, 21.

[8] Ralph Edward Weber, *United States Diplomatic Codes and Ciphers, 1775–1938* (Chicago: Precedent Pub., 1979), 246.

| Code word P | Code No 609 | Message or true reading |
|---|---|---|
| Promotes ........ | 00 | Russia |
| Promoting ...... | 01 | Agreement between Russia and |
| Promotion ....... | 02 | Agreement with Russia |
| Promotions ...... | 03 | Ambassador from Russia |
| Promotive ........ | 04 | Ambassador of Russia |
| Prompt ......... | 05 | Ambassador to Russia |
| Prompted ....... | 06 | And Russia |
| Prompter ....... | 07 | Army of Russia |
| Prompters ....... | 08 | Authorities of Russia |
| Promptest ........ | 09 | Authority of Russia |
| Prompting ...... | 10 | By Russia |
| Promptings ..... | 11 | Cabinet of Russia |
| Promptly ........ | 12 | Charge d'affaires of Russia |
| Promptness ..... | 13 | Commerce of Russia |
| Prompts ......... | 14 | Consul of Russia |
| Promulgate ..... | 15 | Consul-general of Russia |
| Pronate ......... | 16 | Consuls of Russia |
| Pronation ....... | 17 | Convention between Russia and |
| Pronator ........ | 18 | Convention with Russia |
| Prone ........... | 19 | Czar of Russia |
| Pronely ......... | 20 | Embassy of Russia |
| Proneness ....... | 21 | Emperor of Russia |
| Prong ........... | 22 | Empire of Russia |
| Pronged ......... | 23 | Empress of Russia |
| Pronghorn ...... | 24 | Flag of Russia |
| Prongs .......... | 25 | Forces of Russia |
| Pronity ......... | 26 | From Russia |
| Pronoun ........ | 27 | From the Government of Russia |
| Pronounce ...... | 28 | Government of Russia |
| Pronounced ..... | 29 | Head of the Government (by whatever title) |
| Pronouncer ...... | 30 | Her Majesty the Empress of Russia |
| Pronounces ..... | 31 | His Majesty the Emperor of Russia |
| Pronouns ....... | 32 | Imperial Government of Russia |
| Pronubial ....... | 33 | In Russia |
| Pronuncial ...... | 34 | Legation of Russia |
| Proof ........... | 35 | Minister for foreign affairs of Russia |
| Proofless ........ | 36 | Minister for foreign affairs of Russia (by name) |
| Proofs .......... | 37 | Minister from Russia |
| Prop ............ | 38 | Minister of Russia |
| Propagable ...... | 39 | Minister of Russia at |
| Propaganda ..... | 40 | Minister to Russia |
| Propagate ....... | 41 | Naval vessel of Russia |
| Propagated ...... | 42 | Naval vessels of Russia |
| Propagates ...... | 43 | Navy of Russia |
| Propagator ...... | 44 | Of Russia |
| Propel .......... | 45 | People of Russia |
| Propelled ....... | 46 | Policy of Russia |
| Propeller ........ | 47 | Possessions of Russia |
| Propellers ....... | 48 | Secretary of embassy of Russia |
| Propelling ....... | 49 | Secretary of legation of Russia |

**Fig. 2.3** A page from the 1899 State Department Blue Code (note that code numbers all start with 609xx).[a] (National Security Agency)

[a] John H. Haswell, "State Department Cipher" (U. S. Government Printing Office, 1899); Ralph Edward Weber, *Masked Dispatches: Cryptograms and Cryptology in American History, 1775–1900*, vol. 2nd (Fort George G. Meade, MD: Center for Cryptologic History, National Security Agency, 1993), 205.

with what he thought was most surely a very challenging cryptanalytic task. It took him just 2 hours to break the cipher and read the message.[9] The message itself, sent after House's trip to Berlin and while he was on his way home and in Berne, Switzerland, is really only 301 code words, although Yardley may have been referring to plaintext words in the decrypted message. House and Wilson were using the State Department Blue Code, along with a superencipherment designed by House.[10]

No wonder Yardley was astounded at the contents of the message and aghast that he could decode it so easily. His description in his later book does not give any hints as to how he did his decryption, but it is full of commentary on the weakness of American codes and the small-mindedness of its leaders; this would be a theme in Yardley's later writings as well. However, while a very good example of cryptanalysis on Yardley's part, this is not as significant an achievement as it appears at first. Yardley was working in the State Department code room and thus had access to both the Blue Code book and the Holocryptic Code book addendum. House's variation on the Blue Code used the Blue Code book but created a novel way of creating numeric codewords using that book. In House's system, the correspondents renumbered the pages starting at the back and finishing at the first page of the code. Then, when looking up a plaintext word or phrase, the person creating the coded message would count down the words on the page to the word or phrase they wanted and then append those two digits to the end of the reworked page number. While tricky, if one has possession of the Blue Code codebook and determines the renumbering of the pages and the reworking of the numeric codewords as a book cipher, then the decryption is simple. This decryption is a commendable feat for a beginning codebreaker, but nothing spectacular. Nevertheless, it showed Yardley that he had some talent at codebreaking and that creating good, secure ciphers and codes was much harder than it appeared.

This was still a very disturbing development for State Department cryptology. Yardley knew that House was in Europe and on his way home from his peace mission, so House's telegram would have gone through both French and English telegraphic cables on its way to the trans-Atlantic cable. He also knew that both countries were in the habit of examining all traffic that passed over their cables. Surely if an amateur like Yardley could break messages in these weak codes and ciphers, England and the other European powers, with their professional codebreaking organizations, were having a field day. In fact, while the British MI1(b) Army cryptographic organization that had intercepted House's message had not yet fully broken the Blue Code, it would do so by the fall of 1915, followed quickly by its break of the Green Code before the end of the year.[11] This would make the

---

[9] Yardley, *ABC*, 22.

[10] Ralph Edward Weber, "State Department Cryptographic Security, Herbert O. Yardley, and Woodrow Wilson's Secret Code," in *In the Name of Intelligence: Essays in Honor of Walter Pforzheimer*, (Washington, DC: NIBC Press, 1994), 594–595. and Daniel Larsen, "Creating An American Culture Of Secrecy: Cryptography In Wilson-Era Diplomacy," *Diplomatic History* 44, no. 1 (January 1, 2020): 102–32, https://doi.org/10.1093/dh/dhz046

[11] Larsen, *American Culture*, 123.

messages—again mostly in the Blue Code—between House and Wilson during House's second peace-making mission in early 1916 transparent to the British.

Yardley was also distressed that nowhere in the American government was there the equivalent to these European Black Chambers that routinely read the diplomatic messages of other countries and had for centuries. This was not just in Yardley's imagination. John H. Haswell had written to the Secretary of State in 1898 as he was creating the Blue Code that the European governments all had Black Chambers and could all likely read American State Department coded messages.[12]

Yardley decided that he needed to do something about the weakness of the American codes. But, what could he do? He was just a lowly code clerk, and it was his boss who was responsible for many of the State Department codes. Besides, he did not think that President Wilson would be pleased to know that a State Department clerk was reading the secret messages between him and his most trusted advisor.[13] What he did in the end was to spend nearly 2 years learning as much as he could about codes, ciphers, and cryptanalysis and then find as many weaknesses as he could in the State Department codes and ciphers. This exercise made Herbert Yardley the first civilian peacetime professional codebreaker in American history. Late nights when there was little to no traffic, Yardley would look through the days' messages and figure out how an enemy cryptanalyst would attack them. Over the course of the years, he worked through the State Department codes and the Holocryptic code and wrote up everything that he found in a 100-page report. Finally, in early 1917, as America was becoming increasingly nervous about the war in Europe, he presented the report to his boss, David A. Salmon, who had just been named chief of the Office of Indexes and Archives. Salmon was shocked and impressed by Yardley's report, calling it a "fine piece of work." Just about a month later, Salman presented Yardley with a series of messages using a new set of rules for the superencipherment of State Department coded messages and asked him to break it. Several weeks later and likely just after the United States had declared war on Germany, Yardley presented his solution to Salmon, who confirmed it. Yardley then asked Salmon for a recommendation letter so that he could apply for a commission in the Army and go to work for them breaking codes. Salmon was reluctant to let Yardley go but was finally convinced to write the letter. Yardley then went about finding the right person to talk to at the War Department and was ultimately pointed to one Major Ralph Van Deman who was head of the newly created Military Intelligence Section of the Army General Staff.[14]

At its entry into the war in April 1917, the United States had no military intelligence organization.[15] This state of affairs was finally rectified on 3 May 1917—nearly a month after war had been declared—when the War College Division created

[12] Weber, *State Dept Cryptographic Security*, 564.

[13] Yardley, *ABC*, 21–22.

[14] Yardley, *ABC*, 31–36.

[15] James L. Gilbert, *World War I and the Origins of U.S. Military Intelligence* (Lanham, MD: Rowman & Littlefield Publishing Group, Ltd., 2015), https://rowman.com/ISBN/9780810884601/World-War-I-and-the-Origins-of-U.S.-Military-Intelligence, 1–5.

the Military Intelligence Section (MIS), later the Military Intelligence Division (MID), under Major Ralph Van Deman.[16] Van Deman, a Harvard graduate who also had both law and medical degrees, had been in the Army since 1891. He was in the first class of the Army War College in 1904 and had organized and run the Military Intelligence Division in the Philippines during the Philippine-American War (1899–1902). He was the ideal person to run the new MID and would become known as the "Father of American Military Intelligence" (Fig. 2.4).[17]

Van Deman lost no time in organizing the MID. Beginning with just a couple of enlisted soldiers and some civilians, Van Deman had, by the end of 1917, an organization of several hundred soldiers and civilians and a budget of over $1 million, modeled on the British military intelligence organization. One of the subsections that Van Deman created was Subsection 8, the Code and Cipher Section, MI-8.

In early June, when Yardley dropped into his office, Van Deman was intrigued with Yardley's idea for a War Department Cipher Bureau. However, Yardley was not Van Deman's first choice for MI-8. He really wanted a Regular Army officer who

**Fig. 2.4**  Ralph Van Deman during World War I. (US Army photo)

[16] Gilbert, *Origins*, 28–29.
[17] Gilbert, *Origins*, 11–13.

had been trained in cryptology. However, at the beginning of the American entry into the war, there were exactly three Regular Army officers trained in codes and ciphers—Captains Parker Hitt, Frank Moorman, and Joseph Mauborgne, and, in a brilliant bit of Army wisdom, none of them were ultimately assigned to strictly cryptographic duties.[18] Hitt would become the Chief Signal Officer of the American 1st Army in France, Moorman would be the chief of the American Expeditionary Force's (AEF) Radio Intelligence Section G-2 A-6, and Mauborgne would head up the Signal Corps research division. So, after convincing the State Department to let Yardley go, Van Deman had him commissioned a first lieutenant in the Signal Corps of the National Army on 29 June 1917, and he was assigned to active duty in Military Intelligence on July 5th. On July 11th, Van Deman put Yardley, then twenty-eight years old, in charge of the Code and Cipher Section of Military Intelligence, section MI-8. According to David Kahn, when Yardley took command of MI-8, "He had broken some codes and believed he could crack others. He was ambitious. And now he had, via cryptology, a chance to be not an underling, but a boss. Sure that he could handle the opportunity, he seized it."[19]

Thus, unbeknownst to either Yardley or Friedman began the competition that would follow them through the next 25 years.

---

[18] Gilbert, *Origins*, 44.

[19] David Kahn, *The Reader of Gentlemen's Mail: Herbert O. Yardley and the Birth of American Codebreaking* (New Haven: Yale University Press, 2004), 21.

# Chapter 3
# Beginnings: William Friedman and Elizebeth Smith

Wolfe Frederick Friedman was born on September 24, 1891, in Kishinev, Russia (now Chisinau, the capital of Moldova), a city near the Romanian border. His father was an interpreter and translator for the Russian Postal Service, and his mother was the daughter of a well-to-do merchant in Kishinev. The late 1800s were not a good time to be Jewish inside the Russian Empire. The pogroms in the southwestern part of the Empire from 1881 to 1884 resulted in a series of laws restricting Jewish settlements and occupations. Sensing the approach of more restrictions and the increasing tensions that heralded more pogroms, the Friedmans emigrated to the United States in 1892 and 1893; Wolfe's father Frederick left in 1892, headed west, found a job, and established himself. The rest of the family followed the next year, all of them settling in Pittsburgh, Pennsylvania. Not finding a job as an interpreter, Frederick ended up as a door-to-door salesman, selling sewing machines for Singer, and the family settled into their new life in America. Wolfe's name was changed to William shortly after the family landed in Pittsburgh when his parents became citizens. William grew up as a typical first-generation immigrant boy in early twentieth-century urban America. Graduating from high school in 1910, William at first embraced a back to the land movement that was having its day and attracting many young Jewish immigrants to the rural, farming life, enrolling at Michigan Agricultural College in Lansing. It turned out that farming was not exactly to William's city-raised liking, and so after 1 year he transferred to Cornell University in upstate New York and switched his major from agriculture to genetics. He graduated in February 1914 and then stayed on at Cornell to start graduate school. However, a little over a year later, William's graduate study plans would be upended by an opportunity that he could just not pass up (Fig. 3.1).

George Fabyan was a decidedly successful American businessman. Born in 1867 into a wealthy industrial family, he was the elder son of George Francis and Isabella Fabyan. The elder Fabyan had founded and built a successful dry goods and textile company in Boston. George decided early on that he did not want to follow in his father's footsteps and work in the family business; he would leave that to his younger

© The Author(s), under exclusive license to Springer Nature
Switzerland AG 2023
J. F. Dooley, *The Gambler and the Scholars*, History of Computing,
https://doi.org/10.1007/978-3-031-28318-5_3

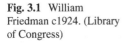

**Fig. 3.1** William
Friedman c1924. (Library
of Congress)

brother Francis. Instead, he threw it all over, quit school at 16, and spent several
years roaming the western United States, working here and there as, among other
occupations, a salesman, a tie and timber agent, and a cotton broker, acquiring a
nonstandard education in the process.[1] While working for a timber company in
northern Wisconsin, George met and married Nelle Wright, the daughter of a local
merchant. Nelle was anxious to be out of the northern forests and live in a big city,
so the young couple headed to Chicago. Landing there in 1892, Fabyan went to
work in his father's Chicago office as a warehouse assistant under an assumed name.
Working his way up, he did so well that his manager insisted on introducing him to
the senior George Fabyan during one of his visits to the Chicago operation.
Reconciled to his family, George became the Chicago managing partner of Bliss
Fabyan & Company and grew the business substantially during the Gilded Age in
the 1890s and early 1900s. In 1905, George Fabyan bought the first of what was
ultimately several hundred acres about 40 miles west of Chicago along the Fox
River in the little town of Geneva and proceeded to convert the existing farmhouse
into a modern mansion—designed by Frank Lloyd Wright and called the "Villa." He

---

[1] Richard Munson, *George Fabyan* (North Charleston, SC: CreateSpace Independent Publishing
Platform, 2013), 17.

then set about creating one of the first private research laboratories in the United States, Riverbank Laboratories. Fabyan would hire scientists and engineers and allow them a free hand to do research as long as it was in an area in which Fabyan himself was interested. The laboratories specialized in acoustics (a spin-off acoustics company still exists today), genetics, and in an obscure area that Fabyan found fascinating—proving that Sir Francis Bacon wrote all of William Shakespeare's plays and left coded messages in the plays verifying that authorship. On the estate, Fabyan built a lavish Japanese garden, a spacious lodge, laboratory buildings, a Roman-style swimming pool, a lighthouse, and housing for many of the more than 150 workers. He even imported a complete windmill that he had erected on the banks of the Fox River (Fig. 3.2).[2]

Fabyan acted like a feudal lord. Tall and heavyset with a goatee and always in a riding outfit and boots, even though he did not ride, he would stride around his estate every day, micromanaging his workers and sharing his opinions on everything. As a manager, he was rude, loud, and imperious. He paid his workers as little as possible, lied to them in order to get his way, and inserted himself into their private lives to the point of intercepting and reading their mail. He was everyone's least favorite boss, a bully. However, for the scientists and engineers on his staff, he gave them the opportunity to work on interesting problems (Fig. 3.3).

**Fig. 3.2** The grounds of Riverbank looking across the gardens and toward the windmill (author's collection)

---

[2] Munson, *Fabyan*, 47–56.

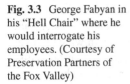

**Fig. 3.3** George Fabyan in his "Hell Chair" where he would interrogate his employees. (Courtesy of Preservation Partners of the Fox Valley)

For the 23-year-old William Friedman, it was the genetics laboratory that attracted him to Riverbank in the spring of 1915 when George Fabyan asked the faculty at Cornell for any bright young men who wanted to do research in crop hybridization. Friedman's faculty adviser recommended him to Fabyan, and after some negotiations, William left Cornell and arrived at Riverbank in the summer of 1915 as the head of the new Department of Genetics. He lived on the second floor of the windmill across the Fox River from Fabyan's villa and the Lodge where Mrs. Elizebeth Wells Gallup was in charge of the Bacon/Shakespeare cipher project.

Mrs. Gallup's obsession was to prove that Francis Bacon had embedded coded messages into the works of Shakespeare using a cipher of his own invention called the biliteral cipher. The biliteral cipher used two different fonts to create two different types of letters in the plays. The two letter types, called A and B, were used in groups of five to encipher individual letters of the alphabet. In Bacon's cipher system, the letter "a" is represented by AAAAA, "b" is AAAAB, "c" is AAABA, etc., on down to "y" encoded as BABBA and "z" as BABBB. The complete alphabet from Bacon's time (where I = J because there was no J in the English alphabet in the late sixteenth century, and U = V because there was no V) is[3]:

| a | AAAAA | b | AAAAB | c | AAABA |
|---|-------|---|-------|---|-------|
| d | AAABB | e | AABAA | f | AABAB |
| g | AABBA | h | AABBB | i = j | ABAAA |
| k | ABAAB | l | ABABA | m | ABABB |
| n | ABBAA | o | ABBAB | p | ABBBA |
| q | ABBBB | r | BAAAA | s | BAAAB |
| t | BAABA | u = v | BAABB | w | BABAA |
| x | BABAB | y | BABBA | z | BABBB |

For example, if the A type font is a regular Times font and the B is the italic version of the Times font, then the sentence "I am Fr Bacon" might be enciphered using the sentence "N*ow* is the win*ter of* our *dis*content *m*ade glorious su*mm*er *by this* sun of York" with a few extra letters at the end.

Mrs. Gallup's objective was to identify the two different font types and then to extract the cipher letters and read pages from Shakespeare's First Folio to uncover the secret coded messages. In order to do this, and because the differences in the type fonts were minuscule, she needed blown up pictures of the individual pages of the First Folio. So, she required a good photographer to take pictures of each of the pages and blow them up to a useful size so she and her assistants, using magnifying glasses, could identify the two font types.

It turned out that William Friedman was a very good amateur photographer, and as a result, for increasingly long periods of time during 1916, he was dragged away from his plants and genetics work to take pictures of Shakespearean plays for Mrs. Gallup. Not that he minded being diverted from his primary work that much, because starting in the summer of 1916 he was increasingly distracted by one of Mrs. Gallup's assistants, a young lady from Indiana named Elizebeth Smith.

Elizebeth Smith—the spelling is deliberate; her mother did not want her being called Eliza—was the tenth and last child of John Marion Smith, a Quaker farmer and local Republican office-holder in Huntington, Indiana, and his wife Sopha Strock Smith. By the time Elizebeth was born on August 26, 1892, most of her siblings were already grown and out of the house. Growing up, Elizebeth was closest to her next older sister, Edna, who was just two years her senior. Elizebeth was a precocious, fidgety, and talkative child who had, over the years, a strained relationship with her father. John Smith did not want his youngest child to go to college; he thought that it was a waste of money for a woman to get a higher education. When Elizebeth insisted and went behind his back to apply to several small colleges, he was furious. Instead of giving her the money for her college tuition, he loaned some of it to her at an interest rate of 4 percent—and she paid it back. She attended the College of Wooster in Wooster, Ohio, between 1911 and 1913. When her mother

---

[3] Sir Francis Bacon, *The Advancement of Learning*, ed. Joseph Devey (New York, NY: P. F. Collier & Son Company, 1901), http://oll.libertyfund.org/titles/bacon-the-advancement-of-learning, 124.

became ill, Elizebeth returned home and transferred to Hillsdale College in Michigan, which was much closer to home. While studying there, she earned tuition and room and board money as a seamstress. Majoring in English Literature and picking up Latin and German along the way, Elizebeth graduated in the spring of 1915.

She took a job as an English instructor and substitute school principal at a country high school near her home. However, she was not content with the then traditional female job of school teacher and she was tired of Indiana and was looking for adventure. Therefore, in the spring of 1916, she quit her job and moved back in with her parents while deciding what her next steps would be. At home, Elizebeth was reminded of why she had left in the first place as her strained relationship with her father picked up where it had left off and then soon deteriorated even more. In June 1916, Elizebeth packed her things, took a deep breath, and boarded a train for Chicago determined to find interesting work and a new life. Little did she know how different and interesting her life would soon become (Fig. 3.4).

**Fig. 3.4** Elizebeth Smith Friedman c1917. (Courtesy of the George Marshall Foundation Library)

Sleeping on the couch in the apartment of a college friend, Elizebeth haunted the personnel offices of companies and the employment agencies looking for work. She was interested in things that engaged the mind, rather than traditional clerical work. Office after office told her there was nothing like that available. After a week, exhausted and nearly out of money, Elizebeth was on the brink of having to head back to Huntington. On what was probably her last day in Chicago, she decided to treat herself and headed over to the Newberry Library to have a look at one of their treasures, a rare original copy of a 1623 Shakespeare First Folio. At the Newberry, Elizebeth started chatting with the reference librarian and mentioned her fruitless job search. The young woman mentioned that she knew a library patron, a wealthy Chicago businessman, who was looking for assistants to help with a research project and suggested that she could call him to see if he would like to interview Elizebeth. The next thing Elizebeth knew, a large black limousine pulled up in front of the library, a large man with a goatee got out and strode up to her and said, "Will you come to Riverbank and spend the night with me?"[4] Whereupon she was whisked out of the library, hustled into the black limousine, and driven to the railway station where the two boarded a train and headed for Geneva.

In Elizebeth's trip to Geneva that June afternoon with the man who turned out to be George Fabyan, she got her first glimpse of Riverbank, met Mrs. Gallup, several of her assistants, including Dr. J. A. Powell, who was working on the typography of Mrs. Gallup's Folio copies,[5] and had dinner in the main dining room of the Lodge. She also met the young head of the Department of Genetics, William Friedman. At dinner, Mrs. Gallup and her sister and partner, Miss Kate Wells, discussed the Bacon-Shakespeare project and Mrs. Gallup's 1899 book that revealed her decryption of a number of Bacon's cipher messages. "When she spoke about the details of her investigations and findings, no one interrupted her to ask skeptical questions. It was obvious to Elizebeth that people here were used to treating Mrs. Gallup with great deference, that she was an important person at Riverbank, and that dinner conversations like this had probably happened many times before, with Mrs. Gallup holding court and the others nodding and smiling."[6]

The next day, Fabyan took Elizebeth on a tour of the Riverbank grounds, including the farm, the gardens, the windmill, and the Villa, and ended up back at the Lodge, where Elizebeth had a long conversation with Mrs. Gallup about the details of the Bacon-Shakespeare project, the possible position, and her expectations. Mrs. Gallup claimed that she had already found all of Bacon's coded messages inside the First Folio, but in order to convince skeptics, she needed others to reproduce her work using the rules that she had set down for reading the Folio pages. That would be the largest part of Elizebeth's job.[7] While Elizebeth was not initially convinced

[4] Jason Fagone, *The Woman Who Smashed Codes*, hardcover (New York, NY: William Morrow, 2017), 5–6.

[5] J. A. Powell, *The Greatest Work of Sir Francis Bacon*, Hardcover (Geneva, IL: Riverbank Laboratories, 1916), 1916.

[6] Fagone, *Smashed*, 30–31.

[7] Fagone *Smashed*, 33–34.

of Mrs. Gallup's theories, the offer of a job, including room and board, and interesting research work on Shakespeare was too tempting to pass up. Who knew? Mrs. Gallup might be right.

Elizebeth accepted Fabyan's offer of employment, moved to Riverbank, and started working on Mrs. Gallup's team trying to duplicate her process and to find Francis Bacon's cryptograms within the Shakespeare plays.

One of the things that George Fabyan did to gin up the visibility and interest in Riverbank Laboratories was to invite scholars who might have an interest—either positive or negative—in the work in which the different departments at Riverbank were engaged. One of these scholars was Dr. John Matthews Manly, the chair of the English Department at the University of Chicago and an expert in late Medieval English literature and in literary codes and ciphers. Manly and his associate Dr. Edith Rickert would spend more than 16 years in the late 1920s through the 1930s compiling what would be, at the time, the most important work on the texts of the *Canterbury Tales* by Geoffrey Chaucer.[8] In addition, Manly and Rickert would be cryptanalysts in the Code and Cipher section of Military Intelligence—MI-8—during the coming war. Manly visited Riverbank in the fall of 1916 and spent several days examining Mrs. Gallup's work with a more than skeptical eye. Because Elizebeth Smith had an interest in late Medieval and Elizabethan literature, Fabyan asked her to shepherd Manly around Riverbank. Elizebeth was not impressed with Manly and thought he was a "pompous ass."[9] Much later she recalled showing Manly some of Mrs. Gallup's deciperments, "I well remember his reading over me... I was sitting at a typewriter, and I had a sheet of paper in there;... And I remember his leaning over me and pushing me on the shoulder, and this and that, you know, getting quite angry and upset that anybody would challenge the great John M. Manly! Oh, my! That was too much to take."[10] Interestingly, Elizebeth seems to be fairly alone in her opinion of John Manly. William Friedman and John Manly became friends at right around this time and corresponded frequently on many topics, including cryptology, the Bacon-Shakespeare controversy, and the Voynich manuscript until Manly's death in 1940. Elizebeth did change her opinion of Manly as the years went on, however, and she came to enjoy his company.

Elizebeth's work threw her into close proximity with William Friedman, who was doing all the photographic work for the project. As two of the youngest and nearly the only single people at the Laboratories, William and Elizebeth started spending more time together in the fall and winter of 1916, bicycling, taking walks through the gardens, taking their meals together, and talking about Bacon, Shakespeare, and

---

[8] John M. Manly and Edith Rickert, *The Text of The Canterbury Tales* (Chicago, IL: University of Chicago Press, 1940).

[9] Fagone *Smashed*, 55.

[10] Elizebeth S. Friedman and Virginia T. Valaki, "Oral History of Elizebeth Friedman (1976) – Part 1," Oral History Collection (Ft. George G. Meade, MD: National Security Agency, Center for Cryptologic History, November 11, 1976), NSA Archives, Center for Cryptologic History, https://www.nsa.gov/Portals/70/documents/news-features/declassified-documents/oral-history-interviews/nsa-OH-1976-16-efriedman.pdf, 13

the biliteral cipher. William was spending more and more of this time working on the Bacon-Shakespeare project and leaving more of the genetics work to his assistants. Elizebeth and William started learning more about cryptology together as well. William was clearly smitten with Elizebeth and told her so early on, and while she liked him and enjoyed his company immensely, she was slightly slower to reveal her growing feelings toward him.

Starting in early 1917, things at Riverbank changed. The European war had been going on for 2 and a half years at this point, and the United States was inching ever closer to joining the war on the side of the Allies and against Germany. Germany resumed unrestricted submarine warfare on 1 February 1917, and within a few weeks, several American merchant vessels were sunk. On 28 February, the Zimmermann Telegram exploded onto the American press, leaked to them by the State Department. In the telegram, the German Foreign Minister Arthur Zimmermann instructed the German ambassador in Mexico City to approach the Mexican government with a proposition. In return for a Mexican declaration of war against the United States, Germany would provide Mexico with weapons and money for the war effort and would guarantee that Mexico would recover its lost territories in Arizona, New Mexico, and Texas.

The United States Congress immediately passed a law—which had been held up by Congressional isolationists—to arm American merchant vessels. Within 3 days President Wilson broke diplomatic relations with Germany. The United States was rapidly approaching war with Germany.

George Fabyan, ever looking for an opportunity to increase the visibility of Riverbank, shot off a letter on 15 March 1917 to "The Intelligence Office, War Department" offering his extensive library of books on cryptography and the services of his Cipher Department to the Army. This letter was received by the sole officer in the Intelligence Branch of the General Staff, Major Ralph Van Deman.[11] Van Deman sent Fabyan's letter off to his friend and the current Head of the Army Signal School, Captain Joseph Mauborgne. Van Deman asked Mauborgne to contact Fabyan and see if his organization could help the Army with its lack of code and cipher expertise. Mauborgne wrote to Fabyan, who immediately invited him to Riverbank to see the Cipher Department for himself. Mauborgne visited Riverbank in early April 1917. In the midst of his visit, the United States declared war on Germany on 6 April 1917. On 11 April, Mauborgne wrote a memorandum about his visit to the head of the War College Division (where Military Intelligence was housed). He waxed enthusiastic about the abilities of the Riverbank cipher organization, which at that time was William Friedman, Elizebeth Smith, Dr. J. A. Powell, the typographer who was later the head of the University of Chicago Press, and a couple of assistants, and encouraged Van Deman to start sending intercepted coded messages from the War, State, and Justice Departments to Riverbank for decoding.

---

[11] George Fabyan, "Fabyan to MID," March 15, 1917, William Friedman Collection, Item 734, George Marshall Foundation Research Library.

Fig. 3.5 Joseph
Mauborgne. (U.S. Army
photo)

Mauborgne also encouraged Van Deman to consider helping Riverbank set up a training course for army officers in elementary cryptanalysis (Fig. 3.5).[12]

Powell was later inducted into the Army, commissioned a Captain, and sent to the Army Signal School at Ft. Leavenworth, Kansas, for cryptographic training. When Powell returned to Riverbank, he brought with him the course materials from the Signal School, and he joined in the effort by William and Elizebeth to design a course in cryptanalysis for Army officers as suggested by Mauborgne. He was later assigned to Riverbank to be the Army point of contact with the civilians and the head of security for all the classified materials with which the new organization was dealing. The original basis for the Riverbank cryptology course was Parker Hitt's slim volume, *Manual for the Solution of Military Ciphers.*[13] This was later supplemented by material that William and Elizebeth developed on their own. Needless to say, their working relationship on the new cryptographic tasks brought William and Elizebeth even closer together.

---

[12] J. O. Mauborgne, "Mauborgne to War Dept Re: Riverbank Labs," April 11, 1917, RG59, Box #210, National Archives, College Park, MD.

[13] Parker Hitt, *Manual for the Solution of Military Ciphers*, paperback, SRH-004 (Fort Leavenworth, KS: Press of the Army Service Schools, 1916).

**Fig. 3.6**  William and
Elizebeth Smith Friedman
on their wedding day.
(Courtesy of the George
Marshall Foundation
Library)

William Friedman and Elizebeth Smith were married by a rabbi in Chicago on
21 May 1917 just as war fever was erupting and as a torrent of coded messages
began to arrive at Riverbank. They skipped their honeymoon (Fig. 3.6).

# Chapter 4
# The Great War: Meetings

When the United States entered the Great War on 6 April 1917, the country was woefully unprepared to wage a modern war, particularly with respect to military intelligence. On 11 July, the newly commissioned First Lieutenant Herbert Yardley was put in charge of the Code and Cipher Section (MI-8) of the War Department's nascent Military Intelligence Division (MID). At their Riverbank site outside of Chicago, William and Elizebeth Friedman were already showing Captain Joseph Mauborgne what they could do to help the Army with coded messages. On Mauborgne's recommendation, they would soon be flooded with intercepted cryptograms ready to be deciphered (Fig. 4.1).

As the Americans began to organize, the commander of the American Expeditionary Force (AEF), General John J. Pershing, set up his staff organization along the lines of the British and French. As such, he had an Intelligence Section (G-2) headed by Major Dennis E. Nolan, a friend and contemporary of Ralph Van Deman's. Early on, Van Deman and Nolan agreed that the AEF G-2 organization in France and the MID in Washington would remain completely separate but would share as much information as possible. MID would also be charged with training many of the intelligence officers and cryptologists who would become part of the AEF. MID would concentrate on counterintelligence, diplomatic messages, and domestic US matters, while AEF G-2 focused on military intelligence gathering and counterintelligence in France. Over the course of the war, the two organizations worked closely together to the point of even sharing personnel.[1]

In Washington, Yardley started with two clerks and an avalanche of coded messages from the Army, the Navy, and the Justice and State Departments. He was under orders to ramp up the new Army cryptanalytic unit in Washington as quickly as possible. Yardley's first job was to find people in or out of the Army who had

---

[1] James L. Gilbert, *World War I and the Origins of U.S. Military Intelligence* (Lanham, MD: Rowman & Littlefield Publishing Group, Ltd., 2015), https://rowman.com/ISBN/9780810884601/World-War-I-and-the-Origins-of-U.S.-Military-Intelligence, 31–33.

© The Author(s), under exclusive license to Springer Nature Switzerland AG 2023
J. F. Dooley, *The Gambler and the Scholars*, History of Computing, https://doi.org/10.1007/978-3-031-28318-5_4

what he called "cipher brains," that peculiar twist of mind that allowed someone to see deeply complex patterns in encrypted messages and unravel them. Yardley was convinced that only people with this talent would make good cryptanalysts. Of course, Yardley assumed that he had this talent. Finding people with "cipher brains" was not easy at first. There were very few Army officers with any cryptologic experience, and most of them were on their way to France, and George Fabyan's training course at Riverbank was not yet functioning.

Yardley spent the summer and fall of 1917 searching the country for people talented enough to become expert cryptologists. There were none in the Regular Army that were not already accounted for; Parker Hitt, Frank Moorman, and Joseph Mauborgne were the three best trained and talented Army cryptologists, and all three were already assigned to other duties. There were also no cryptologists on the Civil Service rolls. So, Yardley took to advertising, putting contests in newspapers, and trying to milk every contact he had to find people with "cipher brains." Yardley's real coup was to hire Dr. John Matthews Manly (Fig. 4.2).

Manly had already volunteered his services to Major Van Deman back in March 1917 and was anxious to help the new MID. Yardley contacted Manly, and he was commissioned a Captain and joined MI-8 in Washington in October 1917. It turned out Manly was a terrific cryptanalyst and a good organizer and leader, so Yardley placed him in charge of the cryptanalytic subsection of MI-8 and made him his

**Fig. 4.2** Captain John
Matthews Manly in 1917.
(Courtesy of University of
Chicago Special
Collections)

second-in-command.[2] Manly brought along several of his colleagues from the
University of Chicago, including Dr. Edith Rickert, Manly's former student and
now an English professor at Chicago who would also prove to be an excellent cryptanalyst. She and Manly would together solve one of the most important cryptograms that MI-8 would see during the war (Fig. 4.3).[3]

Yardley also recruited Dr. Charles Jastrow Mendelsohn from the City College of
New York. Mendelsohn was a classicist who was also interested in mathematics and
who had a years-long interest in cryptology. Mendelsohn would also be commissioned a Captain and would head the subsection of MI-8 dedicated to decrypting
German code messages during the war. He would write one of the seminal works on

---

[2] Herbert O. Yardley, "A History of the Code and Cipher Section during the First World War"
(College Park, MD: National Archives, Record Group 457, 1919); Herbert O. Yardley, *The
American Black Chamber* (Indianapolis: Bobbs-Merrill, 1931), 38–39.

[3] Herbert O. Yardley and John M. Manly, "From the Archives: The Achievements of the Cipher
Bureau (MI-8) During the First World War; Documents by Major Herbert O. Yardley, Prepared
under the Direction of the Chief Signal Officer," *Cryptologia* 8, no. 1 (January 1984): 62–74,
https://doi.org/10.1080/0161.118491858791

German diplomatic codes after the Armistice.[4] Mendelsohn continued to work for
Yardley after the war and would also have a multiyear friendship with William
Friedman. Mendelsohn and Friedman would write the official Army report on the
Zimmermann Telegram.[5]

Another key player in Yardley's codebreaking section was Victor Weiskopf.
Weiskopf immigrated to the United States from Bavaria as a child and was fluent in
German and Spanish. Before the war, he had been working for the Justice Department
breaking Mexican ciphers at the southern border. After the war, Weiskopf would
also continue to work for Yardley part-time, and for a couple of years in the
mid-1920s, he also cracked rumrunner coded messages for the Treasury Department.

As Yardley continued to organize and find new talent, MI-8's responsibilities
grew. Eventually, there would be six subsections within MI-8: *Code and Cipher
Solution* (headed by Manly and which included the *Training* subsection), *Code and*

---

[4] Charles Mendelsohn, "Studies in German Diplomatic Codes Used During the World War" (War
Department, Washington, DC: Office of the Chief Signal Officer, Government Printing
Office, 1937).

[5] William F. Friedman and Charles J. Mendelsohn, "The Zimmermann Telegram of January 16,
1917 and Its Cryptographic Background" (Washington, DC: Office of the Chief Signal Officer,
1938),   https://www.nsa.gov/news-features/declassified-documents/friedman-documents/assets/
files/lectures-speeches/FOLDER_198/41766889080599.pdf

*Cipher Creation* (headed by Altus E. Prince, a former State Department official), *Shorthand* (headed by F. W. Allen who owned a court reporters company in New York), *Communications* (headed by James E. McKenna, another former State Department code clerk), and the *Secret Ink Laboratories* (one in New York at the Postal Service Censorship Office headed by Emmett K. Carver, and one in Washington headed by then Lt. A. J. McGrail, both Ph.D. chemists).[6] Yardley organized and managed the overall work of MI-8 and contributed to solving messages in Manly's area. By the end of the war, MI-8 would have a staff of more than 165 people, military and civilian.

MI-8's most famous and spectacular success during the war was the breaking of the Pablo Waberski cipher message in May 1918 by John Manly and Edith Rickert. "Pablo Waberski" was the alias of a German spy named Lothar Witzke. Born in 1895, Witzke served as a junior officer on board the *SMS Dresden*, a German light cruiser that saw action in the South Atlantic and off the Pacific coast of South America early in the war. The *Dresden* was damaged by the British Navy at the Battle of Más a Tierra off the coast of Chile and later scuttled on March 14, 1915. Witzke was interned with the rest of the crew at Valparaiso, Chile. He escaped later in 1915 and made his way via Mexico to San Francisco, where he joined a cell of German saboteurs that was run out of the German Consulate there. Witzke was suspected of being involved in several acts of sabotage against American factories and ships, including a massive explosion of ammunition at Black Tom Island in New York Harbor on 30 July 1916 and an explosion at the Mare Island Naval base in San Francisco harbor in March 1917. Once the United States declared war, Witzke decamped for Mexico. During the rest of 1917, Witzke made several trips across the border on reconnaissance missions. On 16 January 1918, Lothar Witzke, along with two other German agents, set out from Mexico City with the objective of crossing the United States border at Nogales, Arizona. Their job was to stir up and radicalize labor union members against the war. Unfortunately for Witzke, both of the other agents he was traveling with were also Allied spies. William Graves, a Black Canadian dockworker who had lived in the United States, was working for British intelligence; his job was to disrupt German intelligence operations in Mexico. Paul Altendorf, a Pole with a medical degree from the University of Krakow and who had been in the Mexican army, had been recruited by the Treasury Department's Bureau of Investigation to do the same thing. These two joined Witzke on his travels north from Mexico City toward the United States border. The three made their way north at a leisurely pace and finally arrived at Nogales at the end of January. Along the way Altendorf claimed he'd had a change of heart and left the group. In reality, he headed to Nogales on his own and met up with his contact from the Bureau of Investigation, Special Agent Byron S. Butcher, to report and to set a trap for Witzke. When Witzke crossed the border on 1 February 1918, Butcher and his men were waiting for him. On searching Witzke, a 424-letter cryptogram was

---

[6] Herbert O. Yardley, *The American Black Chamber* (Indianapolis: Bobbs-Merrill, 1931), 47.

found folded up and sewed in his jacket.[7] This was dispatched to MI-8, where it then languished on Herbert Yardley's desk for many weeks as just one of a large number of messages that the overworked cryptanalysts at MI-8 needed to decrypt. Finally, in early May 1918, after several other MI-8 cryptanalysts had given up, John Manly got hold of the message, and he and Edith Rickert set to work deciphering the Waberski cipher. The original cipher message is

## 15-01-18

```
seofnatupk  asihelhbbn  uersdausnn

lrsegglesn  nkleznsimn  ehneshmppb

asueasriht  hteurmvnsm  eaincouasi

insnrnvegi  esnbtnnrcn  dtdrzbemuk

kolseizdnn  auebfkbpsa  tasecisdgt

ihuktnaeie  tiebaeuera  thnoieaeen

hsdaoaiakn  ethnnneecd  ckdkonesdu

eszadehpea  bbilsesooe  etnouzkdml

neuilurnrn  zwhneegvcr  eodhicsiac

niuanrdnso  drgsurriec  egrcsuassp

eatgrsheho  etruseelca  umlpaatlee

clcxrnprga  awsutemair  nasnutedea

errreoheim  eahktmuhdt  cokdtgceio

eefighlhre  litfiueunl  eelserunma

znai
```

Manly and Rickert's work on decrypting the Waberski cipher is masterful. Manly's essay on the solution, written in the mid-1920s, is a classic explanation of how gifted cryptanalysts approach an unknown message and solve it. After a long 3-day weekend of work, Manly and Rickert teased out the solution of Witzke's message.[8] Translated into English, it reads:

---

[7] Gilbert, *Origins*, 93–95.

[8] John M. Manly, "Waberski," 1927, Item 811, Friedman Collection, George Marshall Foundation Research Library, Lexington, VA; John F Dooley, *Codes, Ciphers and Spies: Tales of Military Intelligence in World War I*, (New York, NY: Springer Verlag, 2016); Yardley *ABC*.

To The Imperial Consular Authorities in the Republic of Mexico.

Strictly Secret!

The bearer of this is a subject of the Empire who travels as a Russian under the name of Pablo Waberski. He is a German secret agent.

Please furnish him on request protection and assistance, also advance him on demand up to one thousand pesos of Mexican gold and send his code telegrams to this embassy as official consular dispatches.

Von Eckardt

Lothar Witzke was charged with espionage. Manly and Rickert traveled from Washington to Fort Sam Houston in San Antonio, TX, in August 1918 for the trial. Manly gave testimony on the cipher message and the methods the pair had used in its decryption. Lothar Witzke was convicted and became the only German spy sentenced to death in World War I. His sentence was later commuted by President Wilson, and he was released and sent back to Germany in 1923.

William and Elizebeth Smith Friedman, J. A. Powell, and four assistants from Mrs. Gallup's Bacon-Shakespeare group were already breaking coded messages that Van Deman and Yardley had been sending them since June 1917. Many of the messages sent over from Washington to Illinois were intercepted diplomatic cables between Mexico and Germany. The Riverbank group had good luck with these, mostly because the Mexican ciphers were old and many times their code clerks were sloppy. There is no indication that the Riverbank group solved any German diplomatic code messages, but they did have luck with solving messages from other smaller European and South American countries. Van Deman also sent Riverbank caches of Mexican military cipher messages, which William and Elizebeth were also able to solve with little trouble (Fig. 4.4).

The most spectacular solution that the Friedmans uncovered during this period was not from the US government, though, and was not famous for the solution so much as for its aftermath. In the autumn of 1917, a large heavyset man arrived at Riverbank. He was a police inspector from Scotland Yard who had been referred to George Fabyan by the Justice Department. In the inspector's briefcase were a large stack of enciphered messages that he would like to have deciphered. Scotland Yard was investigating a conspiracy by a group of some 200 Hindus in the United States and Britain, aided by Germany, to buy arms and ship them to India as part of a plot to start a revolution against British rule in the Indian subcontinent. The messages had been intercepted by British postal censors and were addressed to a number of people in India. The only thing that the inspector knew was the names of a few of the suspects, which he gave to the Friedmans.[9]

Looking at the messages, William and Elizebeth quickly discovered that the letters used a combination of numbers and plaintext words. The writers had only encrypted the parts of the letters that they thought were important to hide. Unfortunately, this technique gives the cryptanalyst a substantial amount of

---

[9] David Kahn, *The Codebreakers; The Story of Secret Writing* (New York: Macmillan, 1967), 371–372; Jason Fagone, *The Woman Who Smashed Codes*, (New York, NY: William Morrow, 2017), 80–83.

**Fig. 4.4** Elizebeth and
William Friedman in the
summer of 1917. (Courtesy
of the George Marshall
Foundation Library)

information through the context of the encrypted words inside the plaintext sentences; it allows them to guess the hidden words with a high degree of probability. The Friedmans were able to divide the letters into three groups that appeared as if they were using three different cipher systems. In the first group, all the enciphered elements were in five-digit numerical groups, such as 38425 24736 47575 93826. Guessing that these were not codewords, but sets of encrypted letters, William and Elizebeth then broke the 5-digit groups into pairs of numbers, as in 38 42 52 47 36 47 57 59 38 26. These pairs of digits were reminiscent of a technique known as a Polybius square, where the letters of the alphabet are arranged in a rectangle with numbers across the top and down the side allowing each letter to be referenced by a pair of digits. This technique is known as *fractionating*. A traditional Polybius square looks like:

|   | 1 | 2 | 3 | 4 | 5 |
|---|---|---|---|---|---|
| 1 | A | B | C | D | E |
| 2 | F | G | H | IJ | K |
| 3 | L | M | N | O | P |
| 4 | Q | R | S | T | U |
| 5 | V | W | X | Y | Z |

However, the pairs of digits in the letters were significantly larger than many of the pairs from the Polybius square. The Friedmans then guessed that while something like a Polybius square was used, a keyword was also used whose value from the square was added to the numeric value of each letter. They also determined the size of the rectangle (it was not a square) and the key.[10] The square used by the Hindus and the key that the Friedmans uncovered are:

|   | 1 | 2 | 3 | 4 | 5 | 6 | 7 | Key | Value |
|---|---|---|---|---|---|---|---|-----|-------|
| 1 | A | B | C | D | E | F | G | L | 25 |
| 2 | H | I | J | K | L | M | N | A | 11 |
| 3 | O | P | Q | R | S | T | U | M | 26 |
| 4 | V | W | X | Y | Z |   |   | P | 32 |

And a decryption of the ciphertext 38 42 52 47 36 47 57 59 38 26 looks like:

| Ciphertext | 38 | 42 | 52 | 47 | 36 | 47 | 57 | 59 | 38 | 26 |
|------------|----|----|----|----|----|----|----|----|----|----|
| Key | 25 | 11 | 26 | 32 | 25 | 11 | 26 | 32 | 25 | 11 |
| Difference | 13 | 31 | 26 | 15 | 11 | 36 | 31 | 27 | 13 | 15 |
| Plaintext | C | O | M | E | A | T | O | N | C | E |

Once they had figured out the method, William and Elizebeth had no trouble decrypting all the letters that used this particular system.[11]

In the second batch of letters, the cipher words used one or two digits in groups of three, for example, 22-7-6, 97-2-14, 35-1-17. The Friedmans' immediate guess was that this cipher was what is known as a *book cipher*. In a book cipher, the encrypted words are usually triples, with each representing *page, number-line, letter-number,* in the triple. To decrypt the message, the recipient leafs through the book finding the proper page, line, and letter within the line. Without any context, ciphers such as these are normally practically impossible to break without knowing which book is being used. However, the Friedmans had context; the conspirators had only encrypted certain words and phrases in the letters, leaving the rest in plaintext. In addition, the letter writers were lazy. While they had the entire book to choose from, they largely limited their selection of letters to pages near the front of the book and to the first few lines on a page. These two mistakes on the part of the conspirators gave the Friedmans the clues they needed to decrypt better than 95 percent of the words in this group of letters and to find probable words in the book—all without knowing which book was used to do the encryption—a remarkable achievement.

The third cipher system was a variant of a book cipher called a *dictionary cipher*. While with a book cipher, any type of book can be used, as long as the sender and recipient have the same edition of the same book. With a dictionary cipher, the book is usually—a dictionary—and the sender and recipient must have the same edition

---

[10] Helen Fouche Gaines, *Elementary Cryptanalysis; a Study of Ciphers and Their Solution,* (Boston: American Photographic Publishing Company, 1939), 164–167.

[11] William F. Friedman, "The Hindu Cipher," Signal Corps Information Bulletin (Washington, DC: Office of the Chief Signal Officer, U.S. Army, December 1, 1921), VF096-015, National Cryptologic Museum Library, Ft. Meade, MD.

of the dictionary. The Friedmans figured out that the Indians were using a dictionary cipher because the middle number of the three for each cipher word was always either a 1 or a 2, indicating either the first column or the second column of the page. The third number in the triple was also not a letter number, but a word number in that column on the appropriate page. So, the cipher word 35-1-17 means page 35, column 1, 17th word down the column. Once again, William and Elizebeth had lots of context in the letters with which to work, and they were able to largely decrypt these letters as well, even without having a copy of the dictionary.

Once all the conspirators' letters were largely decrypted, the British and American governments set about arresting them and bringing them to trial. Two trials were held in late autumn of 1917, one in Chicago and one in San Francisco. William—but not Elizebeth—was summoned to both trials to give testimony as an expert witness on cryptology. This is when luck smiled on the Friedmans once again. William's testimony would be greatly strengthened if he could identify the actual books used to encrypt the letters, but up to this time neither the Friedmans nor George Fabyan had been able to find them. When in Chicago, as William was walking to the Federal Courthouse from his hotel, he stopped in a random bookstore for one last attempt at finding the book for the first cipher. Because of their work, he and Elizebeth could identify certain words on certain lines on certain pages to confirm that a particular book was used. Here is where the Friedmans' luck enters the picture again. One of the Hindu conspirators, when confronted with one of the deciphered messages, broke down, confessed, and named the book used, *Germany and the Germans*, by American historian Price Collier that had been published in 1913. Friedman picked up a copy of the book in Chicago and discovered that all the words, pages, and lines matched his and Elizebeth's solution. Literally hours before his testimony, William had found the book.[12]

Several weeks later, in San Francisco for the second trial, William, on the advice of a friend from Cornell University, dropped by the University of California bookstore where an elderly salesclerk rummaged around and brushed off a copy of a German-English dictionary from 1880. All the page, column, and word numbers for the dictionary cipher worked. Luck had smiled again. However, William's testimony at the San Francisco trial was overshadowed by an event that made headlines across the nation. One of the Indian conspirators who was turning state's evidence was on the stand testifying when a man in the gallery stood up and shot the witness dead. A US marshal promptly shot the gunman dead as well, firing above the heads

---

[12] Ronald Clark, *The Man Who Broke Purple* (Boston: Little, Brown and Company, 1977), 52. There are actually two different versions of this story. In the Elizebeth Smith Friedman Collection at the Marshall Library, there is a document in Box #6, File #13 where Elizebeth, in a handwritten comment, claims that William, browsing through a Chicago bookstore, finds Collier's book by accident and discovers that it is the correct text. Later, a different part of the document, almost certainly written by William, gives the account found in Clark's biography.

of the spectators.[13] William's testimony sealed the case for the prosecution, essentially convicting the defendants out of their own mouths.

One of MI-8's most essential jobs was the training of cryptanalysts for both MI-8 and the AEF, but in fact, in July 1917, there was no training program, no curriculum or training materials, and no one yet hired to do the training. The Army Signal Corps' Signal School did have a cryptography course—the same course that Captain J. A. Powell took—but it was somewhat dated and not set up for handling a large number of students. Additionally, the Signal Corps was extremely busy ramping up for the war itself and so was not anxious to accommodate the new Intelligence Section. MI-8 was in quite a fix. This is where the Friedmans and Riverbank came in.

Over the summer and fall of 1917, in between cryptanalyzing cipher messages, the Friedmans and Powell began designing an updated version of the Signal School's cryptography course. They started with the Signal School materials that Powell had brought back with him, and the Friedmans began to add new materials, using some of the enciphered messages they were working on as examples and homework assignments. William Friedman designed much of the curriculum. William and Elizebeth also began putting together a series of eight pamphlets that described how to solve different types of cipher systems. These pamphlets, which would become known as the Riverbank Publications, began appearing in the fall of 1917.

The eight pamphlets authored by William Friedman—and most of them probably also authored and edited by Elizebeth—are:

- #15 *A Method of Reconstructing the Primary Alphabet From a Single One of the Series of Secondary Alphabets*, 1917
- #16 *Methods for the Solution of Running-Key Ciphers*, most likely written with Elizebeth Smith Friedman, 1918[14]
- #17 *An Introduction to Methods for the Solution of Ciphers*, 1918
- #18 *Synoptic Tables for the Solution of Ciphers and A Bibliography of Cryptographic Literature*, 1918
- #19 *Formulae for the Solution of Geometrical Transposition Ciphers*, written with Capt. Lenox R. Lohr, 1918
- #20 *Several Machine Ciphers and Methods for their Solution*, 1918
- #21 *Methods for the Reconstruction of Primary Alphabets*, written with Elizebeth Smith Friedman, 1918
- #22 *The Index of Coincidence and Its Applications in Cryptography*, 1920 (but not published until 1922).[15]

By far, the most famous of Friedman's Riverbank Publications is #22 *The Index of Coincidence*. By itself, *The Index of Coincidence* would change the trajectory of

---

[13] Fagone *Smashed*, 83; Kahn *Codebreakers*, 372; Clark *Purple*, 54; Elizebeth S. Friedman, "Autobiography of Elizebeth Smith Friedman – 1st Draft" (Memoir, Lexington, VA, 1966), George Marshall Foundation Research Library, https://www.marshallfoundation.org/library/wp-content/uploads/sites/16/2015/06/ESFMemoirComplete_opt.pdf, 23.

[14] Fagone, *Smashed*, 77.

[15] Fagone, *Smashed*, 77–78.

American cryptanalysis forever by solidifying the use of statistical analysis in crypt-analytic techniques. From this point on, modern cryptanalysis would increasingly depend on mathematical tools and less on just linguistic tools.

By late October 1917, the Riverbank 2-month long cryptanalysis curriculum was ready to go. The first group of four Army officers arrived early in November, fin-ished the course before the new year, and left for France shortly thereafter with the best training that William and Elizebeth could give them. William did most of the instruction himself in the mornings. The entire Riverbank team graded problem sets in the afternoons in between solving encrypted messages from the government. By this time, December 1917, the flow of coded messages from the War Department had started to slow down. Herbert Yardley's MI-8 section was getting staffed up, and John Manly and his compatriots from the University of Chicago were trained and beginning to take up the increasing flow of messages from the War, State, Justice, and Treasury Departments. The Riverbank school's next class in January 1918 was drawn from all over the Army and numbered 78 officers. Fabyan rented out the larg-est hotel in nearby Aurora, Illinois, to house them all. On the last day of class at the end of February, William lined up the entire class, plus Fabyan, Elizebeth, and two of the Riverbank assistants for a class photograph. However, this would not be a typical class photo. William arranged all the participants in rows and told some of them to face straight ahead and others to look to their left or right. In the photo, William created a live example of a Baconian biliteral cipher using his class of new cryptanalysts; each of the students represented a single letter in one of the two "fonts" in the biliteral cipher message. The message spelled out Francis Bacon's motto, "Knowledge is Power" (Fig. 4.5)[16]

Between November 1917 and March 1918, the Riverbank school trained over 80 Army officers, the majority of whom joined the AEF in France. In March 1918, MI-8 took over training and moved the cryptology school to Washington.[17]

By the spring of 1918, the flow of encrypted messages sent to Riverbank for solution had also nearly dried up because Yardley's MI-8 Code and Cipher Solution section was fully operational. William Friedman was now anxious to enlist and serve in France. Unbeknownst to him, the Army in the guise of Major Mauborgne and Colonel Van Deman also wanted William in the Army, so they could use his skills as a teacher and cryptanalyst. As early as October 1917, Van Deman had writ-ten to Fabyan suggesting that Friedman be commissioned and sent to France, "as Prof. Friedman is subject to draft and you may lose him later, do you not think it advisable to ask for a commission for him and send him to France?"[18] Fabyan coun-tered with a suggestion that Friedman be commissioned and assigned to Riverbank

[16] It turned out that Friedman needed 80 people to spell out "Knowledge is Power," but he only had 76 people in the photograph. So, the message really spells "Knowledge is Powe" with one person left over.

[17] Wayne G. Barker, *The History of Codes and Ciphers in the United States during World War I, Volume 2 (SRH-001)*, vol. 21 (Laguna Beach, Calif.: Aegean Park Press, 1979), 3–8.

[18] Ralph Van Deman, "Van Deman to Fabyan, Re: Friedman Commission," Letter, October 27, 1917, Friedman Collection, George Marshall Foundation Research Library, Lexington, VA.

# KNOWLEDGE IS POWER

**Fig. 4.5** "Knowledge is Power" photo, 1918. (Courtesy of the George Marshall Foundation Library)

instead of going to France. Van Deman replied that "I am obliged to say that I do not consider such action advisable."[19]

The situation was actually even more convoluted than this exchange of letters makes it appear. Van Deman and Mauborgne had also been sending letters to William Friedman with the same suggestions of a commission and deployment to France. However, Friedman never answered any of their letters. That was because George Fabyan was intercepting all the correspondence addressed to the Friedmans and was not giving them any of the letters from the War Department. So, for a period of about 7 months, when he was desperate to enlist and do his bit for his country, William Friedman had absolutely no idea that the War Department was trying to recruit him. Friedman would not learn any of this until much later, well after he was already in the Army and in France.[20]

In April 1918, William and Elizebeth Friedman were wrapping up all the work that Riverbank had done for the War Department. William would then be free to join the Army. Before that, he and Elizebeth had one more request from the Army to fulfill. In early 1918, the British Army proposed a new cipher device to be used near the front lines on the Western Front. The device was invented by J. St. Vincent Pletts of the Marconi Wireless Telegraph Company who was working with the British Army cryptologic organization MI.1(b). Pletts' device was an improvement of a device invented by Charles Wheatstone in 1857 called the *cryptograph*. Pletts' cryptograph was composed of two concentric rings. The outer ring, or *stator*, had 27 cells and was fixed. This ring had the 26 letters of the alphabet written in a mixed order, one letter per cell, and left one cell empty. The user would use the outer ring for their plaintext letters. The inner ring, or *rotator*, had 26 cells on which were also written a mixed alphabet and which gave the ciphertext. The device used two keywords to set up the alphabets, one per ring (Fig. 4.6).

The British Army cryptologic organization, MI.1(b) tested the new device and found it to be secure. The British had Yardley's MI-8 group in Washington test the

---

[19] Ralph Van Deman, "Van Deman to Fabyan, Re: Friedman Commission," Letter, March 23, 1918, Friedman Collection, George Marshall Foundation Research Library, Lexington, VA.

[20] Friedman, *Autobiography*.

**Fig. 4.6** Pletts'
cryptograph. (Courtesy of
the Imperial War Museum)

device as well, and they also thought it would be secure in the field. As one last test, five test messages, each with a length of approximately 40 characters—which is very short—were sent to Riverbank, and William and Elizebeth Friedman were asked to try to break the messages. William determined that the keyword for one of the alphabets was the word **CIPHER**. However, he was stuck on the second keyword. In their experience thus far, the Friedmans knew that many cryptographers were just terrible at making up keywords that did not give away too much information; even worse, many of the pairs of keywords were related to each other, so if the cryptanalyst guessed one, the other was easy. So, what keyword would go along with **CIPHER**? Friedman tried several words, but none of them produced coherent plaintext. Finally, he decided to ask his wife, who was across the room working on another cipher message. As related by Elizebeth:

> He asked me to lean back in my chair, close my eyes, and make my mind blank, at least as blank as possible. Then he would propound to me a question to which I was not to consider the reply to any degree, not even for one second, but instantly to come forth with the word which his question aroused in my mind. I did as he directed. He spoke the word "cipher," and I instantaneously responded, "machine." And in a few moments Bill said I had made a lucky guess. The officer in Washington had broken a fundamental rule, that is, when choosing a key word, never choose one which is associated with the project ... Bill had not attempted to use it because his meticulous mind's eye saw a device, not a machine. ... The five test messages were solved and on their way back to Washington within three hours of the time they had been received.[21]

---

[21] Friedman, *Autobiography*.

Unfortunately, for him, it was Herbert Yardley who had to telegraph the British the next day and tell them "that messages enciphered by Pletts machine have been broken by method of attack different from any considered by inventor, and that system is considered dangerous in presence of enemy."[22] Despite the fact that several hundred of the machines had already been manufactured, the Pletts device was never used in the field.

William Friedman enlisted in the US Army in May 1918 and was commissioned as a First Lieutenant. He sailed for France in June 1918 and was assigned to the Radio Intelligence Section of Military Intelligence in the AEF, G-2 A-6, under Major Frank Moorman at AEF headquarters in Chaumont. Friedman asked to be assigned to the Code Solution section because, while he'd had nearly 2 years experience with cipher systems, he'd had very little practice on codes, and he wanted to learn more about how to cryptanalyze codes. Friedman would rise to be a leader of the cryptanalytic Code Solution section of G-2 A-6 for the remainder of the war.[23]

---

[22] David Kahn, *The Reader of Gentlemen's Mail: Herbert O. Yardley and the Birth of American Codebreaking* (New Haven: Yale University Press, 2004), 26.

[23] Clark, *Purple,* 65.

# Chapter 5
# Wars End

By July 1918, Herbert Yardley had MI-8 organized, up and running. From a section in July 1917 that consisted of Yardley and two clerks, by this time MI-8 had grown to 18 officers, 24 civilian cryptographers, and 109 clerks and typists. The section was handling hundreds of intercepted cipher messages every week, creating new codes, uncovering messages hidden by secret ink and shorthand, and handling the Army's overseas communications with the AEF. Yardley was exhausted. Toward the end of July, Yardley asked Colonel Van Deman to be reassigned because his nerves were shot and he could not take the stress any longer. Instead, Van Deman passed along a request from the AEF commanding General John J. Pershing that Yardley be put on a special mission for the AEF to be a liaison to the British and French cryptologic bureaus. Yardley agreed, and by early August, he was on a troopship that would drop him off in London. John Manly was placed in charge of MI-8 and would remain in that post through the Armistice and the rapid demobilization of the section and his own discharge from the service in mid-1919. The couple of weeks spent crossing the Atlantic with no worries about MI-8 revived Yardley's spirits and settled his nerves. He arrived in London on 29 August 1918 and checked into the Ritz Hotel, stayed one night, and promptly checked out and moved into less expensive lodgings. However, what he saved in hotel bills, he made up for in food and drink by treating British officers to lavish dinners at posh restaurants. Herbert Yardley always liked comfort, especially if someone else was paying for it.[1]

Yardley's goal in London was to establish a relationship with British Military Intelligence, MI.1(b), and to create contacts with the Admiralty organization that handled intercepting and decoding of diplomatic and naval correspondence—Room 40. Despite plying the British Army officers with food, drink, and camaraderie, his first few weeks attempting to gain entry into the inner workings of MI.1(b) proved fruitless, as the British did not really want to share information with the Americans

---

[1] David Kahn, *The Reader of Gentlemen's Mail: Herbert O. Yardley and the Birth of American Codebreaking* (New Haven: Yale University Press, 2004), 45.

© The Author(s), under exclusive license to Springer Nature     43
Switzerland AG 2023
J. F. Dooley, *The Gambler and the Scholars*, History of Computing,
https://doi.org/10.1007/978-3-031-28318-5_5

whom they judged as late to the party and rather loose-lipped. However, Yardley finally cracked the MI.1(b) nut by succeeding at a challenge presented to him by the British Army: breaking a series of messages in a proposed British field cipher. After that, he was welcomed into the MI.1(b) cryptanalytic bureau offices, and information between the two sides was freely shared. Yardley also learned a lot from the British in terms of techniques and methods of cryptanalysis, saying "I felt like I was finishing my education."[2]

However, with the Admiralty and access to Room 40, Yardley had no luck at all. Partly this was because the Americans, who were still just starting their work in cryptanalysis, had nothing to offer the British in return for British information on German codes and ciphers. Yardley was persistent though, and this made matters worse because he then just reinforced British attitudes about pushy, talkative Americans who could not keep a secret. Yardley was also running up against the Director of Naval Intelligence at the Admiralty, Admiral Sir William Reginald "Blinker" Hall. In early 1917, Hall was anxious to get America involved in the war. It was Hall's Room 40 cryptanalysts who had decoded the Zimmermann Telegram in January of that year. Hall worked with Edward Bell of the American Embassy in London to release the Zimmermann Telegram to the US State Department in late January, warning of the imminent beginning of unrestricted submarine warfare by the Germans, and their plot to entice the Mexicans into declaring war on the United States in return for money, arms, and the return of their territories in the American Southwest. Therefore, Hall had been instrumental in getting the Americans to declare war on Germany. That said, Hall was also not anxious to share any of Room 40's secrets with their new allies. "Hall was very willing to share his secrets whether diplomatic or naval with the Americans, where he could see that it was to the advantage of the Allied cause. What he would not do, despite continual requests from both the Office of Naval Intelligence, the U.S. Army, and the State Department, was to impart to them any cryptographic expertise or to assist them in any way to establish their own cryptographic bureau."[3] Through the early period of America's entry into the war, the State and War departments supplied Hall and Room 40 with copies of intercepted German messages, and Hall gladly returned decrypted versions of the telegrams. The Americans wanted more, but Hall was completely unwilling to give it to them. As late as July 1918, Bell reported to the State Department in Washington that Hall "is absolutely opposed to any definite arrangement for the general pooling of this class of information because he feels certain that it would end in the source becoming compromised through leakage, particularly if certain Allies were in regular receipt of it."[4]

So when Yardley arrived in late August 1918 and several weeks later spent much time trying to get Hall to give him German codebooks and to give him access to

---

[2] Kahn, *ROGM*, 46; Herbert O. Yardley, *The American Black Chamber* (Indianapolis: Bobbs-Merrill, 1931), 216–217.

[3] Patrick Beesly, *Room 40: British Naval Intelligence 1914–1918*, (New York, NY: Harcourt, Brace, Jovanovich, 1982), 247.

[4] Beesly, *Room 40*, 248.

Room 40, Hall became even more intransigent. Hall ended up disliking Yardley immensely, largely because Yardley was something of a showman and a glad-handing type of sales guy, but also because he was rather pushy about trying to obtain the things that the Americans wanted their allies to provide to them. Hall just did not like his personality. Hall used the excuse that he did not trust the Americans not to leak the work that Room 40 was doing. Those characteristics that made Yardley a terrific poker player did him no good at the Admiralty.[5] After several more weeks of fruitlessly trying to gain admittance to Room 40, Yardley was finally ordered to move on to France, where he visited the cryptanalytic section of the British Expeditionary Force on the coast at Le Touquet, meeting there with Captain O. T. Hitchings, the head of the BEF's cryptanalytic section. Here, just as with MI.1(b) ) in London, Yardley was welcomed and learned more from the front-line British cryptanalysts.

Shortly thereafter, Colonel Van Deman, who had been transferred and was now in charge of intelligence for the AEF, ordered Yardley to move on to Paris to make contact with the French military's cryptanalytic agency.

Yardley's stay in Paris duplicated what had happened in London. While he was welcomed into the French Army's intelligence offices by Colonel (later General) Francois Cartier, the head of French military intelligence, Yardley was once again denied access to the part of the French intelligence services that was charged with handling diplomatic correspondence. In fact, the French denied to Yardley that they even had an agency that dealt with diplomatic communications. As David Kahn describes Cartier and Hall's attitude toward Yardley, "The American exaggerated his importance and that of his work, a trait that irritated his transatlantic allies. His openness had been intensified by his need to sell his program, and no harmful effects had taught him to boast less. Moreover, though the French had indeed cooperated with Moorman (this is Major Frank Moorman, the head of the Radio Intelligence Section of the AEF's General Staff) and Yardley on the tactical level, they weren't going to teach the Americans how to break diplomatic codes—which they themselves were using and whose solution produced their best intelligence."[6]

However, Yardley did gain some access to the military cryptanalytic bureau and was given access to people and materials related to German military codes and ciphers. He also met Captain Georges Jean Painvin, the greatest cryptanalyst of the war. The two became friends and had interesting discussions about German cipher systems, particularly the ADFGVX cipher that Painvin had broken earlier in the year. In Yardley's book *The American Black Chamber*, even though he misquotes a 1920 lecture by Colonel Frank Moorman on the American opinion of Georges Painvin, the spirit of Moorman's words is correct, "Captain Georges Painvin, the chief code expert of the French, an analytical genius of the highest order, was a regular wizard in solving codes...."[7]

[5] Beesly, *Room 40*, 250; Kahn, *ROGM*, 46.

[6] Kahn, *ROGM*, 46.

[7] Yardley, *ABC*, 223.

Yardley's next stop was AEF Headquarters in Chaumont. But, by the time he got there, the Armistice had already been signed and the war was over. Nevertheless, Yardley reported to the AEF head of intelligence and was sent off to meet with Colonel Moorman, the head of the Radio Intelligence Division, G-2 A-6. Moorman provides some insight into the relationship between G-2 A-6 in France and MI-8 in Washington in the same lecture referenced above:

> ... we lacked liaison with Washington. I do not think that Washington understood our problems in the beginning. We did not understand Washington and did not make any particular effort to appeal to them for help. Later we discovered that there was such an organization as Washington, and at the same time they found out that we were in existence in France, and then a real effort was made to work together. This would have made more efficient work had not the timing of the armistice made further efforts in this line unnecessary.
>
> Major Yardley was sent over but got lost somewhere between London and Paris, and so never got to us until after the Armistice was signed. On that account we never got the advantage of what he was going to tell us, nor to tell him what we needed.[8]

To be fair to both Moorman and Yardley, the jobs that MI-8 and G-2 A-6 were doing were similar, but quite a bit different as well. The AEF's G-2 (intelligence) section and its Signal Corps brethren were interested only in solving German military codes and ciphers, traffic interception and analysis, managing intra-AEF communications, and the creation of tactical level trench codes for the US Army in France. MI-8, on the other hand, did none of these things. Instead, it was interested in solving mostly diplomatic codes and ciphers of a number of different countries and solving the code and cipher systems used by enemy spies and prisoners of war inside the United States. It did this work for the War, State, and Justice Departments and the US Navy. It also created codes for use by the top-level military organizations in Washington and France, solved secret ink and shorthand messages, handled all the communications between the War Department in Washington and the AEF in France, and trained new cryptographers and cryptanalysts for service in France. (The AEF G-2 created its own training organization, but not until the fall of 1918.) So, the overlap between the two organizations was fairly small, largely having to do with training and communications security. Also, as we will see later, Moorman occasionally and Yardley frequently strayed beyond the bounds of facts in their writing.[9]

One would think that with both Herbert Yardley and William Friedman in the US Army, in France, and in military intelligence in 1918 that they would meet. And they did. When Yardley visited AEF's G-2 A-6 headquarters in Chaumont, France, the two met in late November 1918. While Yardley and Friedman knew of each other and had likely corresponded, this was their first in-person meeting. They were an odd pair. Yardley was quite short—five feet five inches—and somewhat stocky

---

[8] Frank Moorman, "Code and Cipher in France," *Infantry Journal* XVI, no. 12 (June 16, 1920): 1039–44, 1042.

[9] Betsy Rohaly Smoot, "Sources and Methods: Uncovering the Story of American Cryptology in World War I," *Cryptologia* 45, no. 1 (January 2021): 81–87, https://doi.org/10.1080/01611194.202 0.1858371, 83.

and already losing his hair. He was a sloppy dresser and was slightly careless in appearance, even in uniform. Friedman was slightly taller, thin and later in life sported a neatly trimmed mustache. He was always impeccably dressed, even in the field. The two men's personalities, Friedman somewhat bookish, intense, stern, and Yardley outgoing, brazen, and boisterous, clashed immediately. There is nothing in Yardley's correspondence about the meeting, but William wrote to Elizebeth on December 16th about encountering Yardley. He was not impressed:

> In one of your letters you ask about Yardley. Well, I wrote you he came just a couple of days before my leave, and I told you I had talk with him in which he told me about the offer that Wash. made to Col. F for me. Well, Y said they knew all along he wasn't playing the game square and all that. At the same time I must confess to considerable distaste for Y. Frankly, I didn't like him at all, though he was not overbearing or patronizing to me. There was something very distasteful though about his air and manner. I had him down to dinner one night at the mess and he acted like a wooden Indian. I certainly wouldn't have asked him had I thought he'd be that way. But he is talkative enough around with ---Childs.[10] Those two were as thick as thieves when he got here, and what those two didn't talk about as wasn't worth mentioning I suppose.[11]

Surely not an auspicious beginning to a rivalry, friendship, and professional relationship.

By early January 1919, Yardley had been ordered back to Paris, where he reported to Colonel Van Deman, who was the head of Military Intelligence for the American Commission to Negotiate Peace. Van Deman ordered Yardley to create a Cipher Bureau for the Peace Commission. With help from two officers from G-2 A-6, Lt. Frederick Livesey and Lt. J. Rives Childs and a few clerks, Yardley set up his organization near the Place de la Concorde. Yardley's team needed to provide codes to be used by the President and the rest of the American commissioners to communicate with MID in Washington. They were also in charge of American communications between Paris and Washington.[12] Finally, Yardley and his crew were charged with breaking new German substitution and transposition ciphers created later for the German delegates to the Peace Conference who had arrived in March 1919, although by the time Yardley left France late in March 1919, they had not made any

---

[10] This is Lt. J. Rives Childs, who was trained in cryptanalysis at Riverbank by Friedman in November–December 1917. Childs was shipped off to France in January 1918 and was assigned to the Cipher Solutions Section of G-2 A-6. He also acted as the liaison to the British Military Intelligence Section in France. It was Childs who was given a number of superenciphered code messages in the new American Trench Code in May 1918 and broke the superencipherment within just a few hours. This exposed a dangerous weakness in this newly developed code, and it was never released to the field. Instead, the Code Compilation Section of the Radio Intelligence Section under Captain Harold Barnes went on to develop an entirely new set of 2-part codes known as the "River" codes because they were named after American Rivers. When the US Second Army was created in September 1918, a new set of codes, the "Lake" codes, were created for that Army.

[11] William F. Friedman, "WFF to ESF Re: Yardley," Letter, December 16, 1918, Box 2, Folder 19, Elizebeth Smith Friedman Collection, George Marshall Research Library, Lexington, VA.

[12] Kahn, *ROGM*, 47.

significant breaks in these new ciphers. The French were luckier and had broken them before the end of the Peace Conference the following June (Fig. 5.1).[13]

It turned out that once things were set up and the set of diplomatic codes used for communications created, Yardley and his team did not really have much work to do during the Peace Conference. They did intercept some diplomatic communications of both allies and Germans, but the small group that made up Yardley's team made little progress in decrypting these messages. Yardley decided that there was not enough work to keep all three of them and the clerks busy all the time, so he divided their work into shifts. Yardley worked mornings, Childs in the afternoon, and Livesey took the evening shift. All three, in particular Yardley and Childs, were then free to take advantage of their downtime to indulge in the recently resuscitated Parisian nightlife.

**Fig. 5.1** Lt. J. Rives Childs and Captain Herbert Yardley in Paris, 1919. (US Army photo)

---

[13] Alan Sharp, "'Quelqu'un Nous Écoute': French Interception of German Telegraphic and Telephonic Communications during the Paris Peace Conference, 1919: A Note," *Intelligence and National Security* 3, no. 4 (October 1, 1988): 124–27, https://doi.org/10.1080/02684528808431974, 124

Childs and Yardley were initially booked into the elegant—and expensive—
Hôtel de Crillon on the Place de la Concorde, where the American Peace Delegation
was being housed. However, it did not take long for them to realize that their per
diem from the Army would go much further at a pension. So, they first moved to a
small pension off the Avenue de Wagram just north of the Arc de Triomphe and
finally to a furnished apartment that they shared with two other American officers at
18 rue Gustave Zédé near the Bois de Boulogne and a Metro line that was about
6km from the Crillon.[14]

Paris in early 1919 was a city set free from the troubles and devastation of 4 years
of war, and with a large number of young foreign soldiers still housed in the city, a
months-long celebration ensued, much to the chagrin of the French authorities who
were still preaching austerity. Childs and Yardley jumped in with both feet, hosting
dances, attending parties, and meeting and wooing all the willing young Parisian
women they could find; Yardley, despite the fact that he was married. They had sur-
vived the war, and it was time to celebrate. Childs, in his autobiographical novel
*Before the Curtain Falls*, describes their days:

> ...Breakfast in bed in the morning about ten, reading of the Paris edition of the Herald in
> order to find out what was actually taking place at the Conference, a stroll along the Rue de
> Rivoli and perhaps a beer at the Café de la Paix, to work at twelve, then the afternoon off
> with Barkley [Yardley's character in the book] after four and a tour of the bars on the
> Champs Elysées, looking the women over and sighing between drinks at the necessity of a
> daily confinement to the office, to one of the semi-public clandestine dance-halls at five,
> public dancing not then being permitted, perhaps dinner with any agreeable dancing part-
> ners disposed to dine with us, the Folies Bergères or the Casino after dinner and dancing
> again after the theater. ... They were great days, if irresponsible ones, and there will never
> be their like again. Through it all there ran the temporary mad reaction from the war, and if
> we were all irresponsible it was an irresponsibility begotten of an inability to find any rea-
> son in our lives since 1914, or to relate our experiences with life's old expectations.[15]

However, all good things must come to an end, and in March 1919, Van Deman
ordered Yardley back to America via Rome so he could make contact with the Italian
Army's cryptanalytic organization and see what he could find out about their methods. Apparently, the Italians were not as sophisticated as Van Deman thought
because Yardley was not impressed. He finally departed from Genoa on 31 March
1919, arrived back in New York in mid-April, and headed immediately to
Washington.

After the Armistice on November 11th and while Yardley was still in France,
MI-8 in Washington was rapidly turning into a ghost town. Nearly as soon as the
Armistice was signed, many of the civilian employees were discharged, and the
Army cryptographers and clerks began to be demobilized. By the time Yardley
returned to Washington in April 1919, MI-8 was at approximately half-strength, a
shell of its former self. John Manly was still there, but he would be demobilized

---

[14] Kahn, *ROGM*, 48.

[15] J. Rives Childs, *Before the Curtain Falls*, (Indianapolis, IN: Bobbs-Merrill Company Publishers,
1932), 158, 160.

himself in early summer. Most of his colleagues from the University of Chicago were already gone, back to their faculty positions. Manly and Yardley wrote up a history of MI-8 and spent some time storing files and considering the future of the organization. Over the course of the 19 months, the United States was involved in the war MI-8 had decrypted over 10,000 foreign ciphered messages and solved more than two dozen different systems from eight countries.[16]

After the armistice, Friedman was anxious to get home, but the Army had other work for him. Major Moorman told Friedman he was to stay in France for a few more months and write the history of the Code Solving Section of G-2 A-6 and a separate description of the German military codes encountered by the unit and their methods of solution. Despite being desperate to get back to his wife, William stayed in France for 4 more months and produced an admirable history of his unit. In his masterful report on German codes, *Field Codes Used by the German Army During the World War*, Friedman does an excellent job of describing and dissecting the structures of the two main types of German field codes, the *Satzbuch* (sentence book) or three-letter codes, called the KRU codes by the Americans because all their codewords began with the letters K, R, or U, which were used down to the regimental level, and the *Schluesselhuft* or three-number codes, which were used within three kilometers of the front.[17] One note that brings out Friedman's thinking after more than 2 years working on ciphers and another 8 months on German codes comes just after his description on identification of the KRU codes and the methods used to solve them:

> It should be added that in this whole process the part played by chance, by the happy coincidences which were always lurking everywhere for the watchful eye of the worker to note, by the mistakes of a foolish or a careless encoder, and by a fortunate 'long shot' or guess by the decoded cannot be overestimated. Often the minutest and most insignificant of clues formed the starting point for the unravelling of a whole chain of groups."[18]

Once Friedman had finished his history of the Code Solving Section and his methods paper, he was more than ever ready to go home.

Over the course of his time in France, William and Elizebeth had kept up a lively and intimate correspondence; one clearly fitting for a young couple that were still newlyweds and still very much in love. Unfortunately, while most of William's letters from this period remain, nearly all of Elizebeth's letters are gone, possibly destroyed by her at some later time. This is a possibility because, based on the content of his letters to her, William would almost certainly have never destroyed her letters to him.

One of the more significant topics of their letters was their future. Before William made his way home, the Friedmans had an important life decision to make; should

---

[16] Kahn *ROGM*, 50.

[17] William F. Friedman, "Field Codes Used by the German Army during the World War (SRMA-012)," 209 (Washington, DC: War Department, February 5, 1919), RG457, Friedman Collection, National Archives, College Park, MD, 6; John F Dooley, *Codes, Ciphers and Spies: Tales of Military Intelligence in World War I*, (New York, NY: Springer Verlag, 2016), 61–62.

[18] Friedman, *Field Codes*, 51.

they return to Riverbank and continue working on Colonel Fabyan's hobby projects or strike out into something new? Elizebeth had left Riverbank in the fall of 1918 and returned home to Indiana to help take care of her father. But rural Indiana was not where either of the Friedmans wanted to be. One option on their list was for William to go back to graduate school and finish his Ph.D. in genetics. In December 1918, William had even gone as far as writing to Dr. John M. Colter, the chair of the Botany Department at the University of Chicago inquiring about graduate research positions in the department.[19] The second option, of course, was for them to return to work for Colonel Fabyan at Riverbank. Fabyan was anxious to have them back and had been saying so in nearly every piece of correspondence he exchanged with the pair.

The Friedmans' correspondence with Colonel Fabyan over the course of late 1918 into early 1919 was increasingly acrimonious. In early October, William received a letter from Elizebeth dated 21 September 1918 in which she told him that she had discovered that Fabyan had intercepted an offer of employment for her from Washington—probably from MI-8—and had declined it on her behalf. They were both livid. William responded to Elizebeth on 07 October (italics added):

> Honey, I could have committed several crimes after reading what it had to tell me about that old nameless rascal. I was upset all day as a result. To think that he would do such a thing after all we have done. ... When I read that they asked for you at Wash. and how he handled that I could have either wept or murdered. I don't know which emotion was the more powerful. And you so deserving of doing your share down there; so capable of doing much, especially when they were after you, unsought of by you. What a blow that is to my faith in men. It would possibly have meant so much to both of us, because now I know we shall never return to Riverbank. ... I am most anxious to hear what reply Capt. M (probably John Manly, who was in charge of MI-8 beginning in late July 1918) made to your letter. It must have surprised him. ... Well, I shall be jobless now for sure, but as I told you I am not worrying one bit and I know you will trust in my ability to make ends meet when that time comes. It may be the making of us. *I am afraid we were getting chained to the job at R(iverbank) and I am glad that we are free now once and for all.*[20]

And their feelings for Fabyan and Riverbank did not improve over the rest of 1918. In a letter to Elizebeth just one week later, William says, "I've had about enough of Kaiserism and have no fear of anything he (Fabyan) can do. He can make a lot of noise at R but no place else I know of. I know pretty well what they think of him at Washington."[21] On the same day, 14 October, William sent Elizebeth a cablegram (an extravagant expense at the time) saying "DONT WANT YOU RETURN RIVERBANK. ADVISE FABYAN EITHER LEAVE ABSENCE DURATION WAR OR PERMANENT LEAVE DIRECT VACATION LEAST TWO

---

[19] William F. Friedman, "WFF to ESF Re: Fabyan," Letter, December 8, 1918, Box 2, Folder 19, Elizebeth Smith Friedman Collection, George Marshall Research Library, Lexington, VA.

[20] William F. Friedman, "WFF to ESF Re: Fabyan," October 7, 1918, ESF Collection, Box 2, Folder 17, George Marshall Foundation Research Library.

[21] William F. Friedman, "WFF to ESF Re: Fabyan," October 14, 1918, ESF Collection, Box 2, Folder 17, George Marshall Foundation Research Library.

MONTHS. LOVE, FRIEDMAN." And the same theme was continued in a letter from William dated the next day (italics added):

> Your fears, Love Girl, of the letter of Sep 5 are entirely unfounded with respect to what he could do to me. He can do absolutely nothing. *I am through with him and the place for good.* He couldn't be square and on the level and do those things you tell me of at the same time.... I want to be free to live with my Darling as most people do and get a little fun out of life and some happiness and a share of the world's goods with and for my Darling. There, it is impossible. For it would be against his interest to have anybody get ahead far enough to be independent for then he'd lose his hold. That explains why he acted so despicably underhanded with regard to your Washington opportunity. He wanted you to stay and blocked the doorway to your advancement for his own personal gain. And not even to consult with you was more dastardly yet."[22]

For his part, Fabyan ignored all the trouble he was causing and continued to pursue both the Friedmans while lying about his actions. In a letter to Elizebeth dated 07 November 1918 Fabyan says, in two obvious lies "I confess, I don't quite understand your letter of November 4th as I have religiously answered every communication I have had from you, neither do I understand your references to Washington."[23]

Then, in an end-run around Elizebeth, Fabyan writes directly to William on 13 November, just after the Armistice (italics added):

> The war is over and I presume that you could work indefinitely in the Army but I do not think it holds anything for your future and *I think the sooner you resign and return to Riverbank, the better for both you and Riverbank. You have had six months vacation.* As far as I know, you have accomplished your purpose and I feel certain that there are better things waiting for you and I wish you would cable me on receipt of this letter, when you think you can be at Riverbank, because there are a lot of things I want to hold up if there is a chance of you coming in the near future.... *You have had a long enough vacation, your salary has been going on, and I do want you to get back at the earliest possible moment.*[24]

Fabyan followed that up with a letter the following day that closed with "I sincerely trust that there will be no necessity of your remaining longer on the other side and that there will be no obstacle in the way of your immediate return."[25]

With the length of time it took for letters to cross the Atlantic in 1918—typically 3 weeks to a month—William did not receive Fabyan's missives until around December 8th. It turns out that this was shortly after he'd gotten back on December 6th from a leave where he visited Nice and Paris, and just after Yardley had visited Chaumont and had dinner with Friedman. At that dinner, Yardley told Friedman that Van Deman had tried to get him commissioned into Army Military Intelligence as

[22] William F. Friedman, "WFF to ESF Re: Fabyan," October 14, 1918, ESF Collection, Box 2, Folder 17, George Marshall Foundation Research Library.

[23] George Fabyan, "Fabyan to ESF," November 7, 1918, ESF Collection, Box 1, Folder 41, George Marshall Foundation Research Library.

[24] George Fabyan. Letter to William F. Friedman. "Fabyan to WFF," November 13, 1918. ESF Collection, Box 2, Folder 20. George Marshall Foundation Research Library.

[25] George Fabyan to William F. Friedman, "Fabyan to WFF," November 14, 1918, ESF Collection, Box 2, Folder 20, George Marshall Foundation Research Library.

far back as October 1917 but that it appeared as if Fabyan had rejected the offer—without telling William.

One would think that after the two letters from Fabyan and after the exchange with Elizebeth about Fabyan interfering with her offer from Washington, and the new information from Yardley about Fabyan's interference in William's commissioning into the Army that William's response to Fabyan's letters would have been blistering and unequivocal. Well, almost.

In a five-page typewritten letter dated December 9th (William sent the handwritten letter to Elizebeth, and she had it transcribed and notarized before sending it on to Fabyan on January 2nd), William started by correcting Fabyan about his idea that one can just "resign" from the Army. "As to my resigning as you suggested, I was considerably surprised and somewhat amused to read that, because I don't think it would be advisable to waste good energy and good paper in trying such an impossible thing. If it were possible, there would be about 100,000 resignations handed in tomorrow, for we all want to go home and we all have to be very patient."[26] Next, William began to lay out one by one the Friedmans' grievances with Fabyan, including dropping the bombs that he knew from Yardley that Van Deman wanted to commission him back in 1917 and that they knew that Fabyan squashed an offer of a job in Washington for Elizebeth. He also called out Fabyan in a lie that Riverbank was still doing decryption work and training for the Army. But then, when it came to telling Fabyan that he and Elizebeth will definitely not be coming back to Riverbank once he is demobilized, William choked (italics added):

> I may say that Elizabeth (sic) is absolutely opposed to a return to Riverbank, and indeed, without any desire on my part to put things in a bad light, I may add that she seems to be exceedingly embittered about many things that happened there. *As for myself, we both know that during my three years at Riverbank we never had any serious differences, that I can recall at least. If it were not for the fact that I like to work with you and for you, that there are certain advantages to be had at Riverbank that do not obtain elsewhere perhaps, and if it were not for the fact that I believe that you have tried to do what is best for Elizebeth and myself, together with the rest of Riverbank, I would not be writing you at length now.*
>
> ...
> I certainly cannot and will not take Elizebeth back to a place where she is going to be unhappy. To do so would be to endanger and perhaps destroy our own perfect happiness, a circumstance which no prospects of material success or academic achievement could induce me to be willing to risk or to endure with equanimity.
>
> ...
> *I consider myself in honor bound to write you here and know my views and feelings in the matter, so that you may not be proceeding falsely on the assumption that my return to Riverbank as a member of the staff is certain.*
>
> ...
> *Please do not conclude that I have already made up my mind definitely not to return to Riverbank, or that I intend to stay with the government, or that I have already established connections with some other institution. As a matter of fact, I have absolutely no idea as to what I shall do, at the present writing.* I am only trusting that with continued good health

---

[26] William F. Friedman, "WFF to Fabyan," Letter, December 9, 1918, Box 2, Folder 19, Elizebeth Smith Friedman Collection, George Marshall Research Library, Lexington, VA.

and with the application of effort and a fair amount of ability, I shall find some means of earning a good livelihood for Elizabeth and myself."[27]

A week after sending his letter off to Fabyan, William received yet another missive; the two letters must have crossed somewhere in the Atlantic. In it, Fabyan lays down his terms in stronger language, "The facts in the case are that you are practically loaned for the emergency. That emergency no longer exists and in justice to yourself, your own future and myself, I think the sooner you return to Riverbank, the better."[28] Fabyan is treating both the Friedmans more like indentured servants than employees; he lies to them, he intercepts and opens their mail, he takes credit for their accomplishments, and he expects them to be grateful and loyal. He lets them know that he expects them to get his permission to take other employment. Unfortunately, this was typical of Fabyan's management style at Riverbank.

Fabyan and the Friedmans correspondence then takes the holidays off, only to resume with yet another letter from Fabyan to William, presumably after Fabyan has received William's letter of December 9th; the letter forwarded by Elizebeth on January 2nd. Fabyan's letter—one can imagine that it is a classic letter from a bully to one being bullied—reads in its entirety

> January 6, 1919
> Dear Lieutenant Friedman:
> I have your letter putting the future up to Elizabeth (sic) and I have written her as per the enclosed carbon. I don't know as anything could be gained by going into detail at this long distance.
> I have never received any letters from you which have not been acknowledged. You are conversant with the antagonism displayed and the desire to break up the Riverbank activities in a number of directions. Further, you are informed of the different methods undertaken to sow discord and the unwarranted criticisms. *At a proper time and place, I shall prefer charges and ask for a court martial or investigation.*
> *Man never knows where the blow is coming from. It is, of course, impossible to know what your career would have been had you not come to Riverbank* but I wish it were possible, in your case and in the case of Elizabeth.
> There are some things in your letter that I do not understand. *Riverbank is not an employment office. I am keenly disappointed.*
> Sincerely yours,
> [signature][29]

Fabyan is clearly using a lot of misdirection and gaslighting here. He blames Elizebeth for not wanting to return to Riverbank—and thus keeping William from returning—and for "antagonism displayed" and for "methods undertaken to sow discord." He also clearly implies that neither of their careers would have come about without him—because Fabyan sees his identity and Riverbank's as being inseparable. He then falls back on the implied threat of "Man never knows where the blow

---

[27] Friedman, 09 Dec 1918, italics added.

[28] George Fabyan to William F. Friedman, "Fabyan to WFF," December 16, 1918, Box 2, Folder 20, Elizebeth Smith Friedman Collection, George Marshall Research Library, Lexington, VA.

[29] George Fabyan to William F. Friedman, "Fabyan to WFF," January 6, 1919, William Friedman Collection, Item 734, George Marshall Foundation Research Library.

is coming from," and finally ends with the tried-and-true guilt trip "I am keenly disappointed." This last emphasizes the point that Fabyan sees himself as a feudal lord who controls all his serfs, sees them more as his children rather than as his employees, and expects their complete obedience, loyalty, and gratitude. Neither of the Friedmans ever directly addresses this letter in any future correspondence.

William Friedman was finally allowed to go home, leaving France in late February 1919 and arriving in New York some weeks later.[30] Elizebeth was there to meet him. He was demobilized on 5 April 1919, shortly after his arrival in New York. The Friedmans spent a few days in New York, then traveled to Pittsburgh to visit William's family, and then finally continued west to Elizebeth's family home in Huntington, Indiana.

Huntington is where Herbert Yardley finally caught up with them.

---

[30] George Fabyan to William F. Friedman, "Fabyan to WFF," March 12, 1919, William Friedman Collection, Item 734, George Marshall Foundation Research Library.

# Chapter 6
# What Might Have Been

Herbert Yardley's return to Washington in April 1919 brought home to him the fact that he would soon be out of a job. The prospect of returning to the State Department Code Room was unthinkable. For the last 22 months, he'd been in charge of a vibrant, important part of the Army General Staff, and the idea of going back to being a code clerk was not even in the realm of possibility. He was a very talented manager and organizer, a competent cryptanalyst, and he enjoyed being in charge. Over the course of his service in the war, Yardley had become increasingly convinced that the US government needed to have a permanent code and cipher breaking organization that would rival all the Black Chambers of America's European allies and enemies. Yardley believed that for the USA to maintain its position as a powerful and respected member of the world community, it needed to do just what everyone else was doing on the sly and intercept and read the secret communications of any nation that represented a threat or an interest to the country.

He was not alone in this. As early as November 1917, US diplomat Leland Harrison, then head of the State Department's Bureau of Secret Intelligence and later the diplomatic secretary of the US Peace Delegation in Paris, wrote to Ralph Van Deman that "it would be most desirable that we should have an organization along the lines now existing at Riverbank Laboratories." Harrison went on to say that Secretary of State Lansing had "promised me any financial assistance that might be required for this purpose." And that "it would seem desirable that the staff be selected with a view to keeping them on after the war."[1] Bruce Bielaski, the head of the Justice Department's Bureau of Investigation, the forerunner of the FBI, and the man responsible for the arrest of Lothar Witzke, was also in favor of a permanent cryptologic organization inside the War Department. Surprisingly, the US Navy also expressed its support. General Marlborough Churchill, Van Deman's replacement as head of Military Intelligence, was also behind the idea, writing from France,

---

[1] David Kahn, *The Reader of Gentlemen's Mail: Herbert O. Yardley and the Birth of American Codebreaking* (New Haven: Yale University Press, 2004), 51.

© The Author(s), under exclusive license to Springer Nature
Switzerland AG 2023
J. F. Dooley, *The Gambler and the Scholars*, History of Computing,
https://doi.org/10.1007/978-3-031-28318-5_6

where he too was at the Peace Conference, "I consider the establishment of M.I. 8 on a permanent peacetime basis most essential and believe that both Yardley and Manly should be included, with Yardley as Chief."[2] By the end of January, both Harrison and Churchill had agreed to a basic format for a peacetime organization but had not yet worked out all the details.[3] However, just because mid-level diplomatic and military officials wanted something to happen, did not mean it was a sure thing.

As soon as he returned to Washington, Yardley began working on a memorandum he would use as his evidence to convince his superiors in the War Department and in the State Department that it was essential to continue MI-8 as an organization that would give the USA expertise in code and cipher solutions in both war and peace.

In the memorandum, Yardley laid out the history of the work of MI-8. He detailed its creation and growth through 1917 and 1918. He included some details on the number of diplomatic code and cipher systems broken; Yardley claimed 579 distinct systems were broken, but he's counting every minor variant of many Mexican systems. The real number was about fifty distinct diplomatic systems, which was still an impressive number for an organization that had only been in existence for approximately 22 months.[4] This number did not include all the different cipher systems that MI-8 personnel solved from messages intercepted via radio interception and the Postal Service from German spies, prisoners of war, and American collaborators. Yardley mentioned that the Secret Writing Laboratories of MI-8 were reviewing about 2000 suspicious letters a week for several months running that were forwarded to it by the Postal Censorship office.

Yardley also tried to convince the Army General Staff of the value of MI-8 as a part of a larger military intelligence operation. "Although MI-8 as an organization did not take part in any of the work on the front, it was in constant communication with G-2 A-6, and furnished and trained most of its personnel. The distinction between MI-8 and G-2 A-6 should be taken into consideration in estimating the value of an organization for code and cipher attack."[5] He then spent a couple of paragraphs praising the work of G-2 A-6 at the front, and Colonel Frank Moorman, its chief, in particular. Yardley then emphasized the value of a permanent cryptanalytic organization in peacetime:

> If it is worthwhile to know exactly what instructions foreign powers give to their representatives at Washington, it is important to maintain MI-8 with a sufficient personnel in time of

---

[2] Kahn, *ROGM*, 51.

[3] Lawrence L. Winslow, "Winslow to Leland Harrison," Personal Letter, May 2, 1919, RG 59, Entry 349, Box 3, Folder: German Codes and Ciphers, National Archives and Records Administration, College Park, MD.

[4] Kahn, *ROGM*, 50.

[5] Herbert O. Yardley and General Marlborough Churchill, "Permanent Organization for Code and Cipher Investigation and Attack: Plans for MI-8 (SRH-161)" (Washington, DC: War Department, Military Intelligence Division, May 16, 1919), RG457, Entry 9032, National Security Agency, Box 777, Folder "Origin of MI-8 1919," National Archives, College Park, MD, 3.

peace. ... Intimate knowledge of the true sentiments and intentions of other nations may often be an important factor in determining whether we are to have peace or war.[6]

Yardley wrapped up the justification section of the memorandum with the "but everyone else is doing it, so we can't be left behind" argument:

> Code attack is indeed still in its infancy. It is capable of rapid and incalculable development. If we do not take part in this development, we shall be helpless when the next war comes,... It is definitely known to us that two at least of our most important allies have arranged to maintain in the future large and powerful organizations for code and cipher attack, for the development of new methods, and for the training of an adequate personnel. It is probable that other nations, of whose plans we know nothing, will pursue the same policy.[7]

The memorandum then moved on to recommendations for the structure and funding of the organization. First, it was to be a joint cipher bureau, reporting to and funded by both the War and State Departments. It was to be secret and, given MI-8's success with recruiting civilians during the war, staffed entirely with civilians. Salaries were to be set at levels for civilian professionals rather than civil servants or Army staff; this included a very generous salary for the day of $6000 per year for the chief of the organization. Finally, the Military Intelligence Division of the Army would contribute $60,000 of its annual funding, and the State Department would contribute $40,000 for a total budget of $100,000 per year. In a final bit of a wrinkle, the new Cipher Bureau would not be able to be headquartered in Washington because all the State Department budgets since 1916 had included a clause forbidding the addition of spending on new personnel in the nation's capital.

Yardley then sent his memorandum on to General Churchill, who signed it on May 16th and forwarded it on to the Army Chief of Staff and the State Department, urging them to "plan for a permanent organization for code and cipher work to be maintained by joint annual appropriation. ... and to be controlled by the Director of MID."[8] Yardley and Churchill's arguments fell on ears that were more than ready to hear them. The plan was approved by Frank L. Polk, the Acting Secretary of State, on 17 May and signed off by Army Chief of Staff General Peyton C. March on 19 May.[9] Congress authorized funding for the new MI-8—to be called the Cipher Bureau—in the Army bill at end of June.

Yardley's gamble had paid off and he was in.

The new Cipher Bureau would be headquartered in New York City. Yardley liked the idea of New York because it would mean that direct supervision was 250 miles away, so he could organize and run the new Bureau as he saw fit.[10] Another reason to move to New York was that it was the hub of cable traffic to Europe and was close to new powerful radio transmitters that were also sending and receiving sensitive messages. The censorship rules that had allowed the diversion of diplomatic

---

[6] Yardley & Churchill, *Permanent Organization*, 4.

[7] Yardley & Churchill, *Permanent Organization*, 4–5.

[8] Yardley & Churchill, *Permanent Organization*, 2.

[9] Yardley & Churchill, *Permanent Organization*, 1.

[10] Kahn, *ROGM*, 53.

cablegrams to the Army stopped at the end of the war. This meant that Yardley could not legally divert any cable (and later radio) traffic to his organization. Never one to be stopped by rules he thought unnecessary, Yardley created side arrangements with several cable companies to acquire copies of diplomatic messages for a good part of the 1920s.[11]

While the Cipher Bureau had sufficient funds to rent office space, Yardley's personnel aspirations were almost immediately reduced because instead of a total of $100,000 per year for the new organization, the Cipher Bureau never received more than about $60,000 of its projected budget in any fiscal year. This was largely because after the war, Congress spent the next decade or so being as frugal as possible with the nation's tax revenue and, in particular, decimated the War Department's budget to the point where Yardley did not normally receive more than around $20,000 of the anticipated $60,000 in War Department funds in any given year. Luckily for Yardley, Congress did not cast its frugal eye as much on the State Department, and they continued to contribute most or all of their monetary commitment over the years.

Yardley now began to think about personnel for the new Cipher Bureau. But, with nearly all of the US Army's soldiers demobilized by the summer of 1919, including most of the personnel of MI-8, Yardley was having a hard time finding qualified cryptanalysts. Also, he could not recruit Army soldiers for his organization because it was explicitly made up of civilians.

He did have one—really two—possibilities in mind, however, William and Elizebeth Friedman.

Yardley was very impressed with William's abilities and thought that both he and Elizebeth would make valuable additions to his team in New York. So, in late April 1919, he set about trying to recruit them as civilian employees of the newly constituted Cipher Bureau.

By April 1919 the Friedmans were back at Elizebeth's family home in Huntington, Indiana, and still trying to decide what William should do for a career. At this point, William had apparently given up the idea of pursuing his Ph.D. in genetics and was trying to find a position in "business." He'd corresponded with a number of companies, had some interviews, and had come up empty every time. Why he wasn't able to find a job is somewhat unclear, but there might be several reasons. First, his skill set was limited to just a few types of positions. He had a bachelor's degree in genetics and nearly 2 years of experience in that field, first at Cornell as a graduate student and instructor, and then at Riverbank as head of the Department of Genetics, but no other experience in industry and no advanced degree. He then had over 2 years of experience as a cryptanalyst, a skill set for which there was very little demand in 1919. Second, and William himself wrote about this, it seems as if Colonel Fabyan was spying on the couple and throwing roadblocks in William's path by corresponding with companies to which William had applied, discouraging them from hiring William, and by showering the couple with telegrams telling them

---

[11] Kahn, *ROGM*, 57–58.

to come back to Riverbank in every city where they went for William's interviews.[12] Third, with nearly four million men being released from the US Armed Forces between November 1918 and the end of 1919, there was an enormous amount of competition for all available positions. Finally, there was anti-Semitism and anti-immigrant sentiment as a feature of hiring practices in the early part of the century. Friedman's family were Jewish immigrants from eastern Europe, and although he had come to this country when he was just two years old and the USA was the only home he had ever known and that he had served his adopted country in the US Army during the war, William was still tarred with the same brush. The early twentieth century saw a wave of nativist anti-immigrant sentiment, particularly for immigrants from eastern and southern Europe. American nativists were intent on keeping America White and Protestant, and these new immigrants were largely Jewish and Catholic. So, the long history of discrimination in employment in the USA persisted after the war. Whether it was obvious and overt, or hidden and subtle, the message was the same; foreigners and Jews were not wanted.

In the midst of his job search, a blast from the past appeared in the Friedmans' mail one day in late April in the form of a letter from Herbert Yardley. As part of his argument for the new Cipher Bureau, Yardley wanted to be able to point to a cadre of experienced cryptanalysts that he could hire and be ready for work as soon as the Army and State Department approved his new organization. Yardley had tracked the Friedmans down to Indiana, and on April 28th he wrote William Friedman a letter with a couple of interesting propositions:

> 04/28/19
>
> Dear Friedman:
>
> Just got back about 10 days ago and find fair prospect for permanent organization, but nothing will be known definitely until the Army bill is passed.
>
> If everything goes as I hope I may be in a position to offer you:
>
> (1) 1st Lt. in Regular Army
>
> (2) $3,000 per annum as civilian provided I can get Mrs. Friedman with you. I can offer her $1,520 per annum.
>
> Please consider this confidential and let me know if foregoing is satisfactory, within how many days both of you could report.
>
> In replying address on personally: 542 Shepherd St., Washington
>
> > Sincerely,
> >
> > H. O. Yardley, Captain[13]

This letter begins a chain of correspondence between Friedman and Yardley that would last for the next several months. Friedman, on one of his job hunting trips, replied immediately:

---

[12] Elizabeth S. Friedman. "Autobiography of Elizabeth Smith Friedman – 1st Draft." Memoir. Lexington, VA, 1966. George Marshall Foundation Research Library. https://www.marshallfoundation.org/library/wp-content/uploads/sites/16/2015/06/ESFMemoirComplete_opt.pdf

[13] Herbert O. Yardley, "HOY to WFF Initial Offer," Letter, April 28, 1919, William Friedman Collection, Item 734, George Marshall Foundation Research Library.

Chicago, Ill
May 1, 1919

Dear Capt. Yardley –

I was very glad to hear you got back safely and I beg leave to acknowledge receipt of yours of the 28th ult. which was forwarded to me from Huntington.

The proposition labelled number 2, namely $3,000 per annum for my services as a civilian, with Mrs. Friedman whose salary would be $1,520 per annum is satisfactory.

We could report within a week after receipt of notice, and within less time if urgent.

We shall regard this as confidential as per your request.

Thanking you very much for this opportunity and hoping to hear from you just as soon as affairs shape themselves, I am,

Sincerely yours,
W. F. Friedman[14]

This is a very good and positive offer from Yardley. The Friedmans were each making about $1200 per year at Riverbank (plus room and board), and despite Colonel Fabyan's insistence that "your salary has been continuing," neither Friedman really expected the Colonel to live up to that promise—and he did not.

Upon receipt of this letter from William Friedman, Yardley thought he had just recruited a pair of excellent cryptanalysts, and the core of his team was set. However, the Friedmans were not quite recruited yet.

Two and a half weeks later, on 18 May, William wrote a letter to Yardley updating him on their situation—they were already back at Riverbank and still apparently waiting for formal confirmation from Yardley. William says to Yardley:

When I arrived from France, my mind was fully made up to go into business. After looking around for a length of time, and conferring with friends it seemed inadvisable to do so just at present on account of unsettled business conditions. Having left some work unfinished at R(iverbank) at the urgent request of C. Fabyan I have returned to complete it. This, I hope, will be only temporary. I do not want to stay longer than I can help it. Had circumstances been different I certainly would not have come at all.[15]

So, the good news here was that William and Elizebeth were still interested in Yardley's offer, but the really bad news was that they were back in Riverbank and under Colonel Fabyan's thumb again. Elizebeth was against the move and had advised against it, but William could not say no to Fabyan just yet.

Despite the fact that the Friedmans were back at Riverbank and under Fabyan's thumb, Herbert Yardley was not giving up on them. On 16 June, he wrote to Friedman that "The present indication is that there will be a permanent organization and I shall know definitely by June 30th."[16] The end of June was the deadline for the passing of the Army bill by Congress. Friedman replied on 27 June not to this letter from Yardley, but to a different one of 23 June talking about a new cipher machine from AT&T that Riverbank was testing. In his note, Friedman asks for more test messages.

---

[14] William F. Friedman to Herbert O. Yardley, "WFF to HOY," May 1, 1919, ESF Collection, Box 2, Folder 20, George Marshall Foundation Research Library.

[15] William F. Friedman to Herbert O. Yardley, "WFF to HOY," May 18, 1919, ESF Collection, Box 2, Folder 20, George Marshall Foundation Research Library.

[16] Herbert O. Yardley, "HOY to WFF Job2," Letter, June 16, 1919, RG 457, Entry 9032, National Security Agency, National Archives, College Park, MD.

Yardley then sends a telegram to Friedman on 30 June saying "...will probably wire you officially tomorrow" and urging him to talk to Fabyan and finally tell him about the offer from the new Cipher Bureau "...much better to be frank about matter. Realise your position but have always been frank with Fabyan. Believe that course will cause less friction."[17] He then follows up with a second telegram on 1 July, "General Churchill has today approved the plans for you and Mrs. Friedman out-lined and agreed to in the exchange of informal letters while you were in Huntington Indiana. Report at earliest possible date. Yardley"[18] Now the Friedmans had a firm offer from the War Department in hand, and it was time to make the break from Fabyan and Riverbank.

On 2 July Friedman first telegraphs Yardley, letting him know "Your wires received. Will report earliest possible date. Letter follows." In his follow-up letter, written the same day, Friedman relates his meeting with Fabyan, where he told the Colonel about the offer from MID and his acceptance. The Colonel did not take it well. Friedman says:

> He immediately came to the conclusion that the offer and its authorization was made with the direct object of getting me down at Washington on account of the AT&T cipher affair... I straightened him out on that score...But he refuses to see it that way in spite of the fact that, as I pointed out to him, I had nothing to do with the AT&T affair, he expressed in no uncer-tain terms his determination of making it exceedingly uncomfortable for everybody con-nected with MI-8. Otherwise, he has been no more upset than I expected him to be at the news.[19]

What is upsetting Fabyan are two things. The first is the prospect of losing his star cryptologist and his wife. Over the course of 1917 and 1918, Fabyan had considered himself and Riverbank to be the saviors of America with regard to codes and ciphers as the country ramped up its participation in the war, and he had basked in the grati-tude and praise of the War Department, indeed of the entire government. Fabyan was addicted to adulation and was loathe to give it up. William and Elizebeth were the keys to the continuation of that recognition and praise, and he was not going to let them go without a fight. The second was Fabyan's image of himself as a feudal lord, with an estate full of loyal and obedient serfs. The very idea that one of his servants would go behind his back and make an arrangement for other employment was anathema to him. Needless to say, William bore the brunt of Fabyan's ire and bullying. It also seemed that William was not quite up to resisting the relentless pressure that Fabyan put on him to stay loyal and stay at Riverbank.

Later, in the same 2 July letter to Yardley, Friedman says, "In order to placate him as far as is possible under the circumstances I have agreed to finish one or two things for him which may take two weeks. But I shall work day and night to finish up and

---

[17] Herbert O. Yardley, "HOY to WFF Job3." Telegram, June 30, 1919. RG 457, Entry 9032, National Security Agency. National Archives, College Park, MD.

[18] Herbert O. Yardley, "HOY to WFF FormalOffer." Telegram, July 1, 1919. RG 457, Entry 9032, National Security Agency. National Archives, College Park, MD.

[19] William F. Friedman to Herbert O. Yardley, "WFF to HOY," July 2, 1919, RG 457, Entry 9032, National Security Agency, National Archives, College Park, MD.

report as soon as possible. Please advise if this is satisfactory. ... I hope that I will not be the cause of further trouble. We are anticipating very congenial and satisfactory relations with MI-8. Thanking you again for the opportunity."[20] This is not good news for Yardley. William is clearly caught between a rock and a hard place here. He sees the opportunity for both he and Elizebeth to continue to work for the Army, but is under enormous pressure from Fabyan to stay at Riverbank. Elizebeth also does not want to stay at Riverbank and would love for the two of them to head to Washington immediately.

Further illustrating William's troubles is a letter to Yardley on 13 July asking for another 2 weeks of grace before they report for work. "Need at least one more week but could use time until August 1st to round out all work. If this is not consistent with your interest I will come at once leaving Mrs. Friedman here to finish."[21]

Yardley would really like the Friedmans to join him in the new Cipher Bureau and responds on 14 July via telegram "AUGUST FIRST OK." At this point, Yardley is in the process of finalizing details about the move of his Bureau to New York and is frantically trying to find more personnel for the Cipher Bureau.

Things continued to move apace. On 22 July, a little over a week after Friedman's letter, Yardley sends a memo to General Churchill with a list of the cryptographic personnel he has selected for the Cipher Bureau, along with their proposed salaries. Notably absent from the list at this point are William and Elizebeth Friedman.[22]

On the very next day, Yardley telegrams Friedman with the address of the new Cipher Bureau "July 31st permanent office opens no. 3 East 38th St. New York instead Washington. This for your information only."[23] Yardley still has confidence that the Friedmans will show up.

Friedman then missed his August 1st date to show up at MI-8 in New York. From the dates of the next set of communications and references in those letters, it appears as if Yardley and Major Mauborgne, the head of research for the Signal Corps, visited Riverbank to talk about the AT&T cipher machine in early August, possibly around the weekend of 1, 2, and 3 August. In any event, Yardley and Friedman had at least one long conversation about Yardley's job offer and Friedman's hesitancy and delay in accepting the offer. This sets Fabyan off because he thinks that Yardley and Mauborgne are trying to poach the Friedmans (they are) and move the work on the analysis of the AT&T cipher machine to MI-8 (they aren't). In a letter to General Churchill dated 6 August, Fabyan lets loose on Yardley for not knowing the details of how to decrypt messages sent via the AT&T cipher machine, something that Riverbank was supposed to be doing along with then telling the Signal Corps the

[20] Friedman, 02 July 1919.

[21] William F. Friedman to Herbert O. Yardley, "WFF to HOY," July 13, 1919, RG 457, Entry 9032, National Sec;urity Agency, National Archives, College Park, MD.

[22] Herbert O. Yardley, "HOY Memo: Cipher Bureau Personnel List," Memorandum, July 22, 1919, RG 457, Entry 9032, National Security Agency (also in SRH-161), National Archives, College Park, MD.

[23] Herbert O. Yardley, "HOY to WFF Re NYC Location." Telegram, July 23, 1919. RG 457, Entry 9032, National Sec;urity Agency. National Archives, College Park, MD.

results of their work. "I was disgusted to ascertain that Major Yardley did not go into the decipherment of the AT&T cipher machine to the extent which I had arranged and which I thought he had when he told me he understood it and could do it. ... The time he spent with Friedman was evidently spent on personalities and giving Friedman the information on the correspondence between Riverbank (meaning Fabyan himself) and the MID (this is Van Deman), including the fact that I had requested the MID to withdraw the offer they made to the Friedmans, etc."[24] Fabyan then spends the rest of the letter unwittingly disclosing that he does not understand how the AT&T cipher machine works either, and asking for an officer from the Signal Corps who does know about the AT&T machine to come out to Riverbank.

Yardley then gets busy. On 14 August he sends two different memoranda to General Churchill and a letter to Friedman. Yardley's first note to Churchill basically refutes the argument that Fabyan has been making that he never received a letter from Van Deman in October 1917 suggesting that William Friedman be commissioned and sent to France. Yardley does this by including a copy of Van Deman's letter from the MID files. He also suggests sending a copy to Friedman and relates to Churchill that Friedman "...feels that he missed one of the big opportunities of his life by not being commissioned in 1917, for had he been sent to France at that time, he would have had an opportunity to make a name for himself."[25] In a bit of snark, Yardley then suggests that Churchill can send a copy of Van Deman's letter to Fabyan as well.

In his second letter to Churchill on the 14th, Yardley lays out his conclusions about Riverbank's work on the AT&T cipher machine, based on what he and Mauborgne had learned during their visit earlier in August. His recommendations amount to (1) the machine as it is currently being used is insecure, (2) the Signal Corps should stop using it and if they want to use it again, MID should be consulted, (3) we should send Fabyan a memo expressing MIDs thanks and appreciation, and (4) MID should hold off telling all the details to the Signal Corps until Mauborgne returns from his leave.[26]

Finally, Yardley's letter to Friedman references Van Deman's letter from October 1917 that Fabyan had intercepted and then denied getting. Yardley intends to include it, but it is missing and Yardley says he will send it later in August, but it gets forgotten again; Churchill sends Fabyan a copy of Van Deman's letter and that is the one that Friedman eventually sees. Yardley then tells Friedman that he needs to make up his mind about where he wants to work—and soon.

---

[24] George Fabyan, "Fabyan to Churchill Re: WFF & HOY," August 6, 1919. RG 457, Entry 9032, National Sec;urity Agency. National Archives, College Park, MD.

[25] Herbert O. Yardley, Letter to General Marlborough Churchill. "HOY to Churchill Re: WFF," August 14, 1919. National Security Agency, Herbert Yardley Collection. https://www.nsa.gov/news-features/declassified-documents/yardley-collection/

[26] Herbert O. Yardley, Letter to General Marlborough Churchill. "HOY to Churchill Re: Riverbank & AT&T," August 14, 1919. National Security Agency, Herbert Yardley Collection. https://www.nsa.gov/news-features/declassified-documents/yardley-collection/

So far as I can see, the situation has not been materially changed by our visit. Whether you should stay at Riverbank or come to New York is a question for you to decide, but I do feel that I have put off as long as I reasonably can the selection of someone to do the work I have in mind for you and Mrs. Friedman. However, I will, because I promised you that I would, delay action until the first of September. This will have given you two months to definitely make up your mind and I feel sure that you must agree that I have been fair to you.[27]

Yardley writes Friedman again on 20 August, but this letter is all about the content of a manuscript that Friedman is working on. Friedman responds on 22 August, and we finally get to see his answer:

I wish that I had known what you told me last Sunday with regard to my chances for advancement before I made my final decision. I believe it would have been different. However, that's all past now, and maybe it will all turn out for the best. The photostat of the letter you mention was not enclosed and I presume it was overlooked in mailing. General C(hurchill). Sent Colonel F(abyan). a copy of that correspondence and sometime I'll tell you how the latter tried to straighten it out. About once a week I get to wondering whether I didn't make a mistake, and if I didn't feel that our personal relations are unchanged by my decision, it would be considerably harder to get along.[28]

So now it is clear that Friedman has given in to Colonel Fabyan's incessant pressure tactics and he and Elizebeth will be staying at Riverbank rather than working in Yardley's new Cipher Bureau in New York. It is also clear that William is having second thoughts about his decision already and is trying not to burn his bridge to Yardley by saying he feels that their personal relationship will not be affected by this new arrangement.

One wonders how much Fabyan's bullying and pressuring of the Friedmans informed their decision, and how much William's initial somewhat negative reaction to Yardley in France gave him pause about working closely with him for years to come. Regardless, we can only imagine how American cryptology would have been different if probably the two best cryptologists of the twentieth century, William and Elizebeth Friedman, had worked through the next decade with the organizational and marketing wizard that was Herbert Yardley. The two men were both outstanding in their fields but for different reasons and different skill sets. While Herbert Yardley was the manager's cryptologist, William Friedman was the mathematician's.

---

[27] Herbert O. Yardley, Letter. "HOY to WFF Re: Last Chance." August 14, 1919. RG 457, Entry 9032, National Security Agency. National Archives, College Park, MD.

[28] William F. Friedman to Herbert O. Yardley, "WFF to HOY," August 22, 1919, RG 457, Entry 9032, National Security Agency, National Archives, College Park, MD.

# Chapter 7
# The Cipher Bureau: Early Days

Once Herbert Yardley had the approval of General Churchill and the War and State Departments in early July 1919 for the creation of his new Cipher Bureau, he got to work on logistics.

Yardley first went looking for space for the Cipher Bureau in New York City and found that his friend F. W. Allen, who had been in charge of MI-8's shorthand section during the war, owned a building at 3 East 38th Street that he could rent for a very reasonable rate of $5500 a year. It even had an apartment on the third floor that Yardley and his wife, Hazel, could move into for an additional $900 per year. So, by the end of July 1919, the Cipher Bureau was approved, had a budget, and a home.[1] The Yardleys and the files from the old MI-8 were moved in, and work was to start in August. What the Cipher Bureau now needed was people.

Yardley's original plan for the Cipher Bureau called for an all-civilian organization with himself as the Chief, along with 25 cryptographers and 25 clerk typists. Because of a reduction in his initial budget, Yardley had to drastically scale down his personnel requirements. Instead of a staff of fifty, the initial personnel contingent of the Cipher Bureau was to be no more than two dozen. Yardley was reduced to employing only half a dozen or so cryptanalysts including himself, a couple of secretary/typists, and about a dozen code clerks who would do most of the more menial work in terms of initial analysis of intercepted cryptograms.

It also appeared by early August that he would not be getting the Friedmans, whom he had counted on as the core of his team. Nor would he get any of the cryptanalysts from the University of Chicago, including John Manly and Edith Rickert. They had all returned to their faculty posts and were not interested in working for the government. He was, however, able to recruit some old MI-8 hands and a couple of new cryptanalysts.

---

[1] David Kahn, *The Reader of Gentlemen's Mail: Herbert O. Yardley and the Birth of American Codebreaking* (New Haven: Yale University Press, 2004), 52–56.

© The Author(s), under exclusive license to Springer Nature Switzerland AG 2023
J. F. Dooley, *The Gambler and the Scholars*, History of Computing, https://doi.org/10.1007/978-3-031-28318-5_7

These included Frederick Livesey, who had worked in G-2 A-6 and, along with J. Rives Childs, was Yardley's aide in Paris during the Peace Conference and who would later work at the State Department. Yardley brought Livesey on as his chief cryptanalytic assistant. Robert Arrowsmith, who was recommended by General Churchill, came on board. Dr. Charles J. Mendelsohn, who worked at MI-8 during the war, was the head of the German Code subsection and who taught at CUNY in the morning ended up working part-time in the Cipher Bureau in the afternoons. Henry D. Learned, who worked in codes and ciphers in France, was hired, as was Claus Bogel, another MI-8 veteran who was an expert in Mexican codes and ciphers.[2] Bogel worked at the Cipher Bureau until 1921 and then for several years for the Navy cipher department before spending the rest of his career at the Library of Congress.

Ruth Willson, the only woman cryptanalyst, had worked in MI-8 during the war. She had a degree in Romance Languages from Syracuse University and became an expert in Central and South American ciphers and codes during her service in MI-8. In the Cipher Bureau, she would also become a Japanese linguist and eventually the leading—and best paid—cryptanalyst right behind Yardley.[3] Ruth Wilson (she changed her name—dropping one "l," to the confusion of all writers since—when she married Howard L. Wilson, an accountant, in 1925) would stay at the Cipher Bureau during the entirety of its existence, only leaving in 1929 when it was closed. Ruth never worked in cryptology after that, nor did she ever talk about her work in the Cipher Bureau, even to her family. She and Howard raised a daughter, Julia, and Ruth went back to school, earning a Master's degree in Far Eastern Studies from Columbia University in 1947. She and Howard moved from New York to Florida in the late 1940s, and Ruth passed away at age 68 in 1958.[4]

Finally, the last cryptanalyst was Victor Weiskopf, another Mexican and Spanish cipher expert from MI-8 who was also a Justice Department employee who had broken Mexican ciphers at the southern border before and during Pershing's Punitive Expedition of 1916–1917 and worked for Yardley part-time, splitting his time between the Cipher Bureau and the Justice Department.[5]

Yardley also hired a number of secretaries who doubled as code clerks. Among these were Marguerite O'Connor, who was Yardley's personal secretary, and Edna Ramsier, an attractive and energetic 17-year-old from New Jersey. Ramsier started as a secretary/clerk, transcribing incoming coded messages onto index cards for linguistic sorting, and worked her way into helping with Japanese code messages.

---

[2] Herbert O. Yardley, Memorandum. "HOY Memo: Cipher Bureau Personnel List." Memorandum, July 22, 1919. RG 457, Entry 9032, National Security Agency (also in SRH-161). National Archives, College Park, MD.

[3] NSA      https://www.nsa.gov/about/cryptologic-heritage/historical-figures-publications/women/Article/1620974/ruth-wilson/

[4] Ruth Wilson Craig, "Lineage of Ruth Willson, Wife of Howard Leon Wilson, Ascending to Her Paternal Grandparents: Vital Clues From a Minor Name Variation," March 2016. Author's personal copy. Used with permission.

[5] Kahn, *ROGM*, 55.

While not a full-fledged cryptanalyst and certainly not paid as one, over the years, Edna contributed substantially to solutions, particularly of Japanese diplomatic messages. She also took on the task of scouring the New York and Washington newspapers for references to Japanese diplomatic initiatives and troubles in the hopes that those stories would end up in diplomatic messages (Fig. 7.1).

Ruth Wilson took Edna under her wing and became her mentor, helping her with both Japanese language lessons and cryptology. It did not take long for Edna to become smitten with Herbert Yardley, despite the 13-year difference in their ages and the fact that he was married. Their soon to commence 39-year on-again-off-again relationship would survive Yardley's marriage, separation, and divorce, Edna's own marriage and divorce, unemployment for them both, and several long separations, including a 2-year separation while Yardley was in China in the late 1930s. Edna stayed with the Cipher Bureau until it was closed in 1929 and by that time was a gifted cryptanalyst in her own right.[6] Finally, Yardley hired another MI-8 veteran,

**Fig. 7.1** Edna Ramsier c1919. (David Kahn Collection, National Cryptologic Museum Library)

---

[6] Edna Yardley, "Oral History: Interview with Edna Yardley by NSA Historians (SRH-016)," Oral History (Ft. George Meade, MD, February 3, 1977).

John Meeth, to be his chief clerk and second-in-command. Meeth took care of the day-to-day running of the office while Yardley was cryptanalyzing intercepted messages. Meeth and Marguerite O'Connor would later marry. John Meeth would leave the Cipher Bureau in the mid-1920s during one of its nearly annual rounds of budget cuts, but Marguerite would be one of the half dozen employees to stay on until the final closure in 1929.[7]

By the end of August 1919, the Cipher Bureau and its roughly two dozen employees were moved into their new quarters on 38th Street, organized, and working.[8]

The real estate arrangement on 38th Street that Yardley had negotiated with F. W. Allen would last less than a year before the Cipher Bureau moved again—twice. The first move was to 141 East 37th Street in 1920 because the Cipher Bureau's lease at the 38th Street building was sold, and 3 years later, the second move came after an attempted break-in—with the team ending up in an office building at 52 Vanderbilt Avenue where the Cipher Bureau occupied locked offices in the rear of a suite. The front office of the suite was the location of a commercial code business, The Code Compiling Company that the Bureau used as a legitimate front. The Code Compiling Company was incorporated in New York on May 3, 1920, by Herbert Yardley and Charles J. Mendelsohn. Yardley owned 49 shares of the company, Mendelsohn owned 49 shares, and their attorney, William Magee, owned the remaining two shares. The Code Compiling Company's first code was for the Tanner's Council and contained hundreds of codewords for calfskins.[9] The company then produced the *Universal Trade Code*, created by Yardley and Mendelsohn and published in 1921 (Fig. 7.2), which contained 100,000 codewords and a proposed cipher system used to produce a superencipherment of the coded messages and which sold rather well.[10]

The last thing that Yardley did that summer of 1919 was to disengage himself from the Army; he received his honorable discharge from the National Army on 30 September 1919. However, the Army still wanted to have some control over Yardley going forward, so he was encouraged to enlist in the Army Reserve Corps as early as March 1920. No doubt to sweeten the offer, General Churchill and his replacement as Director of Military Intelligence A. B. Coxe both recommended that Yardley be enlisted in the Army Reserve at the rank of Lieutenant Colonel, a promotion from his former rank of Major. In a strange and unfortunate twist of fate, Yardley spent the better part of a year unaware of Churchill's advance and the offer of promotion because the Army misplaced his change of address memo and all the letters related to his promotion and the physical exam it required were sent to the Cipher Bureau's original address on 38th Street, rather than the building on 37th Street where they

---

[7] Kahn, *ROGM*, 83.

[8] Kahn, *ROGM*, 52–56; David Kahn, *The Codebreakers; The Story of Secret Writing* (New York: Macmillan, 1967), 357.

[9] Kahn, *ROGM*, 57.

[10] Herbert O. Yardley and Charles Mendelsohn, *Universal Trade Code*, (New York, NY: Code Compiling Company, 1921), https://archive.org/stream/universaltradeco00code#page/n691/mode/2up

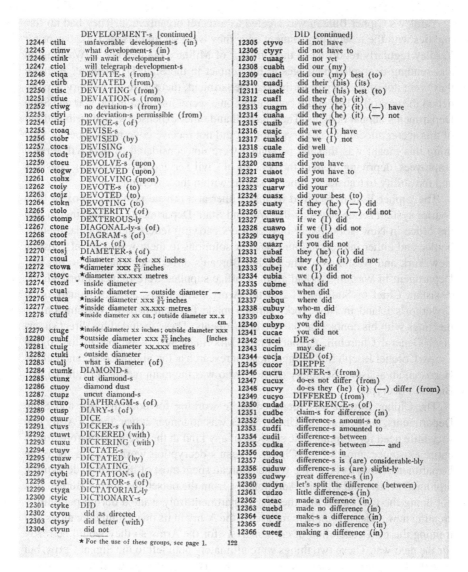

| | | | | | |
|---|---|---|---|---|---|
| | | DEVELOPMENT-s [continued] | | | DID [continued] |
| 12244 | ctilu | unfavorable development-s (in) | 12305 | ctyvo | did not have |
| 12245 | ctimv | what development-s (in) | 12306 | ctyyr | did not have to |
| 12246 | ctink | will await development-s | 12307 | cuaag | did not yet |
| 12247 | ctiol | will telegraph development-s | 12308 | cuabh | did our (my) |
| 12248 | ctiqa | DEVIATE-s (from) | 12309 | cuaci | did our (my) best (to) |
| 12249 | ctirb | DEVIATED (from) | 12310 | cuadj | did their (his) (its) |
| 12250 | ctisc | DEVIATING (from) | 12311 | cuaek | did their (his) best (to) |
| 12251 | ctiue | DEVIATION-s (from) | 12312 | cuafl | did they (he) (it) |
| 12252 | ctiwg | no deviation-s (from) | 12313 | cuagm | did they (he) (it) (—) have |
| 12253 | ctiyi | no deviation-s permissible (from) | 12314 | cuaha | did they (he) (it) (—) not |
| 12254 | ctizj | DEVICE-s (of) | 12315 | cuaib | did we (I) |
| 12255 | ctoaq | DEVISE-s | 12316 | cuajc | did we (I) have |
| 12256 | ctobr | DEVISED (by) | 12317 | cuakd | did we (I) not |
| 12257 | ctocs | DEVISING | 12318 | cuale | did well |
| 12258 | ctodt | DEVOID (of) | 12319 | cuamf | did you |
| 12259 | ctoeu | DEVOLVE-s (upon) | 12320 | cuans | did you have |
| 12260 | ctogw | DEVOLVED (upon) | 12321 | cuaot | did you have to |
| 12261 | ctohx | DEVOLVING (upon) | 12322 | cuapu | did you not |
| 12262 | ctoiy | DEVOTE-s (to) | 12323 | cuarw | did your |
| 12263 | ctojz | DEVOTED (to) | 12324 | cuasx | did your best (to) |
| 12264 | ctokn | DEVOTING (to) | 12325 | cuaty | if they (he) (—) did |
| 12265 | ctolo | DEXTERITY (of) | 12326 | cuauz | if they (he) (—) did not |
| 12266 | ctomp | DEXTEROUS-ly | 12327 | cuavn | if we (I) did |
| 12267 | ctone | DIAGONAL-ly-s (of) | 12328 | cuawo | if we (I) did not |
| 12268 | ctoof | DIAGRAM-s (of) | 12329 | cuayq | if you did |
| 12269 | ctori | DIAL-s (of) | 12330 | cuazr | if you did not |
| 12270 | ctosj | DIAMETER-s (of) | 12331 | cubaf | they (he) (it) did |
| 12271 | ctoul | *diameter xxx feet xx inches | 12332 | cubdi | they (he) (it) did not |
| 12272 | ctowa | *diameter xxx $\frac{xx}{64}$ inches | 12333 | cubej | we (I) did |
| 12273 | ctoyc | *diameter xx.xxx metres | 12334 | cubia | we (I) did not |
| 12274 | ctozd | * inside diameter | 12335 | cubme | what did |
| 12275 | ctual | inside diameter — outside diameter — | 12336 | cubos | when did |
| 12276 | ctuca | *inside diameter xxx $\frac{xx}{64}$ inches | 12337 | cubqu | where did |
| 12277 | ctuec | *inside diameter xx.xxx metres | 12338 | cubuy | who-m did |
| 12278 | ctufd | *inside diameter xx cm.; outside diameter xx.x cm. | 12339 | cubxo | why did |
| | | | 12340 | cubyp | you did |
| 12279 | ctuge | *inside diameter xx inches ; outside diameter xxx | 12341 | cucae | you did not |
| 12280 | ctuhf | *outside diameter xxx $\frac{xx}{64}$ inches [inches | 12342 | cucei | DIE-s |
| 12281 | ctuig | *outside diameter xx.xxx metres | 12343 | cucim | may die |
| 12282 | ctuki | , outside diameter | 12344 | cucja | DIED (of) |
| 12283 | ctulj | what is diameter (of) | 12345 | cucor | DIEPPE |
| 12284 | ctumk | DIAMOND-s | 12346 | cucru | DIFFER-s (from) |
| 12285 | ctunx | cut diamond-s | 12347 | cucux | do-es not differ (from) |
| 12286 | ctuoy | diamond dust | 12348 | cucvy | do-es they (he) (it) (—) differ (from) |
| 12287 | ctupz | uncut diamond-s | 12349 | cucyo | DIFFERED (from) |
| 12288 | cturo | DIAPHRAGM-s (of) | 12350 | cudad | DIFFERENCE-s (of) |
| 12289 | ctusp | DIARY-s (of) | 12351 | cudbe | claim-s for difference (in) |
| 12290 | ctuur | DICE | 12352 | cudeh | difference-s amount-s to |
| 12291 | ctuvs | DICKER-s (with) | 12353 | cudfi | difference-s amounted to |
| 12292 | ctuwt | DICKERED (with) | 12354 | cudil | difference-s between |
| 12293 | ctuxu | DICKERING (with) | 12355 | cudka | difference-s between —— and |
| 12294 | ctuyv | DICTATE-s | 12356 | cudoq | difference-s in |
| 12295 | ctuzw | DICTATED (by) | 12357 | cudsu | difference-s is (are) considerable-bly |
| 12296 | ctyah | DICTATING | 12358 | cuduw | difference-s is (are) slight-ly |
| 12297 | ctybi | DICTATION-s (of) | 12359 | cudwy | great difference-s (in) |
| 12298 | ctyel | DICTATOR-s (of) | 12360 | cudyn | let's split the difference (between) |
| 12299 | ctyga | DICTATORIAL-ly | 12361 | cudzo | little difference-s (in) |
| 12300 | ctyic | DICTIONARY-s | 12362 | cueac | made a difference (in) |
| 12301 | ctyke | DID | 12363 | cuebd | made no difference (in) |
| 12302 | ctyou | did as directed | 12364 | cuece | make-s a difference (in) |
| 12303 | ctysy | did better (with) | 12365 | cuedf | make-s no difference (in) |
| 12304 | ctyun | did not | 12366 | cueeg | making a difference (in) |

★ For the use of these groups, see page 1.     122

**Fig. 7.2** A code page of the Universal Trade Code. (From archive.org)

had moved in the spring of 1920. Yardley received none of those letters. In May 1921, Yardley was finally enlisted in the Army Reserve at his former rank of Major, rather than the new rank of Lieutenant Colonel. He would remain in the Army reserve for another 10 years and never get that promotion to Lieutenant Colonel.[11]

[11] Herbert O. Yardley Collection. "A Selection of Papers Pertaining to Herbert O. Yardley (SRH-038)." College Park, MD: NARA (Record Group 457, Entry 9037), Various Dates, 83–98.

Yardley's Cipher Bureau was created as a secret organization. They had no formal ties with the federal government once they were set up in New York except for Yardley regularly reporting to the Director of Military Intelligence in Washington and sending decrypted messages to his contact in the State Department. Because they were not officially part of the War Department, there were no military personnel on the payroll. Their entire budget was on a secret line item in the War and State Departments annual budgets. Their payroll and other expenses were distributed out of this secret allocation. The cryptologists did not receive government checks. One thing this meant was that the personnel were not considered to be Civil Service employees, depriving them of the benefits of Civil Service jobs, including pensions and the ability to transfer to other positions within the government.

The Cipher Bureau received its mail either at a private post office box or by a courier system set up between the War and State Departments in Washington and the office in New York. Every day, couriers carrying letters, memoranda, reports, books, and either intercepted messages or solutions to them would travel between New York and Washington. The Cipher Bureau's direct telephone line to the War Department in Washington and all their office supplies were funneled through the Assistant Chief of Staff for G-2 at the Army's 2nd Corps Area headquarters on Governor's Island in New York. Yardley made frequent trips to Washington for meetings with his contacts at the two departments. These included his direct supervisor General Churchill, Colonel Frank Moorman, who was now in the Signal Corps, Colonel Joseph Mauborgne, head of research at the Signal Corps, and Leland Harrison, an assistant Secretary of State who was the main recipient of the Cipher Bureau's decrypts.

The Cipher Bureau was supposed to be working for both the War and State Departments, but because the United States was no longer at war, the US Army had very little need for cryptanalytic services of any kind in the 1920s. Therefore, for its entire existence, most of the Cipher Bureau's decryption work was for the State Department. From its birth, the Cipher Bureau spent most of its time on decrypting diplomatic codes and ciphers. Additionally, from the outset, the Cipher Bureau was not doing the two things that the War Department truly wanted during peacetime: creating new codes and ciphers for use by the Army in its own communications and training the next generation of cryptanalysts for the Army so they would be ready for the next war. These two things were ultimately both left to the Signal Corps, but by default rather than intention. When MI-8 was being demobilized in early 1919, Yardley and Manly had shut down the Shorthand Section and the Secret Inks Laboratories, transferred the Code Compilation Section to the Signal Corps, and stopped training within the Code and Cipher Solution section. The new Cipher Bureau never picked up these discarded operations. Yardley's excuse was that his bureau was primarily devoted to breaking foreign government codes and did not have the manpower to create new Army codes or to set up a training program.[12] In reality, Herbert Yardley had no interest in these two endeavors. Solving foreign

---

[12] Kahn, *ROGM*, 82.

coded messages for the State Department made the Cipher Bureau much more visible and valuable to his superiors. This reasoning would come back to haunt Yardley and his organization a decade hence.

What the Cipher Bureau was doing was decrypting foreign diplomatic code messages that were being sent to them by three different cable companies, Western Union, All-American Cable Company, and the Postal Cable Company. Yardley convinced the upper management of all three companies that it was their patriotic duty to turn over the cablegrams to his office. This was regardless of the fact that two different laws—the Mann Elkins Act of 1910 and the Radio Act of 1912—made this type of action illegal. The Mann-Elkins Act expanded the jurisdiction of the Interstate Commerce Commission to include regulating telegraph, telephone, and cable communications and forbade the disclosure of the contents of all these communications to third parties.

> It shall be unlawful for any common carrier subject to the provisions of this Act, or any officer, agent, or employee of such common carrier,... *knowingly to disclose to or permit to be acquired by any person or corporation other than the shipper or consignee, without the consent of such shipper or consignee,* any information concerning the nature, kind, quantity, destination, consignee, or routing of any property tendered or delivered to such common carrier for interstate transportation,... and *it shall also be unlawful for any person or corporation to solicit or knowingly receive any such information which may be so used.*[13]

The Radio Act of 1912, which mostly had to do with regulating radio broadcast licenses, added wireless telegraphy to the mix of regulated communications and forbade the disclosure of radio messages to anyone other than the intended receiver: "No person or persons engaged in or having knowledge of the operation of any station or stations, shall divulge or publish the contents of any messages transmitted or received by such station, except to the person or persons to whom the same may be directed, or their authorized agent, or to another station employed to forward such message to its destination."[14]

However, in his quest to get the cable companies to give him coded messages, Yardley seems to have overlooked the next paragraph in the Mann-Elkins Act, which states in part that "... nothing in this Act shall be construed to prevent the giving of such information in process, response to any legal process issued under the authority of any state or federal court, or to any officer or agent of the Government of the United States, or of any State or Territory, in the exercise of his powers...."[15] The wording here appears to be a way for Yardley to intercept his diplomatic communications as an "agent of the Government of the United States." This seeming oversight on Yardley's part would also have consequences several years hence.

---

[13] "Mann-Elkins Act of 1910," Pub. L. No. 61–218, 36 Stat. 539 539 (1910), https://govtrackus. s3.amazonaws.com/legislink/pdf/stat/36/STATUTE-36-Pg539.pdf, 553, italics added.

[14] Radio Act of 1912, Pub. L. No. 62–264, 37 Stat. 302 6 (1912). https://govtrackus.s3.amazonaws. com/legislink/pdf/stat/36/STATUTE-36-Pg539.pdf, 19.

[15] Mann-Elkins 1910, 553, italics added.

Yardley was acutely aware that his supply of messages from the cable companies could dry up at any time. He was also cognizant of the fact that as time went on, an increasing number of Japanese diplomatic messages were being sent by radio instead of by cable. So he was constantly on the lookout for new sources of messages, to the point of continuing to ask Moorman for new supplies of radio intercepts.[16] At one time, he became aware of a new machine employed by a competitor of the Radio Corporation of America (RCA) that would automatically intercept radio messages and transcribe their sending and receiving stations and message contents. He communicated this information to Moorman and suggested that the Signal Corps should acquire one of these machines so that the Cipher Bureau could have a continuous, reliable supply of Japanese diplomatic radio messages. "Now the question I should like you to consider is our installing an automatic receiving wireless set in this building (in New York) to copy San Francisco. ... I think that there are great possibilities in this idea, it will cost us little or nothing ... and there would be no danger of observation as amateurs in New York have innumerable antennae strung on the housetops."[17] Unfortunately, for Yardley, Moorman never seemed to have been taken with this idea and Yardley never got his machine.

Given the postwar posture of the United States as a newly emergent dominant world power, Yardley and his team concentrated on five different countries that the State Department deemed crucial to American foreign policy. In reverse order, these countries were Russia, Germany, Mexico, Great Britain, and most importantly, Japan.[18]

The Japanese exploded on the world scene in the early part of the twentieth century as a result of the collapse of the nearly 220-year-old exclusion and isolation policy (*sakoku*) of the Tokugawa shogunate. The increase in foreign trade during this period led to a disruption in Japanese society and resulted in the re-establishment of the power of the Emperor and the Meiji Restoration of 1868, and an increase in Japanese military might and the subsequent blossoming of Japanese economic and technological development. The first Sino-Japanese War (1894–1895) and the Russo-Japanese War (1904–1905) proved that Japan was a power to be reckoned with in the western Pacific. Its entry into World War I during August 1914 and its subsequent capture of most of Germany's Pacific colonial empire and its mandated territories in China gave Japan a seat at the Paris Peace Conference. Japan's demands at the Peace Conference for the mandate to all the German central Pacific territories that would allow it to block access to the new American territories in the Pacific, notably the Philippines, its planned naval expansion, and its refusal to return the Chinese province of Shantung all increased the concern in Washington about Japan's increasing power. Additionally, its naval strength and belligerency in an area that the

[16] Gregory J. Nedved, "Herbert O. Yardley Revisited: What Does the New Evidence Say?," *Cryptologia* 44, no. 5 (June 25, 2020): 1–27, https://doi.org/10.1080/01611194.2020.1767706, 12.
[17] Herbert O. Yardley, Letter to Frank Moorman. "HOY to Moorman," November 22, 1922. 6647320. NSA Archives, Herbert O. Yardley Collection. https://www.nsa.gov/news-features/declassified-documents/yardley-collection/
[18] Kahn, *ROGM*, 61–62.

United States had marked as crucial to American commercial interests were very worrying.[19]

Yardley himself began working on the Japanese diplomatic code during the summer of 1919 at the behest of General Churchill. It was tough going. He didn't know the language, and there was no one in the Cipher Bureau who did. Ruth Willson was in the process of learning Japanese but was still quite a way from being fluent. Fred Livesey knew a little Japanese and Yardley also had him enrolled in Japanese language classes, and it was he who would contribute the most to the Japanese work early on.[20] Yardley would later hire a Japanese linguist, a missionary who had lived in Japan for many years and who would leave after only 6 months because he was morally conflicted about solving stolen diplomatic messages. Yardley and Livesey were on their own. Yardley had motivation to learn some Japanese and break the Japanese diplomatic code because he had promised General Churchill in July that he would solve it within a year or tender his resignation.[21]

Things did not look good at the beginning. Yardley only had a hundred or so intercepted Japanese messages of varying lengths to work with, along with 25 cleartext messages in Japanese. Given his brief study of written Japanese, Yardley knew that there were several different systems for written Japanese. *Kanji* was the ideographic system that used variations on Chinese ideograms. *Kana* were simplified versions of ideographs that were based on the sounds (phonemes) of different syllables in spoken Japanese. There were two versions of kana, *hirogana* and *katakana*, with approximately 110 symbols in total.[22] Any handwritten Japanese message could contain any or all kanji ideograms and both types of kana characters. However, none of these written systems could be sent via telegraphic cables, so the kana characters were converted into representations using one, two, or three Latin alphabet characters based on their syllabic sounds. These were used to transcribe Japanese into English spelling (orthography) using phonemes that are familiar to English speakers—making it easier for them to read and pronounce Japanese, a process called *Romanization*. This method of using the Latin alphabet to write the Japanese language is called *romaji*.[23] Any Japanese diplomatic code would likely include codewords for every Romanized kana equivalent, plus some unknown number of other codewords for important diplomatic terms, place names, proper names, etc. Yardley and Livesey would have to identify as many of these codewords as they could in order to break the current Japanese diplomatic code.

Yardley started by setting his code clerks to work compiling frequency charts of all the possible codewords in the intercepted messages and the romanized words in the clear-text messages separately. A Japanese-English dictionary helped the two

[19] Kahn, *ROGM*, 63–64.

[20] Herbert O. Yardley, *The American Black Chamber* (Indianapolis: Bobbs-Merrill, 1931), 273–274.

[21] Yardley, *ABC*, 251.

[22] Wolfgang Hadamitzky, "Linguapedia: Japanese Related Textbooks, Dictionaries, and Reference Works," September 2005, https://www.hadamitzky.de/english/lp_intro.htm

[23] Wikipedia—Romanization of Japanese 2021, https://en.wikipedia.org/wiki/Romanization_of_Japanese. Retrieved 11 November 2021.

cryptanalysts to determine the romanization and to read parts of the twenty-five plaintext Japanese telegrams. This then gave them clues to the coded messages.

The first thing to decide was how long the codewords were in the coded messages. All the words in the body of the coded telegrams were ten characters, but this is probably because the cable companies charged by the word and so having long words that could later be broken up were cheaper. The divisors of ten are 2 and 5, so the thought was that the Japanese codewords were either 2 characters long or 5, and they were combined to form the ten-letter sequences. In the end, by examining the frequency tables created by his code clerks, Yardley correctly guessed that the codewords were two letters long each. This made the job of breaking the code considerably easier.

Five months later they were still at it. At this point, in early December, they were questioning their assumption that the codewords were two letters long, and they had yet to identify enough romanized kana to make reliable decryptions of enough words. Livesey had made several suggestions as to equivalences between codewords and romaji, but Yardley remained unconvinced. Already looking for the glory of being first to a solution, he kept his own guesses largely to himself. Growing increasingly depressed and desperate, Yardley even took several strolls past the Japanese consulate in New York with an eye to staging a break-in and copying the codebook.[24] Later, in a letter to General Churchill on 1 December, Yardley even suggested that they try to fool the Japanese Military Attaché into sending a message to Tokyo with some text planted by MID in it in the hopes that a response would be coded and would give Yardley the ability to try a known-plaintext attack on the code. Churchill actually acted upon Yardley's suggestion, but by the time that a reply reached the MID, it was late February 1920, and it was no longer necessary.

Livesey was also busy.

> Livesey observed that the codegroups BA IL LY, which often appeared as a group in the messages, started only in the odd-number positions. This all but proved that the codegroup unit was two. Studying the dictionary, he found that the Japanese word for "conclusion" was owari, and he connected this with some codegroups near the end of the cryptograms (AF FY OK, suggested by Yardley). The kana ri was a common one because it served often as a verb ending, and Yardley and Livesey "went on prowling through the texts for various possible identifications of the more frequent symbols preceding ri but three identifications [o, wa, and ri ] were an insufficient basis to write into the texts" to make skeleton words that would lead to further identifications. The cryptanalysts were stymied.[25]

All through this period, Yardley's wife, Hazel, would be in their upstairs flat every evening waiting for him to finish for the day, providing a sympathetic ear, words of encouragement, and a late dinner no matter the hour.[26] He also corresponded with John Manly, who was now back in the English Department at the University of Chicago. Yardley "sadly missed his originality of mind."[27] Manly wrote to Yardley, "I can't tell you how delighted I am to hear that you have yourself begun to work on

---

[24]Yardley, *ABC*, 264.

[25] Kahn, *ROGM*, 65.

[26] Kahn, *ROGM*, 66.

[27]Yardley, *ABC*, 263.

those important messages, and that you have made so promising a beginning ...
your method is fine and your results are probably right ... How I wish I were with
you ...."[28]

Finally, Yardley's big break into the code came about early in the morning of 13
December 1919.

> Finally one night I wakened at midnight, for I had retired early, and out of the darkness
> came the conviction that a certain series of two-letter code words absolutely must equal
> *Airurando* (Ireland). Then other words danced before me in rapid succession: *dokuritsu*
> (independence), *Doitsu* (Germany), *owari* (stop). At last the great discovery! My heart
> stood still, and I dared not move. Was I dreaming? At last—and after all these months! I
> slipped out of bed and in my eagerness, for I knew I was awake now, I almost fell down the
> stairs. With trembling fingers I spun the dial and opened the safe. I grabbed my file of
> papers and rapidly began to make notes. ... I had suspected for a long time that *AS FY OK*
> which occurs several times in the messages means some word for stop. The Japanese word
> must end in *ri*, for I have already identified OK (*ri*) in the word for independence. I try the
> Japanese word *owari*, which means conclusion, AS = o, FY = wa, OK = ri. This looks very
> good indeed, though of course it is not absolute proof. I make a chart now in order to see
> how nearly correct I am ... Even this small chart convinces me that I am on the right track.
> For an hour I filled in these and other identifications until they had all been proved to my
> satisfaction. Of course, I have identified only part of the kana ... Most of the code is devoted
> to complete words, but these too will be easy enough once all the kana are properly filled
> in. The impossible had been accomplished! I felt a terrible mental let-down. I was very
> tired. ... I was unbelievably tired, and wearily climbed the stairs. My wife was awake.
> "What's the matter?" she asked.
> "I've done it," I replied.
> "I knew you would."
> "Yes, I suppose so."
> "You look dead."
> "I am. Get on your rags. Let's go get drunk. We haven't been out of this prison in
> months."[29]

The following morning, a Saturday, Livesey and Yardley sat down and worked to
confirm Yardley's guesses of the night before. Livesey added several more code-
kana matches to the list and the two became convinced that they had enough to
continue breaking the code. In Livesey's own words:

> Yardley called me in the morning after his inspiration and we spent the morning writing in
> his eleven guesses under the code texts. We found no place where they were near together
> and no confirmations until, just as I was going to late lunch, I found three of them spelling
> "*ku a u*." I knew just enough Japanese to prefix "*joo*" making the words "*jooyakuau*"—
> "draft treaty" and a moment later found "*jooin*"—"senate." That proved all the previous
> identifications. Not till then was Yardley sure that he was right. By night we had seven or
> eight more identifications.[30]

---

[28] Yardley, *ABC*, 264.

[29] Yardley, *ABC*, 269–271.

[30] William F. Friedman, *Annotated Copy of The American Black Chamber. Item 604.* (Lexington,
VA: George Marshall Foundation Research Library, 1931), Quote is from Livesey, 272; Wayne
G. Barker, *The History of Codes and Ciphers in the United States during the Period Between the
Wars: Part II. 1929–1939 (SRH-001, Volume 3)*, ed. Wayne G. Barker, vol. 54, (Laguna Park, CA:
Aegean Park Press, 1989), 99.

On Monday December 15th, Yardley sent a memo to General Churchill in Washington informing him of their break into the code, which they were now calling "Ja," the J for Japan and the A because it was the first Japanese code they'd solved. Yardley gives a brief description of the code and the method of breaking it and then, with an eye toward the Cipher Bureau's future budgets, concludes:

> I did not want to write to you until I was sure, and to be quite frank I was not sure until Saturday. With the aid of a good Japanese scholar there is no doubt but that I can have the Japanese code complete for you and probably some important messages before you go to Congress for the MID appropriation. I may, because I am so interested in this code, overestimate its value, but I cannot feel that if you go before an executive committee with this information, you will have no small argument for MID.[31]

There are a few things to note in this letter. First, Yardley—and later Friedman—characterizes the Japanese system as both a cipher and a code.[32] Both men are wrong in this assessment. A cipher is a system where plaintext units—all of the same length, such as letters—are replaced by ciphertext units. A code is a system where plaintext units of varying length are replaced by ciphertext units of regular length. Using this definition, the Japanese Ja system is clearly a code. In Ja, all of the replacements are two-character code words, but some of the replacements are for single character kana, some for 2-character kana, some for 3-character kana, and some of the replacements are for complete words or ideographs. This is clearly a code.

Next, in the memo to Churchill, there is no mention of Livesey or any of the considerable help that he gave to Yardley in breaking the code. This is the first example of a behavioral trait that will plague Yardley many times during his career—failing to give credit for the assistance of others. Nevertheless, the bulk of the decryption is due to Yardley, and it is he who should get the lion's share of the credit for breaking Ja.

As the Cipher Bureau continued work on the Ja code, they also worked on other Japanese systems. By the end of spring 1920, they had broken three more Japanese codes, named Jb, Jc, and Je. (Jd was a navy system that they skipped.) By July 1920, they were working on Jh, which was a considerably larger diplomatic code, eventually thought to be some 50,000 code groups, and Jf and Jk, which were military attaché codes.[33] By early 1921, the Cipher Bureau had identified more than 2000 code groups in the Jj code. This gave them enough information to read nearly all the intercepted messages and to recover a few more code groups for each message. Many of these codes were relatively easy to break because many of them were very similar to previous codes, and they were all one-part codes (so the codewords and their plaintext equivalents were in alphabetical order) and nearly all of them encoded

---

[31] Herbert O. Yardley, Letter to General Marlborough Churchill. "HOY to Churchill Re: Japanese Codes," December 15, 1919. National Security Agency, Herbert Yardley Collection. https://www.nsa.gov/news-features/declassified-documents/yardley-collection/; Barker, *History*, 95–99.

[32] Friedman, *Annotated ABC*, 263.

[33] Barker, *History*, 100–101.

the 100 or so romanized kana as part of the code and used these code groups to spell a large number of words in each message.[34]

This period was also approaching the height of the success of the Cipher Bureau. In addition to gaining expertise in Japanese code systems, they were actively breaking German, South American, and Mexican code systems on a regular basis. This newfound expertise was readying them for their biggest challenge, which arrived just a few months later.

---

[34] Barker, *History*, 102.

# Chapter 8
# The Lone Cryptologists: Escape from Riverbank

In late August 1919, William Friedman had finally declined the offer of employment in Yardley's new Cipher Bureau. William had been unable to resist the pressure brought to bear on him by Colonel George Fabyan to stay at Riverbank. So now William and Elizebeth were back in Illinois, doing pretty much the same work they'd left in the summer of 1918 when William left for France and the AEF and Elizebeth headed home to Huntington, Indiana. William and Elizebeth, however, cut a deal with Fabyan before they made their move permanent. Their conditions were that they would live in their own residence in Geneva, not at Riverbank, they would be free to examine the Baconian ciphers in their own way, with no preconceptions as to their truth or falsehood, and finally, they would live their personal lives without interference from Fabyan. Fabyan agreed to all of their conditions and promised them a raise. However, agreeing and complying with the conditions were two different things. While the Friedmans did live in Geneva, Fabyan continued to badger them about the Baconian ciphers and refused to publish anything that showed that the idea was flawed. They also did not get a raise. William also did not get any of the back salary that Fabyan had insisted in his letters to him in France was "still going on."[1]

What initially got William back to Riverbank in late spring of 1919 was Fabyan's request that he finish some work that had languished for over a year while Friedman was in France. The unfinished work that William returned to Riverbank to complete was the analysis of a new cipher machine designed by an engineer at AT&T that the US Army was eager to begin using.

AT&T had developed a teletypewriter machine that would allow an operator in one location, say New York, to send a message over a telephone line to, say Chicago, without any other human intervention. The operator in New York simply typed the

---

[1] Elizebeth S. Friedman, "Autobiography of Elizebeth Smith Friedman – 1st Draft" (Memoir, Lexington, VA, 1966), George Marshall Foundation Research Library, https://www.marshallfoundation.org/library/wp-content/uploads/sites/16/2015/06/ESFMemoirComplete_opt.pdf, 35, 47.

J. F. Dooley, *The Gambler and the Scholars*, History of Computing, https://doi.org/10.1007/978-3-031-28318-5_8

message into the machine, and it appeared on an identical machine in Chicago. AT&T was eager to sell this machine to the government, and the Army was eager to buy it so that it could be used to transmit messages between Army posts quickly and easily. The only problem was security. The AT&T cipher machine used a publicly available cipher called a Baudot code. The Baudot system coded all the letters of the alphabet and 6 control instructions into a 5-element unit based on whether an electric current was on (representing a "mark" or 1) or off (representing a "space" or 0). Because the code was publicly available, the Army was concerned that anyone who tapped one of their phone lines could intercept all their messages. In December 1917, an AT&T engineer named Gilbert Vernam devised a way to encrypt teletypewriter traffic using an add-on device with a key tape and a mechanism to combine plaintext and key signals using the mathematical logic operation exclusive-or (XOR). This operation had the advantage of being self-invertible, so that the original plaintext letter could be recovered at the destination using the same operation on the same key tape.

One of the requirements for Vernam's add-on system to be secure was that the sequence of letters on the key tape could not repeat.[2] Otherwise, if the sequence of key letters was too short, the key would repeat, and the resulting operation was just a regular polyalphabetic cipher that could be broken.[3] This was the main problem that the Army had with the system. Vernam and a colleague, Lyman Morehouse, along with the Army's Joseph Mauborgne, devised a two-tape system that would have two different length key tapes where each letter would be combined using XOR to create a new key letter that would be combined with the plaintext letter to give the ciphertext.[4] This operation would be undone at the destination by an identical machine with identical key tapes. The number of random key letters in this system was the product of the lengths of the two key tapes used.

While this was not a perfect system, in the summer of 1918, Morehouse and Mauborgne's extension was deemed sufficiently secure by AT&T, the Signal Corps, and Military Intelligence in the form of Captain Herbert Yardley. The Signal Corps set up a trial between locations in New York, Hoboken, New Jersey, Washington, and Newport News, Virginia.[5] These machines entered service later in 1918, and soon more than 150 messages a day were being transmitted.

Mauborgne, however, wanted to hedge his bets on the security of the dual-tape version of Vernam's ciphering machine. He asked AT&T to contact Fabyan at Riverbank and see if Fabyan and his Cipher Department would test some messages

---

[2] Steven M. Bellovin, "Vernam, Mauborgne, and Friedman: The One-Time Pad and the Index of Coincidence," in *The New Codebreakers*, Hardcover, Lecture Notes in Computer Science 9100 (Berlin, Heidelberg: Springer-Verlag, 2016), 40–66, https://doi.org/10.1007/978-3-662-49301-4_4, 1.

[3] David Kahn, *The Codebreakers; The Story of Secret Writing* (New York: Macmillan, 1967), 394–398.

[4] Bellovin, *Vernam*, 2.

[5] General Marlborough Churchill and Herbert O. Yardley, "Churchill to Mauborgne Re AT&T Cipher Machine," August 8, 1918, RG457, Herbert O. Yardley Collection, National Archives, College Park, MD.

to see if they could break the cipher. "I am not a cipher expert," AT&T's assistant chief engineer Bancroft Gherardi wrote Fabyan on June 11, 1918, enclosing seven test cryptograms, "and would not presume to say what can and cannot be done, but should you and Professor Friedman decipher messages Nos. 1, 5, 6, and 7, I shall feel that I owe you both a good dinner. I have no doubt that you can decipher Nos. 2, 3, and perhaps 4. These, however, as you understand, are not the arrangement which we propose."[6] Unfortunately for Gherardi, Fabyan's best cryptanalyst, William Friedman, had just joined the Army and left for France and his stint in the AEF's G-2 A-6 code solutions office.

However, 1 year later, William Friedman was now back.

Fabyan had been sitting on Gherardi's seven test messages since June 1918, and he wanted Friedman to break those messages so that Fabyan and Riverbank could get the credit for the solution. In particular, he did not want Friedman to stay in the Army or work for anyone but him and do the same work.

When Friedman returned to Riverbank, he went to work on the test messages (Fig. 8.1). Of the messages that Bancroft Gherardi had sent, numbers 2, 3, and 4 were enciphered using a single 2000 key letter tape. Message numbers 5, 6, and 7 were enciphered using the dual-tape attachment. The final message, number 1, was created using a true one-time use random key tape whose length was longer than the message. Friedman promptly solved Gherardi's message numbers 2 and 3 and most of 4, illustrating the weakness of using short key tapes. Friedman did not have enough text to use to make entries into messages 5, 6, and 7—the messages were only a few hundred letters each—and since message number 1 was enciphered using the true one-time pad method, it was not decipherable, something of which Friedman was well aware.[7]

Throughout the rest of 1919 William continued to work with the War Department to consider the security of the modified AT&T Vernam cipher machine. Despite a memo from Herbert Yardley dated 14 August 1919, responding to Friedman's early results and declaring the modified Vernam machine insecure, Mauborgne was not ready to give up on the two-tape solution. On 6 October 1919, Mauborgne sent Friedman 150 messages all enciphered and transmitted on the same day using a machine with the dual-tape attachment. Two months later, on 8 December 1919, Friedman sent the deciphered messages back to Mauborgne along with an enciphered message using the reconstructed key tapes that required the Signal Corps officers to use their original key tapes to decipher.[8] Part of the reason it took Friedman and his team so long to decrypt the Signal Corps messages was because

---

[6] Kahn, *Codebreakers*, 401.

[7] Kahn, *Codebreakers*, 401; Ronald Clark, *The Man Who Broke Purple* (Boston: Little, Brown and Company, 1977), 60–63.

[8] William F. Friedman, "Six Lectures in Cryptology" (Government Document, Fort George G. Meade, MD, 1965), https://www.nsa.gov/news-features/declassified-documents/friedman-documents/publications/, NSA Archives, https://www.nsa.gov/Portals/70/documents/news-features/declassified-documents/friedman-documents/publications/ACC15281/41785109082412.pdf, 166

**Fig. 8.1** William Friedman at an AT&T Vernam cipher machine c1920. (George Marshall Foundation Research Library)

one of his clerks had mis-typed a single letter in one of the messages as it was being transcribed. Once this error was found, Friedman was able to work out a correct decryption quickly.[9]

After receiving Friedman's deciphered test messages in December, the Signal Corps stopped using the Vernam devices with the dual-tape modifications. General Churchill sent a very gracious congratulatory letter to George Fabyan in which he said, "Your very brilliant scientific achievement reflects great credit upon you and your whole personnel. It would be impossible to exaggerate in paying you and Riverbank the deserved tribute for this very scholarly achievement."[10] The Army would not come back to a machine of this type until World War II when the Army began using the SIGTOT machine created by engineers in William Friedman's Signal Intelligence Service in 1943.

To conclude the work for the War Department, in December 1919 Friedman wrote up a monograph on *Methods for the Solution of the AT&T Machine Cipher* in which he detailed his solution of the Vernam machine using the two-tape attachment.[11] Many years later, in 1963, in a series of lectures on the history of cryptology that he gave at the NSA, Friedman wrote:

---

[9] Clark, *Purple*, 75–76.

[10] Friedman, *Lectures*, 167.

[11] William F. Friedman, "Methods for the Solution of the AT&T Machine Cipher" Item 669, (Lexington, VA: George Marshall Foundation Research Library, December 1919).

The solution was accepted with mixed feelings in Washington, especially on the part of Brigadier General Marlborough Churchill, the Director of Military Intelligence, who had signed a letter to the Chief Signal Officer, dated 8 August 1918, prepared by Captain Yardley to the effect that the cipher system in question "is considered by this office to be absolutely indecipherable."[12]

What Friedman says is technically true because in 1918, before Gherardi's messages had been solved by Friedman, Mauborgne and Yardley had thought, based on what Vernam and Morehouse had told them, that the system, with sufficiently long tapes (the tapes used in the Signal Corps trials were 999 characters and 1000 characters long, for a total unique key length of 999,000 characters), was secure. However, by 14 August 14 1919, after Friedman had solved some of the ciphers from the first set of messages from Gherardi and after Yardley and Mauborgne had visited Riverbank in early August to talk to Friedman and Fabyan, Yardley was writing to Churchill that the system as configured was not secure and should no longer be used; something that Friedman conveniently left out of his lecture.[13] Note that this was well before Friedman had figured out the more general method of solving the two-key-tape version of the AT&T cipher machine that he wrote about in December, after he had considerably more ciphertext to work with.

However, by 1963 when Friedman gave his lecture, there was much more water under the bridge of the Friedman-Yardley relationship.

A good part of the winter and spring of 1920 Friedman spent finishing and editing the final manuscript for the Riverbank Publication, #22 *The Index of Coincidence and Its Applications in Cryptography*.

On its face, the *Index of Coincidence* details a new method of finding the number of different alphabets used in a polyalphabetic cipher message using a system such as a Vigenère cipher. The monograph examines two different cipher systems. One was called the Vogel Cipher after its creator E. L. Vogel, who published it in 1917 (Fig. 8.2). The second was created by French Army officer L. Schneider in 1912. Each one uses a set of mixed cipher alphabets to perform encryptions.

In his monograph Friedman examines the ciphers and dissects their methods of selecting keys, constructing the mixed alphabets, and performing the encryption. He then writes a detailed analysis of each system, examining them from the perspective of the cryptanalyst and asking the questions "How can I break this system? Where are the weaknesses?" His fundamental objective is to find the key. One way to do this is to first guess the key length. Because both of these systems use finite length keys, those keys will repeat across the length of a long message, so that some number of the letters of the enciphered text will have been encrypted using the same mixed alphabet. This idea is the heart of the Babbage-Kasiski method to solve polyalphabetic cipher systems, which dates to the 1850s when Charles Babbage independently proposed it, and 1863 when Prussian Army Major Friedrich Kasiski first

---

[12] Friedman, *Lectures*, 166.

[13] Herbert O. Yardley to General Marlborough Churchill, "HOY to Churchill Re: Riverbank & AT&T," August 14, 1919, National Security Agency, Herbert Yardley Collection, https://www.nsa. gov/news-features/declassified-documents/yardley-collection/

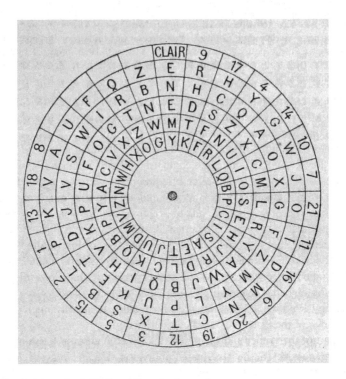

**Fig. 8.2** Vogel cipher wheel. (National Security Agency)

published the method. Friedman was well aware of this method, and its central idea of repeating keys and repeating pieces of plaintext must have been his starting point.

Friedman's new method, a statistical test, is more precise and more consistently correct than the Babbage-Kasiski method, although it is not foolproof. He does not require looking for overlapping pieces of key and ciphertext as Babbage-Kasiski does, but instead relies on the probability of recurrences of letters in a given language. In short, Friedman's index of coincidence is the "probability two randomly chosen letters from a text of length N will be the same."[14]

If we use just one cipher alphabet (or even none—just use plaintext), then the index of coincidence is a reflection of the letter frequencies of the language. In English, for a single alphabet, the index of coincidence is approximately 0.066. However, if we add more alphabets to the encryption algorithm, then any given letter in the plaintext can be substituted by several different letters—a different letter for each of the cipher alphabets. This is why polyalphabetic substitution ciphers are so much harder to cryptanalyze than monoalphabetic substitutions. This multiple substitution means that the frequency distribution becomes flatter, the probability of two letters matching decreases, and so does the index of coincidence. For a large number of alphabets, the index decreases to approximately 0.038. Therefore,

---

[14] Craig P. Bauer, *Secret History: The Story of Cryptology* (Boca Raton, FL: CRC Press, 2013), 76.

because the more alphabets we use in a polyalphabetic encryption scheme, the flatter the frequency distribution of the ciphertext, "the value of the index of coincidence can be said to measure the flatness of the frequency distribution"[15] and as a side effect gives us an estimate for the number of alphabets used in the encryption—the length of the key.

This idea of Friedman's was monumental. No longer did cryptanalysts need to search many times through long cryptograms for short pieces of identical texts. Now they could count the frequencies of each letter in the cryptogram, crank the frequencies through the formula, and come up with a fairly good guess as to the key length. This fundamentally changed how the cryptanalysis of substitution ciphers was done and taught.[16]

However, the index of coincidence method itself is not the most important part of Friedman's monograph. The crucial piece of this result is that his work is the first time that anyone published a method that firmly put the art of cryptanalysis in the camp of science and mathematics. With the publication of *The Index of Coincidence* cryptanalysis changed from an art to a science. From this point on, all new cryptanalytic techniques would be grounded in mathematics and statistics. This is the reason that, if William Friedman did nothing else with respect to cryptology for the rest of his life—and he did a lot—he would still be remembered as one of the greatest cryptologists of all time.

Friedman's work is truly the start of a groundswell of new knowledge that was accumulating over many years, including advances in technology (e.g., wireless telegraphy and the computer) and the introduction of mathematics and mathematicians into cryptologic work that all combined to produce the enormous gains in techniques and theoretical knowledge in cryptology in the first three-quarters of the twentieth century. Friedman was arguably the first, and an important part of this, but only a part. The seminal theoretical work of Claude Shannon on both communications theory and cryptology established both as mathematical disciplines.[17] Lester Hill developed new types of mathematical cryptosystems based on modular arithmetic and matrix algebra and worked on mathematical error detection in communications.[18] In the 1930s, three Polish mathematicians, Marian Rejewski, Jerzy Rozycki, and Henryk Zygalski, provided the key ideas to breaking the German

---

[15] Bauer, *Secret History*, 77.

[16] There is yet another graphical and statistical method of solving polyalphabetic cipher systems that was developed in the early 2000s. See Thomas H. Barr, *Invitation to Cryptology*, (Upper Saddle River, NJ: Prentice Hall, 2002), 143–154.

[17] Claude Shannon, "A Mathematical Theory of Communication, Parts I and II." *Bell System Technical Journal* 27 (October 1948): 379–423, 623–56; Claude Shannon, "Communication Theory of Secrecy Systems," *Bell System Technical Journal* 28, no. 4 (April 1949): 656–715.

[18] Lester S. Hill, "Cryptography in an Algebraic Alphabet," *The American Mathematical Monthly* 36 (July 1929): 306–12; Chris Christensen, "Lester Hill Revisited," *Cryptologia* 38, no. 4 (October 2014): 293–332, https://doi.org/10.1080/01611194.2014.915260

Enigma cipher machine using group theory.[19] During World War II, British mathematician Alan Turing not only provided further ideas and new machines to break Enigma, but he also provided the theoretical basis for computers that would spawn a whole new generation of important work in cryptology.[20] Later, Diffie and Hellman formalized the ideas of public-key cryptography,[21] and Rivest, Shamir, and Adelman provided the first and longest-lasting implementation of a public-key system[22] based on number theory. All of this work turned cryptology into a science, and it all started with Friedman.

In a typical burst of egoism and control, George Fabyan failed to put William Friedman's name on the title pages of any of the Riverbank Publications and had himself put down as the copyright owner. In an even more outright theft of William's intellectual property, in 1920, after Friedman had given him the finished manuscript, Fabyan sent the manuscript of *The Index of Coincidence* to General Francois Cartier, head of the cryptanalytic bureau for the French General Staff. Cartier, unaware of Friedman's authorship, had the pamphlet translated into French and published in Paris. Over time, this French version was attributed to Cartier, not Friedman. Cartier also had a number of copies of the English version printed and bound and sent them to Fabyan. Fabyan then had three of these copies stripped of their covers and replaced them with new covers that contained William Friedman's name and gave them to Friedman; he did not put Friedman's name on the title page of the monograph. These are the only three original copies of *The Index of Coincidence* known to have William Friedman's name on them. Friedman's name does not appear on any of the other copies.[23]

By the fall of 1920, both William and Elizebeth were done with Riverbank. Fabyan was not living up to the promises he'd made a year earlier, and the environment there was becoming more hostile and difficult to tolerate. Both the Friedmans were also coming to the realization that they had nothing more to learn by staying at Riverbank and that it was a dead end for their careers. Government code and cipher work was being done either at Yardley's Cipher Bureau in New York or at the Army Signal Corps and the Navy Division of Communications in Washington. The work on the Baconian biliteral cipher was also a dead end. They didn't believe Mrs. Gallup's ideas or her bizarre reading of Shakespeare, trying to extract different font types in the text that were just not there. There was nothing more for them on the Illinois prairie.

---

[19] Wladyslaw Kozaczuk, *Enigma : How the German Machine Cipher Was Broken, and How It Was Read by the Allies in World War Two*, Foreign Intelligence Book Series. (Frederick, MD: University Publications of America, 1984).

[20] Andrew Hodges, *Alan Turing: The Enigma*, (New York: Walker & Company, 1983).

[21] Whitfield Diffie and Martin Hellman, "New Directions in Cryptography," *IEEE Transactions on Information Theory* IT-22, no. 6 (November 1976): 644–54.

[22] R. L. Rivest, A. Shamir, and L. Adleman, "A Method for Obtaining Digital Signatures and Public-Key Cryptosystems," *Commun. ACM* 21, no. 2 (February 1978): 120–26, https://doi.org/10.1145/359340.359342

[23] Clark *Purple*, 77–78.

Luckily for them, Friedman's old friend, Major Joseph Mauborgne, was now the head of research and development for the Army Signal Corps. After the war, the Signal Corps was tasked with code compilation for the Army (a job that Yardley, who reported to Military Intelligence, was not doing), and Mauborgne was looking for people to do the work. On 2 October 1920, Mauborgne wrote to William and suggested that because of his work in the Code Solution section of G-2 A-6 during the war, he was one of only three or four people in the country who had the skill set to take on this new task.[24]

Mauborgne's initial offer was for William to rejoin the Army and be assigned to the Signal Corps in Washington. The Friedmans were intrigued, but William wanted to be commissioned as a Captain, rather than his old rank of Lieutenant. Mauborgne started investigating this, and in the meantime, William went to take a battery of tests for commissioning in the Signal Corps and went for a medical exam. Neither of these went well. William did well on all the tests except for one on electricity, which he—surprisingly—failed. His college-level physics courses had included the usual topics of electricity and magnetism, but those had been nearly a decade ago and because he had not been told about the electricity test, he'd not prepared. He was also upset because the test section on codes and ciphers—where his job would require him to spend all his time and at which he was expert—was a minuscule part of the exams. He complained and would have been allowed to retake the electricity exam, but at this point the medical exam came into play. When he went to his medical examination at Camp Grant outside of Rockford, Illinois, he was surprised to be turned down by the examining board because they claimed he had a heart problem. This was news to William, who had just turned 29, and he promptly went to a civilian doctor for a second exam and was given a clean bill of health. However, by then it was too late, and the Signal Corps board would not rehear his case. At the same time, Mauborgne also informed William that after the war, a new Army regulation had been put into effect that basically said that anyone who wanted to be recommissioned in the Army after having left the service could not be commissioned at a rank that was higher than the rank they had held when they left the Army. These two things pretty much put an end to Mauborgne's idea of having William rejoin the Army and work for the Signal Corps.

However, Mauborgne wasn't finished. In November, he wrote to the Friedmans again, with a new suggestion. He would hire both William and Elizebeth into the Code Compilation section of the Signal Corps as civilians on a temporary six-month contract to create a new Army Staff code and three new field codes.[25] This contract could be renewed, and there was the possibility of permanent placement in the Signal Corps. If this was approved and the salary offers satisfactory (they were basically the same salaries that Yardley had offered to them 18 months before), then they could start as soon as possible. Mauborgne then put the icing on the cake:

---

[24] Joseph Mauborgne, Letter, "Mauborgne to WFF," October 16, 1920, RG457, Entry 9031, Box #1, Folder 10, National Archives, College Park, MD.

[25] Joseph Mauborgne, Letter, "Mauborgne to WFF," November 27, 1920, Item 734, Folder 1, Friedman Collection, George Marshall Foundation Research Library, Lexington, VA.

The point is, Friedman, that we need your services with the Government and that we would like to have them for a continuing period of time regardless of what kind of a job we call it or what work it is that has to be done, so long as it has to do with codes and ciphers. We feel that it would be a great misfortune if the Friedman family were to retire to some other kind of a job.[26]

The Friedmans were finally hooked, and in early December they wrote to Mauborgne accepting his offers. On 16 December, Mauborgne replied that everything was settled:

I turned over your formal letters of acceptance to the proper division of this office upon arrival, which is all that is necessary for you to start operations with the Signal Corps. I expect a lively row when the news breaks upon Colonel Fabyan's portly frame and expect that no little of his fury will be vented upon me. I am sure I shall be asked to explain why I did not ask his permission before making an offer of any kind to you. Perhaps you had better fix up that side of it – if you can.

We shall be very glad to give you all the office space you need here and to look after you in the way of files, office furniture, etc. ... I certainly hope to see you soon and wish you and Mrs. Friedman a very Merry Christmas.[27]

The same day that Mauborgne wrote his letter, William Friedman wrote his resignation letter to George Fabyan:

Having for some time become thoroughly convinced of the futility of working for someone else under even the most favorable conditions, and feeling that the Cipher Department at Riverbank holds nothing in the present or future to make my staying worth while, and since an opportunity has presented itself at this time to go into business for myself, I hand you herewith my resignation as a member of the staff of the Riverbank Laboratories.

Inasmuch as I have finished all the work it is possible for me to finish, and all the work is in order, I ask that this resignation take effect immediately. I shall be glad to proofread such manuscripts of mine as you see fit to have published.[28]

However, William didn't give the resignation to Fabyan until the day that he and Elizabeth were packed, in their traveling clothes, and ready to leave Riverbank for the last time. They had already packed up their house and shipped their belongings to Washington. With some trepidation, William and Elizabeth stopped by Riverbank on their way out of Geneva, handed Colonel Fabyan the resignation letter, and told the Colonel they were leaving that day. Much to their surprise, Fabyan did not explode and rant and rave at them. He just offered a weak rebuttal and wished them well in Washington. That was it, they were free.

After spending Christmas with Elizabeth's father in Huntington, Indiana, William and Elizabeth arrived in Washington the last week in December and immediately discovered one of the classic problems with a capital city in the aftermath of a war; there were precious few places to live. In fact, they could not find a suitable apartment to rent anywhere in the city. So for the first year they were in Washington, they

---

[26] Mauborgne, November 27, 1920.

[27] Joseph Mauborgne, Letter, "Mauborgne to WFF," December 16, 1920, RG457, Entry 9031, Box #1, Folder 10, National Archives, College Park, MD.

[28] William F. Friedman, "WFF Resignation," December 16, 1920, RG457, Entry 9032, National Security Agency, National Archives, College Park, MD.

rented a music studio from a piano teacher, complete with a baby grand piano in it. It didn't matter. They were out of the rural Midwest and in the big city, for during the war Washington had transformed from a sleepy somewhat Southern capital city into the booming capital metropolis of a world power. There were restaurants, theater, new exciting friends, and although the Friedmans had been married for nearly 4 years at this point, they were able, for truly the first time, to act like newlyweds. They started work at the Signal Corps on Monday, 3 January 1921.

To say that their new employment with the Signal Corps was refreshing is clearly an understatement. In a letter to John Manly in February, William briefly described his feelings about Riverbank, their departure, and their new life:

> I shall say but little here concerning our many grievances against Colonel Fabyan and Riverbank, some inkling of which you undoubtedly already have from even your very limited experience with the latter person and place. They were serious, and I was too long-suffering, or perhaps blind, or both. My balance sheet, after five years association with Riverbank shows losses on all sides, in health, wealth, and happiness. I deeply regret my failure to take more careful heed to the good counsels of Mrs. Friedman, firstly on my return from France, and secondly, when we were offered the opportunity of going with the M.I.D. in July, 1919. ... Our present environment is much more conducive to a normal, healthy, happy existence in this hard, cruel world, as they say. We find the work very interesting, and useful, and with a more cheerful prospect in view for the future. The rust of five years' hibernation has not yet begun to peel off, and it will take time. Mrs. Friedman calls upon me every now and then to be witness to the unmistakable improvement in her disposition. And I am forced to admit that it was I who made her run the risk of an utterly ruined disposition! I fear that she is a bit more worldly wise than I am – or should I now say, was? The Colonel hated her most fervently because she saw through him and his wiles very early in the game.[29]

---

[29] William F. Friedman, "WFF to Manly," February 12, 1921, John Matthews Manly Collection, Series II, Box 2, Folder 12, University of Chicago Library.

# Chapter 9
# The Cipher Bureau: Success and Decline

By the summer of 1921, Yardley's Cipher Bureau was consistently solving the code and cipher systems of several nations, both allies and potential enemies. Their small numbers—there were approximately 16 people on the payroll at this point—belied the amount and quality of the work that they produced. If there was a fly in the ointment, it was that the Cipher Bureau was already beginning to have difficulties in acquiring intercepted cable telegrams.

In July 1921 the Japanese Foreign Ministry changed its high-level diplomatic code and introduced what the Cipher Bureau would call the Jp code. The Bureau received the first message in the new code on 18 July 1921. The Jp code was somewhat larger and more sophisticated than earlier Japanese diplomatic codes, and because it was new, initially there were few intercepts to be had. By mid-August, the Cipher Bureau had received just 15 messages in the new code, and initially, the Americans were stymied by it.

Jp was significantly different from the earlier two-character Japanese codes. At first glance, while messages in Jp looked like those in previous codes, none of the Bureau's techniques seemed to work. Yardley even had his Japanese cryptanalysts working through the weekends. Finally, around August 11th, Yardley had a breakthrough. This new code used both two-character and four-character codewords. Some of the two-letter codewords existed on their own and only used those two letters in that order. For example, DO = ka never appeared in any other codeword. For the four-character codewords, there was a two-character prefix that was used for all the codewords in a group, with a different two-character suffix that distinguished each of the remaining codewords that may or may not have been a separate two-letter codeword. For example, the two-letter codeword EC was decoded as the Latin alphabet letter *S*, while a number of the four-letter codewords prefixed with EC were ECEC = *hakari*, ECEG = *guu*, ECET = *haka*, and ECEW = *hiki*. While the codewords EW = *h* and AK = *z*, the four-letter codeword EWAK decrypted as *sigataki*. A Japanese cryptanalyst would immediately recognize that the decrypted pair "*hz*" made no sense but that the word *sigataki* did. This system took the Americans some

J. F. Dooley, *The Gambler and the Scholars*, History of Computing, https://doi.org/10.1007/978-3-031-28318-5_9

time and more intercepts to figure out.[1] However, because of their increasing experience with all types of Japanese codes, the team at the Cipher Bureau (mostly Frederick Livesey with some help from Yardley and Ruth Willson) took only 5 weeks from the receipt of the first Jp message to produce their first translation of the new code.[2] They produced their first translations by 23 August and continued to build up new codewords in what turned out to be a 700-element code rapidly thereafter. The Cipher Bureau was hitting its stride.

The end of World War I did not mean the end of armament manufacturing. All the participants adopted an attitude that it was necessary for them to maintain or increase their armed forces to prepare for the next conflict. This was particularly true when it came to naval forces. At the end of the war, the United States and Great Britain had the two largest navies in the world. They justified this because of their two ocean exposures. The two countries each had colonies and economic interests in both the Atlantic and Pacific Oceans; hence, they needed larger forces to be able to respond to any aggression or emergency in both oceans. They also, despite being allies during the war, did not quite trust each other in regard to the protection of their relative spheres of influence. With the Germans defeated and the Russians looking increasingly inward, there were also opportunities both in the Atlantic and the Pacific for these two powers to increase their influence and economic strength. Then, there were the Japanese. After their participation in the Great War, Japan now considered itself one of the four Great Powers (which also included the United States, Great Britain, and France).

Immediately after the war, the United States, Great Britain, and Japan all embarked on massive naval capital ship building programs. If the First World War had proven anything, it was that modern armed forces needed to improve their use of technology to be competitive. For naval forces, this meant larger capital ships—battleships, battle cruisers, aircraft carriers—with larger guns and more airplanes. The problem with these capital ship building initiatives was the cost and the unwillingness of the resident populations and political parties to pay for them. After more than 4 years of the war to end all wars, people around the world were tired of war and not inclined to readily support or pay for vast increases in armaments. Politicians were listening to the public sentiment and reducing military budgets in all the former combatant countries. However, the navies in all of the Great Powers were

---

[1] Herbert O. Yardley, *The American Black Chamber,* (Indianapolis: Bobbs-Merrill, 1931), 289–290; David Kahn, *The Reader of Gentlemen's Mail: Herbert O. Yardley and the Birth of American Codebreaking* (New Haven: Yale University Press, 2004), 69–71; Wayne G. Barker, *The History of Codes and Ciphers in the United States during the Period Between the Wars: Part II. 1929 – 1939 (SRH-001),* ed. Wayne G. Barker, vol. 54, (Laguna Park, CA: Aegean Park Press, 1989), 105; Satoshi Tomokiyo, "A Specimen of Yardley's Deciphering of Japanese Diplomatic Code Jp (1921)," *Cryptiana* (blog), June 2, 2013, http://cryptiana.web.fc2.com/code/redciphermachine. htm. Yardley's account in *The American Black Chamber* differs from both Kahn and Barker. Yardley makes no mention of the four-letter codeword combination scheme, but does mention both three- and four-letter codewords in addition to the more standard two-letter codewords in Jp. Kahn *ROGM,* 263 says that Yardley is confusing Jp with the earlier Jg code.

[2] Barker, *History of Codes,* 105.

pushing hard for upgrades to their fleets. The politicians finally won the day, and in March 1921, the British First Lord of the Admiralty called for an international conference on arms reduction and to settle a number of remaining issues from the war. The United States, which was in the process of rapidly reducing the size of its army already, took this as a way to save more money and immediately agreed. After some back and forth on location for the conference, US Secretary of State Charles Evans Hughes proposed that the conference be held in Washington starting in November and that nine countries, the United States, Great Britain, France, Japan, Italy, China, Portugal, the Netherlands, and Belgium, be invited. The agenda items included naval disarmament, the status of Shandong Province and Siberia—both of which Japan had occupied during the war—the status of Germany's overseas possessions and control of its trans-Pacific cable routes, and the defense of these countries' colonies in the Pacific.

For his part, Yardley wanted to give the American negotiating team information about the negotiating positions and the instructions each of the other Great Powers (Britain, France, and Japan) were receiving from their home governments detailing their intentions. That meant that he had to be able to read their diplomatic codes. Yardley and the Cipher Bureau did not have much luck with the codes of either the French or British. Like the Americans, the British continued to support a cryptanalytic bureau after the war. Unlike the Americans, the British had much more experience protecting their diplomatic communications, and Yardley had no luck in breaking any of the high-level British diplomatic codes. The French had even more experience because their Black Chamber had been in existence for hundreds of years in one form or another and was arguably the best in the world. Yardley also had no luck with breaking French codes. As for the Americans, they did not need to send many, if any, coded diplomatic cables during the conference since its location was in their capital and all their delegates and State Department officials could talk in person. This was especially lucky because both the British and French were able to read the current State Department codes.[3] Finally, we have seen that the Cipher Bureau could already read the Japanese diplomatic code, Jp.

As the opening day of the Conference approached, Yardley and the Cipher Bureau prepared for a large influx of messages and work. As Yardley modestly stated a decade later:

> Thousands of messages pass through our hands. The Black Chamber, bolted, hidden, guarded, sees all, hears all. Though the blinds are drawn and the windows heavily curtained, its far-seeking eyes penetrate the secret conference chambers at Washington, Tokio (sic), London, Paris, Geneva, Rome. Its sensitive ears catch the faintest whisperings in the foreign capitals of the world. … the Black Chamber trembles lest new codes be suddenly installed. It establishes swift courier service to and from Washington and awaits the opening gong.[4]

---

[3] At this time the State Department was using its Blue and Green codes. See Chap. 2 for a description.

[4] Yardley, *ABC*, 305–306.

The gong sounded, and the conference opened on 12 November 1921. The courier system that Yardley and the State Department devised worked well. The messages had to be transported by courier from Washington to New York. The cryptanalysts at the Cipher Bureau then had to decrypt the messages. The plaintext messages then had to be translated from Japanese to English. Finally, the translated plaintexts needed to be typed up and then shipped back to Washington by courier. This whole process took anywhere from one to sometimes several days.

The opening session started with a stunning proposal by the American Secretary of State Charles Evans Hughes. In his welcoming remarks, he suggested to the representatives of the eight other nations that "not only that their governments not build major warships for ten years, but that they scrap sixty-six of their capital ships"[5]—more than 1.9 million tons of shipping.[6] To add gravitas to his proposal, Hughes said that thirty of the ships to be scrapped would be American. He then went on to name the exact ships in the navies of each nation that he was suggesting should be demolished. These included four of the British Navy's new superbattle cruisers of the *Hood* class and Japan's latest and most modern Nagato-class dreadnought battleship, the *Matsu*.

Hughes went on to suggest limits for the total size of the remaining ships in each navy, with the United States and Great Britain each allowed 500,000 tons of capital ships, the Japanese 300,000 tons, and the French and Italians 175,000 tons each. The ratio of 10:10:6 for the three largest navies was the key to the proposal and the center of negotiations for the next three and a half months. From the beginning, the United States and Great Britain pushed the Hughes proposal, and the Japanese firmly rejected it. The Japanese wanted to hold out for at least an allowance of 350,000 tons of capital ship tonnage, and they wanted more so they could cement their position as the newest member of the Great Power club. The other countries were also pushing hard for the Japanese to give up their occupation of the Shandong Peninsula and to remove their troops from Siberia, again, something the Japanese were loathed to do.

Even before the conference officially opened, Yardley and his Cipher Bureau crew were reading intercepted messages. Their courier system was set up, and a State Department employee gathered messages intercepted overnight and early each morning rode the train up to New York, where they handed over the newly intercepted messages and picked up the latest batch of decrypted and translated messages before returning to Washington. The volume of messages decrypted and translated was significant. Most messages were turned around in just one day.

---

[5] A "capital ship" is generally considered to be the most important ship or ships in a fleet. From the advent of the first dreadnoughts (aka battleships) in the early twentieth century through World War II, a navy's battleships and battlecruisers (which were nearly the same size as the battleships) were considered it's capital ships. Battleships of this era usually displaced 20,000 tons or more. Battlecruisers were nearly the same size as battleships, but usually had lighter armor and slightly smaller caliber guns. Aircraft carriers were not considered capital ships until the beginning of World War II.

[6] Kahn, *ROGM*, 73.

Yardley later claimed that the Cipher Bureau had solved more than 5000 messages during the conference (another analysis decades later puts the number at a more modest, but still impressive 1600). Yardley's team—Frederick Livesey, Ruth Willson, and Yardley himself as cryptanalysts and Edna Ramsier and Marguerite O'Connor as clerk typists—worked 12–18 hours most days and even worked weekend shifts. The clerk typists would transcribe the messages onto legal-sized pads, identify the code system, and do some of the matching of discovered codewords to plaintext. The cryptanalysts would finish the decryptions, and then Livesey and Willson would translate the Japanese plaintext into English. The clerks would then retype the messages and plaintexts for the State Department. Secretary of State Hughes rarely saw any of these decrypted messages but did receive summaries. Most of the solutions—since they were decrypts of Japanese messages—went to the State Department's Far Eastern Division.[7]

During the conference, the Japanese continued to use the Jo and Jp diplomatic codes. At the conference, they also used a code called Ji by the Americans, which was a naval attaché code that used five-letter codewords that Yardley had reported on in June 1921.[8] Both of these codes had already been broken by Yardley and his team, so that all of the messages sent back and forth between Tokyo and Washington were an open book to the Americans. However, were they really useful to the Americans during their negotiations with the Japanese? Surely not every one of the 5000 messages Yardley claims to have deciphered was earth-shatteringly important? It turns out not. Many of the messages were merely housekeeping reports, requests for financial information (including complaints from Tokyo that the delegation was spending too much money on their food and lodging), and routine status reports. It also turned out that the American press did an excellent job of infiltrating the various delegations and extracting interesting tidbits of information that the Cipher Bureau's decrypts would confirm, but sometimes days later. While Yardley and his team would do a masterly job of turning around decrypts of most messages within a day or two, their decrypts weren't always timely. This was because bureaucracies being what they are, many times it took the State Department several days to get intercepted messages into the queue to be sent to New York and then more days to get the decrypted plaintexts to the right people in the Department. There were also occasional messages that required much more work on the cryptanalysts part than normal, probably because there might be codewords in the messages for which the Cipher Bureau had not yet recovered the plaintext equivalents. In cases such as this, cryptanalysts might need to wait for more material to arrive so they can make an educated guess on the meaning of the codeword. This, of course, slowed down some of the decryptions.

The most important messages that crossed the Cipher Bureau's desks were those that related to the ratios of capital ship tonnage being negotiated between the United

---

[7] Kahn, *ROGM*, 75–76.

[8] Satoshi Tomokiyo, "A Specimen of Yardley's Deciphering of Japanese Diplomatic Code Jp (1921)." *Cryptiana* (blog), June 2, 2013. http://cryptiana.web.fc2.com/code/redciphermachine.htm

States, Great Britain, and Japan. A solution to this problem based on Secretary Hughes' original proposal would have the effect of stopping the capital ship arms race that had begun as soon as the Armistice had been signed and would reduce the overall number of capital ships that each navy possessed.

The British were interested and involved in keeping the number of Japanese capital ships low to protect their Pacific fleet and their colonial possessions, including Hong Kong and Singapore. The Americans were concerned with Japanese expansion in Eastern Asia and the protection of their own possessions in the Pacific, particularly Hawaii and the Philippines. For their part, the Japanese were vitally concerned with protecting their new territories in Korea, mainland China, and the former German colonial islands in the Pacific. They were also convinced that their most likely next naval opponent would be the United States.[9]

The Americans and the Japanese were both doing the same type of calculations with regard to the possibility of a conflict between the two nations and control of the western Pacific. To the Japanese, the difference between a 10:7 ratio of capital ships and a 10:6 ratio was the difference between victory and likely defeat in an encounter with the Americans. This is why the Japanese naval officers on their negotiating team were adamant about insisting upon the 10:10:7 ratio between the fleets. However, the naval officers were not in charge of the Japanese negotiating team. The Navy Minister, Admiral Baron Kato Tomosaburo, was the senior Naval representative, and after hearing Secretary Hughes' proposal on the first day of the conference, he was convinced that the United States would never budge from the 10:6 ratio outlined. However, Tomosaburo reasoned that holding the line on a 10:7 ratio would give the Japanese negotiating room to obtain concessions on other issues they wanted, notably a freeze on building and improving defensive fortifications in the western Pacific by all sides and particularly the American bases in the Philippines, Hawaii, and Guam.[10]

With regard to the negotiations over capital ship ratios, Yardley and his cryptanalysts found themselves in competition with the American news media in providing information on these negotiations. The newspapers, especially the *New York Times*, had a number of reporters on the ground in Washington and apparently had access to a number of people within all the delegations. While Yardley had to wait approximately 4 days for a telegram from Tokyo to reach him in New York via the State Department in Washington, the *Times* reporters were conducting interviews with participants on a daily basis. These stories occasionally conflicted with each other. On 30 November, the *New York Times* headlined two different stories, one "Kato's View Personal Declares Tokugawa: Prince Says No Ratio Decision Made – Early Agreement Is Predicted" contained a Japanese refutation of a quote by Vice Admiral

---

[9] Thomas H. Buckley, *The United States and the Washington Conference, 1921–1922*, (Knoxville, TN: University of Tennessee Press, 1970), 23–24.

[10] Sadao Asada, "From Washington to London: The Imperial Japanese Navy and the Politics of Naval Limitation, 1921–1930," in *THE WASHINGTON CONFERENCE, 1921–22: Naval Rivalry, East Asian Stability and the Road to Pearly Harbor*, (Newberry Park, Ilford, Essex, UK: Frank Cass & Co, LTD, 1994), 147–91, 152–153.

Kato Kanji, "Naval men criticised today the statement made yesterday by Vice Admiral Kanji Kato, who pleaded for 70 per cent as the least with which Japan could maintain effective defense of her territory and interests."[11] A second story in the same issue of the *Times* "Ratio Agreement Depends On Japan: British Observer Says American Delegation Will Not Yield On This Question" says "The expectation that an agreement would be reached this morning on the five-five-three capital ship ratio has been disappointed. The Japanese naval experts are still unable to proceed, and are awaiting final instructions from Tokio. The American attitude still remains unshakably one of take it or leave it."[12] All these stories carried the same warning that the Japanese delegation to the Conference was "waiting on Tokio" before any progress could be made. This was the one thing where Yardley had an advantage over the newspapers despite the amount of time it took him to receive and decrypt the Japanese messages and communicate the answers to Washington. In fact, approximately 4 days before the *Times* 6 December article, the Cipher Bureau had decrypted a message they had received from Tokyo to the Japanese Delegation. Dated 28 November, this message reached Yardley around 1 December, and the decryption was in Washington on either December 2nd or 3rd. It was the breakthrough that Hughes and the American delegation had been waiting for. In the telegram, the Japanese Ministry of Foreign Affairs told Baron Kato:

> Referring to your conference cablegram No. 74, we are of your opinion that it is necessary to avoid any clash with Great Britain and America, particularly America, in regard to the armament limitation question. You will to the utmost maintain a middle attitude and redouble your efforts to carry out our policy. In case of inevitable necessity you will work to establish your second proposal of 10 to 6.5. If, in spite of your utmost efforts, it becomes necessary in view of the situation and in the interests of general policy to fall back on your proposal No. 3, you will endeavor to obtain a wording which will make it clear that we have maintained equilibrium with the American fleet by limiting its power of concentration and maneuver of the Pacific through a guarantee of reducing or at least maintaining in status quo, the Pacific defenses. No. 4 is to be avoided as far as possible.[13]

With the information provided by this telegram, the American delegation was assured that if only they would wait long enough, the Japanese would agree to the 10:6 ratio. As Yardley put it a decade later, "Stud poker is not a very difficult game after you see your opponent's hole card."[14] Yardley thought that for the Cipher

---

[11] New York Times, "Kato's View Personal Declares Tokugawa," *New York Times*, November 30, 1921, sec. News.

[12] New York Times, "Ratio Agreement Depends on Japan," *New York Times*, November 30, 1921, sec. News.

[13] Kahn, *ROGM*, 77; Yardley, *ABC*, 313. Note that Yardley's translation in The American Black Chamber takes some license with the text of the telegram, explicitly adding at the end "...maintain the status quo of Pacific defenses and to make an adequate reservation which will make clear that [this is] our intention in agreeing to a 10 to 6 ratio." It appears that Yardley does this for dramatic effect; the translation in Kahn says essentially the same thing.

[14] Yardley, *ABC*, 313.

Bureau, this telegram was "the most important and far-reaching telegram that ever passed through its doors."[15] He was undoubtedly right.

Finally, on 10 December and after a number of telegrams from Baron Kato pleading for instructions, the Foreign Ministry cabled their capitulation:

> We have claimed that the ratio of 10 to 7 was absolutely necessary to guarantee the safety of the national defense of Japan, but the United States has persisted to the utmost in support of the Hughes proposal, and Great Britain also has supported it. It is therefore felt that there is practically no prospect of carrying through this contention. Now therefore in the interests of the general situation and in a spirit of harmony, there is nothing to do but accept the ratio proposed by the United States.[16]

Unfortunately, for Yardley, this telegram was not decrypted by his team until after the formal Japanese agreement on 12 December. Nevertheless, the 28 November telegram previously decrypted gave the American delegation the ability to wait the Japanese out, which they did. This telegram of 10 December was the final confirmation of the Cipher Bureau's work.

At the end of the conference on 6 February 1922, three main treaties and several smaller agreements were signed by the participants. The most significant treaty was the Five-Power Treaty (also called the Washington Naval Treaty).

That treaty, signed between Great Britain, the United States, Japan, France, and Italy, was the naval limitation treaty and the one that formalized the 5:5:3 ratio of capital ship tonnage. It also restricted the expansion of defensive fortifications on the Pacific territories of the signatories. This meant that for the duration of the treaty, the United States could not add to their defensive fortifications on Guam, the Philippines, or Hawaii, nor could the Japanese improve the fortifications on their newly acquired former German territories.

Overall, the Washington Conference was hailed as a success in international relations; it maintained the status quo in the Pacific for over a decade and effectively stopped the capital ship arms race that had started after the war. However, even after the conference, the major naval powers remained suspicious of each other and proceeded to find and exploit loopholes in the treaties to continue to build smaller ships including submarines, cruisers, and destroyers. They would also turn some of their scrapped battle cruisers and battleships into aircraft carriers. A new turn in naval warfare that would come to fruition in just 18 years' time. Subsequent conferences in Geneva in 1927 and 1932 and London in 1930 were not nearly as successful, and by the mid-1930s, the Japanese were chafing under the restrictions of the Five-Power Treaty and withdrew from it at the first opportunity in 1936.

After the end of the Washington Naval Conference, all the members of the Cipher Bureau were mentally and physically exhausted. Yardley, Livesey, Willson, Ramsier, and O'Connor had worked 12-hour days, 6 or 7 days a week for the last several

---

[15]Yardley, *ABC,* 312.

[16]Kahn, *ROGM,* 78. It turns out that, because of the delays in receiving telegrams from Washington, the Cipher Bureau received and translated this cablegram on December 14th, 2 days after the Japanese had actually made and communicated their final decision. Nevertheless, the Cipher Bureau's work had allowed the Americans to out-wait the Japanese and win their point.

months, and the effort had taken its toll. Yardley, in particular, was worn out and physically a wreck. He wasn't sleeping well, he'd lost weight, and he had a chronic upper respiratory infection that was initially mis-diagnosed as influenza that he'd come down with in late January 1922.[17] However, he did not get better. By mid-February, Yardley was diagnosed by a second doctor with pleurisy, and his pleural sac on the left side was filled with fluid. A week in bed helped this condition but did nothing to cure his chest pain and respiratory problems. Finally, in early March, a third doctor correctly diagnosed Yardley with a mild case of tuberculosis complicated by pleurisy and recommended that he spend the next 6 to 8 weeks in a warm, dry climate to clear up his chest.[18] Yardley spent a couple of days arranging for John Meeth to take charge of the Cipher Bureau while he was away. His letter to Colonel Locke, by this time his immediate superior at MID, recommending Meeth as the person to take temporary charge of the Cipher Bureau, is an excellent example of a good manager supporting one of his employees. In part, Yardley says:

> Mr. Meeth has been identified with our work almost from its inception, very shortly after the war broke out. He was the first civilian who reported to me when I began organizing MI8 and has grown up with the work. ... He has not only grown up with the work, but he himself has grown and broadened. ... He's familiar with the details of the office; necessarily knows its secrets from its inception; and can be trusted with anything. He makes an ideal assistant and can be left in charge for reasonable periods .... [19]

Finally, Yardley cleared his extended leave with his superiors at MID in Washington and headed to Arizona on the evening of 10 March.[20]

He spent a week or so in Phoenix and then headed east up the Apache Trail to Roosevelt, Arizona, where he spent the next 6 weeks at the *Apache Lodge at the Dam*. By the end of March, he was writing to Major Frank Moorman in Washington that he was feeling much better and had wired his wife, Hazel, to join him.[21] The Yardleys stayed in Arizona until the first week of May when they headed home to

---

[17] Herbert O. Yardley, "HOY to Moorman Re: Illness," February 13, 1922, National Security Agency, Herbert Yardley Collection, 6647080, https://www.nsa.gov/news-features/declassified-documents/yardley-collection/

[18] Herbert O. Yardley, "HOY to Locke Re: TB & Arizona," March 8, 1922, National Security Agency, Herbert Yardley Collection, 6647114, https://www.nsa.gov/news-features/declassified-documents/yardley-collection/

[19] Herbert O. Yardley, "HOY to Locke Re: AZ and Meeth," March 15, 1922, National Security Agency, Herbert Yardley Collection, 6647122, https://www.nsa.gov/news-features/declassified-documents/yardley-collection/

[20] Herbert O. Yardley, "HOY to Locke Re: AZ and Codes," March 10, 1922, National Security Agency, Herbert Yardley Collection, 6647120, https://www.nsa.gov/news-features/declassified-documents/yardley-collection/

[21] Herbert O. Yardley, "HOY to Moorman Re: TB & Arizona," March 27, 1922, National Security Agency, Herbert Yardley Collection, 6647134, https://www.nsa.gov/news-features/declassified-documents/yardley-collection/

Worthington, Indiana, to visit relatives and arrived back in New York on 21 May. Yardley was back in the office the next day, fit and anxious to get back to work.[22]

The remaining exciting events for Yardley in 1922 both related back to the Washington Naval Conference and the Cipher Bureau's success with the Japanese encoded correspondence. First, Secretary of State Charles Evans Hughes expressed his appreciation for the work done by the Cipher Bureau by writing a letter to Congress in support of the military intelligence appropriation in the annual budget. He wrote in his recommendation that the "daily contact between this Department and the Military Intelligence Division … which has developed its facilities to a very high degree, is of the utmost value to the Department of State through the information which it is able to supply."[23]

Second, the head of the MID, Colonel Stuart Heintzelman, recommended Yardley for the Distinguished Service Medal. The DSM is the highest noncombatant honor that the Army awards. According to its description, the DSM is "awarded by the President to any person who, while serving in any capacity with the Army shall hereafter distinguish himself or herself, or who has distinguished himself or herself by exceptionally meritorious service to the Government in a duty of great responsibility in time of war or in connection with military operations against an armed enemy of the United States."[24] However, as noted, the DSM is only given for acts that occur during hostilities, so Yardley was recommended for the award for his work during the War, rather than for what it was really in recognition of—his work during the Washington Naval Conference.

Not only was Yardley granted the DSM, but the new Army Chief of Staff, General John J. Pershing, concurred with the recommendation, "I am familiar with the remarkable work of Major H. O. Yardley, O.R.C., in connection with the Communications Section … Major Yardley has distinguished himself by exceptionally meritorious service."[25] Yardley received his award in Washington in December 1922 directly from the Secretary of War, John Weeks. Weeks, of course, knew of the subterfuge with the wording of the DSM citation for Yardley, and while he was pinning the award on Yardley's chest, he gave him a wink. Yardley later said, "The wink pleased me immensely."[26]

1921 and 1922 were stellar years for the Cipher Bureau, and both the War and State Departments were happy with the organization, its output, and Yardley's

---

[22] Herbert O. Yardley to Frank Moorman, "HOY to Moorman," May 5, 1922, 6647162, NSA Archives, Herbert O. Yardley Collection, 6647162, https://www.nsa.gov/news-features/declassified-documents/yardley-collection/; Herbert O. Yardley to Frank Moorman, "HOY to Moorman," May 22, 1922, 6647168, NSA Archives, Herbert O. Yardley Collection, 6647168, https://www.nsa.gov/news-features/declassified-documents/yardley-collection/

[23] Kahn, *ROGM*, 81.

[24] Wikipedia 2021. https://en.wikipedia.org/wiki/Distinguished_Service_Medal_(U.S._Army). Retrieved 11 November 2021.

[25] Anonymous, "A Selection of Papers Pertaining to Herbert O. Yardley (SRH-038)" (College Park, MD: NARA (Record Group 457, Entry 9037), Unknown, but after 1958), 102.

[26] Kahn, *ROGM*, 82.

leadership. However, the Washington Naval Conference and their work during 1922 was the high point of the Cipher Bureau's achievements. Three different things conspired to reduce their effectiveness and their visibility in Washington in the coming years.

First, the Cipher Bureau's output began to decline starting in 1923 and continued to decline for the rest of the 1920s. The cable companies were becoming increasingly uneasy about handing over foreign cable correspondence to Yardley and his organization. Once the war was over, the Radio Act of 1912 came into force again, and a subsequent law, the Radio Act of 1927, which replaced the 1912 law, further strengthened the privacy provisions. Section 27 of the 1927 Act states, in part, that:

> No person receiving or assisting in receiving any radio communication shall divulge or publish the contents, substance, purport, effect, or meaning thereof ... and *no person not being authorized by the sender shall intercept any message and divulge or publish the contents, substance, effect, or meaning of such intercepted message to any person;*[27]

This further eroded the cable companies' confidence in supplying cablegrams to the Cipher Bureau. They were all afraid of getting caught because they would be breaking the law by intercepting communications and giving copies to Yardley. It also didn't help the Cipher Bureau that the last 7 years or so of the 1920s were relatively quiet on the international scene. There were no major conflicts in either Europe or the Americas; Japan was working hard to solidify its gains in East Asia but had complied with the terms of its agreements with China. After the Russian Civil War, the new Soviet Union was turned inward, cleaning house and solidifying the new regime; otherwise, things were calm. Therefore, the number of cables available to the Cipher Bureau decreased year after year from this point on. Within a year or so, Yardley was reduced to bribing employees of the cable companies in order to receive intercepted cablegrams.[28] Fewer cables made it much more difficult for the cryptanalysts to have enough material to break new codes and ciphers, so their output decreased steadily. In addition, while Yardley occasionally considered radio interception as a way to acquire new foreign diplomatic messages, he never really pursued this technology, leaving it up to the Navy and the Army Signal Corps to do the work, but never trying to establish the network of people the Cipher Bureau would need to request and be granted any intercepted messages. His attitude would change somewhat later in the decade, but for now he was giving up on a promising new source of interceptions.

Second, despite the War and State Department's satisfaction with the Cipher Bureau's work, the Congress continued to reduce the budgets of both departments year after year. These reductions were passed on to Military Intelligence and subsequently to the Cipher Bureau. Yardley lost two more employees shortly after the Naval Conference, mostly because of the workload, but he was unable to replace them due to budgetary constraints. By fiscal year 1924, which started in July 1923, the Cipher Bureau's budget was down to $35,000 a year, most of it coming from the

---

[27] US Code 1927; https://uscode.house.gov/statviewer.htm?volume=44&page=1172; italics added.
[28] Kahn, *ROGM*, 84.

State Department. However, these restricted budgets did not stop Yardley from asking for and getting a raise for himself to $7500 per annum. In October 1923, to save money in the new fiscal year, Yardley was forced to move the Cipher Bureau to an office suite at 52 Vanderbilt Avenue near Grand Central Station. This would be their last move. By this time, they were also down to just six employees and Yardley. Claus Bogel had left for the Navy, stayed there for a couple of years and then moved on to the Library of Congress where he would close out his career. Fred Livesey also left—he thought he wasn't being paid enough—and became an economist in the State Department. John Meeth went to work for the Consolidated Edison utility as a manager, and several more of the code clerks had to be dismissed because of lack of funds. The only cryptanalysts left were Victor Weiskopf, who was on the Justice Department payroll until he was officially transferred to the War Department in 1924; Charles J. Mendelsohn, who continued working part-time; and Ruth Wilson,[29] who was a cryptanalyst and the Japanese language translator and had the second highest salary in the Cipher Bureau, behind Yardley. Yardley's secretary, Marguerite O'Connor Meeth, continued her position but doubled as a code clerk as well. The only full-time code clerks left were Alice Dillon and Edna Ramsier, who had also gotten married and was now Edna Hackenburg. This is the group that would last until the final closure of the Cipher Bureau in 1929.[30]

The last thing that conspired against the Cipher Bureau after the conference was a confluence of things that nearly all pointed back at their boss, Herbert Yardley. Nobody on the Cipher Bureau's staff was getting any younger, nor were they learning any new techniques or systems so that they could perform cryptanalysis better, nor were they performing any work that one of their employers, the War Department, found particularly useful. This was again partly because budgetary constraints prevented Yardley from hiring any new cryptanalysts. However, it also had to do with Yardley himself. In Yardley's estimation, the most visible and personally rewarding part of cryptology was solving other countries' code and cipher systems. Neither creating new codes and ciphers for the State or War Departments nor training new cryptanalysts or even updating the skills of his existing staff would help him increase his own visibility or move him up in the ranks of the government. These other duties were not anything that Yardley was particularly interested in having the Cipher Bureau pursue. Finally, because the country was not at war, there were precious few encrypted military telegrams to decrypt.

After the successes of the Washington Naval Conference, Yardley was in no mood to change his mind. He was also not very interested in the new field of cipher machines, which was blossoming in the 1920s and beginning to pass him by. He did occasionally mention machine ciphers, but it was nearly always just in passing, and he never seriously looked into using any machines to help with either creating new ciphers or to enable and facilitate cryptanalysis. This was in contrast to William

---

[29] Kahn, *ROGM*, 83. Ruth Willson married an accountant named Howard Wilson in 1925. Her subsequent name change—dropping a single "l" from her name to use her husband's—continues to cause no end of confusion.

[30] Kahn, *ROGM*, 83.

Friedman, who was interested in both radio interception and cipher machines. The head of the new Navy Code and Cipher section Research Desk, Lt. Laurance Safford, was investigating and purchasing cipher machines as early as 1924, and he worked to have the Navy set up several radio interception stations in the Pacific. Both Friedman and Safford were moving American cryptanalysis forward, while Yardley was allowing the Cipher Bureau to stagnate.[31] In addition to the Americans, the Europeans and Japanese were also very interested in cipher machines during the 1920s. The Germans in particular were switching their military and naval communications to the newly developed Enigma rotor cipher machine. The German Navy adopted the Enigma in 1926, with the Army and Air Force following in 1928. The Japanese Army and Foreign Ministry had also begun an active program to investigate and develop rotor-based cipher machines, including purchasing and reverse engineering a commercial Enigma as early as 1927. At that time, they also began a program to develop their own cipher machine. Yardley and the Cipher Bureau were doing none of this, which would make them and their work less and less relevant in the coming years. As David Kahn puts it:

> The worldwide shift from breakable codes to unbreakable cipher machines was getting under way, with Swedish, German, and American inventors offering such systems and the Reichsmarine and the U.S. Navy adopting them. Yardley was not interested. He never cryptanalyzed them nor considered them for military or diplomatic use. Moreover, though he knew of the weakness of State Department cryptography, had criticized its systems as "sixteenth-century codes," and had once proposed the American Telephone and Telegraph Company's Vernam-Mauborgne online unbreakable cipher machine as the answer and could have known that it could take paper-and-pencil form, he never battled the bureaucracy of the State Department—admittedly an all but hopeless task—to improve its cryptosystems. American cryptology stagnated. Yardley had failed to lead it energetically. [32]

In 1925, after the Cipher Bureau had moved out of the building in Manhattan where they had an apartment, and after the housing allowance that he had negotiated had run out, Herbert and Hazel moved out of Manhattan to the newly flourishing suburb of Jackson Heights in Queens. They bought an apartment, joined the golf club, and became part of the new middle class that was flocking to Queens during the 1920s. Their son Jack was born in October 1925, and 2 years later they moved to a larger apartment. Yardley spent much of his free time golfing and was an excellent player, winning at least three club championships during this period. He would commute into Manhattan to the Cipher Bureau, work a few hours a day—fewer and fewer hours as the years went on—and then head back to his suburban life in Queens. It was also at this time that Yardley earned his real estate broker's license and began to dabble in New York real estate, to make more money, to hide his real work, and to reinforce his reputation as a businessman. He took advantage of the booming real estate market in Queens and bought and sold a number of lots and buildings in the area. He worked for several real estate firms over the course of several years, arranging financing, setting up deals, and becoming involved in constructing new

---

[31] Kahn, *ROGM*, 91.

[32] Kahn, *ROGM*, 91.

apartment buildings. He also helped other buyers and sellers close deals, working on commission. He bought and sold frequently himself. Among his clients were his colleague Charles J. Mendelsohn, from whom he bought a couple of lots in 1928, and his former colleague from MI-8 John M. Manly, to whom he sold a lot in early 1929.[33]

At this point, Yardley was being paid by the War Department, was working in real estate, was also receiving money from the Code Compiling Company for sales of the *Universal Trade Code*, and allegedly earning several thousand dollars a year consulting on commercial codes and ciphers in New York City.[34] Yet he seemed to be always broke or nearly so. Herbert Yardley was not a saver, he was a spender. The more money he earned, the more he spent. He was supremely confident in his ability to succeed at whatever he put his hand to, and for many years this turned out to be the case. However, he was also a person who desperately needed to be admired and respected by those around him, and one of the ways he did this was by spending lavishly. This worked well as long as the money was coming in, but not so well when it began to dry up.

Herbert Yardley and William Friedman's relationship was cordial and friendly throughout the 1920s. Friedman was still grateful for Yardley's attempts to hire him in 1919, and Yardley still admired Friedman's skills. Friedman was working as a civilian in the Signal Corps, so Yardley, technically working as a civilian in Military Intelligence, had any number of occasions to correspond with him about many things related to codes and ciphers. Cryptology and its history was not just their profession but also an avocation for both men, and they would write back and forth on a number of topics. They talked about the Voynich manuscript and Edgar Allan Poe, among other things. Later in the decade, Friedman had a source for intercepted radiograms in the Coast Guard and forwarded a number of intercepted Japanese messages to Yardley. On several of his trips to Washington, Yardley would meet up with Friedman and they'd talk and occasionally have dinner. Friedman visited Yardley in New York on a number of occasions, and they went to at least one baseball game together in Washington. Friedman would also occasionally send Yardley copies of some of the monographs and training materials he was writing for his review and comments. All in all, they were friendly coworkers who had some similar interests even if they were drastically different characters. As Kahn puts it:

> He [Yardley] contrasted sharply with his rival, William Friedman... Their motivations differed fundamentally. Yardley sought money; Friedman, knowledge. Friedman was driven not by egoism but by intellectual curiosity. ... He loved the field not for its rewards, but for itself. And he changed it. ... He constantly looked forward, seeking to improve things. Yardley, in contrast, wanted to maintain the status quo, which preserved his privileges. From the start, he moved politically. ... He was never disinterested. He did not hunt for opportunities to improve codebreaking. ... Yardley never considered [cipher machines]. Improvements like these might have led eventually to promotions and raises, but seeking

---

[33] Kahn, *ROGM*, 88–90.

[34] William F. Friedman, *Annotated Copy of The American Black Chamber (Item 604)* (Lexington, VA: George Marshall Foundation Research Library, 1931), 273; Kahn, *ROGM*, 90.

and implementing them would have distracted him from the outside work that was bringing him money. Thus he never sought them. While Friedman became the wave of the future, Yardley languished, and so did his agency.[35]

Kahn is overly harsh with respect to Yardley here and too soft on Friedman. While Yardley was indeed interested in money and prestige, he was also dedicated to his work, managed his employees well, and sincerely wanted the Cipher Bureau and by extension the United States to succeed. Friedman was by far the better cryptanalyst and the better cryptologist in general. He was indeed looking forward and did a far better job than Yardley in advancing the field in the United States. However, he was also ambitious, harsh in his criticisms of others, and insecure at times. He was required to work harder and longer because he was both an immigrant and Jewish in an era when both were handicaps even in government service.

Herbert Yardley and John Manly continued their friendship through the 1920s. Manly was back at the University of Chicago, where he was a Professor of English and the chair of the English Department. The two men corresponded regularly, and like Yardley and Friedman, they talked about their shared interests in cryptology and its history. Manly was particularly interested in the Voynich Manuscript and had written a lengthy magazine article in response to a series of lectures on the Voynich given by Dr. William Newbold of the University of Pennsylvania in 1921.[36] Starting in 1924, Manly traveled to England every year for the spring semester and summer to work with his colleague Dr. Edith Rickert on their joint research on Geoffrey Chaucer and his *Canterbury Tales*. Since Manly took a ship from New York to England and back, he and Yardley would often get together as Manly was passing through the city. Their most interesting encounter occurred in the summer and fall of 1927 when they collaborated on a series of articles that Manly was writing for *Collier's* magazine on the history of MI-8 during the Great War.

Manly had been interested in telling the story of MI-8 during the war and of his own experiences as a member of the Military Intelligence Division. He was fully aware that much of what he could say was constrained by the secrecy demanded of everyone in MID with regard to their intelligence work during the war, but he thought he could tell enough of a tale to interest readers. In late 1926, the editor of *Collier's Weekly Magazine*, William Chenery, wrote to Manly and suggested that Manly write a series of articles on the role of MI-8 during the war. After some back and forth, finally, in August 1927, Manly decided to write a series of articles for *Collier's* on his war experiences. He was to write between 7 and 12 articles, each 4000 words, and was to be paid $2000 for each article, a tidy sum for 1927.[37] In early September 1927, Manly went to New York, rented an apartment, engaged a secretary, and commenced to write. He was assisted by Yardley, although the extent

---

[35] Kahn, *ROGM*, 91–93.

[36] John M. Manly, "The Most Mysterious Manuscript in the World: Did Roger Bacon Write It and Has the Key Been Found?," *Harper's Monthly Magazine*, July 1921, 186–197.

[37] Anonymous, "Manly vs. Collier's. Facts." (George Marshall Foundation Research Library, 1927), William Friedman Collection, Item 811.

of their collaboration is not completely known. Manly didn't publish anything that the War Department didn't want him to make public, but he probably did use some of the MI-8 documents that Yardley had to refresh his memory of the war years. By the end of September, Manly and Yardley had eleven articles finished and were ready to work on editing them with an experienced magazine journalist that *Collier's* had engaged.[38] Then, things took a distressing turn.

First, there was disagreement about the timing of payments for each article. Next, after initially expressing pleasure with the articles, Chenery started to back off, claiming the articles were too scholarly for the general audience that *Collier's* catered to and needed to be pretty much completely rewritten. By late October Chenery informed Manly "...that the material was such that it was impossible for *Collier's* to accept the articles and offered to return the manuscript of the eleven articles..."[39] After considerable back and forth, on 29 November 1927 John Manly received from *Collier's* the manuscripts he had submitted and kept the $2000 he had already been paid.

Two questions about Manly's articles arise. The first is how much input did Herbert Yardley have in their creation? Second, did Yardley borrow some of Manly's stories when he was writing his own book 4 years later? Manly and Yardley were good friends. Manly rented an apartment in New York City, and he and Yardley did collaborate on the articles. In 1927, Yardley was still working for the War Department as head of the Cipher Bureau, and he had access to all of the records of MI-8 from the war so that some of the stories in Manly's articles may have had their origin there. Additionally, several of the stories from Manly's articles—notably the stories about the German spies Madame Victorica and Patricia and stories about the G-2 A-6 organization in the AEF in France during the war—also appear with some variations in Yardley's 1931 book *The American Black Chamber*. So who wrote what?

It seems clear that Manly and Yardley collaborated in creating the arc of the stories in the articles, so they clearly shared their memories of each of them during September 1927. However, since both Manly—in his articles—and Yardley, in his book, are writing about the same time period and about an organization in which they were both members, it seems likely that there would be some natural overlap in their narratives. It also seems probable that Yardley shared cryptograms and their solutions with Manly from the MI-8 files—else where did Manly get them? Therefore, Yardley's reuse of those cryptograms and anecdotes in writing his own book makes sense. Additionally, analysis of the writing styles of Manly's articles and Yardley's book indicates that the articles and book were written by two different people,[40] so that while Yardley may have used some of the same anecdotes and

---

[38] Anonymous, *Facts*, 6.

[39] Anonymous, *Facts*, 7.

[40] John F. Dooley and Elizabeth Anne King, "John Matthews Manly: The Collier's Articles," *Cryptologia* 38, no. 1 (January 2014): 77–88, https://doi.org/10.1080/01611194.2013.797049

materials, he did all his own writing. It really seems that Manly wrote all eleven of the *Collier's* articles and that Yardley put his own unique spin on each of the stories, and aside from the facts of the stories themselves, the writing and the yarns in *The American Black Chamber* all seem to be Yardley's.

# Chapter 10
# The Lone Cryptologists: Washington Life

For all their excitement about being in Washington and working as civilians in the Army Signal Corps, the Friedmans were still temporary employees. Their contracts with the Army were for a fixed salary—just about the same amount of money that Yardley had offered them in April 1919[1]—and for a 6-month period. Their initial jobs were to create several new codes for the Army, a new Staff code for messages that required some extra security, and several smaller Field codes of a few thousand codewords each for shorter-term tactical messages. William had worked with codes during the war, and Elizebeth, while having little experience with them, was a very quick study. After the experiences in the war, all the Allied militaries knew that two-part codes were more secure than one-part codes. So William and Elizebeth proceeded to design and create new two-part codes for the Army. Things went well, and their contracts were extended for a second 6-month tenure in the summer of 1921. Near the end of their second contract with the Signal Corps, Elizebeth decided to spend her time finding them a place to live and working on a children's book on cryptography that she'd been hoping to do for some time and so she did not pursue permanent full-time employment with the Army. William did. In November 1921, he was offered and accepted the position as the Signal Corps' civilian Chief Cryptanalyst at the middle-class salary of $4500 per year, a position he named himself and which he would hold for the next decade.

Because Herbert Yardley's operation in New York was doing code and cipher solution work, William's arrangement with the Signal Corps included code and cipher compilation and training Army cryptanalysts, as well as studying novel cipher machines and other cipher systems that the Army might consider using, and proposing and initiating the setup of a radio interception service. For the entire decade of the 1920s, his entire section consisted of himself and a single clerk named James J. Skelly, plus an occasional reservist on temporary duty.

---

[1] Katie Letcher Lyle and David Joyner, *Divine Fire: Elizebeth Friedman, Cryptanalyst (The 1910s–1930s)*, (Lexington, KY: CreateSpace Independent Publishing Platform, 2015), 109.

J. F. Dooley, *The Gambler and the Scholars*, History of Computing, https://doi.org/10.1007/978-3-031-28318-5_10

While William was busy reinventing the Code and Cipher Compilation Section of the Signal Corps, Elizebeth was finding them a place to live. Scouring the Washington papers practically every day, she finally found them a spacious five-room apartment in a building called the Argyle at the corner of Park Road and 17th Street NW in Washington, where they moved in late 1921. The foyer of their new apartment was so spacious that they purchased a used baby grand piano and continued the musical ensemble they'd assembled in their tiny piano studio apartment.[2] They settled in and enjoyed the life of a young professional couple in Washington.

After slightly more than a year in their apartment and with a baby on the way, they decided that they needed more space, and in the summer of 1923 they rented a house outside of Washington on five acres in what would become the city of Bethesda. At that time, the house was in the country, right at the end of a local rail line. They named it Green Mansions and quickly got used to domestic life in suburbia. Their home soon became a favorite spot for friends from the city to stop by for a day in the country. This was entirely to William's liking, as in addition to being a workaholic and never wanting to be idle, he was also quite a social person and loved entertaining and going out of an evening. Their house was so much a favorite for their city friends that Elizebeth began to complain that "we learned that anyone who has a country place or a watering place never becomes lonely; indeed, one hardly has an opportunity to do what one wishes, or even one's chores on the place because everyone who needs entertainment, or wants to pass the time at week-ends and summer evenings, invariably drops in."[3]

Despite the minor complaints, both Friedmans loved their time at Green Mansions. It was also at Green Mansions that the Friedmans' daughter, Barbara, was born in October 1923.

William wasn't just involved with Army cryptology in the early 1920s. During this period he kept up a lively and interesting correspondence with John Manly. In their letters, they chatted about the biliteral cipher and other cryptologic topics of mutual interest. One of these was the Voynich manuscript.

The Voynich manuscript is a 204-page illustrated vellum codex that is written in an unknown language and alphabet. It is named after Wilfrid Voynich, a Polish book collector and dealer who acquired it from a Jesuit monastery outside Rome in 1912. Nearly every page is a combination of text and illustrations (Fig. 10.1). Of the approximately 170,000 letters in the manuscript, an alphabet of 20–30 symbols would account for most of them. The vellum has been carbon-dated to the early-to-mid-fifteenth century, and the ink in which the text is written was traced to a slightly later date, giving a date range for the creation of the manuscript between about 1450 and 1550. After his acquisition of the manuscript in 1912, Voynich tried to get experts involved in examining and deciphering the manuscript.[4] He made photostatic copies of many of the pages and sent them to various linguistic,

---

[2] Lyle and Joyner, *Divine Fire*, 113.

[3] Ronald Clark, *The Man Who Broke Purple* (Boston: Little, Brown and Company, 1977), 88.

[4] David Kahn, *The Codebreakers; The Story of Secret Writing* (New York: Macmillan, 1967), 866.

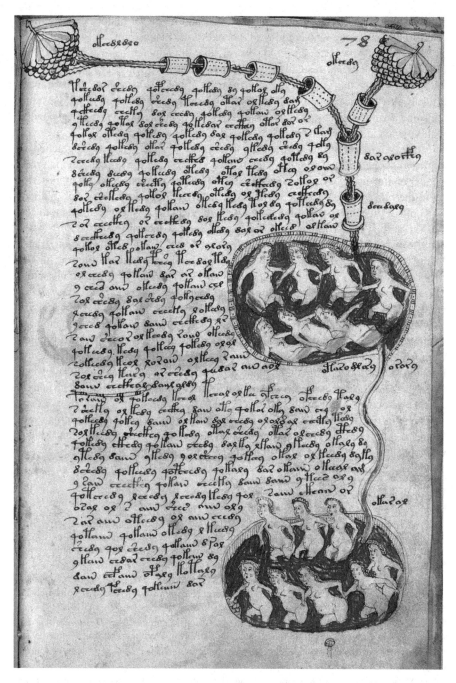

**Fig. 10.1** Page 78r from pharmaceutical section of the Voynich manuscript. (Beinecke Rare Book and Manuscript Library, Yale University)

paleographic, medieval literature, cryptologic, and medieval history experts in an effort to find someone who could read the text of the manuscript.

Like many American cryptologists of the day, including Yardley and the Friedmans,[5] Manly and his Chicago colleague Dr. Edith Rickert became interested in the mystery of the Voynich manuscript from about 1917 onward.[6] In particular, Edith Rickert corresponded with Wilfred Voynich several times in 1917, questioning some assumptions about letter positions in the manuscript. Manly corresponded with Voynich at about the same time as well.[7]

Manly's interest in the Voynich manuscript as a ciphertext was heightened in April 1921 when he and Friedman attended a lecture in Philadelphia. Voynich read a paper on his discovery of the manuscript and related the history of the manuscript up to the current day.[8] Voynich was immediately followed by Professor William Newbold of the University of Pennsylvania, who read his own paper and announced that the author of the manuscript was Roger Bacon, the thirteenth-century polymath. Newbold also advanced a possible solution to the mysterious cryptogram.[9] Manly wrote a sympathetic description of Newbold's method of solution for the *American Review of Reviews* published in July 1921.[10] Later, in 1921, Manly wrote a second, more detailed paper on the Voynich, *The Most Mysterious Manuscript in the World*, in which he dissected Newbold's analysis, concluding that it was faulty.[11]

Manly and Friedman also corresponded about articles that each of them was writing about Edgar Allan Poe and his influence on American cryptology. Both men were having trouble getting their articles accepted. Manly's was too academic and Friedman's was too long and mathematical. Friedman's article was finally published as *Edgar Allan Poe, Cryptographer* in the journal *American Literature*.[12] Manly's article on Poe was never published.

The two friends also talked about Friedman's work in cryptology. Friedman sent Manly a draft copy of his manuscript for *The Index of Coincidence*, and Manly wrote back with praise and a few grammatical suggestions:

[5] Elizabeth S. Friedman, "Voynich Manuscript," *Washington Post*, August 5, 1962.

[6] Kahn, *Codebreakers*, 863–872.

[7] John M. Manly, "Manly Letter to Voynich," July 9, 1921. John Matthews Manly Collection, Box 2, Folder 8. University of Chicago Library; Nill, Anne. "Anne Nill Research Notes on Cipher Manuscript," 1961. http://www.as.up.krakow.pl/jvs/library/0-8-2008-05-23/nill_ring_binder.pdf

[8] Wilfred Voynich, "A Preliminary Sketch of the History of the Roger Bacon Cipher Manuscript," in *Transactions of the College of Physicians*, vol. 43 (Philadelphia, PA: College of Physicians of Philadelphia, 1921), 415–30, https://archive.org/stream/transactionsofco3431coll#page/n5/mode/2up

[9] William Romaine Newbold, "The Voynich Roger Bacon Manuscript." In *Transactions of the College of Physicians*, 43:431–74. Philadelphia, PA: College of Physicians of Philadelphia, 1921.

[10] John M. Manly, "Roger Bacon's Cipher Manuscript," *The American Review of Reviews* 64, no. 1 (July 1921): 105–106.

[11] John M. Manly, "The Most Mysterious Manuscript in the World: Did Roger Bacon Write It and Has the Key Been Found?" *Harper's Monthly Magazine*, Vol. 143 (July 1921): 186–197.

[12] William F. Friedman, "Edgar Allan Poe, Cryptographer," *American Literature* 8, no. 3 (November 1936): 266–80, https://doi.org/10.2307/2919837

I will say that my enthusiasm for your method by "Index of Coincidence" is immense. I think it is no exaggeration to say that it is the most important advance in the mathematical and statistical analysis of cipher since the formulation of the method of finding length of a circulating key.[13] The colored strip method which Yardley and I devised took mechanical account of non-coincidences as well as coincidences but it lacked the delicacy of your method and it had in itself no special promise of future development. Our method of solving running keys ... was theoretically of no great consequence. You have opened the way to unlimited conquests in the field of "cryptanalytics."[14]

Finally, during this period, the two also had a series of communications discussing Friedman's proposed new words "cryptology," "cryptanalytics," "cryptanalyst," and "cryptanalysis." Manly was again enthusiastic and urged Friedman to continue his work in creating a consistent taxonomy for the field and for getting his words included in dictionaries.

These first couple of years at the War Department were a busy time for William. One of the first things he did in early 1922 as the Army's new Chief Cryptanalyst was to revive the training function for military cryptanalysts. This was the same function that he and Elizebeth had performed at Riverbank in the second half of 1917 and that Yardley's MI-8 section had taken up in early 1918 but that Yardley had subsequently abandoned after the war in the Cipher Bureau. William's experience teaching Army officers in the second half of 1917 at Riverbank stood him in good stead in this new endeavor. The first thing that William needed before beginning a course of instruction was a complete set of training materials. Parker Hitt's book, *Manual for the Solution of Military Ciphers*,[15] and the pamphlets that he and Elizebeth had written during their time training Army officers became the source material for his new curriculum design. He set about writing his new manuals while continuing to create new codes.

The first training manual that he created, called *Elements of Cryptanalysis*, is a gem and a text that has stood the test of time. The first version, approximately 150 pages long, was released in May 1923 as *Training Pamphlet No. 3*.[16] It revolutionized the look, feel, organization, and content of cryptanalysis texts, including down to the present day where US Army *Basic Cryptanalysis* field manuals largely take the same approach as Friedman's first pamphlet.[17]

In *Elements of Cryptanalysis*, Friedman adds a logical organization to the presentation of information on cryptanalysis and expands on previous work. Most importantly, he lays out a consistent and understandable taxonomy for cryptology. This is the book that Friedman used starting with a draft of the work in the fall of

---

[13] Manly is talking about the Babbage-Kasiski method here.

[14] John M. Manly, "Manly to WFF," January 26, 1922, Friedman Collection, George Marshall Foundation Research Library, Lexington, VA.

[15] Parker Hitt, *Manual for the Solution of Military Ciphers*, paperback, SRH-004 (Fort Leavenworth, KS: Press of the Army Service Schools, 1916).

[16] William F. Friedman, *Elements of Cryptanalysis*, Training Pamphlet No. 3 (Washington, DC: Office of the Chief Signal Officer, 1923).

[17] Anonymous, "Basic Cryptanalysis Field Manual" (Department of the Army, 1990), No. 34-40-2, U.S. Army, Washington, DC, https://irp.fas.org/doddir/army/fm34-40-2/

1922 when he began teaching a course on *The Solution of Military Codes and Ciphers* at Camp Vail (later Fort Monmouth) in New Jersey. He would teach this class regularly for the next decade, sometimes with a class of one, sometimes larger. He would later expand *Elements of Cryptanalysis* into a four-volume set, and this version would carry the Army through World War II. Despite the revolutionary aspect of this text, Friedman was modest about its goals:

> This course is intended to give a brief exposition of the general subject of military cryptog-raphy, to show how and why certain types of cryptograms are solved so readily, and to point out and exemplify the various rules and precautions that should be observed in order to maintain the secrecy of our own communications. ... it is believed that the ground covered and the material contained herein afford a firm general foundation for the further training of students in the application of the principles of cryptanalysis to the more complicated types of cryptograms such as would be encountered in any future emergency.[18]

While Friedman was creating his training regimen, he was also evaluating code and cipher systems for use by the Army. He was charged with evaluating new cipher machines and cipher systems submitted by individuals, companies, and other parts of the armed forces for use by the Army. One of his first duties with respect to approving cipher machines was the analysis of a mechanical cipher device invented by his boss, Colonel Joseph Mauborgne.

What was to become the US Army M-94 cipher device was a cylindrical device composed of twenty-five numbered aluminum disks, each approximately 3 inches in diameter that were mounted and rotated around a central shaft (Fig. 10.2). A nut held the disks tightly onto the shaft. Each disk had a mixed alphabet engraved on the outer rim of the disk. All of the alphabets were completely random except for disk number 17, which contained the alphabet **ARMYOFTHEUSZJXDPCWGQIBKLNV**.

**Fig. 10.2** US Army M-94 cipher device (note the third disk from the right is disk #17). (Computer History Museum)

---

[18] Friedman *Elements*, v.

Mauborgne was not the first person to create this device; it has at least four parents. The earliest known version was devised by Thomas Jefferson in approximately 1795. Jefferson's version used disks made of wood but was otherwise very similar to the M-94. In 1891, French Commandant Etienne Bazieres independently created a nearly identical device, and in 1914, Captain Parker Hitt created a device that used strips of paper on which the alphabets were printed instead of disks. It was Mauborgne who, in 1917, took Hitt's idea and turned it into aluminum cylinders. Mauborgne also improved the mixed alphabets, making them more random and increasing the security of the device. None of the latter three inventors knew about Jefferson's first device, and neither Hitt nor Mauborgne was aware of Bazieres' version until much later.[19]

The M-94 was intended for tactical messages between troops near the front lines and for which the message life was short. To encrypt messages, one first had to arrange the disks on the shaft according to a predetermined key of numbers from 1 through 25. Once the disks were arranged, the first twenty-five letters of the plaintext were encrypted. To do this, the user spun the disks around until the letters of the plaintext lined up along the metal guide. The user would then read any of the other lines of text as the first twenty-five letters of ciphertext. This technique was repeated for every group of twenty-five letters of the plaintext message. To decrypt the message, the receiving M-94's disks were arranged using the same key, and the first twenty-five letters of the ciphertext were lined up along the aluminum guide. The user then examined the device until they found readable plaintext. This process was repeated for the entire ciphertext.

Friedman's analysis concluded that the M-94 was sufficiently secure for the types of tactical messages for which it was intended—short plaintext messages that also had a short lifetime. There were more than 15 septillion different ways to arrange the 25 cipher disks on the shaft, creating a key. However, the cipher itself was just a polyalphabetic cipher that used 25 different alphabets that were repeated every 25 characters in the message, so decryption was possible in a reasonable amount of time. The device was approved for Army use in June 1921.[20] The M-94 was also approved for use by the Navy, which called it the CSP-488. The M-94 was in Army service from 1921 through 1942, with a total of 9342 manufactured.

A second cipher machine that Friedman evaluated in the early 1920s would ultimately lead to his greatest success with machines. In 1921, an American named Edward Hugh Hebern filed a patent application for an electromechanical cipher machine that used a rotating disk to change the cipher alphabets after each plaintext letter was typed. Hebern had the idea for his machine as far back as 1917 and had spent the intervening years before his patent application perfecting the idea and building several prototypes. This "rotor" machine was one of at least four that were devised and patented during and immediately after World War I. The others were

---

[19] Various, "The History of Army Strip Cipher Devices (July 1934–October 1947) (SRH-366)" (Washington, DC: U.S. Army Security Agency, November 1948), https://archive.org/details/ticom/Srh-366UsArmyStripCiphers1934-1947/mode/2up?view=theater, 8–18.

[20] SRH-366 *Strip Cipher*, 19.

devised by a Dutchman, Hugo Koch, who filed his patent in 1919, a Swede, Arvind Damm, who applied for a patent in Sweden in 1919, and a German, Arthur Scherbius, who had applied for a patent for a rotor machine in 1918. All of these machines used the same basic idea for the rotor. Each rotor came in two pieces that were joined together by screws. On each side of the rotor were a set of electrical contacts. Inside the rotors, wires connected a contact from one side of the rotor to a random contact on the other side so that when an electrical current was applied to one contact, the resulting current appeared in a different place on the other side of the rotor. All of the rotors had the letters of the alphabet engraved on the outside rim. The effect of the rotor is to create a monoalphabetic substitution cipher using a mixed alphabet. No two rotors are supposed to be wired the same, so each one of them creates a different set of monoalphabetic substitutions. The rotors had pins on one side and flat connectors on the other so that more than one rotor could be installed and would complete an electrical circuit. To change the position of the rotors—and thus change the alphabet used—the rotors also had ratchets on them so they could move once one or more letters were typed. Figure 10.3 shows a picture of typical rotors.

With just one rotor, a cipher machine would not be very secure. However, what all rotor machines have in common is that once the rotor has been used to encipher a single plaintext letter, it is rotated one or more positions, presenting to the user a *different* substitution alphabet, creating a *polyalphabetic* cipher. If the user first types an A and obtains a D as an output and then types an A again, the second output could be an M, etc. Once every 26 letters, the rotor returns to the original alphabet, so we say that the *period* of the rotor is 26. This is still not very secure, being roughly equivalent to a Vigenère cipher. But, if one puts two rotors together, things become much more interesting. The electrical current will then flow into an input contact on the first rotor and pass from an output contact in the first rotor to an input contact in the second rotor and then take the output from the opposing contact on the second rotor, doing, in effect, two substitutions. If the first rotor moves with every letter and the second rotor remains stationary, we still have just 26 alphabets. However, if when the first, fast, rotor has finished a complete rotation, the second rotor then advances one contact, then we have a different set of 26 alphabets to use. The period then becomes $26 \times 26 = 26^2 = 676$, and the machine uses the equivalent of 676 mixed cipher alphabets. This is much more difficult to decrypt. Adding a

**Fig. 10.3** Typical electromechanical rotors. (Wikimedia Commons)

**Fig. 10.4** Edward Hebern's original single rotor cipher machine c1921. (Computer History Museum)

third rotor brings the period to $26^3 = 17,576$. A further complication in a rotor-based machine is that the rotors can be inserted in the machine in any order, so if you have three rotors, numbered 1, 2, and 3, they can be inserted into the machine in six different orders: 1–2–3, 2–1–3, 2–3–1, 1–3–2, 3–2–1, and 3–1–2, causing the machine to perform a different set of substitutions for each ordering. Finally, each rotor can be set to start at a different place for each message sent, greatly complicating the sequence of alphabets used.

Hebern's original rotor machine patent application, filed in 1921 and approved in 1924, only used a single rotor (Fig. 10.4). This would only create a machine that would be able to use 26 mixed alphabets, which was not nearly enough for security.

Later versions of Hebern's machine would use five rotors. This latter version is the one that William Friedman was asked to evaluate around 1923.

Hebern thought that his rotor machines would have excellent security and tried to sell them to the US government, starting with the US Navy in 1922. At this time, all Navy signals intelligence work was housed in the Operations area under the Division of Naval Communications. The Code and Signal Section of the Communications Office was created in 1917, primarily to create new codes for the Navy. During America's time in the Great War, the Navy's cryptanalytic efforts had been delegated to Herbert Yardley's MI-8 organization, and after the war had been moribund. On July 1, 1922, the Navy finally created a Research Desk within the Code and Signal Section. The Research Desk's objective was to resurrect the cryptanalytic operations of the Navy.[21] However, the unit was thinly staffed until January 1924 when Lt. Laurance Safford would be named its commander. Safford would benefit from his senior employee, employed as a code clerk and who had been a yeoman in the Navy during the war, Agnes Meyer.

Meyer, who was born in Illinois, earned a bachelor's degree in 1911 from Ohio State University with a double major in mathematics and music. In June 1918, just a month shy of her 29th birthday, Agnes Meyer enlisted in the US Navy. That decision would change her life.[22]

After spending the better part of a year in the Naval Office of the Chief Cable Censor, and being promoted to Chief Yeoman in the process,[23] Meyer was transferred to the Code and Signal Section in mid-1919. However, because Yardley's MI-8 was doing all the cryptanalytic work for the Navy, Meyer did not get to solve any coded messages just yet. Instead, she was set to work analyzing Navy systems. According to her future boss, Captain Laurance Safford, "She stayed on with us, not attempting any foreign [code or cipher] solutions, but studying our own systems and particularly solving all manner of machine ciphers submitted to the Navy Department for adoption. She solved them all and none of them were taken."[24]

At the end of July 1919, Meyer was taken off active duty (all the women Yeomen were) and moved into the Naval Reserve but stayed in her position in the Code and Signal Section as a civilian. Shortly after that, probably in the fall of 1919, she was given a temporary assignment and was sent to spend 5 months training at Herbert Yardley's newly created Cipher Bureau in New York. Since Yardley and his team were heavily involved in decrypting Japanese diplomatic codes at this point, that is probably what Meyer ended up doing.[25]

Agnes Meyer was honorably discharged—at her own request—from the Naval Reserves in February 1920 and the very next day sat down at a desk in the Code and Signal Section as a civilian employee of the Navy. Shortly after, Meyer was shipped off to spend several more months learning more about cryptanalysis at Riverbank Laboratories, where she first met William and Elizebeth Friedman. So within the first 10 months or so of her civilian employment at the Navy, Agnes Meyer met and was instructed by both William Friedman and Herbert Yardley.[26]

---

[21] Elliott Carlson, *Joe Rochefort's War*, (Annapolis, MD: Naval Institute Press, 2011). 28–36.

[22] Kevin Wade Johnson, "The Neglected Giant: Agnes Meyer Driscoll," Special Series, Volume 10 (Ft. George Meade, MD: NSA Center for Cryptologic History, 2015), https://www.nsa.gov/about/cryptologic-heritage/historical-figures-publications/publications/assets/files/the-neglected-giant/the_neglected_giant_agnes_meyer_driscoll.pdf, 4.

[23] Chief Yeoman was the highest rank a woman could achieve in the Navy at this time.

[24] Johnson *Neglected Giant*, 7.

[25] Robert Hanyok, "Madame X: Agnes Meyer Driscoll and U.S. Naval Cryptology, 1919–1940." (Ft. George Meade, MD: Center for Cryptologic History, National Security Agency, 2002), https://www.nsa.gov/news-features/declassified-documents/crypto-almanac-50th/assets/files/Madame_X_Agnes_Meyer_Driscoll.pdf, 2; Johnson *Neglected Giant*, 8; Jack Holtwick, "Naval Security Group History to World War II (SRH-355), Part 1" (Ft. George Meade, MD: U.S. Navy Security Group, June 1971), 29.

[26] Hanyok *Madame X*, 2; Johnson *Neglected Giant*, 8–9; Holtwick *SRH-355 Part 1*, 29.

Back at the Navy in June 1920, Meyer began work on projects designed to improve the Navy's internal communications. She worked during 1920 and 1921 with the head of the Code and Signal Section, Lt. Cmdr. William Gresham on a mechanical cipher machine, designated as the "CM" or Communications Machine. It used sliding alphabets to produce a polyalphabetic ciphertext in a way similar to a rotor machine but using printed alphabets instead. Finished in 1921, the ungainly machine was designed by Gresham based on a cryptographic idea by Meyer. It was approved for use in 1923 and was used by the Navy as its main cipher machine throughout the rest of the 1920s. This experience with cipher machines allowed her to discover her next project.

In 1921, Edward Hebern put out a challenge message to the Navy created on his original machine; Agnes Meyer solved it without ever seeing the machine. While Hebern was not happy with this turn of events, it spurred him to make more changes to his rotor machine over the next few years. He also started trying to get Agnes Meyer to work for him, which she finally did, leaving the Navy in January 1923 and starting work for Hebern in his company's Washington office in February as a technical consultant. In an odd twist of fate, the person the Navy hired to replace Meyer in the Code and Signal Section was none other than Elizebeth Friedman, who started work in February 1923. However, Elizebeth would only last 5 months compiling codes for the Navy, leaving in June 1923 because she was pregnant with her and William's first child, Barbara. Unfortunately for Agnes Meyer, her work on the cipher machine and her suggestions on improvements mostly fell on deaf ears, and she left Hebern's company in July 1924 and was back at the Navy the following month where she would continue to have a distinguished career until her retirement in 1959. In the summer of 1924, Meyer married Washington attorney Michael Driscoll (Fig. 10.5).[27]

Another reason for Agnes Meyer Driscoll leaving Hebern's company was probably the result of an analysis of Hebern's new machine by the Army's chief cryptanalyst, William Friedman. In early 1924, the Army finally agreed to test Hebern's new five-rotor design to see if the machine was cryptographically secure enough for use in the military. The Navy was already preparing to buy a number of the machines, and the Army's test was the final hurdle that Hebern had to overcome.

Hebern's new five-rotor machine was considerably more complicated than the original machine that Agnes Meyer had solved so easily. In early 1924, William Friedman was given ten test messages by the Navy to use on two Hebern machines that the Army had just acquired. To make things simpler, the same rotor order was used for all ten messages, although the rotor starting positions were different. Unfortunately for Friedman, the internal wiring of the rotors on the Army machines was different than those on the Navy machines, complicating his analysis significantly. Friedman spent approximately 4 weeks thinking about the machine, determining how it worked, and working out a theory for cryptanalyzing it. He then spent

[27] John F Dooley, *History of Cryptography and Cryptanalysis: Codes, Ciphers, and Their Algorithms*, History of Computing (London, UK: Springer-Verlag, 2018), 131–135.

**Fig. 10.5** Agnes Meyer
Driscoll c1925. (National
Security Agency, Center for
Cryptologic History)

2 weeks actively working on the messages and at the end of that time, had broken all ten messages.[28] This was a stunning piece of work; the first time any rotor-based cipher machine was solved. Consequently, neither the Army nor the Navy bought Hebern's machines, and the unfortunate Hebern declared bankruptcy later in 1924. This is not to say that the Army and Navy did not learn anything from Hebern's machines nor that they were completely put off of cipher machines. Friedman's work on the Hebern machine and his analysis of its inner workings led him to examine several other cipher machines, and slightly over a decade later, he and one of his

---

[28] Cipher A. Deavours and Louis Kruh, *Machine Cryptography and Modern Cryptanalysis*, Artech House Telecom Library. (Dedham, MA: Artech House, 1985); William F. Friedman, "Analysis of a Mechanico-Electrical Cryptograph, Part II" (Washington, DC: War Department, 1935), https://archive.org/details/41709409074875

**Fig. 10.6** William Friedman in his office, c1924. (Library of Congress)

colleagues would design their own rotor-based cipher machine that overcame the earlier issues and produced a very secure device.

As the Army's Chief Cryptanalyst, Friedman was occasionally called upon to consult with other organizations and to provide his expertise in decoding intercepted messages (Fig. 10.6). In 1924, Friedman had another brush with fame when he was handed a sheaf of encrypted messages by a US Senator who asked that they be decoded.

The messages were sent to and from associates of Interior Secretary Albert Fall, who was the main focus of the Teapot Dome Scandal. In 1921, shortly after being named Secretary of the Interior, Albert Fall arranged to have the oil reserve lands controlled by the US Navy transferred to the Interior department. He subsequently granted exclusive rights to the Teapot Dome reserve in Wyoming to Harry F. Sinclair of Mammoth Oil Company and exclusive rights to the Elk Hills and Buena Vista Hills reserves in California to Edward L. Doheny of the Pan American Petroleum Company at prices considerably below market value and without any competitive bidding. When the US Senate, in an oversight investigation, questioned these leases, it turned out that Fall and members of his family had received $200,000 in Liberty bonds from another company controlled by Sinclair and that Fall himself had received a $100,000 loan from Doheny that did not seem to have been paid back. The publisher of the *Washington Post*, Edward B. McClean, seems to have been the intermediary for the loan, although he was not believed to know anything about the oil leases.

The coded telegrams that Friedman was given were all very short. He deduced that they were in code, but none of the codebooks to which he had access was the one that decoded the messages. Within days, however, the *New York World* newspaper published the plaintext of several of the messages, claiming that they were encoded using a Department of Justice codebook. Friedman went over to the Justice Department and discovered that the codebook was one that was normally issued to agents of the Bureau of Investigation. It turned out that Fall and McClean had been appointed honorary agents and so had copies of the codebook. With this knowledge, Friedman was able to decode all the messages. He subsequently testified before Congress about these decryptions. He did not relish it. In 1927, the Teapot Dome oil leases were invalidated by the US Supreme Court, and in 1929 Albert Fall was convicted of conspiracy and accepting bribes and spent time in prison, the first former Cabinet secretary to do so.

After Barbara was born, the Friedmans decided that Green Mansions, however nice in the countryside, was too far from Washington for convenience. Therefore, in late 1925 they moved again, building a brand-new house at 3932 Military Road in Chevy Chase, where they would stay for nearly the next 30 years.[29] At the time, Elizabeth was working on two different books, a history of the alphabet book for children and an introduction to cryptography book for teens and interested adults.[30] However, her work on these would be interrupted by another supplication from the government.

By 1925, Prohibition in the United States had been in force for 6 years, and it wasn't going well. Nearly as soon as the Volstead Act, which implemented Prohibition under the 18th Amendment, was enacted in October 1919, illegal manufacture and importation of alcoholic beverages into the United States began. Over the course of the following 6 years, the tenor of bootlegging had changed, from opportunistic charter boat captains and fishermen importing a few cases of liquor from the Bahamas to the much more serious and violent denizens of organized crime running large organizations nationwide. The amount of money to be made and the ease of smuggling liquor into the United States made rumrunning too irresistible to pass up, and a large number of gangs sprang up by the mid-1920s. The Treasury and Justice departments were charged with enforcing Prohibition, and they were barely keeping up. The Treasury department had six different law enforcement agencies inside it: the Coast Guard, the IRS, the Secret Service, Customs, the Prohibition Bureau, and the Narcotics Bureau.[31] As one of its functions, the Coast Guard was charged with finding and apprehending illegal importers of alcohol—

[29] Elizebeth S. Friedman, "Autobiography of Elizebeth Smith Friedman" (Memoir, Lexington, VA, 1966), George Marshall Foundation Research Library, https://www.marshallfoundation.org/library/wp-content/uploads/sites/16/2015/06/ESFMemoirComplete_opt.pdf, 59.

[30] Jason Fagone, *The Woman Who Smashed Codes*, (New York, NY: William Morrow, 2017), 128–129, 133.

[31] Fagone, *Smashed*, 134.

rumrunners. The rumrunners had evolved from simple, single boat operations to multinational corporations with fleets of ships of sizes ranging from speed boats to large cargo ships that could hold upward of 100,000 cases of illegal spirits. With operations this large, the rumrunners began using radio to communicate between their vessels and between the smuggling ships and their destinations onshore. Naturally, they began using codes and ciphers to hide the contents of their messages. During the early 1920s, the Coast Guard set up several radio stations along the American East and Gulf coasts. One of the things these stations did was to intercept rumrunners' radio messages. However, they couldn't read them. This is where Elizebeth Friedman entered the picture. One morning in 1925, shortly after William and Elizebeth had moved into their new house on Military Road, Elizebeth answered a knock on her door to find a Coast Guard officer on her doorstep. The officer was Lt. Commander (later Captain) Charles S. Root. Root explained that he was the Intelligence Officer of the Coast Guard, in charge of a new intelligence division that had been created the year before, and he needed her help. Root's intelligence section was sitting on over 2 years' worth of rumrunner radio intercepts, and more were piling up every day. He was desperately in need of someone to decrypt all these messages. Elizebeth agreed to a 90-day contract, but only on the condition that she could work from home. Root immediately acquiesced, and Elizebeth was soon the proud owner of a leather case containing a metal badge with the words SPECIAL AGENT, U.S. TREASURY stamped in gold. Initially, she stayed on her continuing temporary contract, like the one she had had with the Signal Corps, a part-time employee of the Treasury Department Prohibition Bureau, on loan to the Coast Guard. For those first couple of years, Elizebeth's routine was to drop by Root's office in the Treasury Building across from the White House and pick up a satchel of intercepted messages. She would take them home, decrypt them over the course of a week or so, and bring the decrypts back to Root and pick up a new satchel of messages.[32] Most of the messages were in relatively simple ciphers, but some were in more complicated combinations of substitution and transposition ciphers and codes of different types, including enciphered code. Elizebeth cracked them all, and the Coast Guard's interception of rumrunner cargos began to increase. By the end of her first 3 months, she had solved 2 years' worth of messages, and by the beginning of her third year decrypting rumrunners cryptograms in 1930, she had solved nearly 12,000 messages.[33]

One particular message is instructive. The Coast Guard intercepted a telegram from Havana and sent it on to Elizebeth. She determined that the message was in a transposition cipher, but since it was the only communication she had between this particular sender and receiver, she could not find a method of breaking the cipher except by trial and error, a very time-consuming task. A young Lieutenant in Captain Root's office suggested that perhaps the key was the city from which the telegram

---

[32] Fagone *Smashed*, 135–136.

[33] Eric S. Ensign, "Intelligence in the Rum War at Sea, 1920–1933" (Master's Thesis, Washington, DC, Joint Military Intelligence College, 2001), https://apps.dtic.mil/docs/citations/ADA485809, https://apps.dtic.mil/dtic/tr/fulltext/u2/a485809.pdf, 28.

was sent—Havana. Elizebeth scoffed at the idea that someone would be naïve enough to use such a simple and obvious keyword. However, after she had tried a large number of possible keywords for a considerable length of time, she finally tried the keyword "Havana," and it worked. The Lieutenant had been right. From this Elizebeth learned a valuable lesson, "I decided right then and there that I would not permit my mind to become so rigid as to exclude the obvious but that hereafter, I would try first that very supposition and thus clear away the possibilities that the sender of a secret message had been so foolish as to employ a tool of such naïve practices."[34]

By 1927, Elizebeth's services had become so valuable to the Coast Guard that Root recommended that she be hired full-time as a Cryptanalyst by the Treasury Department at a starting salary of $2400 per annum, given an assistant and permanently loaned to the Coast Guard. So by April 1927, Elizebeth, a Mrs. Anna Wolf, and Root's assistant, Lieutenant J.G. Clifford Feak (who had been trained by William Friedman), became the nucleus of the Coast Guard's Cryptanalytic Unit for the next two decades. While she continued to work from home for a while, eventually it was just more efficient for Elizebeth to go into the office to work. William and Elizebeth's second child, a son, John Ramsay, was born in July 1926. In addition to their housekeeper, Cassie, the Friedmans hired a nanny, named Carlotta, to look after the children during the day, and they both headed into downtown Washington to work just blocks away from each other (Fig. 10.7).

Elizebeth's duties at the Coast Guard continued to expand. In 1927, the Treasury Prohibition Bureau had decided that it needed its own code for internal communications. So, they developed a code and passed it on to the Coast Guard for evaluation. As they learned to their chagrin, "the codes were submitted to the Coast Guard's Intelligence Section for comment and returned by Mrs. Friedman indicating they could be solved in nine minutes and were 'not sufficiently secure for any important use.'"[35]

Within a year, between the efforts of Elizebeth's team and an increase in the number of patrol craft, the rumrunner traffic on the US East Coast was lessening somewhat as the Coast Guard gained more control over the bootleggers. This allowed Elizebeth to start focusing more on West Coast intercepts. Because the process of sending intercepts to Washington from the West Coast, having them decrypted and then sending them back via post, was more time consuming than the Coast Guard liked and because Elizebeth was more concerned with solving new systems than in decrypting messages in simpler, older, cipher systems, in the summer of 1928 Elizebeth headed to San Francisco for several weeks in order to train Coast Guard personnel at the radio intercept station there in cryptanalysis. One officer there, C. A. Housel, was particularly adept and became the person who would do most of the decrypting out of the San Francisco office. This eased Elizebeth's workload somewhat and allowed her to concentrate more on new cipher

---

[34] Friedman *Autobiography*, 59–60.

[35] Ensign *Rum War*, 54.

**Fig. 10.7** A Friedman family portrait from the 1930s. (George Marshall Foundation Research Library)

systems and the Gulf Coast traffic where there was a large smuggling ring in operation. This was not her only business travel. In an article she would write years later for her sorority magazine, Elizebeth explained this part of her career this way:

Some of the interesting developments are being sent from Coast to Coast, being called in court cases as an expert witness, or supplying material for grand juries. ... I am summoned by telegram to a city two or three thousand miles away to read several thousand messages to be used in a court case the *following Monday*, or some equally impossible demand. I think with a sigh of the sheltered life of the man who sits in a museum and spends thirty years deciphering one page of Hittite. But I pack my bag and hug my children a good-bye which is to last for a week or a month or longer, I know not, and board a train with a prayer that the new fields to conquer will not be impossible of conquest.[36]

Meanwhile, half a dozen blocks away in the Munitions Building on Constitution Avenue NW, William Friedman was continuing to create codes, write training materials, give courses in cryptanalysis, and evaluate new cryptographic systems and cipher machines. He also put his knowledge of electricity and engineering to good use by designing new and improved communication and cryptographic devices and processes and patenting the same. His first patent application was made with Paul Sabine in 1920 while both Sabine and Friedman were still at Riverbank Laboratories. It was an "Apparatus for and Method of Rapid Transmission of Telegraphic Messages" (patent #1,503,250 issued 29 July 1924). This patent "relates to mechanical means for sending and receiving wireless messages and to a new method of carrying out this operation, the purpose being to simplify the work and increase the speed of such transmission of messages."[37]

In 1922, Friedman filed four more patent applications. Two of these were for improvements to Gilbert Vernam's AT&T cipher machine that he worked on at Riverbank,[38] and the second two were for other improvements in electrical signaling systems.[39] Throughout his career, Friedman would file applications for and be granted 24 different patents, both alone and with a number of his colleagues in the Signal Corps, nearly all of them classified as secret by the government.

In 1926, Friedman filed his first patent application that was not strictly for a mechanical or electrical device. This patent "Alphabetical Chart"[40] created a new process that:

relates to improvements in means for preparing and constructing symbols for use as identification symbols to designate or distinguish any member of a class of objects from other members in the class … A further object of the invention is to provide means for the scien-

[36] Elizabeth Smith Friedman, "Pure Accident," *The Arrow of Pi Beta Phi*, February 1933, ESF Collection, Box 12, Folder 9, George Marshall Foundation Research Library, https://archive.org/details/ElizebethFriedmanArticlesInTheArrow

[37] Paul E. Sabine and William F. Friedman. Apparatus for and Method of Rapid Transmission of Telegraphic Messages. U.S. Patent Office 1,503,250. Geneva, IL, filed August 7, 1920, and issued July 29, 1924.

[38] William F. Friedman, Secret Signaling Apparatus for Automatically Enciphering and Deciphering Messages, U.S. Patent Office 1,522,775, Washington, DC, filed April 14, 1922, and issued January 13, 1925; William F. Friedman and Louis M. Evans. Secret Signaling System Employing Apparatus for Automatically Enciphering and Deciphering Messages. U.S. Patent Office 1,516,180. Washington, DC, filed June 5, 1922, and issued November 18, 1924.

[39] William F. Friedman, Printing Telegraph System. U.S. Patent Office 1,530,660. Washington, DC, filed July 26, 1922, and issued March 24, 1925; Friedman, William F. Method of Electrical Signaling. U.S. Patent Office 1,694,874. Washington, DC, filed July 10, 1922, and issued December 11, 1928.

[40] William F. Friedman, Alphabetical Chart. U.S. Patent Office 1,608,509. Washington, DC, filed January 7, 1926, and issued November 30, 1926; Louis Kruh, "The Inventions of William F. Friedman," *Cryptologia* 2, no. 1 (January 1978): 38–61, https://doi.org/10.1080/0161-117891852776, 44.

tific construction of the identification symbols ... and to provide charts and a method for using the charts in this construction in order to simplify the production of the symbols.[41]

In other words, he devised a way to generate unique sequences of letters to be used for identification strings. Friedman's example in his patent application was of using his method to generate unique motor vehicle identification tags—license plates. However, this method could just as easily be used—and almost certainly was—to generate unique codewords with particular characteristics for use in a military code-book. But because patent applications are generally not considered to be copyrightable,[42] and unless declared secret by the government, patents themselves are in the public domain, Friedman had to disguise the true purpose of the process he was proposing.

Friedman was also called upon to represent the Army (and by extension the US Government) at international radio and communications conferences. Friedman represented the State Department as a technical adviser to an international communications conference in Washington in 1927, for which he wrote a report on *The History of the Use of Codes and Code Language.* He was subsequently the secretary and technical adviser to the American delegation to the International Telegraph Conference in Brussels, Belgium, in September 1928. Conveniently, Elizebeth, now working full-time for the Coast Guard, was also a delegate to the conference, so they were able to go together. They took a European vacation after the conference and traveled to Sweden on orders from the War Department for William to meet Boris Hagelin, who was manufacturing a cipher machine in which the Americans were interested.[43] Friedman and Hagelin hit it off immediately, and this first meeting would be the first of many in a life-long friendship for both men.

All of this work and the incessant demand for secrecy in it—William and Elizebeth always insisted that they never talked about William's work at home—took it's toll on William's mental health; he was feeling overworked, anxious, and depressed. So much so that in 1927, William consulted a psychoanalyst, Dr. Philip Graven, for 6 months to discuss his mental state and psychiatric difficulties.[44] Apparently, these consultations must have helped William because he did not take any time off from his work during this period and appeared to have just soldiered on. This is the first time that William found the burden of secrecy in his profession overwhelming, but it would not be the last.

---

[41] Friedman, *Alphabetical Chart*, 5.

[42] See https://en.wikipedia.org/wiki/Copyright_on_the_content_of_patents_and_in_the_context_of_patent_prosecution

[43] Clark, *Purple*, 106.

[44] Clark, *Purple*, 113.

# Chapter 11
# Cryptologic Endings and Beginnings

In October 1929, the stock market crashed, and the American Black Chamber closed within 3 days of each other. In April 1930, the US Army's Signal Intelligence Service came into existence with the hiring of three "junior cryptanalysts" and William Friedman at its head. In November 1930, an overworked cryptanalyst in the Coast Guard wrote a seven-page memorandum proposing a new cryptanalytic organization that would service all the enforcement organizations in the Treasury Department.

Before 1929 William Friedman and Herbert Yardley were friends, friendly rivals, and mutual admirers. However, something began to change in their relationship in the late 1920s. By that time, the Army did not think that it was getting the information and service it deserved from Yardley's Cipher Bureau; rather, it thought the Cipher Bureau was primarily working for the State Department, so the Bureau began to be pushed to the side and left behind in the Army's push to grow its own cryptologic resources. William Friedman was at the center of this effort and was also involved with the coming closure of the Cipher Bureau. If not pushing for it, at least not standing in the way.[1]

The latter half of the 1920s had not been kind to Herbert Yardley and his Cipher Bureau. After their work peaked during the 1921–1922 Washington Naval Conference, the output of the Cipher Bureau decreased dramatically, along with its budget. At the beginning of the decade, during fiscal year 1920, the Cipher Bureau was allocated a budget of $100,000, just what Yardley had asked for but never received. By FY 1921, his budget was already down to $50,000, and by FY 1925, it was $25,000: $15,000 from the State Department and $10,000 from the War

---

[1] Major Owen S. Albright to Signal Corps ACoS, "Memorandum for ACoS, Signal Corps," July 19, 1929, SRH-038, pp. 121–124, National Security Agency, Herbert Yardley Collection.

© The Author(s), under exclusive license to Springer Nature Switzerland AG 2023
J. F. Dooley, *The Gambler and the Scholars*, History of Computing, https://doi.org/10.1007/978-3-031-28318-5_11

Department, a level where it would stay for the remainder of the Cipher Bureau's existence.[2]

By 1929, the Cipher Bureau was down to seven people, Yardley, three other cryptanalysts, Ruth Wilson, Victor Weiskopf, and Charles Mendelsohn, Yardley's secretary, Marguerite O'Connor Meeth, and two clerks, Alice Dillon and Edna Ramsier Hackenburg. They were doing very little cryptanalysis because they were mostly unable to acquire any diplomatic cable or radio intercepts. As we have seen, the Radio Act of 1912 made it illegal to copy cablegrams, and the Radio Act of 1927 added a prohibition on radio interception as well.[3] This meant that Yardley's friends at the telegraph companies were increasingly reluctant to pass on any diplomatic cryptograms. Moreover, the War Department was uninterested in Yardley's work because all of it was diplomatic traffic for the State Department. What the War Department was increasingly interested in was the training of cryptanalysts for use in future wars, something that the Cipher Bureau never did.[4] As the decade wore on, Yardley seemed to be increasingly less interested in the actual work of the Cipher Bureau. He sold his 49% share of the Code Compiling Company to Mendelsohn and spent more and more of his time doing code consulting and buying and selling real estate. He seemed to be interested in the Cipher Bureau only as a source of his salary and a way to stay in touch with people of influence in Washington. Thus, by 1929, the Cipher Bureau was barely doing the work it had been tasked to do for the State Department and was doing practically nothing at all for the War Department. This was not a scenario for future success.

For much of the late 1920s, Elizabeth Friedman worked for the Coast Guard with a single code clerk, Anna Wolf, and a part-time junior cryptanalyst, Lt. Clifford Feak, who worked decrypting the code and cipher messages of rumrunners. By 1929, the team had solved several thousand rumrunner code messages and had trained Coast Guard radio operators on the Pacific Coast to intercept and decrypt several of the systems used out there. As the 1920s had progressed, the volume of messages that landed on Elizabeth's desk at the Coast Guard grew to about 2000 messages per month. She, Lt. Feak, and her code clerk were clearly being overwhelmed. Nevertheless, she and her assistants continued to produce volumes of decrypts. From 1927 to 1930, she and her team solved approximately 12,000 rumrunner messages from criminal entities in the Atlantic, Gulf, and Pacific coasts.[5]

By 1929, William Friedman had solidified his role in the War Department and was well known in other areas of the federal government, including the Navy, Justice, and Treasury Departments and Congress. He had testified before Congress

[2] Wayne G. Barker, *The History of Codes and Ciphers in the United States during the Period between the World Wars, Part I. 1919–1929 (SRH-001, Part 3.),* ed. Wayne G. Barker, vol. 22, Cryptographic Series 22 (Laguna Hills, Calif.: Aegean Park Press, 1979), 70–73.

[3] Robert G. Angevine, "Gentlemen Do Read Each Other's Mail: American Intelligence in the Interwar Era," *Intelligence and National Security* 7, no. 2 (February 1992): 1–29, 18.

[4] Major Owen S. Albright to Col. Alfred T. Smith, "Memorandum for Col. Alfred T. Smith, ACoS, G-2," March 24, 1931, SRH-038, NSA Archives, Herbert O. Yardley Collection.

[5] Jason Fagone, *The Woman Who Smashed Codes,* (New York, NY: William Morrow, 2017), 139.

and had written several published monographs on cryptology and the history of cryptology. He had created a number of new, secure codes for the Army and had established a training regimen and curriculum for Army cryptanalysts. In addition, he had reached out beyond the Army and was helping the Navy with their cryptologic organization, OP-20-G, once again under Lt. Laurance Safford. So, when the War Department began to think about reorganizing and centralizing the Army's cryptologic efforts, it was natural that they thought of William Friedman and his tiny organization in the Signal Corps.

In July 1928, US Army Signal Corps Major Owen S. Albright was placed in charge of the communications section of the Military Intelligence Division. Soon thereafter, Albright's gaze fell upon Yardley's Cipher Bureau in New York, and he was not pleased with what he saw. Of the four functions that Albright thought the Cipher Bureau should be performing for the Army—code and cipher compilation, code and cipher solution, radio interception, and training—it was performing none. The Cipher Bureau was performing code and cipher solution, but all its output was targeted at the State Department, not the War Department. When Albright looked at the War Department, he saw a fragmented organization. Code and cipher compilation was the responsibility of Friedman's organization in the Signal Corps; he was also working on creating a radio interception service. There was no official training organization, although Friedman was doing training and was in the process of establishing a regular school at Camp Vail. Publishing, distributing, and storing codes in readiness for war was housed with the Adjutant General's office. In addition, code and cipher solution was really nowhere. This all meant that Albright did not think that the War Department was getting value for all the money it was spending on Yardley's Cipher Bureau. Albright's conclusion was that all cryptologic activities for the Army should be centralized in one place for efficiency and to provide a single point of contact for the General Staff and that place should be the Signal Corps. This conclusion was the first toll of the death knell for Yardley's Cipher Bureau.[6] In early 1929, Albright wrote a memorandum detailing his suggestions and that memo began to work its way through the Army bureaucracy.[7]

On 9 February 1929, Herbert Yardley received a letter from Colonel Ford, the Assistant Chief of Staff, inviting him to Washington from 6 May through 19 May 1929 for a course in cryptanalysis to be given by William Friedman.[8] Two weeks later, Yardley responded to Ford, accepting the invitation to the cryptanalysis course.[9] On the following day, Friedman wrote to Yardley and said, in part,

---

[6] Lt. Col. J. T. Wilson to Col. Stanley H. Ford, "Memorandum to Colonel Ford," March 18, 1929.

[7] Major Owen S. Albright to U.S. Army Assistant Chief of Staff, "Memorandum for the Chief of Staff," April 4, 1929, Herbert Yardley Collection, RG 457, National Archives, College Park, MD.

[8] Col. Stanley H. Ford to Herbert O. Yardley, "Memorandum to Herbert O. Yardley," February 9, 1929, Herbert Yardley Collection, RG 457, National Archives, College Park, MD; Herbert O. Yardley to William F. Friedman, "HOY to WFF," February 19, 1929, Herbert Yardley Collection, RG 457, also SRH-038, NSA Archives.

[9] Herbert O. Yardley to Col. Stanley H. Ford, "HOY to Colonel Ford," February 26, 1929, Herbert Yardley Collection, RG 457, also SRH-038, NSA Archives.

"Understand you have a visitor today, and I will be interested to learn any new developments."[10] The visitor who came to New York to fill Yardley in on the Army's plans for its cryptologic organization was Major Owen Albright. It seems clear that Friedman knew what the Army was planning at this point.

Three days later Yardley responded to Friedman's letter of 26 February, "Major Albright was here Wednesday as you infer in your last paragraph. I went over the entire matter with him and he no doubt will have something to say to you."[11] Albright had clearly told Yardley about his plans to move the Cipher Bureau to the Signal Corps. What did Yardley think of all this? David Kahn, in his biography of Yardley says, "It did not concern Yardley very much. Moving the Cipher Bureau from one part of the army to another was a nuisance, perhaps, but not much more: agencies in bureaucracies are often shifted around."[12]

However, this could not have been good news for Yardley. His Cipher Bureau was to be moved under a new organization housed in the Signal Corps, not Military Intelligence and almost certainly not run by him, but by Friedman, who was already doing quite well in the Signal Corps and likely had Albright's ear. Albright also intended to have the organization headquartered at the War Department in Washington and would not have wanted to keep a New York office. Yardley's hope may have been to continue the Cipher Bureau's work with the State Department alone and possibly move the whole organization there and out from under the War Department. Yardley had been cozying up to the State Department throughout the 1920s at the expense of doing any serious work for the War Department.

Three weeks later, a memo from Lt. Col. Wilson of the War Plans and Training Division of the Signal Corps to Colonel Ford contained the formal recommendation that all Army cryptologic activities (except printing and distribution of codes) be moved to the Signal Corps.[13] Two weeks after that, a memorandum from Ford to General George Gibbs, the Chief Signal Officer, made the formal recommendations on moving cryptologic activities.[14] On the following day, 5 April, the Chief Signal Officer approved the recommendation.[15]

Sometime in here, Yardley must have been notified by Albright of General Gibbs's approval of his recommendations. Friedman was also still in the loop. Yardley wrote to Friedman on 22 April 1929, "Thanks for your information. I had a letter from Albright dated the 15th which in effect contains about the same

---

[10] William F. Friedman to Herbert O. Yardley, "WFF to HOY," February 27, 1929, Herbert Yardley Collection, RG 457, also SRH-038, NSA Archives.

[11] Herbert O. Yardley to William F. Friedman, "HOY to WFF," March 2, 1929, Herbert Yardley Collection, RG 457, also SRH-038, NSA Archives.

[12] David Kahn, *The Reader of Gentlemen's Mail: Herbert O. Yardley and the Birth of American Codebreaking* (New Haven: Yale University Press, 2004), 95.

[13] Wilson, *Memo to Ford*, 18 March 1929.

[14] Col. Stanley H. Ford to General Gibbs, "Responsibility for the Solution of Intercepted Enemy Secret Communications in War," April 4, 1929, Herbert Yardley Collection, RG 457, also SRH-038, National Archives, College Park, MD.

[15] Barker, *History of Codes*, 181.

information as your letter. As to my reaction about the matter I hardly know what to say. Do you think you and Albright will be up between now and the time I go to Washington May 6th."[16] The boom has really been lowered on Yardley and the Cipher Bureau at this point.

On 23 April, in a letter to Yardley responding to a letter from the previous day, Friedman—who clearly wanted any confrontation with Yardley to be on his own turf, noted, "Of course I could hardly expect a detailed letter giving your reaction so quickly, and presume it can wait until you get here. There is no possibility of our coming up before May 6th, so we will see you here first. Things are moving very slowly around here and nothing has yet been done toward organizing the business here."[17] That would change very shortly. Yardley, seemingly ignoring the sword hanging over his head but who was likely working out how to move the Cipher Bureau to the State Department, continued corresponding with Friedman and—at Friedman's request—preparing problems for the cryptanalysis course coming up in May.[18]

In early May—no exact date has been found—Yardley shipped a batch of decoded Japanese diplomatic messages to the new Secretary of State, Henry Stimson.[19] Yardley was no doubt trying to impress Stimson with the output and excellent work of the Cipher Bureau and likely trying to prepare him for Yardley's request to move the Cipher Bureau completely under the State Department. Stimson's reaction is well known, and the next blow fell on the Cipher Bureau when Stimson ordered all State Department funding ($15,000, 60% of the total) to be discontinued immediately but with a reprieve negotiated by the War Department.[20] Stimson wanted the State Department to have nothing to do with intercepting and reading the correspondence of other nations. In his mind, it wasn't just illegal, it was immoral. Diplomats were supposed to come to the table with honest voices and negotiate fairly. In his words from his memoir years later, "Gentlemen do not read each others mail." Given the twin blows from Albright and Stimson, it was clear that Yardley's Cipher Bureau would be out of business very soon.

If he was not terribly surprised by the War Department's decision to transfer his Cipher Bureau, Herbert Yardley seemed genuinely taken aback and puzzled by the abrupt withdrawal of State Department funds that ultimately closed his organization. For nearly a decade, the entire output of his Bureau had been diplomatic traffic of use to the State Department, so the sudden closure of his operation, which meant

---

[16] Herbert O. Yardley to William F. Friedman, "HOY to WFF," April 22, 1929, Herbert Yardley Collection, RG 457, also SRH-038, NSA Archives.

[17] William F. Friedman to Herbert O. Yardley, "WFF to HOY," April 23, 1929, Herbert Yardley Collection, RG 457, also SRH-038, NSA Archives.

[18] Herbert O. Yardley to William F. Friedman, "HOY to WFF," April 25, 1929, Herbert Yardley Collection, RG 457, also SRH-038, NSA Archives.

[19] Herbert O. Yardley, *The American Black Chamber* (Indianapolis: Bobbs-Merrill, 1931), 369.

[20] Colonel S. Cooper to Herbert O. Yardley, "Memorandum for Major H. O. Yardley: Transfer of Code Activities," June 29, 1929, RG 165, Signal Intelligence Service Study, National Archives and Records Administration, College Park, MD.

that the State Department was now totally blind to foreign diplomatic messages, was a colossal mistake in his opinion. The State Department was now out of the codebreaking business for the better part of a decade.

In the midst of this, Yardley started Friedman's cryptanalysis course on 6 May, stayed the full 2 weeks, went to dinner at Friedman's house, and then a week after the course ended he wrote a memorandum on his impressions of the course, proposed a cryptologic "bible" of several thousand pages that he would contribute to, and heaped praise on A.J. McGrail for his lectures on secret inks and on Friedman and the other Signal Corps officers for their contributions to the course. "I should like to take this occasion to express my sincere thanks for the courtesy and goodwill extended to us by both M.I.D. and Signal Corps officers. I should also like to compliment Major Friedman upon the way in which he conducted the classes and to assure him that not only I, but all the officers of the class, hold him in very high esteem indeed." It also appears that Yardley already knew about the name change for Friedman's organization because he mentions the "Signal Intelligence Service" as the organization that should maintain his proposed cryptologic bible (Fig. 11.1).[21]

In the meantime, on 10 May 1929, Change #1 to Army Regulation 105-5 was approved, moving all Army cryptologic activities from the Military Intelligence Division to the Signal Corps. In June 1929, a Colonel Cooper sent a memo to Yardley in New York giving the details of the transfer of responsibilities from the Cipher Bureau to the new Signal Intelligence Service in the Signal Corps. The memorandum contained a copy of AR 105-5 Change #1.[22] In the same month, the State Department agreed to give the employees of the Cipher Bureau three (3) months severance beginning 1 July 1929. After that, the State Department would cut off funds and the Bureau would have no money and would officially shut down. Their work, however, would stop immediately. The deed was done.

At the beginning of 1929, William Friedman had been the sole cryptologist for the US Army since 1921 and had a staff of exactly one clerk.

That all changed dramatically with AR 105-5, Change #1 on 10 May 1929. On that day, the Signal Intelligence Service (SIS) came into being—whatever that was to be. At that point, no one, least of all Friedman, had any real idea of how SIS was to be organized or what exactly it was to do. However, this mystery did not last for long. On 17 July 1929, Major Albright sent a memorandum to General Gibbs, the Army Chief of Staff, that detailed the procedures for closing the Cipher Bureau.[23] Two days later, on 19 July, a meeting was held in the office of the Chief Signal Officer, attended by a number of Signal Corps officers, including General Gibbs, the Chief Signal Officer, Lt. Colonel John E. Hemphill, who had recently been commandant of the Signal Corps School at Fort Monmouth (the former Camp Vail),

---

[21] Herbert O. Yardley, May 27, 1929 in Anonymous. "A Selection of Papers Pertaining to Herbert O. Yardley (SRH-038)." College Park, MD: NARA (Record Group 457, Entry 9037), Unknown, but after 1958.

[22] Cooper, *Code Activities*.

[23] Major Owen S. Albright to General Gibbs, "Memorandum to General Gibbs," July 17, 1929, SRH-038, National Security Agency, Herbert Yardley Collection, 120.

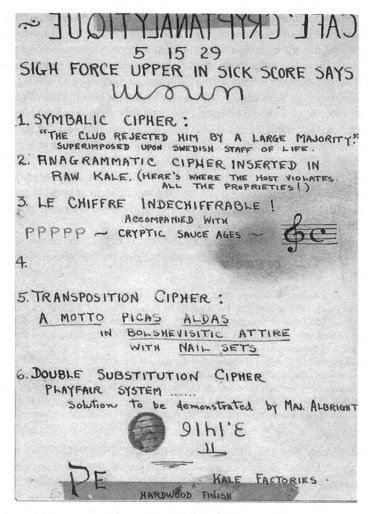

**Fig. 11.1** The dinner menu at Friedman's house in May 1929 which was attended by Herbert Yardley. (National Cryptologic Museum Library)

Major (later Lt. Colonel) William Blair, the head of research and engineering at the Signal Corps Radio Laboratories at Fort Monmouth, Lt. Colonel Albright, and William Friedman.[24] At that meeting, the final bones of the Cipher Bureau were laid to rest so that the SIS could officially be born. The participants discussed how the new SIS would be organized and what responsibilities the new Service would have going forward.

It was decided that the primary function of the SIS would be "training for war rather than of active operations for immediate interception and solution of the

---

[24] Albright, *SRH-038*, 121–124.

communications of foreign armies or governments" and that this training would be targeted toward the four functions of SIS that were essential to the Army during war time and would include training for code and cipher compilation, training for code and cipher solution, radio interception and goniometric services, and secret inks.[25] This emphasis on training did not forbid SIS from intercepting and solving foreign cryptograms, however. According to Colonel Albright, "if information of present or immediate value to G-2 should be intercepted and solved, such information would be acceptable to G-2, but it should always be regarded as a byproduct of the training work and not as the function of the Signal Communication Service in peace-time."[26] The meeting also agreed that radio intercept stations might need to be constructed in Hawaii, Panama, and the Philippines and that SIS would organize and control them. The participants also decided that training would occur at Fort Monmouth (at a newly created Signals School) and that the chemical (Secret Ink) laboratory would also be set up there.

With regard to Yardley's Cipher Bureau and how that work and personnel would be transitioned into the new Signal Intelligence Service, the participants—including William Friedman—agreed that:

> In view of the foregoing it is obvious that the taking over of the present M.I.D. Code Solving Section involves a rather complete breaking up of that section, and a departure from the mission it has had from 1919 to the present, although there can be no doubt that its operation has yielded very important results that would have a definite bearing upon war-time effectiveness of the service. ...
>
>     It is suggested by Colonel Hemphill that the present chief of that section be offered a definite proposal that he come here at a salary considerably below his present, with whatever personnel from his section he wishes, the total to be within the funds available, which is $10,000. It is highly probable that this offer will be inacceptable, in which case this office is free to go ahead and reorganize from the very bottom, with no entanglements from the past.[27]

In the end, Yardley was offered a position in the new SIS at $312.50 per month—exactly half his Cipher Bureau salary—or $3750 per annum and significantly less than Friedman's $5600 per year.[28] Yardley turned the offer down as soon as it was made, perhaps feeling he could make a go of it with his Queens real estate business; it turned out events were to prove that this was a tactical mistake on his part. Interestingly, the offer of $3750 per year to Yardley would have made him the 2nd highest paid person in SIS—and he would have had a job. Victor Weiskopf and Ruth Wilson were offered positions in the new SIS in Washington, but both turned them down, Weiskopf because he had another business (in stamps) that he wanted to keep in New York, and Wilson because her husband was also employed in New York and she didn't want to move. Neither of these rejections bothered Albright, who thought that the Cipher Bureau personnel were all too old to be useful in any military

---

[25] Albright, *SRH-038*, 121.

[26] Albright, *SRH-038*, 121.

[27] Albright, *SRH-038*, 122.

[28] Kahn, *ROGM*, 100.

emergency anyway.[29] None of the clerical employees of the Cipher Bureau were offered employment in the new SIS, as they were deemed "unsuitable for our purposes."[30] Clearly, the participants at the meeting—including Friedman—were determined to start from scratch. Interestingly, a number of later sources refer to the position that Yardley was offered as a "temporary" position.[31] However, nowhere in the notes of the meeting is the word "temporary" used. From these notes, these positions were intended to be permanent.[32]

It took Yardley and his crew a couple of months to sort and pack up all their materials for the move to Washington. Friedman went up to New York in October to take charge of all the records. On 31 October 1929, the Cipher Bureau ceased to exist, 2 days after Black Tuesday and the start of the Great Depression. William Friedman was now in charge of all cryptologic activities within the War Department, code and cipher compilation, radio interception, training, secret inks, and code and cipher solution, and Herbert Yardley was out of a job.

For the rest of 1929 and into 1930, the Army, in its slow, methodical way, proceeded with the organization of the Signal Intelligence Service. Friedman oversaw the move of all the Cipher Bureau's files to the War Department in Washington and made sure they were installed in a locked room in the Munitions Building just down the hall from Friedman's own office. It is not known whether Friedman and Yardley met during this period, but it seems likely that Yardley helped Friedman organize the files for shipment.

The next order of business was to set up the new organization and hire staff. On 26 November 1929, the SIS was transferred to the War Planning and Training Division under the command of Major D. M. Crawford. This move put the SIS into an organization that more closely fit its new emphasis on training and code and cipher compilation. On 16 December 1929, the remaining fiscal year funds from the War Department's allocation for the Cipher Bureau were transferred to the Signal Corps, and on 26 December 1929, Major Crawford wrote a memorandum to the Chief Signal Officer (CSO) suggesting that the remaining funds were sufficient for the hiring of four junior cryptanalysts and one assistant cryptographic clerk for the SIS. On 4 January 1930, the CSO requested authorization from the Secretary of War to hire four junior cryptanalysts for the SIS, and that authorization was given on 13 January 1930. William Friedman was now really ready to go.[33]

Because of the special skills necessary for the Signal Intelligence Service, it was difficult to find people on the current Civil Service roles who would fit the skills requirements for cryptanalysts. Friedman was given permission to write his own requirements for the positions and look further afield. His budget was the remaining

---

[29] William F. Friedman, "A Brief History of the U.S. Cryptologic Operations 1917 – 1929 (SRH-029)," *Cryptologic Spectrum* 6, no. 2 (June 1942): 9–15, 9.

[30] Friedman, *SRH-029*, 12.

[31] Barker, *SRH-001*, 186; Friedman *SRH-029*, 12.

[32] Albright, *SRH-038*, 122.

[33] Major D. M. Crawford to Signal Corps ACoS, "Memorandum for ACoS, Signal Corps," December 26, 1929, NSA Archives, Center for Cryptologic History.

$6668 from the War Department contribution of $10,000 to the Cipher Bureau for fiscal year 1930, all State Department funds already having been withdrawn.[34] His searches bore fruit, and in March 1930, he was able to hire two clerks, Laurence Clark and Louise Nelson, followed by new junior cryptanalysts Frank Rowlett, Abraham Sinkov, and Solomon Kullback. Finding a fourth cryptanalyst with expertise in Japanese proved more difficult, and John Hurt, who was fluent in Japanese but knew nothing of cryptology, was hired on 13 May as a cryptanalyst aide instead. This brought the strength of SIS up to seven, a number at which it would remain until fiscal year 1937.[35]

Frank Rowlett (Fig. 11.2) was born in Lee County, Virginia on 2 May 1908. He received a bachelor's degree with a double major in mathematics and chemistry from Emory & Henry College in the spring of 1929 and began teaching high school the following fall. He took the Civil Service exam and scored well enough that Friedman noticed him on the list. Conveniently, Rowlett had also studied German, a requirement of Friedman's for one of the cryptanalyst positions. Rowlett was the first junior cryptanalyst Friedman hired, and he reported for work on 1 April 1930.

**Fig. 11.2** Frank Rowlett. (National Security Agency)

---

[34] William F. Friedman, "Expansion of the Signal Intelligence Service from 1930 – 7 December 1941 (SRH-134)," trans. U.S. Army Signal Corps (Washington, DC, December 4, 1945), NSA Archives, Center for Cryptologic History, 3.

[35] Barker, *SRH-001*, 203.

Abraham Sinkov (Fig. 11.3) was born in Philadelphia to Russian Jewish immigrant parents in August 1907. His family moved to Brooklyn shortly thereafter, and Abe grew up there, graduating from Boys High School and then earning a B.S. in mathematics from City College of New York. He taught high school—but wasn't happy—while he was also going to graduate school in mathematics. Looking around for new opportunities, Abe also took the Civil Service exam in late 1929, and that is where Friedman found him. He started work on 10 April 1930 as the second junior cryptanalyst. Sinkov continued his graduate education while working and earned his Ph.D. in mathematics from George Washington University in 1933. He filled the French position in the SIS.

Solomon Kullback (Fig. 11.4) was born in Brooklyn, New York, also of Russian Jewish immigrant parents, and also in 1907. Kullback went to Boy's High School and City College in New York and was a classmate and friend of Abe Sinkov. The two graduated with their mathematics degrees in the same year and took the Civil Service exam—at Sinkov's insistence—at the same time. Kullback's offer of

**Fig. 11.3** Abe Sinkov during World War II. (National Security Agency)

**Fig. 11.4** Solomon
Kullback. (National
Security Agency)

employment at the Signal Corps came a few days after Sinkov's, and he reported for
duty on 21 April 1930. Kullback spoke Spanish and so filled that slot in the group.
Kullback also went to graduate school while he was working at the SIS and finished
his Ph.D. in mathematics at George Washington University in 1934.

Friedman had one more cryptanalyst slot to fill, but he could not find a mathematician who spoke and read Japanese, his last language requirement. Word of
Friedman's search for a Japanese speaker made its way across the War Department,
and one day a US Congressman called and offered the services of his nephew. John
Hurt was born in Virginia in 1904 and attended several colleges on and off before
finally earning a bachelor's degree in 1952 from the University of Maryland.[36]
During his college days, John Hurt learned Japanese from two of his college roommates but had never been to Japan. Despite this, he was fluent in spoken and written
Japanese. When his language skills were tested by an Army translator, the translator
said that Hurt was the best non-Japanese Japanese linguist he had ever encountered.
Unfortunately, Hurt wasn't a mathematician. However, the Civil Service waived
that requirement, and Hurt was hired by Friedman as a cryptanalyst aide and started
work on 13 May 1930.

Friedman's roster was now filled, and he could get on with the creation of a new
organization, the one that would evolve over the next 22 years into the National

---

[36] https://ead.lib.virginia.edu/vivaxtf/view?docId=wcc/viwyc00033.xml

Security Agency. The Army was also finally ready to lay out the new organization's structure and responsibilities. On 24 April 1930, in a memo titled "Codes, Ciphers, Secret Inks, Radio Interception and Goniometry," the Adjutant General notified the Chief Signal Officer of the details of the new organization's responsibilities and personnel allocations.[37]

Friedman immediately began a training regimen for his new junior cryptanalysts, using his own materials and a library of classic texts in cryptology he had acquired over the years. However, without a radio interception service and without Yardley's connections in the telegraph companies, Friedman and his students were forced to use old cryptograms from the Cipher Bureau files and some diplomatic intercepts provided by the Navy for their training. Their initial training focus was on breaking code and cipher systems, particularly Japanese systems. But, they did not have much in the way of traffic, especially Japanese Army traffic.[38] This changed somewhat in September 1931 when, after the Japanese invasion of Manchuria, the Navy passed on large numbers of Japanese Army cipher messages it had intercepted at its station in Shanghai.

Ultimately, Friedman always had plenty of work for his new cryptanalysts to do. From compiling codes to reviewing the Cipher Bureau's work, solving Japanese and other nations cipher machines, and working to create and manage the new radio intercept stations, Rowlett, Sinkov, Kullback, and Hurt were kept more than busy. The Army was also now in a better position to work with the Navy and OP-20-G.

The acquisition of military radio traffic from other nations was a particular problem for SIS. By the time of SIS's creation in late 1929, the Navy had radio intercept stations around the Pacific rim and on the East Coast of the United States.[39] The Army had no intercept stations and, because of budgetary constraints, no prospects of building any. In fact, the Army would not start a formal radio interception service until 1933. For most of the 1930s, Friedman and SIS were to be dependent on the Navy and Coast Guard for radio interception services. Of course, those services assigned their own needs higher priority, so the SIS struggled.

In other areas of cooperation there was more light. On 29 October 1931, the Director of Naval Communications wrote a memorandum to the Signal Corps proposing a division of labor and sharing of information between the Office of Naval Communications and the Signal Intelligence Service.[40] The memo proposed that the

---

[37] Barker, *SRH-001*, 189.

[38] Theodore M. Hannah, "The Many Lives of Herbert O. Yardley," *NSA Cryptologic Spectrum* 11, no. 4 (Fall 1981): 5–29, http://www.nsa.gov/public_info/_files/cryptologic_spectrum/many_lives. pdf; Frank R. Rowlett, "Oral History of Frank Rowlett (1976)," Oral History, Oral History Collection (Ft. George G. Meade, MD: National Security Agency, Center for Cryptologic History, 1976).

[39] Captain Laurance Safford, "A Brief History of Communications Intelligence in the United States (SRH-149)" (College Park, MD: National Archives and Records Administration, RG 457 (SRH-149), March 21, 1952).

[40] S. C. Hooper to Chief of Naval Operations, "Memorandum Proposing Allocation of Radio Intelligence Activities between the Army and the Navy," October 29, 1931, RG-165, National Archives and Records Administration, College Park, MD.

Navy be responsible for all Naval codes and ciphers, the War Department be responsible for all Military codes and ciphers, and that the two departments divide diplomatic cipher solutions by country.

Several weeks later, Major Crawford of the Signal Corps War Planning and Training Division responded to the Chief Signal Officer with respect to the Navy's proposal. In his memorandum, Crawford agreed to the split of naval and military codes and ciphers but did not see the reason for formal diplomatic cooperation. "Under the present State Department policy I believe the War Department has no responsibility whatever for interception or solution of diplomatic codes, and hence, no formal discussion or agreement on this subject is advisable. I can, however, see no objection to an informal, verbal working arrangement between the two Divisions directly concerned, with the object of subdividing the field as regards solution of diplomatic codes."[41] Leaving out diplomatic interception and cryptanalysis would prove problematic, but with this memorandum, the Army and the Navy entered into their first long-term, albeit informal agreement to cooperate on cryptology.

Elizebeth Friedman was one busy cryptanalyst in the period from 1928 through 1931. Early in this period she was focusing on West Coast rumrunning operations. In early 1928, there were two main communications systems in the Pacific. One for the Consolidated Exporters Company (CONEXCO) and one for their main rival, the Hobbs Group, both of whom were headquartered in Vancouver, British Columbia. Each of these code systems was changed every 6 months. Elizebeth had been very successful in breaking these systems. As time went on, CONEXCO increasingly controlled the rumrunning traffic in the Pacific at the expense of Hobbs, and they began to change their code systems more often and use more and different systems. By mid-1930, nearly every ship on the Pacific coast was using its own system. For example, in May 1930, CONEXCO had three shore radio stations that used one cryptosystem for communications with their large rumrunning mother ships, and each mother ship communicated with its rumrunners in a completely different system. Between mid-1928 and early 1930, more than 3300 enciphered messages were intercepted by Coast Guard stations on the Pacific Coast.

In addition to her cryptanalytic work on the Pacific coast, Elizebeth began to be called as an expert witness in trials of accused rumrunners. She was also called to decrypt messages for the prosecution for a number of these trials. In October and November of 1929, she was in Houston, Texas, where she decrypted 650 rumrunner messages in 24 different systems in the course of a month for the United States Attorney, who was building a case against a number of rumrunners.

Finally, unable to continue with herself as the only full-time Coast Guard cryptanalyst, in the fall of 1930 Elizebeth, supported by the new head of the Coast Guard Intelligence Office, Lt. Commander Frank J. Gorman, wrote a seven-page memorandum recommending the creation of a Coast Guard Cryptanalytic Unit in the Intelligence Office. As part of their reasoning for an increase in staffing, the two

---

[41] Major D. M. Crawford to Chief Signal Officer, "Memorandum Re: Allocation of Radio Intelligence Activities," November 30, 1931, RG-165, National Archives and Records Administration, College Park, MD.

wrote, "It may be stated that every system employed by the smuggling interests has been solved but in no case has it been possible to read all of the messages in view of the large amount of labor involved and the lamentable lack of personnel to accomplish the work."[42] Her request was approved in June 1931, and on July 1st Elizebeth Friedman was put in charge of the new Cryptanalytic Unit with the new title Cryptanalyst-in-Charge and a hefty raise. Her new department was authorized for a strength of seven, Elizebeth herself as the Cryptanalyst-in-Charge at a salary of $3800 per annum, an assistant cryptanalyst at $2000, a senior cryptanalytic clerk at $2000, a cryptanalytic clerk at $1800, and three assistant cryptographic clerks at $1620 each.[43]

Just like her husband in the spring of 1930, in the summer of 1931, Elizebeth had a very difficult time finding people with the talents to make good cryptanalysts. She insisted on people who were college graduates and who had majored in mathematics, physics, or chemistry—despite having an English literature degree herself. Scouring the civil service lists, she claimed that she was unable to find any women with the required skills, so she only hired men.[44] This seems odd because there were any number of universities and colleges in the United States at the time that were graduating female mathematicians and scientists—Agnes Meyer Driscoll is only one example. But, apparently none of these women took the Civil Service exam. Elizebeth hired three young men who were recent physics, engineering, and mathematics majors, Vernon Cooley, Robert E. Gordon, and Hyman Hurwitz, along with three more cryptographic clerks as the core of her new team. Cooley was a thirty-one-year-old teacher from Kalamazoo, Michigan, Gordon was a twenty-three-year-old math major from Waco, Texas, and Hurwitz was a twenty-one-year-old electrical engineer from Dorchester, Massachusetts. Just as her husband had done, Elizebeth set up a training regimen for her new cryptanalysts, emphasizing codes and elementary cryptanalysis. She set them groups of problems to work every week that she would take home and grade. All three were quick learners and soon became adept at cryptanalysis, helping to take the load of incoming intercepts off her shoulders. The Cryptanalytic Unit would remain this size until the end of the decade.

Regardless of the fact that Elizebeth could not find any women to hire, this new Cryptanalytic Unit was the first of its kind in the Treasury Department and the first unit in any department to be headed by a woman.[45] This was Elizebeth's real

---

[42] Elizebeth Smith Friedman, "Memorandum upon a Proposed Central Organization at Coast Guard Headquarters for Performing Cryptanalytic Work," November 1930, Box 5, File Folder 6, Elizebeth Smith Friedman Collection, George Marshall Research Library, Lexington, VA.

[43] F. J. Gorman, "Memorandum for the Commandant of the Coast Guard," Memorandum (Washington, DC: United States Coast Guard, October 10, 1930), https://www.nsa.gov/Portals/70/documents/news-features/declassified-documents/ cryptologs/cryptolog_103.pdf; David Mowry, "Listening to the Rumrunners: Radio Intelligence during Prohibition" (Ft. Meade, MD: National Security Agency, 2014), 21–23.

[44] Fagone, *Smashed*, 141; Elizebeth S. Friedman, "Autobiography of Elizebeth Smith Friedman" (Memoir, Lexington, VA, 1966), https://archive.org/details/ElizebethFriedmanPartialAutobiography, Archive.org, 53.

[45] Fagone, *Smashed*, 141.

beginning as the expert and go-to person with respect to cryptology for the Treasury and Justice Departments.

While Yardley and Friedman were drifting apart after the closure of the Cipher Bureau, they still did retain some contact. In early 1930, Friedman wrote Yardley, asking him to come to Washington later that year to do his normal 2 weeks of annual Army Reserve duty at the Signal Corps. It seems that Yardley replied with a plea for a temporary job assignment with the Signal Corps. Friedman seemingly made this happen because in early April, Major Crawford sent Yardley a telegram approving his appointment. Yardley, who was back in Worthington, Indiana, by now and was already struggling with monetary problems, replied directly to Friedman that his business dealings were in such a mess that he had to be in New York to straighten them out. He apologized and asked Friedman to just forget the entire temporary work arrangement.[46]

Also, in April 1930, Yardley applied for a job as an instructor in cryptanalysis with the Navy but was rejected.[47] Yardley did actually get a job in the fall of 1930. At the urging of his friend John Matthews Manly, the Scientific Crime Detection Laboratory of Chicago at Northwestern University offered Yardley a part-time position as an associate staff member for "decoding of code messages." His appointment was announced in the November–December 1930 issue of the *Journal of Police Science*, the Laboratory's official house publication. Yardley accepted and he did some lecturing at the Laboratory in 1931, but it is not known if he ever solved any encrypted messages for the Laboratory. He was still on the roster in 1932 when the Journal ceased publication.

Later in 1930, Friedman wrote to Yardley in Worthington with some questions about Cipher Bureau materials he was reviewing. At the end of Friedman's letter, we see the most poignant expression of his feelings (and maybe guilt?) about Yardley's predicament:

> I wish I could keep in closer touch with you. Please, when you are next in Washington, even if you have only an hour or so, give me a ring. You have no idea how badly I feel at the way things turned out for you, not that you need my sympathy, but that I can appreciate what a raw deal you got, and that I was powerless to avert it.[48]

This seems a very interesting expression of Friedman's regrets on how things ended in the Army for Yardley, particularly because he was in the room when all the decisions about the Cipher Bureau were made back in April and July 1929. It seems odd that Friedman thought himself "powerless" through all this, especially because he was the main beneficiary of the demise of the Cipher Bureau.

Friedman continued to try to recruit Yardley into early 1931. He wrote another letter to him in February 1931 once again asking Yardley to spend his active duty

---

[46] Herbert O. Yardley to William F. Friedman, "HOY to WFF," April 1, 1930, William Friedman Collection, George Marshall Foundation Research Library.

[47] Kahn, *ROGM*, 104.

[48] William F. Friedman, Letter to Herbert O. Yardley. "WFF to HOY," December 16, 1930. William Friedman Collection, George Marshall Research Library, Lexington, VA.

time at the Signal Corps in Washington. He even dangles a carrot: "For my part I would be extremely anxious to have you come for several reasons, but in particular, if you want to see some interesting stuff along R(ussian) lines, now is the time. Also I would like to see you because I really miss our former contacts of a personal nature."[49] Unbeknownst to Friedman, by February 1931 Yardley was already deeply committed to writing what would become his blockbuster tell-all memoir. The book that would end their friendship forever.

At the end of this approximately 2 and a half year period, Friedman, Yardley, and American cryptology were all drastically changed.

The Cipher Bureau's 10-year long ride was over. All of its employees were out of government cryptology, most of them forever. All its records were down in Washington. The State Department was out of the code breaking business for the next decade.

The Signal Intelligence Service had been created and was set up to succeed with a clear focus, strong leadership, and support from the Army General Staff. The Army had created a single organization to handle code and cipher compilation, code and cipher solution, training, and radio interception services. It would also soon bring publishing and distribution of war-time codes and ciphers into the Signal Corps from the Adjutant General's office. While underfunded and understaffed throughout the 1930s, the SIS set up the framework for the cryptologic organization that would be necessary in 1941.

The Coast Guard and the Treasury Department had set up a professional intelligence office with a cryptanalytic unit headed by an expert and the first female head of a code and cipher unit in the United States government, Elizebeth Friedman.

With the division of naval and military cryptanalysis work and an informal agreement on diplomatic code and cipher systems, the Army and Navy took the first steps in interservice cooperation. This cooperation, which would deepen during the next decade and into the next war, was made easier by the fact that SIS and OP-20-G were in adjacent buildings on Constitution Avenue in Washington. These two buildings, the nine-wing wide Main Navy Building and the parallel eight-wing Army Munitions Building, were connected by hallways at each floor, making it easy for Army and Navy personnel to go back and forth.[50] These corridors would be traveled time and again by William Friedman as he worked with his Navy colleagues. This time was also the beginning of the intermittent collaboration of the two services on machine cryptology. Both services were interested in moving away from codes and toward using cipher machines to strengthen their communication security. They were also aware that both the Japanese and the Germans were actively investigating machine ciphers. In fact, by this time, the Germans were already actively deploying Enigma machines, and the Japanese were working on developing their own electro-mechanical cipher machine.

---

[49] William F. Friedman to Herbert O. Yardley, "WFF to HOY," February 18, 1931, Friedman Collection, George Marshall Foundation Research Library.

[50] https://web.archive.org/web/20081023151819/http://www.history.navy.mil/library/online/main_navy_bldg.htm

By 1931, both the War and Navy Departments had in place the basic cryptologic organizations that would carry them into and through World War II.

As for William Friedman and Herbert Yardley, they were already going their separate ways. For Friedman, this period was the start of his seemingly inexorable rise to the top of the American cryptologic community. For Yardley, it was the end of his career in professional American cryptology and the start of a series of other occupations: memoirist, novelist, restauranteur, bureaucrat, housing contractor, poker player, itinerant cryptologist; some of them lucrative, some of them interesting, but none of them quite as satisfying as his decade in charge of the Cipher Bureau.

# Chapter 12
# The American Black Chamber

By August 1930 and having been unemployed for nearly a year, Herbert Yardley was feeling the financial pinch. He wrote to John Manly on 29 August that he was broke and was having to sell off all his investment properties. He said, "I'm not certain at all what I shall do."[1] Yardley must have seen this day coming but was in a state of denial throughout most of 1929 and early 1930. His several attempts at creating a living in the midst of the Great Depression failed one after another. It was in the late spring of 1930 that he had an idea for another source of income. One that changed his relationship with Friedman and the War Department forever.

In that spring, Yardley came up with the idea of telling his story to the public. In 1927 Yardley had helped his friend, John Manly, write a series of articles on the work of MI-8 during the war for *Collier's* magazine.[2] While *Collier's* never published Manly's articles, Yardley enjoyed the experience of helping his friend and participating in the writing. As Yardley contemplated telling the story of his Cipher Bureau, the tales of MI-8's work during the war seemed a good starting point. At the suggestion of his friend, the columnist Franklin Pierce Adams, who had worked in military intelligence in the previous war, he took this idea to Viking Press to try to sell it. Unfortunately for Yardley, the publisher at Viking got in touch with Colonel Stanley Ford, the assistant chief of staff of intelligence (MI) at the War Department. Ford thought that the type of revelations such a book would contain would not be good for the Army, and Viking turned Yardley down.[3] Yardley let his idea for a book drop for a few months, but by the fall of 1930 he was in desperate straits. So

---

[1] Herbert O. Yardley to John M. Manly, "HOY to Manly," August 29, 1930, John Matthews Manly Collection, Series II, Box 3, Folder 2, University of Chicago Library.

[2] John F. Dooley and Elizabeth Anne King, "John Matthews Manly: The Collier's Articles," *Cryptologia* 38, no. 1 (January 2014): 77–88, https://doi.org/10.1080/01611194.2013.797049

[3] David Kahn, *The Reader of Gentlemen's Mail: Herbert O. Yardley and the Birth of American Codebreaking* (New Haven: Yale University Press, 2004), 105.

© The Author(s), under exclusive license to Springer Nature
Switzerland AG 2023
J. F. Dooley, *The Gambler and the Scholars*, History of Computing,
https://doi.org/10.1007/978-3-031-28318-5_12

desperate that he asked Manly for a $2500 loan, which Manly, himself struggling with some of his family's company's finances, had to turn down.[4]

During this time, Yardley also decided to get more serious about pursuing his book idea and set about finding an agent in New York. Friends there pointed him at George Bye, one of the most successful and influential literary agents in the city. Just a couple of years older than Yardley, Bye's clients included Charles Lindbergh, Eleanor Roosevelt, Laura Ingalls Wilder, and Yardley's friend Franklin Adams. Bye was impressed with Yardley because he was personable and a raconteur, and he liked his idea. Just before Christmas, he introduced Yardley to Thomas B. Costain, the editor of the *Saturday Evening Post*, the largest and most popular weekly magazine in the country. Costain was also intrigued with Yardley's stories, and they began negotiations for a series of articles on his experiences in MI-8 and the Cipher Bureau to be published in the *Post*.

On 20 December 1930, the same day Yardley dashed off a note to Friedman in which he promised to be in Washington in a few days to help Friedman with some Cipher Bureau files, at George Bye's suggestion, he met with George Shively, the New York editor for the Bobbs-Merrill publishing company out of Indianapolis to discuss a book detailing all his activities with MI-8 during the war and the Cipher Bureau over the past decade. Shively was excited about the idea, writing to his boss in Indianapolis, "Bye may have dug up that best seller. This morning he sent in a chap named Yardley, who was chief of a secret bureau of the Intelligence Dept. during and for some time after the war ... It's an amazing story, and if true ought to make the front page of every paper in the world."[5] After some negotiations, a contract was agreed upon. Shortly after Christmas Yardley signed the contract with Bobbs-Merrill, who promised him a $500 advance once the manuscript was delivered.[6]

With nearly the last of his available cash, Yardley rented a room at 21 Jones Street in Greenwich Village in New York, borrowed a typewriter from Bye, and began to write. It was an excruciating experience for Yardley. As he had never tried this type of writing, a combination of nonfiction and memoir, he had no support structure in place. The best explanation of Yardley's evolving writing process comes from the man himself. After the publication of his book, Yardley wrote what was basically a thank-you letter to George Bye relating how he'd really written *The American Black Chamber* and how he owed any success the book had to Bye. Here are some excerpts (the misspellings are Yardley's).

> I was a cryptographer, not a writer. Friends suggested that I return to New York and consult you. They told me that you could make anyone write, no matter what his training. So I came to New York with my last few dollars, took a room at the Commodore Club Hotel, and called you up. Your suave secretary told me that you were not in; so I left my telephone number and sat around the rest of the day waiting for a call from you. None came. ...

[4] John M. Manly, "Manly to HOY," January 30, 1931, John Matthews Manly Collection, Box 1, Folder 19, University of Chicago Library.

[5] Kahn, *ROGM*, 105–106.

[6] Kahn, *ROGM*, 106.

These I had within a few hours, and moved from the hotel to a dark cheap room. Before me sat a typewriter, and [by] my side laid 500 sheets of paper. But I could do no more than stare into space. For days I pecked out a few lines and threw them into the fire. I utterly detested the job of writing what seemed to me one of America's greatest episodes. All that I had done in life had been done well. ... But I knew nothing about writing. And, George, it seemed to me that I had a thrilling story to tell. You cannot know what it means to sit before a typewriter with a tremendous story with no training, no craftsmanship to tell it. I was desperate.

At last I began to write whole paragraphs, then pages, and I cared nothing for words, for form, for structure. Often after working all night I timidly handed you a chapter, and the next day you told me to keep at it. ...

For New Year's [1931] I drank an ice cream soda and worked all night. I ground out a thousand words a day, then two thousand, then three thousand; and on occasions when the room got cold and I could not sleep as many as seven thousand. (Editor: ABC is roughly 79-thousand words long.) ... I simply pecked away, day after day, night after night.

At last after four weeks I gave you about three quarters of the book and Bobbs-Merrill asked that I come to their office to discuss advance royalties and a contract. Before they would sign, they said I must complete the MS within one month. ...

After telephoning to the Saturday Evening Post, you told me that I must complete the book within two weeks, instead of a month, in order to give them sufficient time to run a few articles before the publication of the book. ...

After delivering the MS I sat around in my room in trembling and fear. Then when the typist delivered the MS to you and you were kind enough to read it and telegraph "Congratulations on magnificent book which is ten times better than my most optimistic expectations"; then all the hours of drudgery slipped from me, and I felt that perhaps I had told my story not too poorly.

In any case, George, for you it must mean something to pick up a person from the street and by your genius for encouragement and criticism inveigle this person to produce a book within a few weeks.[7]

Yardley was afraid that he could not stay an Army Reserve officer and publish his tell-all book without being liable to a court martial, so in the midst of his writing spree, he submitted his resignation from the Army Reserve on 31 January 1931.[8] This immediately began to ring alarm bells in the War Department, and Yardley was asked to explain his cryptic one-sentence resignation letter. In his response, Yardley was equally cryptic: "My reason for resigning is that I do not approve of the policies of the Military Intelligence Division and therefore no longer wish my name identified with this division. My resignation is unconditional and without rancor of any sort."[9] Word of a possible book reached Military Intelligence and the Signal Corps shortly thereafter; lawyers were consulted. Albright called Yardley and warned him about publishing military secrets. Yardley reassured him, but did not promise to

---

[7] Kahn, *ROGM*, xvii–xxi.

[8] Herbert O. Yardley to Secretary of War, "Letter to Secretary of War," January 31, 1931, Herbert Yardley Collection, RG 457, SRH-038, p. 137, National Archives and Records Administration, College Park, MD.

[9] Herbert O. Yardley to Captain M. F. Shepherd, "HOY to Shepherd," February 24, 1931, SRH-038, p. 133, NSA Archives, Herbert O. Yardley Collection.

send the War Department the manuscript for review.[10] In the end, the Army's own lawyers could not find any reason not to accept Yardley's resignation, nor could they find a reason to prosecute him later.[11] Yardley's resignation was accepted on 1 April 1931, just in time for his first article on the Cipher Bureau to appear.[12]

On 17 February 1931, he and Bye had also come to an agreement with Costain, and Yardley signed a contract for three articles—slightly modified excerpts from his book—with the *Saturday Evening Post* at $750 per article. The articles, titled *Secret Inks*, *Codes*, and *Ciphers*, appeared on 4 April, 18 April, and 9 May 1931, respectively. Yardley also worked out the final contract arrangements with Bobbs-Merrill and was paid his $500 advance on the delivery of the completed manuscript on 23 February 1931; after Bye's commission and legal fees, Yardley received $375. At this point, *The American Black Chamber* was written, and Yardley was back home in Worthington, Indiana. Over the next 2 months he made requested changes to the book and delivered updates to the Bobbs-Merrill editors in Indianapolis. The first copies of the book rolled off the presses on 3 May 1931.[13]

For all that was going on in the first few months of 1931, Friedman and Yardley kept up a correspondence, with Friedman still trying to get Yardley back in Washington. On 27 February, Friedman wrote, "It is with considerable regret that I note you do not wish to participate in active duty. I had hoped that you would have changed your mind by this time. Would you be at all interested in undertaking any temporary work of a special character should the necessity therefore develop? I had in mind that something might come up in the near future and it would be well to know in advance how you would feel towards such a proposition. Your brother has been in touch with me and I have tried to get him whatever information he wanted for you. Please do not hesitate to call upon me for anything further."[14] Note that by the end of February Yardley had already resigned from the Army Reserve, contracted with both Bobbs-Merrill and the *Saturday Evening Post*, and finished writing *The American Black Chamber*. None of which he appears to have told Friedman. On the other hand, in light of the Army's concern about Yardley's resignation from the Reserves, it seems likely that Albright had discussed Yardley's resignation with Friedman, yet Friedman continued to implore Yardley to come to Washington for active duty. Friedman never mentioned his conversations with Albright to Yardley.

All this cordiality, however, changed after Yardley's *Saturday Evening Post* articles were published (Fig. 12.1). When Yardley's first *Saturday Evening Post* article,

---

[10] Major Owen S. Albright to Col. Alfred T. Smith, "Memorandum for Col. Alfred T. Smith, ACoS, G-2," March 24, 1931, SRH-038, pp. 138–141, NSA Archives, Herbert O. Yardley Collection, 141.

[11] Lt. Col. W. A. Graham to Col. Alfred T. Smith, "Memorandum for the ACoS, G-2 Re: Disclosure of Confidential Information," March 28, 1931, SRH-038, pp. 143–145, NSA Archives, Herbert O. Yardley Collection.

[12] Adjutant General to Herbert O. Yardley, "Acceptance of Resignation of Reserve Commissionn," April 1, 1931, SRH-038, p. 148, NSA Archives, Herbert O. Yardley Collection.

[13] Kahn, *ROGM*, 109–110.

[14] William F. Friedman to Herbert O. Yardley, "WFF to HOY," February 27, 1931, Friedman Collection, Item 840, George Marshall Foundation Research Library.

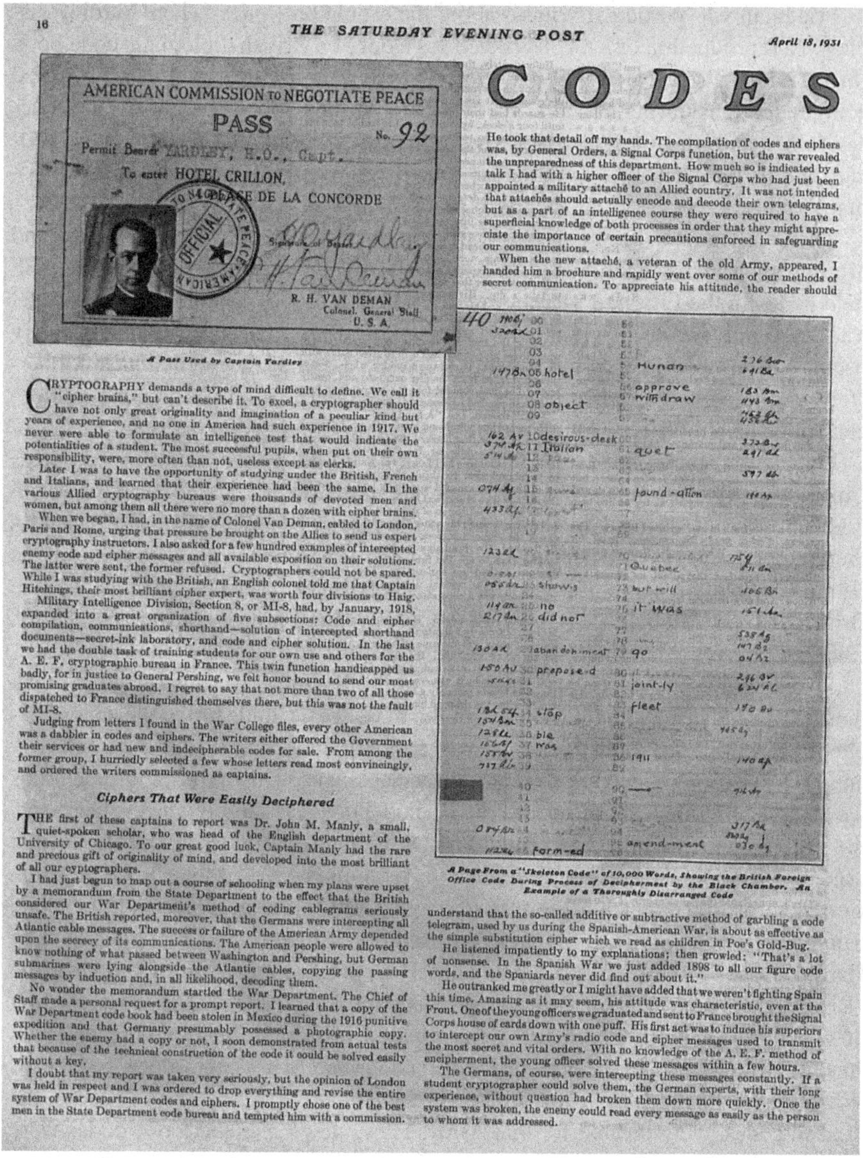


16 THE SATURDAY EVENING POST April 18, 1931

# CODES

He took that detail off my hands. The compilation of codes and ciphers was, by General Orders, a Signal Corps function, but the war revealed the unpreparedness of this department. How much so is indicated by a talk I had with a higher officer of the Signal Corps who had just been appointed a military attaché to an Allied country. It was not intended that attachés should actually encode and decode their own telegrams, but as a part of an intelligence course they were required to have a superficial knowledge of both processes in order that they might appreciate the importance of certain precautions enforced in safeguarding our communications.

When the new attaché, a veteran of the old Army, appeared, I handed him a brochure and rapidly went over some of our methods of secret communication. To appreciate his attitude, the reader should understand that the so-called additive or subtractive method of garbling a code telegram, used by us during the Spanish-American War, is about as effective as the simple substitution cipher which we read as children in Poe's Gold-Bug.

He listened impatiently to my explanations; then growled: "That's a lot of nonsense. In the Spanish War we just added 1898 to all our figure code words, and the Spaniards never did find out about it."

He outranked me greatly or I might have added that we weren't fighting Spain this time. Amazing as it may seem, his attitude was characteristic, even at the Front. One of the young officers we graduated and sent to France brought the Signal Corps house of cards down with one puff. His first act was to induce his superiors to intercept our own Army's radio code and cipher messages used to transmit the most secret and vital orders. With no knowledge of the A. E. F. method of encipherment, the young officer solved these messages within a few hours.

The Germans, of course, were intercepting these messages constantly. If a student cryptographer could solve them, the German experts, with their long experience, without question had broken them down more quickly. Once the system was broken, the enemy could read every message as easily as the person to whom it was addressed.

*A Pass Used by Captain Yardley*

CRYPTOGRAPHY demands a type of mind difficult to define. We call it "cipher brains," but can't describe it. To excel, a cryptographer should have not only great originality and imagination of a peculiar kind but years of experience, and no one in America had such experience in 1917. We never were able to formulate an intelligence test that would indicate the potentialities of a student. The most successful pupils, when put on their own responsibility, were, more often than not, useless except as clerks.

Later I was to have the opportunity of studying under the British, French and Italians, and learned that their experience had been the same. In the various Allied cryptography bureaus were thousands of devoted men and women, but among them all there were no more than a dozen with cipher brains.

When we began, I had, in the name of Colonel Van Deman, cabled to London, Paris and Rome, urging that pressure be brought on the Allies to send us expert cryptography instructors. I also asked for a few hundred examples of intercepted enemy code and cipher messages and all available exposition on their solutions. The latter were sent, the former refused. Cryptographers could not be spared. While I was studying with the British, an English colonel told me that Captain Hitchings, their most brilliant cipher expert, was worth four divisions to Haig.

Military Intelligence Division, Section 8, or MI-8, had, by January, 1918, expanded into a great organization of five subsections: Code and cipher compilation, communications, shorthand—solution of intercepted shorthand documents—secret-ink laboratory, and code and cipher solution. In the last we had the double task of training students for our own use and others for the A. E. F. cryptographic bureau in France. This twin function handicapped us badly, for in justice to General Pershing, we felt honor bound to send our most promising graduates abroad. I regret to say that not more than two of all those dispatched to France distinguished themselves there, but this was not the fault of MI-8.

Judging from letters I found in the War College files, every other American was a dabbler in codes and ciphers. The writers either offered the Government their services or had new and indecipherable codes for sale. From among the former group, I hurriedly selected a few whose letters read most convincingly, and ordered the writers commissioned as captains.

## Ciphers That Were Easily Deciphered

THE first of these captains to report was Dr. John M. Manly, a small, quiet-spoken scholar, who was head of the English department of the University of Chicago. To our great good luck, Captain Manly had the rare and precious gift of originality of mind, and developed into the most brilliant of all our cyptographers.

I had just begun to map out a course of schooling when my plans were upset by a memorandum from the State Department to the effect that the British considered our War Department's method of coding cablegrams seriously unsafe. The British reported, moreover, that the Germans were intercepting all Atlantic cable messages. The success or failure of the American Army depended upon the secrecy of its communications. The American people were allowed to know nothing of what passed between Washington and Pershing, but German submarines were lying alongside the Atlantic cables, copying the passing messages by induction and, in all likelihood, decoding them.

No wonder the memorandum startled the War Department. The Chief of Staff made a personal request for a prompt report. I learned that a copy of the War Department code book had been stolen in Mexico during the 1916 punitive expedition and that Germany presumably possessed a photographic copy. Whether the enemy had a copy or not, I soon demonstrated from actual tests that because of the technical construction of the code it could be solved easily without a key.

I doubt that my report was taken very seriously, but the opinion of London was held in respect and I was ordered to drop everything and revise the entire system of War Department codes and ciphers. I promptly chose one of the best men in the State Department code bureau and tempted him with a commission.

*A Page From a "Skeleton Code" of 10,000 Words, Showing the British Foreign Office Code During Process of Decipherment by the Black Chamber. An Example of a Thoroughly Disarranged Code*

**Fig. 12.1** The first page of Yardley's Codes article in the Saturday Evening Post. Note the illustration of a page from a "British Foreign Office Code" that infuriated Friedman.[a] (National Cryptologic Museum Library)

[a] Herbert O. Yardley, "Codes," *The Saturday Evening Post*, April 18, 1931, David Kahn Collection, DK 68-24, National Cryptologic Museum Library.

titled "*Secret Inks*," came out in early April 1931, it was an instant hit. The second and third articles, "*Codes*" and "*Ciphers*," were also very successful and whetted the public's appetite for the book, which appeared on 1 June 1931.

Friedman was particularly upset about the article on *Codes*, where Yardley displayed a reproduction of a reconstructed page out of a British diplomatic code book (Fig. 12.1). This revealed that the United States was not only intercepting Allied communications during and after the war but that the Cipher Bureau was also successfully decrypting the coded diplomatic messages of our allies well into the 1920s and letting the British, in particular, know that we were breaking their diplomatic codes.

The publications began a flurry of correspondence between Friedman and Yardley about the articles, particularly about Yardley's characterization of the AEF field codes in the First World War which Friedman saw as completely inadequate. Yardley finally wrote to Frank Moorman asking him "...to get Friedman off my back."[15] It turns out that to tell a lively story, Yardley had, accidentally or deliberately, conflated two different stories, inflated the contributions of a young lieutenant, and smeared the reputation of the AEF's Code Compilation Section.

One of the stories involves some work done by the young lieutenant, J. Rives Childs, shortly after he arrived in France in early 1918. Lt. Childs was trained in cryptanalysis at Riverbank by the Friedmans in November–December 1917. He was then shipped off to France in January 1918 and was assigned to the Cipher Solutions Section of G-2 A-6 under Major Frank Moorman. He also acted as the liaison to the British Military Intelligence Section in France. In May 1918, as a test of its security, Childs was given a number of superenciphered test code messages in the new one-part American Trench Code and the codebook itself. Childs was instructed to break the superencipherment and then decrypt the messages. Childs broke the superencipherment within just a few hours—it was a mono-alphabetic substitution cipher—and then used the codebook to decrypt the messages. This exposed a dangerous weakness in this newly developed code; if a codebook was captured by the Germans, the superencipherment would provide no additional security to any messages that used the Trench Code, and American tactical plans would be an open book. Consequently, the Trench Code was never released to the field. Instead, the Code Compilation Section of the Signal Corps Radio Intelligence Section under Captain Harold Barnes went on to develop an entirely new set of 2-part codes known as the "River" codes because they were named after American rivers. These codes, the first of which was named "Potomac," were released in 2-week intervals beginning in June 1918 to minimize the possibility of the German Army capturing a codebook. When the US Second Army was created in September 1918, a new set of codes, the "Lake" codes, were created for that Army. These new Lake and River codes were significantly more secure than the original Trench Code and Barnes, and his Signal Corps subordinates' work on these codes was a masterpiece.

The second story that Yardley drew from was also about communications, but this time it was American radio and telephone communications and the security of

---

[15] Friedman 21 April 1931-a; Friedman 21 April 1931-b; Friedman 29 April 1931; Friedman 11 May 1931; Friedman 3 June 1931; Yardley 15 April 1931; Yardley 26 April 1931; Yardley 30 April 1931. All in William F. Friedman Collection, Item 840, George Marshall Foundation Research Library, Lexington, VA.

those communications. The Radio Security section of the American G-2 organization in France was concerned that American soldiers were not taking radio and telephone security seriously enough. So shortly before the first major all-American action of the war—an attack in September 1918 to flatten the St. Mihiel salient at the southern end of the Allied lines—they began listening in on American radio and telephone conversations. What they heard horrified them. In a matter of days, the intelligence operators were able to reconstruct the entire order of battle of the American forces and the exact time of the start of the attack on the salient.[16] Since the Allies were sure that the Germans were also listening to radio transmissions and, where possible near the front lines, telephone conversations, this was a major breach of security. The Americans promptly instituted new security measures.[17]

In his article on "Codes," Yardley mixes these two stories up, stating that the code messages broken by Childs actually contained all the information about the St. Mihiel attack and that the Germans, also having intercepted and decoded the messages, expected the attack and began a withdrawal just before the Americans attacked. Yardley blames all of this on the inadequate code produced by the Signal Corps Code Compilation section under Captain Howard Barnes.[18] What is true is that the Germans were, in fact, already withdrawing on 12 September as the Americans began their attack, but they had never intercepted or decoded any American communications. They were withdrawing in order to shorten their battle lines and to more securely defend the city of Metz.

Friedman was furious about the apparent slur on the honor of the Signal Corps and, in particular, the Code Compilation section in France. This was the crux of Friedman and Yardley's arguments during April and May of 1931. However, it wouldn't end there. Yardley's response was that he garnered his information from a lecture given by Colonel Moorman in 1920 to a group of Military Intelligence Division officers. It turns out that Moorman's lecture only talks about the radio communications security problem but says nothing about Child's break of the superenciphement of the American Trench Code. So Yardley was only partially correct here. He also gets it wrong when he says it was the Germans who intercepted and decoded the American messages about the St. Mihiel salient attack. That story is in Moorman's lecture, and he makes it clear that it was the Americans who were intercepting their own communications.[19]

Others of Yardley's former colleagues in Military Intelligence and the Signal Corps were also upset about Yardley's articles and turned on him immediately. In particular, A. J. McGrail, who was the chemist in charge of the MI-8 Secret Ink

---

[16] Luckily for the Americans, the one radio operator who gabbed about the date of the attack got it wrong by 24 hours.

[17] Frank Moorman, "Lecture Delivered to Officers of the Military Intelligence Division" (February 13, 1920), RG457, Entry 9032, National Security Agency, Herbert Yardley Collection, National Archives, College Park, MD.

[18] Herbert O. Yardley, "Codes," *The Saturday Evening Post*, April 18, 1931, 16–17, 141–142. Yardley does not mention Barnes' name in the article.

[19] Moorman, *Lecture Delivered*, 14.

Laboratory in Washington during the war, was furious about the techniques and successes that Yardley freely revealed about solving secret ink messages in his first article. These included the development and use of a universal reagent to reveal secret ink messages, how the Secret Ink Lab surreptitiously opened and then reclosed sealed letters, and the fact that MI-8 and its Secret Ink Laboratory intercepted and opened secret diplomatic correspondence. He told this in a letter to Friedman, saying at one point, "Y's resignation is the act of a man with a troubled conscience."[20] Friedman agreed with McGrail, writing:

> Yardley resigned his reserve commission immediately before the first article appeared.... *I got the suspicion that Yardley was preparing something for publication when his resignation was tendered,...*[21] In your letter which I urge you very seriously to write, *please avoid any allusion to what I have said above, and let the matter come with no background other than your present duty and responsibility* as a Reserve Officer... *if anybody was going to publish or had a right to publish on this phase of the work, certainly it should have been you,...* I was also especially irritated by the references to the matter of breaking seals on diplomatic packages, *because the less said about such things the better.*[22]

So Friedman is saying basically "I agree with you, but don't let anyone know I said that. I think it's OK to publish this information, but you should have been the one to do it, not your former boss. Oh, and lets just ignore the whole thing about opening other countries' diplomats mail, shall we?" Which, while he is condemning Yardley's article because Yardley is letting the public know what goes on in the intelligence community in both war and peace, he doesn't seem to condemn the acts themselves that were performed during and after the war in the name of the government.

Curiously, while Friedman and Yardley had a lively correspondence about the articles and Friedman's perceptions of Yardley's mistakes in them, there were also flashes of their old friendship. In a letter dated 21 April 1931, after having read the first two of Yardley's *Saturday Evening Post* articles, Friedman tries to convince Yardley about his errors with regard to the American Trench Code and Rives Childs breaking of the superencipherment of the test messages. However, Friedman's tenor is not outraged or fierce; instead he is trying to calmly present evidence to Yardley and convince him that he's wrong. At one point he says, "Please consider my remarks as friendly, wholly unofficial, and purely my personal reaction to your

---

[20]Capt. A. J. McGrail to Director of Military Intelligence, "Letter to the Director of Military Intelligence," April 8, 1931, SRH-038, 149–150, NSA Archives, Herbert O. Yardley Collection. The universal reagent was iodine vapor, which when sprayed on a secret ink message settles the iodine on the fibers of the paper that have been disturbed by the writing. This reagent was actually known as far back as the end of the nineteenth century, but not to the Americans. Kristie Macrakis, *Prisoners, Lovers, & Spies: The Story of Invisible Ink from Herodotus to Al-Qaeda* (New Haven, CT: Yale University Press, 2014), 148.

[21]Yardley resigned his commission on 31 January 1931. The first Saturday Evening Post article appeared on 04 April 1931. Close, but hardly "immediately before."

[22]William F. Friedman to Capt. A. J. McGrail, "WFF to A. J. McGrail," April 6, 1931, William F. Friedman Collection, Item 840, George Marshall Foundation Research Library, Lexington, VA; *italics added.*

story." At the end of the letter, Friedman adds a hand-written postscript, "P.S. You did a fine job of writing. Weren't you once interested in a literary career? Mrs. F says you write in a thrilling style. Are Bobbs-Merrill going to publish your book?"[23] Unfortunately, this civil discourse will not last long.

The publication of *The American Black Chamber* on Monday, 1 June 1931, was what really set off the fireworks (Fig. 12.2). The complete, original texts of the three *Saturday Evening Post* articles were in the book, along with many other indiscretions related to signals intelligence during the Great War and the decade after. Yardley was not allowed to name many names by his publisher, who was still afraid of getting sued by individuals or prosecuted by the government, but his pseudonyms fooled no one in the small American cryptologic community. Yardley was the hero of his own story, and he took credit for many things that should have rightly been attributed to others. He also let loose with a number of real stories of code and cipher decryptions, German spies, and all the details of the Washington Naval Disarmament Conference of 1920–1921. It truly did not help that Yardley's book became a best seller. Primed by the three *Saturday Evening Post* articles, which were very popular, the public snapped up copies at $3.50 apiece. In short order, the book was also published in the United Kingdom and in translations in Japan, France, Sweden, and China.

Most of the nations mentioned remained quiet with respect to Yardley's stories and revelations, except for the Japanese. The Japanese ambassador to the United States first wrote about the book in a telegram to Foreign Minister Kijuro Shidehara on 6 June. Shidehara was in a particularly sensitive spot because he was the Japanese ambassador to the United States during the 1921–1922 Washington Naval Conference and headed the Japanese delegation. The government was livid about the publication of the *American Black Chamber*. The chief of the Telegraph Section of the JMFA, Shin Sakuma, wrote a memorandum to the Foreign Minister on 10 June, "Regarding the Book by Yardley." Sakuma was not surprised that the Americans were trying to break Japanese codes, but he was upset about the disclosure of Japanese telegrams, and his memorandum spent most of its time exploring ways to get the Americans to charge Yardley with a crime.[24] A second memorandum by Sakuma on 28 July 1931 exposed the heat that the Foreign Ministry was feeling. The topic of the memorandum was proposed answers to questions about the *American Black Chamber* in the Japanese Diet.[25] Japanese newspapers expressed popular anger at both the government and Yardley. Typical was *The Japanese*

---

[23] William F. Friedman to Herbert O. Yardley, "WFF to HOY," Correspondence, April 21, 1931, William F. Friedman Collection, Item 840, George Marshall Foundation Research Library.

[24] Shin Sakuma, "Sakuma to Minister and Vice Minister, 10 June 1931, Subject: A Book Written by Yardley, the Former Chief of the Cryptographic Bureau of U.S. Army Intelligence" (Washington, D.C.: Telegraph Section, Japanese Embassy, 1931), UD 30, Frames 157–174, Archives of the Japanese Ministry of Foreign Affairs, Library of Congress.

[25] Shin Sakuma, "Answers to Hypothetical Questions from the Diet about Yardley's Book 'The American Black Chamber,'" Microfilm (Tokyo, 1931), UD 29, Frames 1 - 28, Archives of the Japanese Ministry of Foreign Affairs, Library of Congress.

**Fig. 12.2** The cover of the first edition of The American Black Chamber (with the permission of Tobias Schrödel)

*American* newspaper, which published a scathing editorial on 5 August 1931. It excoriated Yardley and his book, saying, "It is immoral because it boastfully narrates the pilfering, the snooping, the stealing, the spying practised by agents under his supervision... No decent-minded man can read this book without a sense of revulsion."[26]

---

[26] K. K. Kawakami, "Editorial in the 'Japanese American' Newspaper (SRH-038)" (College Park, MD: NARA (Record Group 457, Entry 9037), August 5, 1931), 158–160.

Despite being derided by the American cryptologic establishment and journalists overseas, Yardley's book sold very well: 17,931 copies in the United States, a phenomenal number for a nonfiction hardcover book, and a whopping 33,119 copies in the Japanese translation. Bobbs-Merrill was into a third printing by the end of June. The book was the number one seller at eight of eleven New York bookstores polled by the publisher.[27] Readers really liked Yardley's writing style, his over-the-top rhetoric, and the feeling of peeking into the inner workings of a secret government bureau (Fig. 12.3). Many of the reviews in the United States were very favorable. Reviewers typically talked about Yardley's ability to tell stories. The *Chicago Tribune* exclaimed "...one of the most gripping and exciting mystery stories I ever came across. And it actually happened." Some reviews, however, were not as effusive. These typically questioned the revealing of government secrets by a former employee. Louis Gannett in the *Herald Tribune* wrote in this vein "... one marvels a little at the code of ethics which permits a professional decoder to keep copies of the messages he decodes and later to publish them, without authorization from any government, apparently solely to tell a good story and to get back at those who banned his bureau."[28] Others chimed in with the same refrain. Kahn writes that "The *New York Evening Post* editorialized that *The American Black Chamber* 'betrays government secrets with a detail and clarity of writing that makes one gasp. Rarely has there come out here a book with such dramatic and important official revelations. We wish Theodore Roosevelt were alive to read to the author of this book a lecture on betraying the secrets of one's country.' The *Brooklyn Eagle* told the government to strengthen its legal restraint against betrayal by former servants."[29] While officially, both the State and War Departments claimed no knowledge of Yardley or his Cipher Bureau, internally they seethed.

The publicity and good reviews also turned Yardley's head, much to the chagrin of his publisher. Laurance Chambers, his chief editor at Bobbs-Merrill in Indianapolis, said, "Yardley is crazy to get his name in the papers. ... This sort of thing is not going to help the sale of *The American Black Chamber*. It is calculated to involve us in obloquy if nothing worse." Chambers also refused to pay for a good part of Yardley's travel expenses.[30]

Yardley went on a book tour anyway and was finally making some money again (Fig. 12.4).

Friedman and many of the other American cryptologists, whether currently working or not, were truly very angry about the publication of the book. Friedman felt that Yardley had betrayed his oath as an Army officer and the secrecy oath that all members of Military Intelligence were required to take—and of which Yardley was the likely author. He also felt that the revelations in the book would increase the burden on his small Signal Intelligence Service because governments and militaries

---

[27] Kahn, *ROGM*, 124.
[28] Kahn, *ROGM*, 122.
[29] Kahn, *ROGM*, 125.
[30] Kahn, *ROGM*, 125.

**Fig. 12.3** The dust jacket of the first edition of "The American Black Chamber" (with permission of Richard Brisson)

around the world would see the book as a reason to update all their code and cipher systems.

Charles Mendelsohn, who was in charge of the Code Solution subsection in MI-8 during the war, who had worked for and with both Yardley and Friedman, and was friends with both men, wrote a lengthy and even-handed review. He examined the different stories in the book and found them all thrilling. "The author has told his story more than well, and has skillfully avoided two temptations that must have

**Fig. 12.4** Advertisement for The American Black Chamber (The Coastal Artillery Journal)

assailed him—the technician's wish to write of the details of his subject as a special-
ist, and the opposing desire to write down to a public that craves sensation above all
else. Thrills there [are] and thrills aplenty; but for the most part they are legitimately
provided by the subject matter and only at times by red fire." He questioned the ethics of Yardley telling the stories of top secret war work, saying he did not think that
Yardley was justified in making his disclosures. He called the Cipher Bureau's
breaking of the Japanese diplomatic codes "a beautiful cryptographic achievement"

and that Yardley's telling of that story "brought a new thrill and a new sensation of admiration."[31]

John Manly was about the only other former colleague who tried to defend Yardley and in some correspondence with Friedman that summer attempted to act as a mediator between the two while trying to be fair to Friedman as well and expressing his own reservations about what Yardley had done. Manly explained that he didn't think that Yardley intended to slur the AEF Code and Cipher section. Yardley exaggerated Childs' talents for the sake of telling a good story. Manly said that Yardley probably distorted facts in the effort to tell a thrilling, dramatic story that would grab the public's attention and possibly get the government to recreate an organization such as the Cipher Bureau. He continued, "Yardley's articles and book are, of course, often inaccurate in details, and I think he has made a serious mistake in not giving due credit to the men who actually did the work in many of the instances he relates. ... In doing this, he has invented conversations, changed details, and made revelations which I do not think he ought to have made. Whether any good will come of what he has written I do not know." Finally, Manly agreed with Yardley that it was a colossal mistake to close the Cipher Bureau and leave the United States defenseless in the cryptologic wars.[32]

Yardley also defended himself in his own personal correspondence, articles published later in 1931, and in letters to various publications that were questioning his ethics and all but accusing him of treason. To the *New York Evening Post* he wrote that since the Cipher Bureau was already closed, "what valid reason could there be for withholding the knowledge of the work of this bureau from the general public?" Yardley responded to a Mr. Lincoln Foster who had written a negative letter to the editor of the *Post* that "It is inconceivable to me that American officials should deny the existence of the American Black Chamber, which was supported secretly by War Department and State Department funds and secluded in a brownstone front in New York." and later, "It is utterly ridiculous for the United States Government to depend upon antiquated methods for the encipherment of its messages."[33] Yardley also knew that what he had written was not all completely true. In a letter to John Manly on 30 April 1931, Yardley says, "To write saleable (sic) stuff one must dramatise (sic). Things don't happen in dramatic fashion. There is therefore nothing to do but either dramatise or not write at all."[34]

Friedman was anything but cordial or gracious in his own reaction to *The American Black Chamber*. He reserved his most biting and angry remarks for the

---

[31] Charles J. Mendelsohn, "Mendelsohn Review of 'The American Black Chamber,'" 1931, William F. Friedman Collection, Item 840, George Marshall Research Library, Lexington, VA.

[32] John M. Manly to William F. Friedman, "Manly to WFF," July 24, 1931, William F. Friedman Collection, Item 840, George Marshall Foundation Research Library, Lexington, VA.

[33] Herbert O. Yardley to Lincoln Foster, "Letter to Mr. Lincoln Foster," June 6, 1931, 6649178, NSA Archives, Herbert O. Yardley Collection, https://www.nsa.gov/news-features/declassified-documents/yardley-collection/

[34] Herbert O. Yardley, "HOY to Manly," Personal Correspondence, April 30, 1931, Manly Papers, Box 3, Folder 3, John M. Manly Archives, University of Chicago Library.

margins of his copy of the book (given to him and signed by Yardley) and for the official histories he later wrote for the War Department about Military Intelligence and its evolution from World War I through the 1930s.[35] Friedman also requested opinions from a number of current and former Army cryptologists about Yardley's book, its truthfulness, and the morality of what he had done. He sent his personal copy of *The American Black Chamber* around to his former colleagues and solicited written comments in the book itself. Particularly vitriolic in their condemnation of Yardley were A. J. McGrail, Frank Moorman, and cryptologist Parker Hitt.[36] Yardley's former cryptanalyst in the Cipher Bureau, Frederick Livesey, also chimed in. J. Rives Childs, from his diplomatic post in Egypt, was mostly indifferent. Colonel Owen Albright got into the act as well, sending a four-page memorandum to the Army Assistant Chief of Staff for Intelligence dissecting *The American Black Chamber*. "The book is a self-glorification of the author's activity. ... While most of the basic facts in the book are correct, the narration of details is in most cases so distorted that the exaggerations would seem to be apparent to the casual reader. ... they may cause protests from foreign governments." Albright was particularly concerned about the Japanese chapters.[37]

Friedman's annotated copy of *The American Black Chamber* is an interesting and revealing read. Friedman starts on the title page with an accusation that Yardley did not write the book at all but had it ghostwritten for a $1000 fee. Friedman and especially A. J. McGrail and Frederick Livesey then litter the next 375 pages with comments on every perceived error in the book. At one point, Friedman complains that Yardley could only find a very few books on cryptography in the Library of Congress because he only spoke English. Later, once again complaining about Yardley's conflating of the two AEF code issues, Friedman writes, "All this is a most amazing piece of misstatement, inaccuracy, and downright falsehood." The word "lie" appears on many pages. In a back-handed compliment, at one point Friedman says, "Yardley was a good executive, not a real cryptographer." When Yardley mentioned that MI-8 was involved in training Army cryptanalysts, Friedman complained that his department at Riverbank trained more of them.[38] A. J. McGrail was upset with many of the things Yardley said, particularly with the chapters on secret inks

---

[35] William F. Friedman, "A Brief History of The Signal Intelligence Service (SRH-029)," *Cryptologia* 15, no. 3 (July 1991): 263–72; William F. Friedman, "Expansion of the Signal Intelligence Service from 1930 - 7 December 1941 (SRH-134)." Translated by U.S. Army Signal Corps. Washington, DC, December 4, 1945; David Kahn, "The Annotated 'The American Black Chamber.'" *Cryptologia* 9, no. 1 (1985): 1–37.

[36] William F. Friedman et al., "Series of Letters from Hitt, Moorman, McGrail to/from Friedman Re: Publication of ABC & SEP Articles," 1931, RG457, NSA, Entry 9032, Herbert Yardley Collection, RG 457, National Archives, College Park, MD. (See also Item 840 in the William F. Friedman Collection at the George Marshall Research Library, Lexington, VA.)

[37] Lt. Col. Owen S. Albright to Col. Alfred T. Smith, "Memorandum for Colonel Alfred T. Smith, ACoS, G-2, Re: 'The American Black Chamber,'" June 5, 1931, SRH-038, 151–153, NSA Archives, Herbert O. Yardley Collection.

[38] William F. Friedman, *Annotated Copy of The American Black Chamber (Item 604)* (Lexington, VA: George Marshall Foundation Research Library, 1931), 120. The Friedmans trained a total of

and the two German spies, Patricia and Madame de Victorica. He was more measured and added in his comments places where Yardley was correct and places where Yardley's revelations were close to the truth. Friedman continued on, pointing out every mistake, area of confusion, mis-statement, exaggeration, falsely taking credit for others work, and lie that Yardley wrote in the book; and there are quite a few. An interesting note with respect to Friedman's own annotations is that they continue on for many years. Friedman dated many of the comments he and others made in the book, and the dates span from 1931 to 1933, 1934, 1935, 1941, 1945, 1946, and into 1950. Finally, toward the end of the book, as the narrative approaches the end of the Cipher Bureau, Friedman gives the reader just a bit of the other side of his feelings toward his now former friend "I think Yardley well deserved the DSM (Distinguished Service Medal) – but not for the reasons he would have us believe. In my opinion he merited it because of his ability as a director of other people's activities – an executive in other words."[39]

So why did Herbert Yardley write his tell-all memoir, and why did he deliberately exaggerate and fabricate some stories and claim credit for work that others had done?

First of all, he needed the money. Yardley was never one to look long down the road where money was concerned; it was earned by hard work and meant to be spent, and the more money you had, the more you could spend and the better off your life would be. So, after more than a year of unemployment during the Great Depression, he was broke and looking for any opportunity to make money to support himself, his wife, and their now five-year-old son. After nearly 17 years working for the government, most of it in secret organizations doing things that would normally be considered illegal Yardley really didn't have many other marketable skills. The other jobs he might be good at, sales and management, were in short supply in 1929 and 1930.

The second reason that Yardley himself gave for having written *The American Black Chamber* was that he felt that for the United States not to pursue a cryptanalytic effort during peacetime put it at an enormous disadvantage compared to other countries that were continuing their cryptanalytic work.[40] In a follow-on article in *Liberty* magazine in December 1931, Yardley gave the clearest statement of this reason: "I had hoped to bring home to my government and to the public the dangerous position that America holds by abolishing the Black Chamber and at the same time retaining antiquated codes to carry our diplomatic secrets. All great powers have their Black Chamber where the best cipher brains in the world puzzle out our

---

about 84 Army cryptanalysts at Riverbank between October 1917 and February 1918. MI-8's training organization operated from early 1918 through November 1918 and trained considerably more.

[39] Friedman *Annotated*, 363.

[40] William F. Friedman, "Notes on a Conversation with Herbert O. Yardley," February 26, 1933, William F. Friedman Collection, Item 840, George Marshall Research Library, Lexington, VA; Herbert O. Yardley, "Are We Giving Away Our State Secrets?," *Liberty Magazine*, December 19, 1931; Barker *SRH-001*, 170.

codes."[41] Interestingly, Friedman wrote in a 1942 report that "It would be of utmost value to the winning of this war if the Government were now in a position to read the codes and ciphers of all the foreign powers whose actions and probable intentions are of interest and importance in our prosecution of the war. It could have been in this fortunate position had it given to cryptanalytic studies the attention which they deserve during peacetime and had provided funds for their continuity on a scale sufficient for the purpose for which they are intended. The matter can be summarized very succinctly in this statement: *Actual or physical warfare is intermittent but signal security warfare, especially cryptanalytic warfare, is continuous.* It is vital that this be understood by those who exercise the control over such studies."[42] Yardley would certainly have agreed.

William Friedman and his colleagues also felt that one of the consequences of the publication of Yardley's book was that both America's allies and potential enemies would use the revelations in the *American Black Chamber* as a reason to make major changes in their own code and cipher systems. These changes would put the American cryptanalysts, particularly the new, young cryptanalysts in Friedman's Signal Intelligence Service in the Signal Corps, back to square one in terms of solving these code and cipher systems. Friedman in particular thought that Yardley's book pushed other countries, especially the Japanese, to scrap all their current code and cipher systems and replace them with newly designed cipher machines. This actually happened, but not immediately as Friedman claimed, nor to the degree he feared, and not for the reasons that Friedman thought.

The Japanese had, in fact, been working on new cipher machines for their diplomatic systems since at least 1927. In that year, Genichiro Kakimoto of the Japanese Navy proposed a new cipher machine. Engineers at the Navy Technical Research Institute under Risaburo Ito, the head of the Navy's Telegraph Section, worked on the machine's design through 1927 and applied for a secret Japanese patent in early 1928. The Ministry of Foreign Affairs used nine prototypes of the new Navy machine at the London Naval Conference from January to April 1930. The initial design was based on the Kryha Standard cipher machine, but later versions switched from the Kryha mechanism to a "half-rotor" mechanism originally designed by Arvid Damm in 1919. In an effort to make manufacturing easier and cheaper, the Japanese changed the design so that the six vowels (AEIOUY) were always encrypted as vowels, and the 20 consonants were always encrypted as consonants. This may have made the device cheaper to manufacture, but it severely weakened it cryptographically.[43] The Japanese Army had also bought and reverse engineered the Enigma cipher machine, using that to design and manufacture cipher machines of their own.

---

[41] Yardley, *State Secrets*, 8.

[42] Friedman, *Brief History*, paragraph 11. [Friedman's emphasis].

[43] Satoshi Tomokiyo, "Japanese Reaction to Yardley's 'The American Black Chamber,'" *Cryptiana* (blog), February 2014, http://cryptiana.web.fc2.com/code/yardley_jp.htm

At the London Naval Conference, the Navy machines received their first real workout. They turned out to be cumbersome, difficult to use, and fragile, but the Japanese Navy learned a considerable amount about the performance of their machines in the field and took that knowledge back to Tokyo to effect a major redesign. In July 1930, Ito wrote a summary of the changes necessary for the machine, and the Navy then suggested to the Foreign Ministry that the updated machines be used for all their high-level communications. In typical bureaucratic fashion, Ito's memo languished at the Ministry of Foreign Affairs for a year. However, in July 1931—just a month after the publication of Yardley's book—Ito met with Shin Sakuma, the Chief of the Telegraph Section of the Foreign Affairs Ministry and the two hammered out an agreement that the Ministry would begin using the Navy machine at the Geneva Naval Conference of 1932. By later in 1931, the Japanese Navy was in the process of finalizing its cipher machine. By the time the Geneva Naval Conference started in April 1932, the Ministry of Foreign Affairs had 20 of the new machines, and the Navy had eight. This new version, dubbed the *Angōki Taipu-A (Cipher Machine, Type A)*, became the main diplomatic cipher system of the Japanese Ministry of Foreign Affairs in September 1932. This is the machine that Friedman and his SIS team would call RED.[44]

However, the Japanese development of the RED machine had nothing to do with Yardley's book. The Japanese had already been working on the machine long before the publication of *The American Black Chamber,* and the Japanese Navy had been encouraging the Ministry of Foreign Affairs to use the new machine since 1930.

Yardley's book caused the Japanese Ministry of Foreign Affairs (JMFA) to issue warnings about code and cipher security to their embassies and consulates and to make some changes to their codes and ciphers. The Ministry of Foreign Affairs went so far as to purchase 138 copies of *The American Black Chamber* and shipped them to embassies and consulates around the world. The book's publication also likely caused the Ministry of Foreign Affairs to speed up their agreement with the Navy and the subsequent release of the new RED machine, but that deployment was something that was going to happen anyway.

The Japanese Army was also alarmed at the publication of Yardley's book, and the Army cryptologic section circulated a memorandum in August 1931 warning about complacency in the use of codes and ciphers and reiterating the rules for their use. Commenting on the contents of the *American Black Chamber*, the Japanese Minister of War said with some emphasis on practicality, "Upon reading it, I did not feel like censuring the United States for such an act but drew a very important lesson that we should be on the alert in future. The next year will see a general disarmament conference and international relations will be more and more complicated, which would call for utmost caution on our side. In the military in particular, it

---

[44] Satoshi Tomokiyo, "Development of the First Japanese Cipher Machine: RED," *Cryptiana* (blog), May 20, 2014, http://cryptiana.web.fc2.com/code/redciphermachine.htm

would be disastrous if operational secrets were to be stolen by the enemy and we must buckle down for utmost security."[45]

The Japanese Navy did make some changes to their code and cipher systems after the publication of *The American Black Chamber*, but many of those, such as their rollout of their cipher machines, had already been planned. One person who was convinced that the Japanese Navy had quickly changed their codes and ciphers after the publication of *American Black Chamber* was Captain (later Admiral) Edwin T. Layton. In 1931 Lt. Layton was stationed in Tokyo, along with Lt. Joseph Rochefort, who would later command the Navy's cryptanalytic unit at Pearl Harbor. Layton would go on to have several stints in Naval Intelligence. Both officers were enrolled in the Navy's Japanese language program at the time. Layton was in Tokyo from 1929 through 1932, so he was there when *The American Black Chamber* was published.

Fifteen years later, in his testimony before the Congressional Pearl Harbor Commission, Layton said, "Senator, you would hardly believe it, but the Japanese naval ciphers in those days were pretty simple. Their call signs were even more simple. … After they read the book (American Black Chamber) they treated us language students with suspicion and rightly so, and they changed their codes and ciphers very fast, and the information we were able to have in the past, which was a prop to national security was knocked out from under us."[46] However, one thing deserves mention here. While Layton was in Tokyo, he was not in Naval Intelligence. That assignment did not occur until he returned to Washington in 1933, so his knowledge of Japanese ciphers and call signs was likely minimal in 1931.

One thing that the JMFA did as an apparent direct result of the publication of *The American Black Chamber* was to try to figure out how to get revenge on Yardley by smearing him in various memoranda and accusing him of being a traitor to his country. In his 6 June 1931 memorandum to Foreign Minister Shidehara, Shin Sakuma accused Yardley of betraying his country by offering to sell decrypted Japanese diplomatic messages and the techniques used to decrypt them in 1930. He went on to say that Yardley delivered some decrypted messages and was paid $7000. Sakuma then said that Yardley went back on his word by failing to tell the Japanese about the cryptanalytic techniques used to decrypt the messages and by printing the messages in his book a year later. This story, first reported in Lladislas Farago's book *Broken Seal* in 1967, depends solely on the Sakuma memorandum, but cannot be

---

[45] Tomokiyo, *Japanese Reaction.*

[46] Anonymous, "Hearings Before the Joint Committee on the Investigation of the Pearl Harbor Attack: Part 10," Transcript, Hearings Before the Joint Committee on the Investigation of the Pearl Harbor Attack (Washington, DC: United States Congress, February 1946), U.S. Archives, College Park, MD, http://www.ibiblio.org/pha/congress/Vol10.pdf., 4909; Lt. Robert Bar, "SIGNAL INTELLIGENCE DISCLOSURES IN THE PEARL HARBOR INVESTIGATION: A Study Based on the Hearings before the Joint Committee on the Investigation of the Pearl Harbor Attack.," Technical Report (Washington, DC: Army Security Agency, July 1, 1947), National Cryptologic Museum Library, https://drive.google.com/drive/u/0/folders/1jQ64F-fsqBCZDV6_ErtQ4zCiVqw_VXWy, 35.

completely discounted because of a lack of evidence.[47] This story has been repeated several times over the years, and each time the only evidence is the Sakuma memorandum of 6 June 1931. For example, in his memoir, *And I Was There*, Admiral Edwin Layton, discussing the uproar over *American Black Chamber*, uses the Sakuma memorandum to tar Yardley with the "selling secrets to the Japanese and then betraying them" brush. In addition, he also appears to blame the Japanese tempest over the *American Black Chamber* for the Mudken Incident in September 1931.[48] This seems a bit too far of a stretch, even for Yardley.

*The American Black Chamber* also apparently did not cause many other countries to scrap their existing code and cipher systems and quickly replace them with new ones. Documents from the British Public Records office and copies of German records in the US National Archives reveal that neither the British nor the German intelligence agencies reported rapid changes in any country's code and cipher systems, especially those of Japan. In fact, both the British and Germans reported increases in the number of Japanese diplomatic messages decrypted by their intelligence agencies in 1931 and 1932, times when a rapid change in codes and cipher systems would have resulted from Yardley's book. However, the changes in countries' systems, including Japan's, were not sudden; they were the usual gradual changes that countries make as a part of their regular upgrades to their security systems. "The change was neither sudden nor total, but gradual. And consequently it crippled neither the American nor foreign codebreaking agencies."[49]

Yardley's book and his revelation of MI-8 secrets may have been an ethical and legal breech and a reneging of his secrecy oath, as detailed in a short authorized biography of Yardley by the NSA: "In today's terms, it would be as if an NSA

---

[47] John Dooley, "Was Herbert O. Yardley a Traitor?," *Cryptologia* 35, no. 1 (January 2011): 1–15. See also Kahn, ROGM, 273–274, where Kahn discusses his researches in an endnote. In addition, no evidence in the form of bank records has been found for the depositing of the $7000. In 2018, Satoshi Tomokiyo reported on an interview by Japanese diplomat Kase Toshikazu for Japanese television from 1982, more than 50 years after the event, in which Kase claims to have been present at the meetings with Yardley in 1930 (although Kase puts the date as 1929). In a personal correspondence (February 11, 2022) between Tomokiyo and this author, Tomokiyo says "I reviewed Kase's interview (3:40) of the 1982 TV program. Kase's testimony is translated below. It offers nothing more than what I already translated on my webpage from the book based on this program."
KASE: "He said outright all our codes were read by the Americans. It was too much of a shock. Rather, we did not believe him, neither Togo nor I. Then, he put a heavy bunch of papers on the table. I took up some and felt uh-oh. About eighty percent was deciphered. Of course I couldn't tell it before Yardley. So I signaled the Secretary with my eyes to the corridor and said, yes, they did read. It was Secretary Togo's turn to be surprised and ask whether it's true. Then, it was reported to the Ambassador. A telegram was sent to the home office. The Ambassador was surprised and petrified. The home office was further surprised." Kase appears again at 10:20 and testifies how warnings of codebreaking of the Japanese diplomatic cipher (PURPLE) were ignored in 1941. Furthermore, according to Japanese Wikipedia https://ja.wikipedia.org/wiki/Kase's writings include historical inaccuracies and exaggeration of his own role.
[48] Layton, Edwin T., Roger Pineau, and John Costello. 1985. *And I Was There: Pearl Harbor and Midway - Breaking the Secrets*. New York, NY: William Morrow & Company, 41–42.
[49] Kahn, *ROGM*, 133.

employee had publicly revealed the complete communications intelligence operations of the Agency for the past 12 years–all its techniques and major successes, its
organizational structure and budget–and had, for good measure, included actual
intercepts, decrypts, and translations of communications not only of our adversaries
but of our allies as well."[50] However, one can also look at it from a different perspective. In today's terms, it would be as if—*after the NSA was dissolved as an organization and all its records destroyed or archived*—that an NSA employee had
publicly revealed the (almost) complete communications intelligence operations of
the Agency for the past 12 years. This is essentially the argument that Yardley was
making when he said that since the Cipher Bureau was defunct, that all bets and
constraints were off and he was telling his story in order to wake the government up
to the danger it was putting itself in by not having a codebreaking unit.

Despite all the vitriol thrown Yardley's way and the best-seller book, this was the
high point of his involvement in American cryptology in the period. He would be in
the news again, he'd write again—mostly fiction this time, and he would start cryptographic bureaus in two other countries, but as far as American professional cryptology was concerned, he was done.

William Friedman and Herbert Yardley had largely fallen out after the 1931 publication of Yardley's best seller and the subsequent uproar over it in the cryptologic
community. The last time that the two men are known to have seen each other and
talked in person was in February 1933 when Yardley invited Friedman to his hotel
in Washington while he was visiting there and just before he left on a lecture tour
about his book. Friedman, now in charge of cryptanalysis for the War Department,
felt the need to keep detailed notes on this meeting and wrote them up as a memo to
his boss the very next day. Even 2 years later, Yardley was defending his publication
of secrets in *The American Black Chamber*. In his notes, Friedman appears somewhat, but not really surprised at Yardley's attitude and his comments on the response
to his book, magazine articles, and lectures. "Y acted as though our personal relations wholly unimpaired; most cordial, friendly, and frank. Re his acts in publishing, lecturing, etc. – most unruffled, brazen. Admitted without hesitancy his motives
are merely to support himself and family; no animus or retaliatory motives re his
having been let out. Kept reiterating he had to get money to pay grocery bills."
Yardley also insisted that he had to make a living but that he was now beyond being
a waiter in Denver, where he got his one of his first jobs. Nevertheless, after more
than 15 years in cryptology, he had no other really marketable skills. Yardley did not
think his revealing the work of his Cipher Bureau had been unpatriotic, nor did he
think that he had broken any secrecy oaths. Rather he said the one who had truly
acted unpatriotically was Secretary of State Stimson, who had left the United States
defenseless after shutting the Cipher Bureau. He was also upset with the recent
seizure of his new manuscript *Japanese Diplomatic Secrets* before it was even published. Yardley insisted there were no secrets in the new book and that the book was

---

[50] Theodore M. Hannah, "The Many Lives of Herbert O. Yardley," *NSA Cryptologic Spectrum* 11,
no. 4 (Fall 1981): 5–29, http://www.nsa.gov/public_info/_files/cryptologic_spectrum/many_lives.
pdf, 10.

mostly "hokem." Friedman kept trying to press Yardley on patriotism and betraying his secrecy oath, but Yardley was having none of the ethical arguments that Friedman was making. Friedman does not record all his responses to Yardley's arguments, nor does he say in his notes how they parted.[51]

[51] Friedman, *Notes*.

# Chapter 13
# A Pretty Young Woman in a Pink Dress

By 1931, both of the Friedman's were leading cryptologic organizations in the US government. William had been training his new junior cryptanalysts since April 1930 and putting in place the start of a sophisticated organization in the War Department. With the creation of the Coast Guard Intelligence Office's Cryptanalysis Section in July 1931, Elizebeth Friedman now also had her own team with which to confront drug and alcohol smugglers. Her three cryptanalysts were well into their own training regimen, and Elizebeth was now freer to help the Treasury and Customs agents with the rumrunning cases that resulted from all their work.

While Elizebeth worked with the Coast Guard, she received work and intercepted cryptograms from all six of the Treasury Department's enforcement organizations, the Prohibition Bureau, the Narcotics Bureau, Customs, the Coast Guard, the Internal Revenue Service and the Secret Service.[1]

Over the course of the previous 6 years, Elizebeth's understanding of the code and cipher systems used by the rumrunners had become much clearer while the smuggler's cryptographic systems grew increasingly sophisticated. As Elizebeth said in a 1930 memo, "Some of these are of a complexity never even attempted by any government for its most secret communications."[2]

Early on, the messages she worked on were simple. For example, she decrypted a number of messages in February 1926 for the Prohibition Bureau from rumrunners out of Halifax Nova Scotia. One of the messages from Halifax to an unknown rumrunning ship off the American east coast read

AWJTSSK JQS GBQKWSK LYMSE EJBCG SPEC QPFYEYQD MYHGC PRPYC
    JWKSWE CWI PQTGJW EPFS VBSM AWJEASTCE HJJK.
(signed) BLACKCAM.

---

[1] Jason Fagone, *The Woman Who Smashed Codes*, hardcover (New York, NY: William Morrow, 2017), 134.

[2] David Kahn, *The Codebreakers; The Story of Secret Writing* (New York: Macmillan, 1967), 804.

© The Author(s), under exclusive license to Springer Nature
Switzerland AG 2023
J. F. Dooley, *The Gambler and the Scholars*, History of Computing,
https://doi.org/10.1007/978-3-031-28318-5_13

While looking like gibberish, this message is in a simple mixed-alphabet mono-alphabetic substitution cipher. To find the plaintext, the cryptanalyst must recover the cipher alphabet that was used for the encryption. For a simple cipher such as this one, the cryptanalyst first performs a frequency analysis to try to identify the most commonly used letters in the cryptogram. These letters should match up with the most commonly used letters in English. Building up these equivalents letter by letter, the cryptanalyst can first expose individual words and then the entire message.

For this message, the plain and ciphertext alphabets are:

**PLAIN:**  abcdefghijklmnopqrstuvwxyz

**CIPHER:** P-TKSVHGY-DMLQJA-WECBFR-I-

(Five letters are missing because they do not appear anywhere in the ciphertext.)

Decoded, the message reads "PROCEED ONE HUNDRED MILES SOUTH EAST NAVISINK LIGHT AWAIT ORDERS TRY ANCHOR SAVE FUEL. PROSPECTS GOOD."[3]

The rumrunners quickly moved from simple substitution ciphers to using more complicated enciphered codes, complicating Elizebeth's job considerably. There were many commercial codes and public codes available at the time, and a common technique of the smugglers was to use a commercial code along with a superencipherment. In addition, sometimes numbers were added to each codeword as well.[4] The numbers are called *additives*, and they are used to disguise codewords within a message, making it more difficult for the cryptanalyst to discover the real codeword.

One system used by the rumrunning gang CONEXCO in the early 1930s utilized two different commercial codes and two superencipherments to encode messages. In order to decipher messages in this system, Elizebeth had to perform the following steps:

0. Original message as sent: MJFAK ZYWKB QATYT JSL QATS QXYGX OGTB

1. Decrypt using a mono-alphabetic substitution cipher alphabet to get a mix of plaintext and codewords in a commercial code, the Acme commercial code.

   BARRY OIJYS where and when WINUM fuel

2. Translate the codewords into Acme code numbers, yielding

   08033 53725 where and when 25536 fuel

3. Subtract 1000 from the code numbers

   07033 52725 where and when 24536 fuel

4. Convert the code numbers using the commercial ABC Code, 6th edition yielding the plaintext

   Anchored in harbor where and when are you sending fuel.[5]

---

[3] Fagone, *Smashed*, p. 136.

[4] Katie Letcher Lyle and David Joyner, *Divine Fire: Elizebeth Friedman, Cryptanalyst (The 1910s–1930s)*, (Lexington, KY: CreateSpace Independent Publishing Platform, 2015), 131.

[5] Lyle & Joyner, *Divine Fire*, 132.

In 1933, Elizebeth Friedman served as the star witness in the trial of 23 members of the CONEXCO mafia, which the lead prosecutor in the case, Federal Director of Prohibition Amos Woodcock, called "the most powerful international smuggling syndicate in existence" (Fig. 13.1).

CONEXCO was headquartered in Vancouver, British Columbia, and had extended its operations all up and down the American Pacific coast. The syndicate expanded its operations in 1932 from the Pacific to the Gulf of Mexico, running at least eight rumrunning ships via a clandestine radio transmitter in New Orleans. Over the course of several months, as part of their investigation, Treasury Department

**Fig. 13.1** Artist rendering of Elizebeth Friedman in court.[a] (Washington Evening Star)
[a]Mary Jane Brumley, "Local Matron Decodes Cryptic Messages for Treasury Department," *The Evening Star*, June 5, 1937, sec. Women's Features, chroniclingamerica.loc.gov, Library of Congress, https://chroniclingamerica.loc.gov/data/batches/dlc_1johns_ver01/data/sn83045462/0028060195 0/1937060501/0140.pdf).

agents intercepted a number of messages from the New Orleans hub of CONEXCO and its rumrunning ships in the Gulf. They mailed 32 of these messages to Elizebeth in Washington, and she and her team had decrypted them. Their solutions uncovered many of the details of the operation, including the names of many of the rumrunning ships—*Concorde, Corozal, Fisher Lassie, Rosita,* and *Mavis Barbara*—and how the liquor was off-loaded from the ships, transported via motorboats to small bayou towns in the Mississippi River Delta, and later transshipped via rail north. The messages provided the backbone of the Treasury Department's case against CONEXCO.

On May 2, 1933, Elizebeth was in New Orleans to testify in the trial of 25 members of the CONEXCO syndicate, who had been rounded up by Prohibition Bureau agents, including CONEXCO's man-in-charge in the Gulf, Albert Morrison. Morrison was charged with being the land agent of the CONEXCO scheme and making all the arrangements for smuggling the liquor from British Honduras (now Belize) and Mexico to the United States. His codefendants were all accused of operating the rumrunning boats.[6] All 25 men were in court, along with their lawyers, on the day that Elizebeth testified. They sat in a row, as if they were on the sidelines of a football game, and they switched positions in between witnesses to try to make it difficult for the witnesses to identify them individually.[7]

Elizebeth almost did not get to testify at all because, as she was called, the defense attorneys objected to her testimony on the grounds that cryptanalysis was not a science, so all of her testimony would be opinion, not fact. The presiding judge, Charles Kennamer, overruled their objections, stating that Mrs. Friedman was, in fact, a scientific expert.

Elizebeth took the stand dressed in a pink dress and a hat with a flower pinned to it. The defense attorneys smiled at each other, sure that discrediting a petite woman in a pink dress would be easy. They would not be the first, nor the last, to underestimate Elizebeth Friedman. Lead prosecutor Amos Woodcock started by asking Elizebeth what her occupation was. "Cryptanalyst," she replied. He then asked her what a cryptanalyst did. "A cryptanalyst is a person who analyzes and reads secret communications without the knowledge of the system used," came her reply. Woodcock then proceeded to walk Elizebeth through each of the 32 telegrams and their decryptions that were introduced as evidence. The defense attorneys took turns objecting to each of Elizebeth's responses about the contents of the decrypted cryptograms. They said that no one could possibly decrypt the messages. They accused her of not being able to break the codes, instead receiving the information about the codes from federal agents or informants in the gang. At one point, one of the defense attorneys objected to her testimony on a particular telegram, calling it "incompetent, irrelevant, and immaterial." Finally, irritated, Elizebeth turned to the judge and responded, "I believe I am asked my opinion of the reading of this message? This is not a matter of opinion. There are very few people in the United States, not many it

---

[6] G. Stuart Smith, *A Life in Code: Pioneer Cryptanalyst Elizebeth Smith Friedman,* (Jefferson, NC: McFarland & Company, 2017), 72.

[7] Fagone, *Smashed*, 143–147.

is true, who understand the principle of this science. Any other experts in the United States would find, after proper study, the exact readings I have given these."[8] The judge overruled the objection and the questioning of Elizebeth proceeded.

When the cross-examination started, one of the lead defense attorneys, Walter J. Gex, Sr., tried to get Elizebeth to admit she had not really broken the code.

> Gex: "Before you could properly translate these symbols somebody had to tell you it was symbols in reference to the liquor transportation?"
>
> "Oh, no," Elizebeth replied, innocently. "I might receive symbols related to murder or narcotics."...
>
> Gex: "The same symbols these gentlemen used to mean what you say, whiskey, beer, position, could not have been made up by people in code for transportation of women from Europe?"
>
> ESF: "No, not with the meaning given them here."
>
> Gex: "I know; you gave them the meaning?"
>
> ESF: "No, I did not give them the meaning. The meanings were not created by me and put alongside the code words. I obtained these meanings by scientific analysis. I did not obtain them by any guess work. ...."
>
> "I move that all of the testimony of this lady be stricken out," said another lawyer, Maxwell Slade. The judge overruled him.[9]

Another defense attorney, Edwin H. Grace, tried to raise doubts about Elizebeth's conclusions about the plaintext of certain codewords, claiming that the codeword that translated into "alcohol" could just as easily mean coconuts or bananas. Elizebeth demurred, "Once any particular cipher system is worked out, no doubt can be entertained as to any single word appearing in a sentence....[any other code expert would translate the message] precisely as I have done. It is not a matter of opinion, but a matter of science."[10]

When her ordeal on the witness stand was over for the day, Elizebeth picked up her purse, left the courtroom, and headed back to Washington. Four days later, the trial ended with the conviction of Albert Morrison and another handful of his code-fendants. Morrison was sentenced to 2 years in federal prison and given a stiff fine, but his conviction was appealed. All the while the local and national press found a new prohibition-era heroine. Reporters covering the trial described Elizebeth variously as "a pretty government scrypt-analyst or 'code-reader'," "a pretty middle aged woman," "a pretty young woman with a filly pink dress," and "a pretty little woman who protects the United States."[11] While the articles all intended to be complimentary, Elizebeth was still put out by the mildly sexist and ageist language. She particularly did not like being called a "middle-aged woman." At 40, she certainly did not consider herself a matron.

---

[8] Fagone, *Smashed*, 145.

[9] Fagone, *Smashed*, 146; Anonymous, "USA v. Albert Morrison, et al. (1933) Trial Exhibits and Trial Transcript (Vol. 1 of 4 Volumes)" (Washington, DC: National Archives and Records Administration, 1933), archive.org, https://archive.org/details/usavmorrisonetal1933, 164–166.

[10] Smith, *Life in Code*, 72.

[11] Fagone, *Smashed*, 146.

Elizebeth returned to New Orleans a year later to testify again in Albert Morrison's appeal hearing. Facing off against Edwin Grace, Al Capone's attorney, Elizebeth grew impatient with his attacks on the validity of her science. Once again asked, how she knew which liquor brand names were which, she told the judge she could settle the issue quickly if she had a blackboard. A bailiff found a blackboard in storage and wheeled it into the court. Elizebeth then proceeded to show the jury how the rumrunners' ciphers and codes worked: .

> I was very quickly able to demonstrate the validity of the cipher method which had been used for the names of the liquors in many of the messages because that method was [a] simple mono-alphabetic encipherment. For example, OLD COLONEL has three el's and three o's. I put the words OLD COLONEL on the blackboard in caps and placed beneath the letters their cipher equivalents, thus the three o's were shown in each case to be the identical cipher letter and [the] three el's likewise. E [is] the most frequently appearing letter in English and therefore is usually represented by the letter which appears most often in a frequency table of any mono-alphabetic cipher, was present here only once but there were other names of brands which of course contained one or more appearances of the letter E. … [Scanning the messages in her hand, she then said] My eye was able to catch quickly brand names which contained more than one occurrence [sic] of the letter E and also the word alcohol with el's and o's which, when put upon the blackboard, revealed the same cipher letters as had been used for the el's and o's of the OLD COLONEL. … By this time the defense attornies [sic] were nervously indicating that they had had enough of this black and white proof, that is, the blackboard proof and not black and white whiskey.[12]

She continued until the jurors were nodding their heads and defense attorney Grace was muttering that "this was highly irregular."[13] Once again, the press had a field day with Elizebeth's testimony and performance. One headline read, in all capital letters, "CLASS IN CRYPTOLOGY."

The national press were not the only ones that appreciated Elizebeth's work. Lead prosecutor Woodcock took the opportunity to write to Elizebeth's superiors in the Coast Guard:

> Mrs. Friedman made an unusual impression upon the jury. Her description of the art of deciphering and decoding established in the minds of all her entire competency to testify. It would have been a misfortune of the first magnitude in the prosecution of this case not to have had a witness of Mrs. Friedman's qualifications and personality available.[14]

Elizebeth was now famous, and newspapers, radio stations, and news syndicates all wanted to interview her. All the attention made her uncomfortable, but it was just the beginning.

On October 5, 1933, at Haverstraw, New York, about 40 miles up the Hudson River from its mouth in New York City, the Coast Guard intercepted a small freighter as it worked its way up the river from New York toward Albany. The freighter, named the *Texas Ranger*, was carrying 25,000 cases of liquor to be unloaded in

---

[12] Smith, *Life in Code*, 72–73.

[13] Fagone, *Smashed*, 146.

[14] Elizebeth S. Friedman, "Autobiography of Elizebeth Smith Friedman" (Memoir, Lexington, VA, 1966), George Marshall Foundation Research Library, https://www.marshallfoundation.org/library/wp-content/uploads/sites/16/2015/06/ESFMemoirComplete_opt.pdf, 96–97.

Albany and held there until the end of Prohibition took effect that coming December. It turned out that the freighter was not the *Texas Ranger* at all but a ship of a different name, the *Holmwood*, that the Coast Guard had been watching for at least 3 years.[15]

Elizebeth Friedman and her team in Washington had been following the *Holmwood*'s transmissions since the first radio interception in November 1930 by the New York Intelligence Office of the Coast Guard. The Coast Guard operated a number of stations that monitored rumrunner radio transmissions. Usually, these were in a commercial telegraph code or a cipher but sometimes they were in plain English. Initially, the *Holmwood*'s transmissions were in a digraphic cipher system. In a digraphic cipher, two letters are enciphered at a time rather than just one. The objective here is to disguise the single-letter frequencies of the letters in the substitution cipher. Digraphic cipher systems typically use a rectangular table with a keyword to encrypt and decrypt messages.

Elizebeth and the Coast Guard Intelligence Office in New York kept track of the *Holmwood*'s transmissions from 1930 through 1933. So, in late September 1933, when she began her voyage from Barbados to New York and then up the Hudson, they were ready. Using the encipherment table and code provided by Elizebeth's team, the New York Intelligence Office was able to decrypt the *Holmwood*'s messages as they were transmitted. However, when Coast Guard cutters were sent out into the southern part of New York Harbor to find and board the ship, they could not find the *Holmwood*. It turned out that the *Holmwood* had stopped short of the harbor, changed her flag and painted over her name with the name of a different freighter that was also due in New York, but which had been delayed, the *Texas Ranger*. But then the *Holmwood/Texas Ranger*'s handlers made one mistake, sending one more message that contained the phrase "Stand up the river toward Albany." Radioman First Class B. E. Howell of the New York Intelligence Office intercepted and deciphered the following message at approximately 3:00 p.m. on October 5, using Elizebeth's digraphic table:

> Heave your anchor immediately and get underway. Stand up the river towards Albany.
>    Anchor the boat in good place immediately. Take all men off in one of life boats. Hide the life boat if possible. Come ashore on New York side. Call [undecoded phone number] when you come ashore. PA code.[16]

This was enough to uncover the deception. Howell communicated this to the Coast Guard cutter, which then led to the seizure of the *Holmwood*. Elizebeth Friedman, to ensure that credit for the capture was split between her group in Washington and the New York office, wrote a strong commendation letter for Radioman Howell for his hard work and dedication to service.

In probably her most publicized case, Elizebeth Friedman saved the United States Government approximately $330,000 and a great deal of embarrassment in the *I'm Alone* case. The fast motor-powered sloop *I'm Alone* was built in 1911. She

---

[15] Fagone, *Smashed*, 138.

[16] Smith, *Life in Code*, 77; Lyle & Joyner, *Divine Fire*, 154–155.

had several owners before being sold to a couple of supposed Canadians in 1924, who then entered the liquor smuggling trade in the Gulf of Mexico. The *I'm Alone* made a number of trips from Mexico and Belize to the US Gulf Coast from 1924 to 1929. The Coast Guard knew that the *I'm Alone* was smuggling but was never lucky enough to catch her in the act of picking up or dropping off illegal liquor inside US territorial waters. However, their luck changed in early 1929.

Just before dawn on March 20, 1929, the US Coast Guard cutter *Wolcott* spotted the *I'm Alone* just 10 and a half miles off the coast of Louisiana—within the US territorial waters 12-mile limit. The skipper of the *Wolcott*, Boatswain Frank Paul, sailed up to her and ordered the *I'm Alone* to heave to and prepare to be boarded. Instead, the captain of the *I'm Alone* turned out to sea and sped away. Thus, a more than 2-day chase began across the Gulf of Mexico. Under the doctrine of "hot pursuit," the *Wolcott* radioed the Coast Guard base in New Orleans and headed after the *I'm Alone*. The next day, a second USCG cutter, the *Dexter*, commanded by Boatswain A.W. Powell joined the chase. The Wolcott continued to radio and flag the *I'm Alone*, telling her to heave to. The captain of the *I'm Alone*, John Randell, ignored the messages for a while and then responded that he would shoot if the Coast Guard tried to board his ship. The *Wolcott* and the *Dexter* finally managed to hem the *I'm Alone* in and threw a couple of shots across her bow. Paul crossed over to the schooner and had a more than 1-hour meeting with Captain Randell, who freely admitted he was carrying liquor but refused to be boarded or stopped. According to Boatswain Paul, Randell said "that he would never allow his vessel to be seized by the Coast Guard and that he would permit it to be sunk if necessary."[17]

On the morning of March 23, the commander of the *Dexter* "directed [our] three-inch gun to fire at the *I'm Alone*, instructing my gun crew to hit her in the rigging and on the main deck forward." Randell still refused to stop. Powell ordered his gun crew to continue firing, and at about 8:58 a.m. one shot holed the *I'm Alone* below the water line and she began to sink from the head. The *I'm Alone* sank at 9:03 a.m. One crewman drowned, and the rest, including Captain Randell, were rescued.

Now the case became interesting. The problem with the *I'm Alone* was that the captain and crew claimed they were all Canadians and the ship was a Canadian vessel, while the Americans were sure it was owned by Americans, but sailing out of Nova Scotia. The Canadian government claimed that the sinking of the *I'm Alone*—a Canadian vessel—was not justified and that the Americans had broken a 1924 treaty in which the US promised not to fire on Canadian vessels. They filed a complaint and demanded an apology and $386,000 in reparations and compensation for the crew. The Canadian press vehemently protested the sinking and blamed the Americans for chasing and sinking an innocent Canadian vessel in international waters and killing a Canadian crew member in the process. Relations between the two neighbors sank. The race was on to determine who really owned the *I'm Alone*.

In November 1929, Elizebeth Friedman was sent to Houston, Texas to solve some messages subpoenaed from Western Union in a different smuggling case.

---

[17] Smith, *Life in Code*, 53.

Twenty-seven of these messages originated in the British colony of Belize (British Honduras then) and did not seem to have anything to do with the Houston case but might be related to cases being run out of New Orleans. So Elizebeth stopped off at the Customs Office in New Orleans on her way back to Washington to deliver these now decoded messages. Elizebeth knew that part of each message was encoded using the *Private Supplement* to *Bentley's Complete Phrase Code* but that there were a number of codewords, all seemingly related to either people or goods, that she could not decode without the smugglers' other codebook. Elizebeth did confirm that some of the codewords—notably those that began with W, Y, or Z—were from the *Private Supplement* and were used by the smugglers to name brands and types of liquor, the names of the principals involved in the operation, and amounts of money and liquor in the ships manifest. For example,

> An original message on a Western Union telegram form on January 30, 1929, was a jumble of letters: "MOCANA = NEWYORK (NY) = UGUCK MIOSD EPUJS AFAGS PEJYT USENZ MITEP LPUIS REKRO NY AZ POUDY YIOVB."
> When Elizebeth partially decoded the message, it read: "Belize, January 30, 1929. To MOCANA, New York. Referring to telegram of 29th, 8000 dollars additional required. Total amount 12000 dollars. Shall we pack in sacks YIOVB."[18]

Comparing these messages with others that the Customs investigators had intercepted, Elizebeth was able to begin to make connections, deducing the plaintexts of several words. More codewords related to liquor followed.[19]

The Customs officer in New Orleans, Edson Shamhart, noticed that the dates on the messages corresponded exactly with known sailing and contact dates and known cargo manifests of the *I'm Alone*. Elizebeth and Shamhart quickly made substitutions for many of the unknown codewords. Back in Washington, Elizebeth continued to work on the messages, and Shamhart also continued working in New Orleans on his copies of the messages. Their work confirmed that the *I'm Alone* was smuggling liquor and it pointed to a couple of Americans as the owners of the ship.

One thing that Elizebeth needed to do next was confirm the ports where the *I'm Alone* was sailing from and going to. The port of origin turned out to be fairly easy. "The cable address used was CARNELHA which was easily determined to be a registered cable address for the Melhado Brothers, the foremost suppliers of liquor in the British Honduras area."[20]

Elizebeth and Shamhart had now confirmed the port from which the *I'm Alone* was leaving when she headed allegedly to Bermuda, but really for a rendezvous near New Orleans. Elizebeth had some help with a couple more of the codewords that indicated the *I'm Alone*'s controllers and with whom the ship was in contact.

---

[18] Smith, *Life in Code*, 58; The decrypted messages are from Elizebeth Smith Friedman, "Decoded Messages Used in 'I'm Alone' Smuggling Operations" (Washington, DC: National Archives and Records Administration, 1933), RG26, Entry 297, Box 76, File 8, NARA, https://cryptocellar.org/files/PURPLE_History.pdf

[19] Smith, *Life in Code*, 58.

[20] Smith, *Life in Code*, 57.

"Since my husband was so well known in the world of communication companies," Elizebeth continued, "I asked him to ascertain, if possible, the identities of the New York cable addresses HARFORAN and MOCANA. He learned that both these addresses were used for one Joseph H. Foran, Hotel McAlpine, New York City." The second address, MOCANA, suggested that it had been intended for someone in Montreal.[21]

Shamhart went to New York, looking for Joseph Foran, but could find no hint of him. However, descriptions of Foran given to him led Shamhart to believe that Foran was really a different smuggler, one Dan Hogan who had run afoul of the Customs Office before and was known to operate out of New Orleans from time to time. Hogan also had other aliases, including Daniel Halpern. Shamhart found Hogan's apartment in New York and staked it out. He and his FBI investigators did not have long to wait and soon caught Hogan as he came home. On searching Hogan's New York apartment, police found a car registration in the name of James Clark. It turned out this was "Big Jim" Clark, who was known to the smugglers in New Orleans and who had introduced Hogan as his partner at least once. Captain Randell of the *I'm Alone* also gave up the name of the man in Nova Scotia who gave him his smuggling order, G. J. Hearn of Montreal. All of these men were indicted by a New York grand jury on charges of smuggling. Once this happened one after another, they started to turn on each other and provide the government with more information.

Four years later, a joint American-Canadian arbitration commission was created. After spending over 2 years accumulating evidence, the commission met in Ottawa in 1934 to hear testimony and decide the case. Elizebeth Friedman testified before the commission in Washington about her decryptions in December 1934, escorted by an armed US agent for protection (Fig. 13.2). Once again, on the witness stand, Elizebeth was compelled to give a lesson in cryptanalysis to the members of the commission. And once again, she convinced them that the method of decryption she used and the result that she brought forth was the only correct result for those messages. In addition to Elizebeth's decryptions, the commission was also presented with a sworn affidavit from the now deceased Big Jim Clark that he was one of the owners of the *I'm Alone*, and the testimony of G. J. Hearn that he had been given American dollars by Hogan and another associate to purchase the *I'm Alone* in 1927. The binational commission issued its report in January 1935. They found that the *I'm Alone* was, in fact, owned by Americans but that the sinking was still not justified. They said that the United States should apologize to the Canadian government for the harm done to their sailors and pay an indemnity of $25,000 plus an additional $25,666.50 to compensate the crew of the *I'm Alone*. The American government was happy on both counts and apologized and paid up.[22] Instead of paying nearly $400,000, the United States paid just $50,000, and they won the point that the *I'm Alone* was an American ship involved in smuggling, largely based on Elizebeth Friedman's decryptions.

---

[21] Smith, *Life in Code*, 57.

[22] Smith, *Life in Code*, 52–68; Lyle & Joyner, *Divine Fire*, 133–137.

**Fig. 13.2** Elizebeth Friedman heading for a court appearance, 1934. (U.S. Department of Defense)

Elizebeth continued to be written about in the press and talked about on the new medium of radio. As soon as the *I'm Alone* decision came down, a US newspaper headline blared "MILLIONS ARE SAVED TO NATION BY DECODER." In 1934, she was selected by NBC (National Broadcasting Company) radio correspondent Margaret Santry as one of the first interviewees of a series titled "First Ladies of the Capitol." Elizebeth truly enjoyed this interview. NBC allowed her to bring her children, Barbara, then 10, and John, age 7, to the studio for the recording. Commercial radio was just slightly more than a decade old and was still exciting and interesting to both adults and children. During the interview, Elizebeth admitted that Barbara would send her parents messages in cipher, including while they were onboard ship heading home from the International Radio Telegraph Conference in Madrid. Elizebeth also admitted that Barbara did not want to be a cryptanalyst but instead a dancer.[23]

Her continuing successes eventually led to celebrity status, of which she was leery and eventually weary. Not only were newspaper reporters and columnists giving her complete credit for various solutions, something she thought was completely unfair to all the hard-working Treasury agents and the other members of her Coast Guard team. However, they were also perennially amazed that a woman was outsmarting all these criminal men. Elizebeth much preferred being interviewed by women reporters than men. The only male reporter she said kind words about was

---

[23] Fagone, *Smashed*, 164.

A. H. Williamson of the Vancouver (Canada) *News Herald*. Others she described as "ill-bred," "blaspheming," and "blunderers."[24]

To cap off her weariness with reporters and publicity, in 1937 Elizebeth was profiled in an article in Reader's Digest, titled "Key Woman of the T-Men," in which she is described as the "key woman of codebreaking activities on the crime front" for the Treasury Department.

> She is entrusted with more secrets of the crime world and of federal detection activities than any woman in history. Gang bosses have gone to penitentiaries as a result of her expert efforts. Syndicates have been broken up and millions of dollars worth of outlaw business has been interrupted. Much of her activity is necessarily involved in mystery as deep as that surrounding the Army and Navy code experts. Yet there are definitely "closed" cases on which her work is a matter of public record.[25]

Finally, she had had enough, and in 1938 she wrote to the public relations director of the Treasury Department "requesting that thereafter no one but NO ONE from the world of the press or radio would be given permission to get so far as even an interview with me. … I supplied the Public Relations Treasury Chief with the bare facts of my life and career and told them that they were authorized to use them in any way they deemed essential for the public relations of the department."[26] This, of course, did not stop the stories, but a couple of years later, as the world ground inexorably into war, all this would become silent.

However, attention was not always a bad thing. In June 1938, several months after Elizebeth had wrapped up a high-profile smuggling case, her alma mater, Hillsdale College, awarded Elizebeth an honorary Doctor of Laws degree. As ever, William was her biggest cheerleader. On the day she received her honorary degree, William telegraphed her, "Congratulations, My Darling. Stop. Do you remember me? I'm the man who thinks you're grand. I'm proud as I can be of your renown and well earned crown of Hillsdale's LLD. Stop. Yes, I'm the chump who picked a trump in life's sweet lottery. Yes I'm the man who loves you still—Your doting husband, Bill."[27]

---

[24] Friedman, *Autobiography*, 72.

[25] Leah Stock Helmick, "Key Woman of the T-Men," *Reader's Digest*, September 1937, https://ia800801.us.archive.org/0/items/KeyWomanOfTheTMen/Key%20Woman%20of%20the%20T-men.pdf, 53–55.

[26] Friedman, *Autobiography*, 70.

[27] Smith, *Life in Code*, 100.

# Chapter 14
# One Career After Another

1931 was in many ways a very good year for Herbert Yardley. He published six popular articles in reputable magazines with large circulations, a series of short pieces on solving cryptograms, and his blockbuster book *The American Black Chamber*. He began a book tour, and it turned out he was an entertaining and much-desired speaker. After nearly 2 years of unemployment during the Great Depression, he began making money again and spent it nearly as fast as he made it. On the downside, his sensational revelations about his Cipher Bureau had lost him the friendship and trust of nearly everyone in the American cryptologic community.

Yardley's three articles excerpted from his book were a tremendous hit with the public. Yardley's writing style was energetic and easy to read; he gave many technical details, but nearly all of them were understandable even by people who did not know anything about cryptology. In particular, the first article, on *Secret Inks*, was accessible and thrilling with spies, intrigue, clever English chemists, diabolical Germans, beautiful but fiendish women spies, and desperate searches for chemical agents to develop secret ink messages.

The British publishing house of Faber and Faber bought the UK publishing rights to *The American Black Chamber* that summer and put out a version of the book in September 1931. Later, in 1932, the book was translated into French and published there. The Japanese translation came out in late 1931 and was a sensation there complete with embarrassing denials by the Foreign Ministry and angry editorials by Japanese newspapers. The book sold more than 30,000 copies there. By the end of the 1930s, nearly 60,000 copies of *The American Black Chamber* had been sold worldwide.

Nearly as soon as *The American Black Chamber* was published in June, Yardley engaged an agent and went on a lecture tour, largely in the American East and Midwest. It is not clear whether he made much, if any, money from this tour, but he certainly argued with his agent about expenses and payments fairly constantly. He also kept peppering his literary agent, George Bye, with ideas for new projects and new pieces of writing. To Yardley, while writing was difficult and time-consuming,

© The Author(s), under exclusive license to Springer Nature
Switzerland AG 2023
J. F. Dooley, *The Gambler and the Scholars*, History of Computing,
https://doi.org/10.1007/978-3-031-28318-5_14

it was easier than most other ways he could make a living and as long as he continued to have ideas and was able to sell stories—and as long as the material he had taken from the Cipher Bureau files held out—he could continue to earn money.

Later, in 1931, Yardley published three more nonfiction articles: *Double Crossing America* in October in *Liberty Magazine, Cryptograms and Their Solutions* in the *Saturday Evening Post* in November, and *Are We Giving Away Our State Secrets?* in *Liberty Magazine* in December. *Double Crossing America* and *State Secrets* provided Yardley's most full-throated defense of his publication of *American Black Chamber*, and included his denunciation of the government, and the State Department in particular, for leaving the United States defenseless in the cryptanalytic arena, while all other developed countries were continuing to use and support their own versions of the Black Chamber. By this time, Yardley had been taking a lot of heat from both editorial writers and from his former colleagues in the American cryptographic community for the publication of *The American Black Chamber*, and he was eager to give some back.[1]

In *Are We Giving Away Our State Secrets*, Yardley sets the stage with the fiction that "one of America's leaders" invites him to visit him at his home and talk about Yardley's concerns that the United States is vulnerable to foreign interception and decryption of its diplomatic and military messages. Yardley gives his host a short lesson in pencil-and-paper cryptography, explaining the Playfair cipher and the Bazeries cipher cylinder and how they have both been solved.[2] Yardley then does a very good job with a story about how to design codewords that resist garbling in transmission, echoing the descriptions of unique identifiers in William Friedman's "Alphabetic Chart" patent from 1926.[3] Yardley's host then urges him to write to the State Department and see if an accommodation can be made. Yardley writes, but gets an unsatisfactory response. He surprisingly insists that the only way the State Department can protect its secrets is by using a machine cipher. Claiming to have the design of one, he again offers it to the State Department but is turned down. Yardley ends the article by again extolling the virtues of machine ciphers, something he never seems to have pursued otherwise,

> The whole trend of civilization is toward machinery. So the trend in cryptography should be toward machinery, which means, rapid, accurate, safe communication. With machine ciphers in use, if Secretary Stimson wished to communicate with Ambassador Dawes in London, he could take the elevator to the code room and dictate his message to the cipher-machine operator, who while writing the message on a typewriter, would at the same

---

[1] Herbert O. Yardley, "Are We Giving Away Our State Secrets?," *Liberty Magazine*, December 19, 1931; Herbert O. Yardley, "Cryptograms and Their Solution," *The Saturday Evening Post*, November 21, 1931; Herbert O. Yardley, "Double Crossing America," *Liberty*, October 10, 1931.

[2] The cipher cylinder had been invented by Thomas Jefferson in the early 1800s, reinvented by Bazeries in the 1890s and reinvented again by Parker Hitt in 1914, and improved by Joseph Mauborgne around 1917. By the time Yardley wrote his article, the cylinder was the official US Army tactical cipher device, known as the M-94.

[3] William F. Friedman, Alphabetical Chart, U.S. Patent Office 1,608,509 (Washington, DC, filed January 7, 1926, and issued November 30, 1926).

moment flash the message across the Atlantic. Should England listen in on the wire she would hear nothing but an indecipherable string of letters.[4]

In November and December of 1931, Yardley was also lured out to Hollywood by RKO Pathé pictures with the idea of turning *The American Black Chamber* into a movie. While he loved Hollywood, the star glitter, and the Southern California weather, Yardley was quickly disillusioned. Toward the end of November, he wrote to his agent, George Bye, "Studio is cockeyed. Asked for a love story now they don't want a love story they want a spy story with cryptography. I see what they do not see. Cryptography no good unless I write dialogue. I'll be leaving in two weeks but they will have to have me to make cryptographic pictures successful. … I'm licked unless you can impress them with fact am under contract for lectures, etc. I'm the key to situation. Sounds egotistical but am reporting facts. Today I told them to go to h and they like me for it. Three weeks and nothing done. Have never known such a cockeyed situation."

Bye told him several weeks later (and just before Yardley's contract with RKO was up) "I am terribly afraid you are getting deeper and deeper into some kind of a bad muddle… The lecture tour will help sell more books, and it would keep you in the public eye. In Hollywood you are buried deeper than you will be when you solve the greatest cryptogram of all."[5] Yardley finally broke free of RKO and resumed his lecture tour in January 1932. His tour would take him around the country through August.

Around this same time period, Yardley came up with yet another idea for quick cash—Yardleygrams. Sometime in the fall of 1931, he convinced *Liberty Magazine* to let him write a regular column of short mystery and spy stories that all had a mystery cipher message as the hook. Hints would be given, and the solution would be in an appendix at the end of the column. Dubbed *Yardleygrams*, the column started running at the end of December 1931—the week after his *State Secrets* article appeared. The column ran weekly until 05 March 1932 and again from May through August 1933 (Fig. 14.1).

It was a hit, and Yardley then took the first set of columns and had them published as a book with the same name by Bobbs-Merrill later in the summer of 1932. The British publisher Hutchinson & Co. published a version under the title *Ciphergrams* in the fall of 1932. However, Yardley himself was too busy to actually rework the columns and write the book, so he hired his former neighbor from Jackson Heights, Queens, the AT&T engineer Clem Koukul, to ghostwrite the 190-page book (Fig. 14.2). The book starts with a short introduction by the fictional Alan Crossle, a former cryptanalyst in Yardley's Black Chamber who is giving lessons in cryptology to his young nephew. Crossle drops by his nephew's home of an evening and tells him a story of espionage, the solution of which requires them to solve a cipher message. Crossle explains the type of cipher to his nephew and how to solve

---

[4] Yardley, *State Secrets*, 13.

[5] David Kahn, *The Reader of Gentlemen's Mail: Herbert O. Yardley and the Birth of American Codebreaking* (New Haven: Yale University Press, 2004), 144–145.

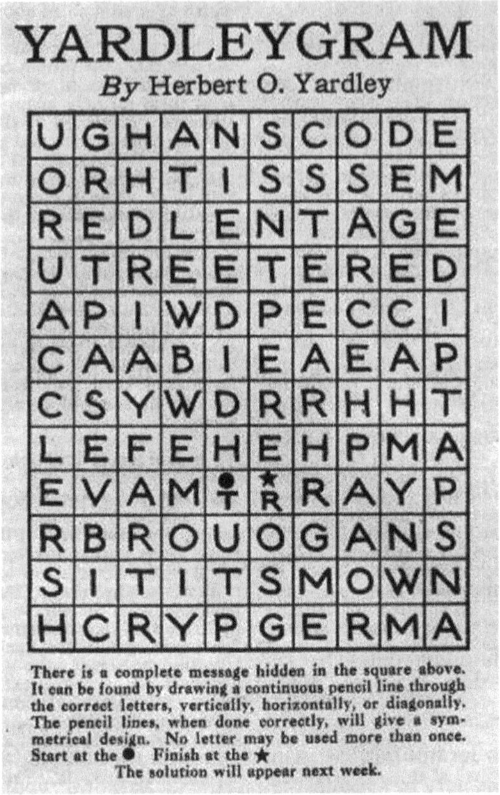
YARDLEYGRAM

*By* Herbert O. Yardley

| | | | | | | | | | |
|---|---|---|---|---|---|---|---|---|---|
| U | G | H | A | N | S | C | O | D | E |
| O | R | H | T | I | S | S | S | E | M |
| R | E | D | L | E | N | T | A | G | E |
| U | T | R | E | E | T | E | R | E | D |
| A | P | I | W | D | P | E | C | C | I |
| C | A | A | B | I | E | A | E | A | P |
| C | S | Y | W | D | R | R | H | H | T |
| L | E | F | E | H | E | H | P | M | A |
| E | V | A | M | ● T | ★ R | R | A | Y | P |
| R | B | R | O | U | O | G | A | N | S |
| S | I | T | I | T | S | M | O | W | N |
| H | C | R | Y | P | G | E | R | M | A |

There is a complete message hidden in the square above. It can be found by drawing a continuous pencil line through the correct letters, vertically, horizontally, or diagonally. The pencil lines, when done correctly, will give a symmetrical design. No letter may be used more than once. Start at the ● Finish at the ★

The solution will appear next week.

**Fig. 14.1** A sample Yardleygrams puzzle from *Liberty Magazine*, July 1933. (Courtesy of Richard Brisson)

it, leaving the actual solution to the boy. Unfortunately, the book was not much of a success, and Bobbs-Merrill never put out a second printing. Like all good ghostwriters, Koukul's name appears nowhere in the book. This will not be the last time that Yardley has his work done by a ghostwriter.[6]

During this period, Yardley was never short of ideas for new projects. In the fall of 1931, he had an idea for another book project, a sequel to *The American Black Chamber*. Yardley was still in possession of hundreds of decoded Japanese Foreign Ministry messages from the 1921–1922 period of the Washington Naval Conference. His next idea was to produce a more comprehensive look at the Naval Conference and the negotiations between the United States, Great Britain, and Japan by publishing these decoded messages with commentary to set them into the context of the conference. However, between his lecture tour, his magazine writing projects and the lure of Hollywood he didn't want to do the actual work of creating the new book. He needed a ghostwriter again.

[6] Kahn, *ROGM*, 140; Herbert O. Yardley, *Yardleygrams*, (Indianapolis, IN: Bobbs-Merrill Company Publishers, 1932).

**Fig. 14.2** Cover of the *Yardleygrams* book 1932. (Author's photo from his collection)

**Fig. 14.2** Cover of the *Yardleygrams* book 1932. (Author's photo from his collection)

In October 1931, he found one in the form of Marie Stuart Klooz, a journalist who had graduated from Sweet Briar College in rural Virginia in 1923 and had spent several years working for various newspapers and was now working as a freelance journalist and writer. Ms. Klooz had the reputation of being a good and particularly fast writer. Klooz and Yardley entered into an agreement, and he sent her all the decrypted Japanese messages that he had stored in the Bobbs-Merrill vault (probably for plausible deniability if the government ever came looking for them). Over the course of about 7 months, Marie Klooz created a slightly over 1000 page book that they both agreed would be called *Japanese Diplomatic Secrets* and delivered it to Yardley in late May 1932. David Kahn summarizes the book correctly and succinctly, "It is a bore. The book consists of hundreds of intercepted Japanese diplomatic dispatches with scraps of connecting text—impersonal, technical, dry. Moreover, Klooz's prose is dreary: her first chapter title is 'Who Killed Cock Robin?'… Marie Klooz was not the writer Yardley was."[7]

By the late summer of 1932, there were hints in the air in Washington that Herbert Yardley was writing another book, similar in content to *The American Black Chamber*. To try and avoid any more unpleasantness with his former colleagues and bosses in the government, Yardley had Marie Klooz put her name on the title page as the author of the new book. Nobody was fooled, however, mostly because the

---

[7] Kahn, *ROGM*, 159.

idea that a 30-year-old freelance journalist who had still been in college during the Naval Conference had acquired a raft of Japanese diplomatic telegrams, decoded them, and then wrote a scholarly treatise on them was just not to be believed. Despite the transparency of his ruse, Yardley and George Bye submitted a treatment of *Japanese Diplomatic Secrets* to Bobbs-Merrill. D.L. Chambers, the chief editor at Bobbs-Merrill, turned down the book in just 2 weeks, reasoning correctly that another book of this stripe by Yardley was just inviting more trouble with the government. Chambers suggested on August 1, 1932 that Yardley offer the book to a New York publisher instead. Unbeknownst to Bye or Yardley, Chambers also notified Nugent Dodds, the Assistant Attorney General about the new book.[8] Bye and Yardley then offered the book treatment to Macmillan, and they agreed to consider it. However, the publisher, George Brett, the heir to the Macmillan publishing empire and president of the company, ran the treatment by friends in the State and War Departments first—without telling either Bye or Yardley—and the government people were very alarmed. In particular, the State Department strenuously objected to the publication of the book. At this time, the Japanese were invading Manchuria, the Americans were trying to extend the Four Power Treaty that limited Japan's Navy, the Japanese military was expanding its influence in the Imperial government, and the Japanese press was becoming increasingly anti-American. A book with several hundred decrypted Japanese Foreign Ministry telegrams in it was sure to blow the lid off Japanese-American relations. The State Department's senior advisor on Japan wrote to his boss on 12 September "that, in view of the state of excitement which apparently prevails in Japanese public opinion now, characterized by fear or enmity toward the United States, every possible effort should be made to prevent the appearance of this book."[9] The Departments of War and State, bringing in the Justice Department as well, put their heads together to try to figure out a way to quash Yardley's book.

First out of the gate was the War Department. On the evening of September 16, 1932, three US Army officers, led by Colonel Oliver P. Robinson, knocked on Herbert Yardley's front door in Worthington, Indiana. Without even a polite hello, Colonel Robinson began to read the order that he had received earlier that day from the War Department

> The Secretary of War is informed and believes that you have in your possession and under your control diverse original documents that came into your possession during the time that you were an employee of the United States Government in connection with the Military Intelligence activities of the War Department, including those certain documents, reproductions of which are set forth in a book written by you entitled The American Black Chamber between pages numbered 48 and 49, and 168 and 169.
>
> The Secretary of War has also been advised that you have within your possession and under your control diverse other original documents belonging to the United States made and obtained by you while you were connected with the United States Government in the capacity mentioned above.

---

[8] James Bamford, *The Puzzle Palace: Inside the National Security Agency, America's Most Secret Intelligence Organization* (New York: Houghton-Mifflin, 1982), 38.

[9] Kahn, *ROGM*, 159.

It is, therefore, demanded of you that you deliver to the Adjutant General, United States Army, War Department, Washington, D.C., which officer is designated to receive such delivery, all such documents or copies of documents hereinabove described by reason of the relation of such documents and copies of documents to the National Defense, and that you refrain from making or causing to be made any copies thereof any kind or nature whatsoever.[10]

The surprised Yardley first tried to bluff his way out of the situation by assuring them that he was out of the exposé business. He then said, "I have no documents that could injure the strength of the U.S. Government," and continuing, his temper now rising, "I cannot understand why the U.S. Government should attempt to embarrass me."[11] The Army officers left Yardley's door empty handed. Yardley's protestations were technically correct; he no longer had any Japanese diplomatic messages in his possession. Marie Stuart Klooz had them. However, Yardley, of course, did not volunteer that information.

Four months later, the next attempt to muzzle Yardley was an idea that seemed to emerge out of the Justice Department in collaboration with State. What they came up with was edging up to the limit of current law but had the possibility of standing up in court. On Thursday, February 16, 1933, George Bye dropped by the Macmillan company's offices in New York and handed over the complete manuscript of *Japanese Diplomatic Secrets* to George Brett. Brett was allegedly going to have Macmillan's editorial team read the manuscript and give Bye a final decision by the following Tuesday when Herbert Yardley would be in town. Instead, Brett promptly gave the manuscript to Assistant US Attorney for New York Thomas Dewey. Dewey wanted to have the War and State Departments look over the final manuscript to see how to proceed, but with only a few days before Yardley was to be in New York, he didn't have the time to get the manuscript from New York to Washington, have it reviewed, and get it back to New York before the following Tuesday. So instead, on Monday, February 20, Dewey had US Marshalls escort both George Brett and George Bye to the US Federal Courthouse and had them testify about the book to the sitting federal grand jury. The grand jury decided to impound the manuscript under the provisions of the Espionage Act of 1917 and promptly sent it off to Washington. Despite the fact that *The American Black Chamber* also included copies of decrypted Japanese diplomatic telegrams, it was never impounded. The seizure of *Japanese Diplomatic Secrets* was the first, and thus far, only, time that a manuscript was impounded by the government of the United States in order to prevent publication. The manuscript was classified as secret and not declassified until 1979 and not released until 1982, and that release required a Freedom of Information Act (FOIA) request.

However, even the seizure of the manuscript did not guarantee that Yardley and Bye would not be able to get it back and publish the book anyway. More had to be done. The next step that the diplomats at the State Department took was to encourage Congress, specifically Congressman Hatton Sumners, the chair of the House

---

[10] Bamford, *Puzzle Palace*, 39.

[11] Bamford, *Puzzle Palace*, 40.

Judiciary Committee, to create a new law that would outlaw the publication of secret government documents. Called H.R. 4220 and named "For the Protection of Government Records" Act, it was introduced into the House on March 27, 1933.[12]

The House debated the bill on April 3 and passed it largely unchanged the same day. An uproar immediately ensued as the members of the press and some members of Congress presumed that this bill would prevent them from doing their jobs. Nevertheless, the bill proceeded to the Senate for discussion and approval. The Senate Foreign Relations committee took the complaints into account and completely rewrote the bill but kept its intended purpose—to prevent Yardley's book from being published. The new Senate bill was brought to the floor and debated on May 10, 1933. It received a raucous, if polite, reception. The high point of the debate was the oration of the Republican senator from California, Hiram Johnson, who cut through the State Department's obfuscation and got to the heart of the matter

> Mr. Yardley published a book called "The Black Chamber." In that book he purported to set forth certain despatches that had come from the Japanese during the Disarmament Conference in 1922. ... Yardley committed his offense against good taste, against every rule that related to fiduciary relations that we can suggest. I have nothing but indignation for that sort of act upon any man's part, and no sympathy whatsoever with him. ... The proposed statute is one made for a particular and specific case. Statutes of that sort are always doubtful. Sometimes they are necessary, I am willing to concede; ... We may be striking at the very fundamentals that we would preserve in this country untouched and unharmed.[13]

Regardless of Senator Johnson's objections, the new bill was passed that day. Since the House and Senate bills differed, a conference committee was formed, and the House members agreed to keep the Senate's version. On June 7, the Senate approved the amended version, and the House did the same on the next day. The full text of the bill that President Franklin Roosevelt signed on June 10 as Public Law 37 is:

> Whoever, by virtue of his employment by the United States, obtains from another or has or has had custody of or access to, any official diplomatic code or any matter prepared in any such code, or which purports to have been prepared in any such code, and without authorization or competent authority, willfully publishes or furnishes to another any such code or matter, or any matter which was obtained while in the process of transmission between any foreign government and its diplomatic mission in the United States, shall be fined $10,000 under this title or imprisoned not more than ten years, or both.[14]

This bill remains as a Public Law, now called Title 18, Section 952, to the current day, having been slightly amended in 1948 and 1994.[15]

---

[12] Kahn, *ROGM*, 163.

[13] Kahn, *ROGM*, 165–168.

[14] "An Act for the Protection of Government Records," 18 U.S. Code § 952, Diplomatic Codes and Correspondence (1933), https://www.law.cornell.edu/uscode/text/18/952. Updated in 1948 and 1994.

[15] *Japanese Diplomatic Secrets* was finally released as a CD created by Cmdr. Emil H. Levine in 2001. No one tried to get the more than 1000-page book published. Neither Yardley nor Bye ever tried to get the original manuscript back from the government.

Despite the setback caused by the suppression of *Japanese Diplomatic Secrets*, 1933 turned out to be another good year for Herbert Yardley. Taking a break from his new writing career, early in 1933 while still in Worthington, Yardley started developing two secret ink products, one for a children's game and one for advertisers, and began selling ink, developer, and advertising paper. Soon, he had several employees and a local partner, a young man named Virgil Vandeventer. Near the end of April 1933, Yardley cut his hand and shortly thereafter developed a severe infection, ending up in the hospital. Things went from bad to worse, and finally, he was told he must have the second finger of his right hand amputated. This happened on May 21. The operation and Yardley's recovery were both successes, but now Yardley's usual cash flow problems became acute as he needed money to pay the hospital and doctor's bills. Yardley finally sold the secret ink business to Vandeventer to pay his bills and moved on yet again.[16] He continued to give the occasional lecture on his book, and from May 27 through August 12, 1933, he wrote another series of *Yardleygram* columns for Liberty Magazine.

In May 1933, George Bye sold two of Yardley's new short stories to Liberty Magazine, and on December 30, the first short story was published. *The Beautiful Secret Agent* introduced his new hero Nathaniel Greenleaf, modeled after Yardley's image of himself. Even for a first effort at short fiction, this was a truly bad story. The dialogue does not flow well, the story line is thin and obvious, and characters are introduced willy-nilly and not developed well. The beautiful secret agent is a spy for the Germans who is shot when her usefulness is over. She is saved by Greenleaf, and in the end, when the real spy and assassin are exposed, she is discovered to be a double agent, working for the Americans. From her hospital bed, she also wants to date Greenleaf. The plot involves Greenleaf discovering a hidden secret ink message and overnight identifying the type of ink and coming up with a developer from scratch, something neither the British nor the Americans ever did during World War I. He also solves a written cryptogram just magically off the top of his head. Luckily for Yardley, his mastery of the short fiction form improved significantly in his later short stories.[17]

Yardley's next short story appeared in the magazine *Detective Fiction Weekly* in February 1934. *The Commissioner Turns Cryptographer* is a much better effort than his first story, mostly because the story is largely about straight cryptanalysis. The story also has the hero Nathaniel Greenleaf, now identified as the chief of the American Black Chamber, the job that Yardley himself had in the 1920s. In this story, Greenleaf helps his friend, the Washington, DC Police Commissioner, solve what at first appeared to be a double suicide, but which turns out to be a double murder instead. Greenleaf initially gets the decryptions of an alleged suicide note and a second note between two lovers correct, but he misses a couple of subtle differences in the cipher alphabets of the mono-alphabetic ciphers that point toward murder and away from suicide. Once he discovers his mistake, it takes him no time

---

[16] Kahn, *ROGM*, p. 146–147.

[17] Herbert O. Yardley, "The Beautiful Secret Agent," *Liberty*, December 30, 1933.

at all to alert his friend the Commissioner and for the two of them to confront the murderer, who promptly confesses. Greenleaf insists that the Commissioner must take credit for the cryptogram solutions and the solution of the murder to preserve Greenleaf's own identity. This story sets a pattern for much of Yardley's fiction, both short and long. His heroes, mostly Nathaniel Greenleaf, are embodiments of the dashing tall, rakish, personable, and handsome cryptologic genius that Yardley wished himself to be. All of his heroes are Yardley.[18]

April 1934 was a busy month for Yardley. He had a nonfiction essay *Spies Inside Our Gates* published in the Washington *Sunday Sun Magazine* and the *New York Herald Tribune Magazine*, his short story, *H-27 – The Blonde Woman from Antwerp* appeared, and his first novel, *The Blonde Countess*, published by Longmans, Green, & Company appeared[19] (Fig. 14.3).

In *H-27*, Yardley improves his writing yet again. Set in April 1918, just a year after the United States entered World War I, the story is concerned with the sinking of an increasing number of American transports by German U-boats. Since only the President and the British Prime Minister know the exact schedule and rendezvous locations of the transports, there must be a German spy involved. The blonde woman from Antwerp is that spy, and it is Nathaniel Greenleaf's job to catch her. Yardley confuses his spy with a real woman known as Fraulein Doktor. Elsbeth Schragmuller earned her Ph.D. in political science from the University of Freiburg, one of the first German women to earn a Ph.D. During World War I, she joined German military intelligence (Abteilung IIIb) and was head of its spy school in Antwerp. Her most common nickname was Fraulein Doktor. She is said to be the person who betrayed Mata Hari to the French. In Yardley's story, she is a beautiful blonde German spy who is the center of the plot to obtain the American transports rendezvous dates and locations. The Germans changed their cipher system, and Greenleaf has been stumped for weeks. Greenleaf meets with the President to talk about the case, and when given the details of the latest attack on an American transport convoy has an epiphany and goes into a long description of the new German cipher for the President. Yardley does a very good job of explaining the cipher—a simplified version of the German ADFGVX cipher, which is a substitution cipher followed by a transposition. Greenleaf's explanation is easily understood and sensible, but aside from the fact that the cipher has been broken, it really has nothing else to do with the story line. Greenleaf and his team set a trap for the German spy and catch her in the act of stealing the original text of the cipher messages. Confronted with the proof of her espionage activities, the beautiful blonde from Antwerp takes a cyanide capsule and dies in Greenleaf's arms, muttering "c'est la guerre."[20]

---

[18] Herbert O. Yardley, "The Commissioner Turns Cryptographer," *Detective Fiction Weekly*, February 17, 1934.

[19] Herbert O. Yardley, "Spies Inside Our Gates." *Sunday Washington Star Magazine*, April 8, 1934; Herbert O. Yardley, "H-27, The Blonde Woman from Antwerp." *Liberty Magazine*, April 21, 1934; Herbert O. Yardley, *The Blonde Countess*, (New York: Longmans, Green and Company, 1934).

[20] Yardley, *H-27*.

**Fig. 14.3** The cover for
Yardley's first novel, *The
Blonde Countess*.
(Author's photo from his
collection)

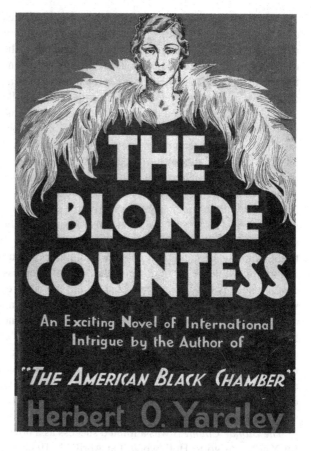

Yardley's real break-out work of fiction is his first novel, *The Blonde Countess*. Although only Yardley's name appears on the title page, his English instructor from the University of Chicago, Carl Grabo, wrote the majority of the book. Grabo was an associate professor of English at Chicago, having been there since 1907. Yardley had signed up for a correspondence course from Grabo in the mid-19-teens but never finished it. He was, however, influenced by two of Grabo's books, *The Art of the Short Story* from 1913 and *The Technique of the Novel*, published in 1928. The ideas in *The Blonde Countess*, the cryptography, details about espionage, etc., all bear Yardley's signature, but the flow of the narrative, the references to literature and music, and the writing style suggest that Grabo wrote much of the book.[21] *The Blonde Countess* takes many of its elements from *H-27*. In this novel, the spy is J-37 and is a blonde woman, married to the Swedish ambassador, a count, hence the novel's name. Nathaniel Greenleaf now heads a much larger Black Chamber

---

[21] John F. Dooley and Yvonne I. Ramirez, "Who Wrote The Blonde Countess? A Stylometric Analysis of Herbert O. Yardley's Fiction," *Cryptologia* 33, no. 2 (2009): 108–17; Kahn, *ROGM*, 152–153.

organization, and the other main protagonist is his female secretary, Joel Carter. In the story, Greenleaf is desperately trying to decrypt a new German cipher, all the while looking for J-37, who is communicating with her German handlers using messages in secret ink and is about to send them the rendezvous coordinates of the first large convoy of American infantry transports heading to France. The story flows very well, a tribute to Grabo's writing skill. Yardley clearly adds the crypto-logic elements, with good descriptions of secret inks and laying bare the means of their solution, including the use of the iodine vapor test to detect secret ink messages. While these techniques may have been top secret during the war, 16 years later, all these techniques have been in the popular press, several of them revealed by Yardley himself. Greenleaf also spends a goodly amount of time on the German cipher, which it turns out is another watered-down version of the German ADFGVX cipher, but with just a cipher square used for substitution and with no added trans-position step. This should make the cipher system easy for any cryptanalytic profes-sional to solve, but Greenleaf is made to struggle with it for weeks and weeks to add to the dramatic element, no doubt. His solution, of course, comes in a moment of inspiration while he is bemoaning the lack of progress on the cipher. Character development is the weakest element of the novel. Greenleaf's character and his motivations, particularly with the two strong women in the novel, are mostly obscure, and in many scenes, he is largely emotionless. Joel Carter vacillates between admiration for and attraction to Greenleaf and exasperation at his indiffer-ence to her, but otherwise is herself pretty emotionless. J-37, the Countess, is also an enigma. She and Greenleaf spar with each other, but the reader is frustrated in trying to really tease out their relationship—even after Greenleaf explains it to one of his Black Chamber agents. Overall, as Kahn puts it, the book is a "pot-boiler," something Yardley put out to make a living.[22]

*The Blonde Countess* was a limited success as a novel, but it led to another offer for Yardley to go to Hollywood. On April 11, 1934, MGM offered to buy movie rights to both *The American Black Chamber* and *The Blonde Countess* and to employ Yardley as screenwriter for 10 weeks. Yardley accepted MGM's offer for both the rights to the two books and for employment as a screenwriter 3 days later. He anticipated working on a screenplay for *The Blonde Countess*. Part of his arrangement with MGM was to be reimbursed for his travel expenses out to California. He booked a train ticket and was in Hollywood by April 19, starting work at MGM.

He was initially put to work on a film titled *Stamboul Quest*, which purported to be based on the work of Fraulein Doktor and which has nothing to do with either of Yardley's two books. Yardley starts as a fact checker for the screenplay, but that did not pan out because the producer did not want to change the script based on facts.[23]

Yardley then started working on a screenplay based on *The Blonde Countess*. Several other screenwriters and "treatments" later, and with the producer and other

---

[22] Kahn, *ROGM*, 153.

[23] *Samboul Quest* was released in July 1934, starring Myrna Loy and George Brett.

writers ignoring Yardley's suggestions, the studio started work on a movie titled *Rendezvous*—which name was suggested by Yardley and which also has no relation to either *The American Black Chamber* or *The Blonde Countess* beyond the fact that the movie takes place during World War I and involves cryptography and German spies.[24] Despite the fact that the movie says "Based on *The American Black Chamber* by Major Herbert O. Yardley," Yardley really had nothing to do with it, except for posing for a couple of publicity pictures (Fig. 14.4). All his story ideas, his information on codes and ciphers, and his script treatments were ignored by the new screenwriters and director. The movie, starring William Powell and Rosalind Russell, was a success when released, with the *New York Times* reviewer calling it "a lively and amusing melodrama."[25]

During the summer of 1934, Yardley went back to Worthington to pick up his wife Hazel and son Jack and drove back to Hollywood with them. Once again, he really liked California, although the movie industry was driving him crazy. "I like the climate and I like the work, but I doubt if I could stick at it for it is a political game and I'm not very diplomatic. I usually say what I think and that is dangerous. Anyway it's swell while it lasts."[26] He also took the time to continue his lecturing, giving a well-received talk at the Los Angeles Athletic Club in late August 1934.

**Fig. 14.4** Herbert Yardley and Rosalind Russell on the set of *Rendezvous*, 1935. (National Cryptologic Museum Library)

---

[24] *Rendezvous* was released in October 1935 and starred William Powell and Rosalind Russell.

[25] Andre Sennewald, "William Powell as the Star of 'Rendezvous,' a Spy Melodrama Now at the Capitol Theatre.," *New York Times*, October 26, 1935, sec. Entertainment, https://timesmachine.nytimes.com/timesmachine/1935/10/26/97147825.html?pageNumber=12

[26] Kahn, *ROGM*, 176.

Following the success of *The Blonde Countess*, Yardley was emboldened to write another book right away and thought he could go it alone this time. In June 1934, he submitted to his agent, George Bye, a novel titled *Red Sun of Nippon*. Unfortunately, an overconfident Yardley was the main author of this novel, and it shows. *Red Sun* is noticeably worse than *The Blonde Countess* in almost every way. David Kahn calls it "overplotted" and "filled with events that would never happen." He also thinks that while Yardley's prose in *The American Black Chamber* "flowed wonderfully," his crack at writing fiction without the help of a collaborator showed that his writing style had deserted him in this novel.[27] Set in late 1932 and into early 1933, it tells the story of a young half-American, half-Chinese woman who is forced to spy for Japan. Torn between the two cultures of her birth, she yearns to have East and West better understand each other and works for more cultural enlightenment on both sides. However, she is forced by her mother and Japanese tutor to report on all her encounters with Americans, and especially the man she loves, an American diplomat named Bruce Caldwell. Rather than spy on her lover, she breaks up with him but is still under a cloud of suspicion. Nathaniel Greenleaf, now a former government employee, eccentric bachelor (evidently his attraction to Joel Carter in *The Blonde Countess* did not work out), and private counterespionage master, is once again our hero and solves a Japanese code, with Caldwell using an idea that Yardley had while he was trying to break a new Japanese diplomatic code in 1921: Greenleaf plants a fake message and name in a message that the Japanese decipher and then re-encipher in their own code, giving Greenleaf a crib to use to help break the code. Unfortunately, this is all we see of the Japanese code or Greenleaf's efforts to decipher it, although there are also several instances of secret ink messages and their development in the novel. Greenleaf's decipherment enables the young diplomat to prevent a war between China and Japan that would have dragged in the United States and to be reunited with his girlfriend, who finally accepts her dual heritage and agrees to marry him. Greenleaf, throwing over his bachelorhood, plans to marry Caldwell's attractive and feisty sister.

A fascinating scene in the novel occurs when Greenleaf and Caldwell encounter the Secretary of State—named Jimson by Yardley, in a thinly veiled reference to Secretary of State Stimson who closed the Black Chamber, on their way to a meeting with the President to reveal the plot by a now deceased Under Secretary of State to foment an American-Japanese war:

> A shocked Secretary of State met them at the White House at the appointed time. Even the Government can move fast on occasion, and the official-minded Jimson had for once been stung to impetuous action. Bruce had needed to utter but a few sentences to galvanize him.
>
> "The President will see us at once," said the Secretary. "What you have said is incredible. I cannot believe it."
>
> "Nevertheless it is true," said Bruce.
>
> "But what," said the Secretary stiffly, as he stroked his beard, "has Mr. Greenleaf to do with it?"

---

[27] Kahn, *ROGM*, 153–154.

He cast a venomous glance at Greenleaf, who smiled benignly in reply. The thanks due to saviors of their country seemed to be slow in coming.

> "It was Mr. Greenleaf who so greatly assisted me in getting the facts."
> "And what is Mr. Greenleaf's official position?" the Secretary asked icily.
> "That of a man who loves his country and places its interests before his own," Bruce retorted.
> The Secretary grew slightly pink and then pale.[28]

Even 5 years after the Black Chamber's closing, Yardley is apparently still annoyed with Henry Stimson and is still defending his decision to publish *The American Black Chamber* as "a man who loves his country and places its interests before his own."

Yardley continued to pour out ideas for new projects. In the fall of 1934, he hooked up with D. Thomas Curtin, who had been a war correspondent and journalist and who was now writing for radio shows in New York. He and Curtin came up with the idea for a radio show titled *Stories of the Black Chamber* that, after assuaging some doubts by both the War Department and their advertising agency, was broadcast on the NBC network. Curtin and Yardley even hired Dr. Charles J. Mendelsohn as a "consulting expert" to ensure that the details of codes and ciphers in the radio plays were accurate. They probably chose Mendelsohn for two reasons: first, Yardley knew him well—they had worked together in both MI-8 and the Cipher Bureau, and second, Mendelsohn lived in New York, so he was easily available should Tom Curtin have any questions. The show ran on 21 different NBC stations nationwide in three consecutive stories of 21 episodes each on Monday, Wednesday, and Friday during the winter, spring, and early summer of 1935.[29] Curtin made sure the show was professionally produced and slick. Each episode ended with a cliff-hanger. Yardley supplied many of the ideas and all the information on codes and ciphers, and Curtin produced and wrote all the episodes. Yardley and Curtin had to collaborate across the country, as Herbert was still in Hollywood and Curtin was running things in New York. Over the course of their partnership, they developed mutual respect and grew to become very good friends. One interesting story about their working relationship is told by Curtin in a 1959 interview,

> But the big pay-off came one night after we decided we must go into a long conference. Renewals were coming up.
> "I can't take time off this movie to go to New York," said Herbert.
> "And I can't leave three shows a week to go out to Hollywood," said I.
> We even tried to figure a point half way. Finally we agreed that we'd take a weekend to fly at other fellows side of the nation on Saturday night—and back again Monday morning.
> "How can we decide which of us goes?" I said.
> "Let's match coins," answered Herb. "I'm matching you, Tom. Got a coin?"
> "A quarter," I answered, beginning to breathe hard.
> "Same, a quarter," from Herb.
> Clank, down went mine on the table. "Heads," I said.

---

[28] Herbert O. Yardley, *Red Sun of Nippon*, (New York: A. L. Burt Company, 1934), 157.

[29] "Stories of the Black Chamber," *Stories of the Black Chamber* (New York, NY: NBC, January 21, 1935).

Clank over the wires from 3,000 miles away.

"Hell, tails. All right, Tom. I'll be at your home Saturday evening. Will fly back Sunday night. O.K.?"

"O.K." I agreed and hung up.

A simple incident, but it endeared me to Herbert Yardley more than ever. Calling the shot he could have cheated. But that wouldn't have been Yardley.[30]

By March 1937, Herbert, Hazel, and Jack were back in Queens, New York. However, after all the tumult of California things weren't going well for the Yardleys and by October of that year Herbert and Hazel were legally separated and Hazel and Jack had moved back to Worthington. Hazel got her old job back as a librarian at the Worthington Library. Herbert hardly ever visited Worthington after this, and he was by and large an absent parent to Jack, who was 12 by this time. By early 1938, Herbert was again working in real estate as a broker in Queens, and he was living with Edna Ramsier in Hasbrouck Heights, New Jersey.

After *The Blonde Countess* and *Red Sun of Nippon*, Yardley continued to try long-form fiction. In 1937, he produced a new novel titled *Shadows in Washington* in just 8 weeks. Written again without a ghostwriter, it is Yardley's only novel that does not include any cryptology or secret inks. Not that they would have helped. Just as in *Red Sun*, Yardley's exciting style of writing nonfiction deserts him again in *Shadows*, beginning with the first paragraph of Chapter 1:

For an hour now he had watched the lights and shadows cast by the flickering embers play on the flushed face of the slender girl in a blue velvet negligee lying asleep on the sofa. He was putting off what he knew was an evil task. But it was one none the less imperative—if he were ever to discover the mystery that surrounded her employer and her secret associates. It scarcely seemed credible that so lovely a creature could be guilty of intrigue if not of actual crime. But lovely or not Larry felt sure that it must be true.

The story is about a journalist, Larry Moore, and his investigations into a freelance spy ring. This spy ring searches out government secrets and then sells them to the highest bidder. They are not patriots and do not represent any particular country; they are interested in money. One improbable scene and accident follows after another. Larry bumbles his way through them all, in the process being shot, bludgeoned, and finally breaking out of a hospital to save the girl.[31]

Needless to say, even George Bye could not find a publisher for *Shadows in Washington*. The closest they came was Jessica Mannon, an editor at Bobbs-Merrill, who shopped the manuscript around internally. The kindest review she received from one of her developmental editors was "There may be a thread of a story here, but it's pretty ragged. I won't attempt to list my objections or to say what it needs— certainly a new start from scratch, or several of them, wouldn't hurt it. But one thing

---

[30] Tom Curtin, Interview with Tom Curtin re: Herbert Yardley, 1959, RG 457, Entry 9032, National Security Agency, National Archives and Records Administration, Herbert Yardley Collection, College Park, MD.

[31] Herbert O. Yardley, *Shadows in Washington*. Unpublished manuscript. National Cryptologic Museum Library, Ft. Meade, MD, David Kahn Collection, DK 82-03, 1937.

it *doesn't* need, as it stands now, is a publisher." Reluctantly, on July 8, 1937, Mannon wrote to Yardley and told him that Bobbs-Merrill was not interested.[32]

By early 1938, Yardley's career as a writer was slowing down considerably, and his writing projects began to taper off. So, it was an opportune time for him to get back into the cryptologic consulting business, this time in China.

---

[32] Kahn, *ROGM*, 185–186.

# Chapter 15
# Red and Purple

About the time that Elizebeth Friedman was made Cryptanalyst-in-Charge of the
new Coast Guard Cryptanalytic Section in July 1931, her husband was deeply
involved in creating the Signal Corps' Signal Intelligence Service (SIS) just up the
street. By July 1930, William Friedman's three junior cryptanalysts had been training for just over 3 months, and it was at that time that he led them on a stroll through
the Army Munitions Building to the locked vault that contained all the records
recovered from Herbert Yardley's Cipher Bureau. This was the next, and probably
most important, phase in their training because Yardley's records were full of
Japanese diplomatic code messages, Japanese Army cipher and code messages, and
all the records of the Cipher Bureau's work on them. The vault also included most
of the records of MI-8 from World War I–those that Yardley had not kept for himself. Friedman had Rowlett, Sinkov, and Kullback go through all the records, putting them in order, and he extracted certain batches of records to be used in their
training.[1]

One of the topics that Friedman had his trio of cryptanalysts look at early on was
all the records and intercepts of the German ADFGVX cipher system. Introduced in
March 1918 just as the Germans began their final set of offensives along the Western
Front, the French cryptanalyst Georges Painvin had solved a special case of the
cipher during the war. Painvin's solution worked quite well, but there was still not a
general solution to the ADFGVX system. So, Friedman set Rowlett, Sinkov, and
Kullback to work coming up with a general solution to ADFGVX. Their solution,
published as a Signal Corps memorandum in 1934—it took them 3 years because
they could only work on it part-time–is a testament to Friedman's instruction and
the talents of the three junior cryptanalysts.[2]

---

[1] Frank R. Rowlett, *The Story of Magic: Memoirs of an American Cryptologic Pioneer*, (Laguna
Hills, CA: Aegean Park Press, 1998), 36–39.

[2] Frank R. Rowlett, Solomon Kullback, and Abraham Sinkov, "General Solution for the ADFGVX
Cipher" (Washington, DC: U.S. Army Signal Intelligence Service, 1934), Friedman Collection

© The Author(s), under exclusive license to Springer Nature
Switzerland AG 2023
J. F. Dooley, *The Gambler and the Scholars*, History of Computing,
https://doi.org/10.1007/978-3-031-28318-5_15

Friedman could only run his training course part-time because the other respon-sibility of SIS was creating new code and cipher systems for the Army. In the early 1930s, this was almost exclusively new field codes; the new cryptanalysts had to spend at least half their time creating these new codes. All the new codes that SIS produced were two-part codes. The cryptanalysts would create a long list of plain-text words and phrases and an equally long list of codewords according to a set of rules created by Friedman and described in his patent #1,608,590 issued in November 1926. These two lists then needed to be paired randomly. There could be no link between a set of codewords and a set of plaintext words and phrases; other-wise, enemy cryptanalysts would have a way they could partially decode a message. To mix up the plaintext words to assure randomness, the cryptanalysts would first write the new plaintext words and phrases onto individual index cards. They would then put themselves inside a small room in the Munitions building, turn on a couple of large standing fans, and then throw the plaintext index cards in the air time after time until the floor of the room was covered in randomly arranged index cards. Gathering up the cards from the floor, they then had a set of random plaintext equiv-alents. They performed the same operation for the list of proposed codewords. They then created piles of plaintext words and code words and paired them one at a time.[3]

Friedman's training regimen also included an introduction to cipher machines. Initially, for the three junior cryptanalysts, this would be examining machines that Friedman had already broken in years past. The three examined the Army's M-94 cipher device, Pletts' cipher machine, and Edward Hebern's single- and five-rotor cipher machines, among others. Cipher machines would become central to the work of SIS during the 1930s, both creating new machines and cryptanalyzing others.

Early in January 1933, Robert C. Birkhahn, an attorney representing a company that had purchased the US rights to a German cipher machine known as the Kryha Standard Cipher Machine wrote a letter to the Chief Signal Officer and copied William Friedman (Fig. 15.1). Birkhahn was interested in obtaining a contract with the Army for the Kryha cipher machine. Friedman and the administrative head of SIS, Major Spencer Akin, tried to put Birkhahn off, but the lawyer was very persis-tent, adding at the end of more than one letter that "I shall only be too happy to submit a 200 word cipher statement to be deciphered without the aid of the machine; or, for that matter, with the aid of the machine but without prior knowledge of the particular key on which the text was enciphered."[4]

Akin and Friedman discussed the Kryha at some length and decided that decrypt-ing a random message enciphered on the Kryha Standard would be a good exercise for Friedman and his three cryptanalysts. So, on January 24 Akin responded to

(online), National Security Agency Archives, https://www.nsa.gov/Portals/75/documents/news-features/declassified-documents/friedman-documents/publications/FOLDER_269/41784769082379.pdf

[3] Rowlett, *Magic*, 53–54.

[4] Lambros D. Callimahos, "Q.E.D.-2 Hours, 41 Minutes," *NSA Technical Journal* XVIII, no. 4 (1973): 13–34, https://www.nsa.gov/Portals/70/documents/news-features/declassified-documents/tech-journals/qed.pdf, 1.

**Fig. 15.1** The Kryha Standard cipher machine. (Wikimedia Commons, with permission from 1971markus@wikimedia.de)

Birkhahn, telling him that if the lawyer was so confident of its security and operational ease, the SIS would accept the challenge, and Akin invited Birkhahn to send in his 200-word cipher challenge as long as it was in standard English and in triplicate.

On February 23, Birkhahn submitted his 200-word—1135 letters—message to Major Akin. It was received in the SIS office and time-stamped "Feb 24 AM 11:12." Friedman and his team sat down with the message and right over the time stamp Friedman penciled in "Commenced work. W.F.F." The team stopped for lunch for 50 minutes and then recommenced work. Friedman next added a new time stamp "Feb 24 PM 2:43" and the notation "Solved. W.F.F." Taking out the time for lunch, Friedman and his team solved the 1135-letter cryptogram in 2 hours and 41 minutes. Not one to miss a chance to impress the War Department with SIS's skills, in a memorandum for Major Akin at the end of February, Friedman said

> Under ordinary circumstances, a single cryptanalyst working alone, no matter how skillful he might be, would require at least 24 to 36 hours to solve such a message. In this case a team of three trained junior cryptanalysts were assigned the problem, under the direction of the principal cryptanalyst. The speed with which the solution was accomplished in this case shows what proper organization, effective coordination, and experienced direction of trained cryptanalysts can accomplish.[5]

In September 1932, the Japanese Ministry of Foreign Affairs began to deploy a new cipher machine to its embassies and consulates worldwide. The machine had been in development since 1927 and had its first real-world trial at the London Naval

---

[5] Callimahos, *Q.E.D.*, 17–18.

Conference in 1930. An updated version was successfully deployed for the *Conference for the Reduction and Limitation of Armaments* in Geneva, Switzerland, in April 1932. Originally based on the Kryha Electrical machine and taking some inspiration from the German Enigma, the machine was thought to have used what is known as a half-rotor to encrypt plaintext.[6] The Americans named the new machine RED. The RED machine separated out the six vowels (AEIOUY) from the 20 consonants and behaved as if it used two half-rotors, one for the vowels and one for the consonants. The Americans called this arrangement the "sixes" and the "twenties." This separation enabled ciphertext to be created in pronounceable sequences that could be transmitted as codewords, which was, at that time, a requirement for transmitting codewords and which for this cipher reduced the cost of sending telegrams. Unfortunately, the separation of vowels and consonants also made the RED machine much less secure and enabled Friedman's team to easily and quickly identify all the encrypted vowels in any message. In addition, the mechanism itself generated the equivalent of a $6 \times 6$ and a $20 \times 20$ Vigenère tableau for each complete rotation, making the system susceptible to Friedman's statistical analysis.

SIS intercepted the first Japanese diplomatic messages using the new machine in early 1933 but did not start serious work on cryptanalysis until a year later. They dubbed the machine RED because it was easier to hide than the two Japanese names, *91-Shiki Injiki* (Type 91 Printing Machine) and *Angoki Taipu A* (Cipher Machine Type A) or their original name, *The Japanese Cipher Machine*. Friedman and his team set about trying to get as many intercepts as possible so they could break it. Frank Rowlett and Solomon Kullback were the two cryptanalysts who spent their time largely on breaking RED. They were aided by the introduction in 1935 of IBM tabulating machines used for much of the statistical grunt work of cryptanalysis.[7] At one point in early 1935 and with Friedman up at Fort Monmouth on business, Rowlett noticed some pattern similarities between three of the intercepted RED messages, all with the same key indicator that he and Kullback were examining. Performing a detailed statistical and frequency analysis, the two men found a pattern in one of the messages that allowed them to decrypt all the vowels and then presented word patterns for the consonants. Moving on to the next two messages, they repeated their technique and again were able to find patterns for both the vowels and consonants. This enabled them to read nearly all of the three messages and took them a long way toward uncovering the inner workings of the RED machine. Rowlett also thought that the indicators were changed every 9 days, which, once they uncovered a particular indicator, would give them a long string of messages they could decrypt. They were in. When Friedman arrived back in Washington the next day, Rowlett and Kullback laid out their technique and the results. Friedman made some suggestions for improvements and confirmed that he thought that they had succeeded. From that point, SIS could reliably read RED messages; 2 years

---

[6] Satoshi Tomokiyo, "Development of the First Japanese Cipher Machine: RED," *Cryptiana* (blog), May 20, 2014, http://cryptiana.web.fc2.com/code/redciphermachine.htm

[7] Rowlett, *Magic*, 116.

later, the Signal Corps Laboratory, along with help from the SIS cryptanalysts, created a prototype of the RED machine that essentially automated the process of decrypting messages—all without ever seeing an actual RED cipher machine.[8] Many years later, in a detailed essay on the breaking of the RED cipher machine, Deavours and Kruh observed

> A point to be made here is that, although the daily solution of the machine was easy, someone first had to determine how the machine worked before this was possible. Determining the inner workings of a cryptograph from ciphertext alone, no matter how simple the mechanism may seem afterwards, is often difficult. One who has not sat before pages of jumbled five-letter groups trying to bring forth sense from nonsense cannot understand the feeling of isolated confusion engendered in the pursuit. To the majority of people such a task would be considered hopeless from the start. Where does one begin? The cryptanalyst scans the ciphertext looking for telltale clues, making counts, comparing texts, and exhausting one idea after another in vain. Hours pass—days—weeks—all with no guarantee that success will ever be achieved. Few persons are capable of such sustained and exhausting work, but US Army and Navy cryptanalysts persevered and, in the end, succeeded.[9]

The breaking of the Japanese RED cipher machine in 1935 was the first big success for SIS in current cryptanalysis of the new cipher machines that all nations and militaries were now using (Fig. 15.2). It impressed the Chief Signal Officer, the head of

**Fig. 15.2** The SIS Team in 1935 (Sol Kullback is the second from the left, William Friedman is in the middle, Abe Sinkov is third from the right, and Frank Rowlett is on the far right. The man between Sinkov and Rowlett is Lt. L.T. Jones of the U.S. Coast Guard, then a student of Friedman's, who later worked for Elizebeth Friedman). (National Security Agency)

---

[8] Rowlett, *Magic*, 112–125.

[9] Cipher A. Deavours and Louis Kruh, *Machine Cryptography and Modern Cryptanalysis*, Artech House Telecom Library. (Dedham, MA: Artech House, 1985), 221–222.

Army Military Intelligence, and his Navy counterpart. This was another example of William Friedman's skill at training and energizing his team.

Another pair of cipher machines that the Army cryptanalysts examined and evaluated, and the first electromechanical devices they worked with, were two of Boris Hagelin's portable cipher machines, the B-21 and B-211. These two B-2xx machines were basically the same, and both were electromechanical machines. The B-21 had a set of lamps that would illuminate the cipher letters in turn as the plaintext was typed in, just the same as an Enigma machine would illuminate its ciphertext. On the other hand, the B-211 had a built-in printer that would create a tape of the ciphertext; the B-211 could also be operated by a hand-crank if no battery was available. Both machines had the same internal cryptographic system; they were about the size of a portable typewriter and weighed approximately six pounds. Hagelin had designed the B-21 in a 6-month period in 1925 in an effort to sell a cipher machine to the Swedish Army. He also sold the B-21 and B-211 to the French Army and to the Soviets. In the latter half of the 1920s, Hagelin made a series of minor improvements to the B-21, introduced the B-211 for the French Army, and sought to sell the B-21 to the Americans. This is likely why William Friedman visited Boris Hagelin after his trip to the International Radio Conference in 1928.

In 1933, Friedman gave his team of cryptanalysts access to a B-211 machine. They removed all its covers and proceeded to try to determine the paths of electrical signals through the device. It took Rowlett, Kullback, Sinkov, and John Hurt approximately a month to figure out exactly how the machine worked and to propose a way to figure out the starting positions of the pin-wheels and the half-rotors for each message. This gave them just what they needed, and the decryptions of a series of test messages were completed shortly after that. They also took the time to write up a report of their work, describing all the techniques they had developed to break the cipher machine. Their analysis of the electrical system and the conversion of that knowledge into a description of the cryptographic elements of the machine would serve the SIS team in good stead in the coming years.

In addition to training his new cryptanalysts and compiling new codes for the Army, William had a number of other activities going on during the 1930s. This period should be considered the most productive of his career. During this period, Friedman filed for eleven different patents, seven of them on his own and two of the other four with Frank Rowlett. All of these patents related to either new cipher machines or improvements on existing cipher machines. Many of them would be developed into products that the Army and Navy would use during World War II. All of them were assigned to the US government; some of them, while being filed in the 1930s, were not officially approved by the Patent Office until the 2000s, decades after Friedman's death. These patents do not include other innovations that Friedman produced in this time period for various cipher machines that were considered so secret by the Signal Corps that patent applications were not even filed for them.

Also, during this period, Friedman played the leading role in formalizing the training courses that he had been running at Fort Monmouth in New Jersey as the curriculum for the new Signal Intelligence School. It's first head was Lt. Preston Corderman, one of Friedman's former students who had stayed on as an instructor at the nascent school in 1934 and was then promoted to be its chief. Corderman would later rise to the rank of Major General and command the Army Signal Security Service from 1943 to 1945 and later the Army Security Agency in 1945 and 1946.[10] Friedman also reprised his role from the 1928 International Radio Conference by being named the chief technical adviser to the American delegation at the 1932 International Radiotelegraph Conference in Madrid, Spain. William sailed for Madrid in August. The conference lasted from September 3 until December 3. Elizebeth was now working full time at the Coast Guard and was deep in rumrunner cryptanalysis, so couldn't immediately join William. It took her more than 2 months to wrap up her current assignments before she could take ship and join William in Madrid in early October, leaving the children with their housekeeper/nanny at her sister's home in Detroit. After the conference ended, the pair took a short vacation in Europe before sailing back to the United States, arriving home just before Christmas.[11]

Just as Yardley had problems finding diplomatic telegram intercepts during the 1920s, William Friedman had the same problems in the 1930s getting military communications intercepts. Because the Federal Communications Acts of 1927 and 1934 both prohibited the interception of cable telegrams between the United States and any foreign country, Friedman was instead looking for radio traffic so that he and his team could discover what types of cipher and code systems foreign armies were developing and using.[12] Early on, Friedman was reduced to getting intercepted correspondence from the Navy and the Coast Guard. However, in 1933 and in conjunction with SIS, a Provisional Radio Intelligence Detachment was formed at Fort Monmouth, New Jersey, and it proceeded to set up several radio intercept stations, helping to alleviate Friedman's lack of material. By 1936, SIS had set up several of its own radio intercept stations in the Eighth Corps Area in Texas and in the Ninth Corps area at the Presidio in San Francisco with their personnel deployed as part of five different signal service companies. The station at the Presidio replaced an ad hoc intercept station that then Colonel Joseph Mauborgne, the Signal Officer for the Ninth Corps Area, had set up in the basement of his house on the base in the early 1930s.[13] Abe Sinkov was assigned to set up and manage a new radio intercept station in Panama, and he spent nearly 2 years there, starting in early 1936. Solomon Kullback performed similar duties in Hawaii for a year. By 1938, Major General Joseph Mauborgne, now the Chief Signal Officer, saw a need to centralize radio

---

[10] David Kahn, *The Codebreakers: The Story of Secret Writing* (New York: Macmillan, 1967), 388.

[11] G. Stuart Smith, *A Life in Code: Pioneer Cryptanalyst Elizebeth Smith Friedman*, (Jefferson, NC: McFarland & Company, 2017), 87.

[12] This was also technically illegal according to the Federal Communications Act of 1934, but the Army and Navy got around that law by claiming that they were just setting up operations that would be used in case of war and that any traffic they intercepted was used for training purposes. They also imposed the tightest secrecy they could muster on the entire intercept operations.

[13] John Patrick Finnegan and Romana Danysh, *Military Intelligence*, Army Lineage Series, CMH Pub 60-13 (Washington, DC: Center of Military History, U.S. Army, 1998), https://history.army.mil/html/books/060/60-13-1/cmhPub_60-13-1.pdf, 48–49.

interception services and to expand their breadth. Therefore, he ordered the creation of the 2nd Signal Service Company at Fort Monmouth, which was effective on January 1, 1939, and centralized all Signal Corps radio interception work. This took William Friedman and the SIS off the hook of having to manage and support radio interception networks. By 1941, the Army had nine radio intercept stations at Fort Hancock in New Jersey, San Francisco, Fort Sam Houston in San Antonio, Panama, Fort Shafter in Honolulu, Fort Mills in Manila, Fort Hunt in Virginia, and Rio de Janeiro.

William also continued his writing during the 1930s, producing three volumes, *Elementary Military Cryptography*, *Advanced Military Cryptography*, and *Military Cryptanalysis* (in four parts), for the Signal Intelligence School. Along with his good friend Charles J. Mendelsohn he also produced a monograph on the Zimmermann Telegram in 1938.[14] The two had hoped to get *The Zimmermann Telegram of January 16, 1917 and its Cryptographic Background* published independently, but the State Department quashed that idea, citing the deteriorating international situation with regards to Germany. Mendelsohn and Friedman met and became friends in the early 1920s. They met over a dinner at Herbert Yardley's apartment in New York in 1924 when Friedman was up from Washington visiting the Cipher Bureau. The two became good friends and worked on the *Zimmermann Telegram* report together; they also wrote a paper on *Notes on Code Words* for the American Mathematical Monthly that talked about the mathematical construction of codewords.[15] Friedman also encouraged Mendelsohn to write several other papers in cryptology, a couple of which Friedman arranged to be published in the Signal Corps Bulletin.[16] In 1937, Mendelsohn, at Friedman's request, also wrote another report, titled *Studies in German Diplomatic Codes Employed During the World War*.[17] In 1938, Friedman requested that Mendelsohn return to active duty and come to Washington and work on some German codes. He signed a 6-month contract and worked for SIS starting in January 1939. In early September he signed on for a second 6-month contract. Sadly, just before he was to begin that work, Mendelsohn contracted meningitis and died 5 days later on September 27, 1939 at the age of 58.[18]

---

[14] William F. Friedman and Charles J. Mendelsohn, "The Zimmermann Telegram of January 16, 1917 and Its Cryptographic Background" (Washington, DC: Office of the Chief Signal Officer, 1938),   https://www.nsa.gov/news-features/declassified-documents/friedman-documents/assets/ files/lectures-speeches/FOLDER_198/41766889080599.pdf; Mendelsohn had worked on German codes under Herbert Yardley in MI-8 during the war. The Zimmermann Telegram monograph was finally declassified and released by the NSA in 2013.

[15] William F. Friedman and Charles Mendelsohn, "Notes on Code Words," *American Mathematical Monthly* 39, no. 7 (September 1932): 394–409, https://www.jstor.org/stable/2300386

[16] David Kahn, "Charles Jastrow Mendelsohn and Why I Envy Him," *Cryptologia* 28, no. 1 (January 2004): 1–17, https://doi.org/10.1080/0161-110491892737

[17] Charles Mendelsohn, "Studies in German Diplomatic Codes Used During the World War" (War Department, Washington, DC: Office of the Chief Signal Officer, Government Printing Office, 1937).

[18] Kahn *Envy*, 13.

Friedman also wrote a number of reports on cipher machine cryptanalysis, notably on the Hebern five-rotor cipher machine and, as we will see, on the cryptanalysis of the Japanese PURPLE machine. Even in his spare time, Friedman found time to think and write about cryptology. In November 1936, he published a journal article on Edgar Allan Poe's skills as a cryptographer, and in 1940, he published an article on Jules Verne and his use of cryptography in his fiction in the *Signal Corps Bulletin*.[19] William continued his correspondence with George Fabyan during this period as well. Distance and time enabled their relationship to mellow, and by the 1930s, they corresponded as old friends. As Fabyan grew older, William tried to get him to commit to donating his considerable book and manuscript collection on cryptography to a library. He failed to convince Fabyan to donate his books before Fabyan's death in 1936, but he did succeed with Fabyan's wife Nelle, who donated George Fabyan's collection to the Library of Congress upon her death in 1939. In addition, many of the remaining papers from the Riverbank Cipher Department—those that Fabyan had not destroyed—were donated to the New York Public Library.[20] After Belle Fabyan died, most of the Riverbank property, including the Fabyan Villa, gardens, and windmill were sold to Kane County, Illinois and are now part of the Kane County Forest Preserve District. The Villa and gardens are open to the public as a museum. The Riverbank Acoustical Laboratories continues to exist, first as part of the Illinois Institute of Technology's Research Institute and now as part of Alion Science and Technology.

While the Signal Corps did not even add any new personnel to SIS beyond its original complement until 1937, there were some changes. Preston Corderman's addition as an instructor and then head of the Signal Intelligence School at Fort Monmouth was the first. The next and most significant was the Army deciding that an Army officer should be in charge of SIS. In 1935, William Friedman was replaced by an Army officer, Major Haskell Allison, as the administrative head of SIS, the first in a succession of officers in this position. William was moved sideways to be the Principal Cryptanalyst of SIS, a post he would hold until another reorganization just after the US entry into World War II. This is one of the old "civilians aren't allowed to manage soldiers" thing that was part of the Army's culture and which also happened in the US Navy.[21] While this eased some of Friedman's workload, the latter half of the 1930s would not be an easy or carefree time for Friedman or the SIS. In fiscal year 1938, the first large increase in the number of personnel at SIS came, with the addition of five new people, including electrical engineers and clerks.

---

[19] William F. Friedman, "Edgar Allan Poe, Cryptographer," *American Literature* 8, no. 3 (November 1936): 266–80, https://doi.org/10.2307/2919837

[20] Jason Fagone, *The Woman Who Smashed Codes*, (New York, NY: William Morrow, 2017), 159–160.

[21] This is likely one reason why Agnes Meyer Driscoll never became a manager in OP-20-G. It also makes Elizebeth Friedman's long tenure as Cryptanalyst-in-Charge of the Coast Guard Cryptanalytic Section all the more remarkable.

From here on in, the numbers, office space, responsibilities, and budget would increase every year throughout the next war.[22]

By the time that 1937 arrived, SIS had been reading Japanese RED machine messages for a couple of years, to good effect. Once they were convinced that the information from SIS was reliable and useful, both the Chief Signal Officer and the head of the Army General Staff's Military Intelligence division (G-2) were active and enthusiastic consumers of all the decrypted intercepts that SIS produced. From the Japanese perspective, however, the RED machine was getting old. The updated version was introduced in 1932, and nearly all high-level diplomatic traffic had been transmitted using the machine since then. So, it was time for the Japanese to create a new, more complex electromechanical cipher machine to replace RED. Their next machine, named *Angooki Taipu B* (*Cipher Machine B*), or *97-shiki O-bun In-ji-ki*, or *Alphabetical Typewriter '97* was created in late 1937 and began rolling out to the major Japanese embassies in the late fall of 1938. In keeping with their color-coded naming scheme, SIS called this new machine PURPLE.

Initially, the new machine went to the Japanese embassies at Washington, Berlin, Paris, London, Moscow, Rome, Geneva, Brussels, Ankara, Beijing, and the consulate at Shanghai. All the rest of the Japanese embassies continued to use the RED machine during this period, and the above embassies also used it, but for lower-level traffic only. This slow roll-out of the PURPLE machine by the Japanese was a gift to the Americans. With many embassies and consulates still using the RED cipher machine, there were a fairly large number of PURPLE messages that were duplicated and also transmitted via the RED machine. Because SIS could read all the RED messages, this gave them a large number of "cribs"—a word or phrase that is known to appear in the plaintext of a message—and thus allowed them to make educated guesses as to the content of some of the PURPLE messages.[23]

SIS intercepted its first messages from this new machine on 20 February 1939, after having been warned just 2 days earlier in a RED message that the switch was being made. Rowlett, who was in charge of the Japanese cryptanalytic team by this time, organized the work, and starting immediately, the team had enough messages to begin to work on the statistical analysis they would need for a break.

Within 6 weeks of starting work on solving PURPLE, Rowlett's team had their first breakthrough. They realized that the new machine used the same technique of breaking up the Roman alphabet letters into two separately encrypted groups, the "sixes" and the "twenties." The difference between the original RED machine and PURPLE was that in the PURPLE sixes, the letters could be any six letters in the alphabet, with the remaining 20 letters making up the twenties. It also looked like the Japanese changed which six letters were chosen for the sixes every day. It turned out, however, that the cryptanalysts could still use frequency analysis to identify the six letters used on each day because by performing a frequency count, they could

---

[22] Kahn, *Codebreakers*, 388–389.

[23] Stephen Budiansky, *Battle of Wits : The Complete Story of Codebreaking in World War II* (New York: Free Press, 2000), 164.

detect which six letters in a message appeared with a different frequency than the other 20. Using the large number of intercepts and the idea of the separate sixes frequency, the Americans soon created a 6 × 25 substitution cipher table—similar to a Vigenère table and a manual method of determining which six letters were used every day and which substitutions were used for each letter. From this, the SIS cryptanalysts could identify all the sixes in a message and decrypt them. This weakness with the sixes in PURPLE also told the Americans that PURPLE could not be a rotor machine like Enigma or RED,[24] because the way the substitutions of the six letters changed over the course of the encrypted message could not be duplicated using a rotor or half-rotor. The problem Rowlett and his team had was that their manual method for recovering the sixes substitution alphabets was very slow and cumbersome. It would be much better if they could automate the work. However, the IBM tabulating machines that SIS typically used for frequency analysis were not up to this task. William Friedman took a gamble and assigned one of the newest members of the SIS organization to Rowlett's team with the hope of solving this problem. Leo Rosen was an MIT graduate in Electrical Engineering who was also in the Reserve Officer Training Corps (ROTC) and had been called to active duty and assigned to SIS earlier in 1939 (Fig. 15.3).

Rowlett gave Rosen the job of trying to automate the cryptanalysis of the sixes. Rosen struggled for a few weeks, but one day, while flipping through an electrical parts catalog, he came upon a machine called a "uniselector." The uniselector took six stepping switches and ganged them together into a single device that would step the six input signals into one of 25 outputs. Rosen thought that this was exactly what he needed to simulate the substitution table for the sixes. The head of the Signal Corps War Planning Division—and William Friedman's boss—Colonel Spencer B. Akin immediately had two of the uniselectors air mailed to SIS. Rosen spent a few days designing and building the new device, and then in September 1939, SIS had a device—dubbed the "six-buster"—that would automatically solve the sixes from a PURPLE message almost immediately. Ironically, Rosen's decision to use the uniselectors in the six-buster was the perfect choice because unknown to anyone in SIS,[25] these switches were exactly the devices that the Japanese used in their own PURPLE machines.

While Rowlett and his team had now solved the "sixes" part of PURPLE, the "twenties" were significantly more difficult. This problem was not helped by the fact that the Japanese, on May 1, 1939, had introduced a shorthand code (called a Phillips code) that used a number of single-letter and short abbreviations for a fairly large number of Japanese words that made the decrypted text even more difficult to

---

[24] Recall that the RED machine uses a single half-rotor to do its encryption. Because of the division of the sixes and twenties in RED, the rotor had 60 contacts (the least common multiple of 6 and 20).

[25] The Americans would not know what devices the Japanese used in PURPLE until after the end of the war when a part of a PURPLE machine—including a uniselector—was found in the ruins of the Japanese embassy in Berlin. The Americans never saw a complete PURPLE machine.

**Fig. 15.3** Leo Rosen. (National Security Agency)

read.[26] More new cryptanalysts were brought onto the PURPLE team, including Genevieve Grotjan, a 26-year-old mathematician from Buffalo, NY, who was hired in 1939[27] (Fig. 15.4).

At one point in 1939, Friedman was relieved of many of his administrative duties and instructed to spend as much time as possible helping Rowlett and his team. For the next year, Rowlett and his team beat their heads against the twenties, looking for a weakness in the machine. This was a very long and tiring year for SIS and tells us just how difficult cryptanalysis is as a profession. "This kind of work, particularly in the early stages of a difficult cryptanalysis, is perhaps the most excruciating, exasperating, agonizing mental process known to man. Hour after hour, day after

---

[26] William F. Friedman, "Preliminary Historical Report on the Solution of the 'B' Machine" (Washington, DC: War Department, October 14, 1940), https://cryptocellar.org/files/PURPLE_ History.pdf, 2. A Phillips Code is a "brevity code" used to shorten the length of telegrams. It was initially devised in 1879 by Walter P. Phillips of the Associated Press. It took hundreds of commonly used words and proper nouns and abbreviated them in news reports. There were special sets of abbreviations for things like commodities and baseball terms.

[27] Genevieve Grotjan married chemist Hyman Feinstein in 1943. During World War II, Grotjan Feinstein worked on Russian cryptanalysis, making key findings in the famous Venona project. She resigned from the government in 1947 and became a professor of mathematics at George Mason University. Her husband was also a faculty member at George Mason.

**Fig. 15.4** Genevieve Grotjan 1935, in her college yearbook. (Courtesy of the University Archives, University at Buffalo, the State University of New York)

day, sometimes month after month, the cryptanalyst tortures his brain to find some relationship between the letters that hangs together, does not dead-end in self-contradiction, and leads to additional valid results."[28]

Success finally came in September 1940. On September 20, Genevieve Grotjan was perusing a long series of tables of information from a number of PURPLE messages, when she noticed a pattern in the repetitions. Working through her guesses, adding more messages to her list and confirming that the same pattern occurred in more messages than her original set, she discovered a cycle in daily messages that repeated itself.

---

[28] Kahn, *Codebreakers*, 21.

With the large quantity of matching plain and cipher text they had to work from, the PURPLE team had already been able to reconstruct the cipher alphabets for the twenties—that is, the patterns in which the letters at successive key positions were shuffled with one another. But there were thousands and thousands of these patterns, and nothing seemed to link to one another. … she noticed that there was a pattern to the patterns. They formed cycles twenty-five key positions long that were related to one another in a systematic fashion that unmistakably showed that they had been generated by a cascade of scrambling units.[29]

Instead of a single uniselector as that used by the sixes, for the twenties, the Japanese had used a cascade of three units, each with a group of four uniselectors ($6 \times 4 = 24$ outputs, enough for the 20 letters of the twenties). The electrical signals for the twenties first entered a plugboard that performed a single monoalphabetic substitution of the input letter. The signals then cascaded from the first through the second and then the third group of uniselectors and then out through a second plugboard, which was the inverse of the input plugboard, and finally to the output typewriter of the machine to print the cipher text. What the SIS team eventually discovered was that each of the uniselectors would "rotate" after each letter to present a different substitution. The three groups of uniselectors would rotate differently but predictably to present different connections. This is part of what Grotjan discovered that day in September. Genevieve Grotjan's discovery of the cyclic nature of the uniselector groups was the key that the team needed to uncover the substitution tables for the twenties. The team was ecstatic, jumping up and down and shouting their elation, enough to bring Friedman out of his office to discover what was going on. When informed by Rowlett of Grotjan's discovery, Friedman briefly joined in the gaiety. Rowlett and his team then celebrated with Cokes and went back to work.

One week later, on September 27, the team was able to present Friedman with the first completely decrypted and translated PURPLE message. This message used only one "indicator" (original key setting of the machine) out of the 120 possible indicators, so much work was yet to be done. However, now that the team knew the system they proceeded to make rapid progress. By the middle of October, they had recovered more than one-third of the possible indicators and were regularly reading messages. At the same time, Frank Rowlett and Leo Rosen worked on creating a device that would allow cryptanalysts to automatically decrypt PURPLE messages. This involved creating the three groups of uniselectors, the plugboards, and determining all the connections between the elements to allow the "rotations." The connections between uniselector groups alone required 500 wires that each had to be soldered absolutely correctly. Late one evening as they finished what they believed was the last of the soldering of the final control board, Rowlett suggested they test the completed machine at once. He had selected three PURPLE messages for the first test. They set up the machine and Rowlett began typing in the ciphertext. The first few letters worked perfectly, but then the machine just stopped and refused to work at all. A close examination by Rosen showed that one of the control relays had shorted out. Luckily, he had a spare. Once replaced, the machine worked without

---

[29] Budiansky, *Battle of Wits*, 165–166.

any problems, and the two men decrypted all three of Rowlett's test messages. Satisfied, they closed up the office and went home to bed. With some help from Rowlett, Leo Rosen had first built the prototype to solve the "sixes" decryption problem, and then designed and built the complete PURPLE prototype machine— all without ever seeing a Japanese PURPLE machine. The solution of PURPLE by Rowlett and his team is arguably the most significant American cryptanalytic accomplishment of World War II.

Once the first PURPLE analogue was completed, the team started informing the rest of the Signal Corps and Military Intelligence brass. Also, on obtaining permission from the Chief Signal Officer and the Director of Military Intelligence, Friedman and Rowlett went across to the Navy Building and told Laurance Safford, head of OP-20-G, about their success with PURPLE and gave him a demonstration as well. They also provided all the technical details of the solution of PURPLE and of the machine they had created to decrypt PURPLE messages. Safford was extremely impressed and, although there were still many bumps in the road ahead, this work was another step in Army–Navy cooperation leading up to the next war.

So, who really broke PURPLE? According to Elizebeth Friedman and William's biographer Ronald Clark, William Friedman was *The Man Who Broke PURPLE*.[30] However, by the time that SIS began working on breaking the PURPLE system in early 1939, Friedman was being consumed with a host of different projects and was managing the technical work of a rapidly growing organization. He also had several people on his staff, including Rowlett, Sinkov, and Kullback, who had been with him for nearly 9 years and were now very capable and experienced cryptanalysts, ad hoc engineers and who were already managing their own teams. In his review of Clark's biography of Friedman in 1977, Frank Rowlett says:

> Some of those who have written about the cryptologic operations of the U.S. have allowed themselves, either through speculation or outright fabrication, to enlarge upon the few facts available. They have generated a considerable body of misinformation which now forms the popular concept of code-breaking operations. Clark has drawn upon this body of misinformation for almost all that he has written about Friedman's official accomplishments. In so doing, he has painted a distorted picture of the more important aspects of Friedman's career. ...
>
> The PURPLE was the most important of these systems, and it was broken by the group responsible for the Army's work on Japanese diplomatic intercepts. Its recovery was too great a task for one person to accomplish. ...
>
> Friedman personally contributed to the breaking of the PURPLE system, notably in the selection and assignment of personnel to the PURPLE team as well as in his part-time participation in the diagnosis and analysis of the system.[31]

Friedman himself generously distributed the credit for the PURPLE solution. In his official report from October 1940 giving details of their work and the solution of the PURPLE machine, Friedman gives nearly all of the credit to others.

---

[30] Ronald Clark, *The Man Who Broke Purple* (Boston: Little, Brown and Company, 1977).

[31] Frank R. Rowlett, "Review of 'The Man Who Broke Purple' by Ronald Clark," *Studies in Intelligence*, Winter 1977, 31–33.

The successful solution of the B-machine is the culmination of 18 months of intensive study by a group of cryptanalysts and assistants working as a harmonious, well-coordinated and cooperative team. Only by such cooperation and close collaboration of all concerned could the solution possibly have been reached, and the name of no one person can be selected as deserving of the major portion of credit for this achievement. The parts played by the individual members of the team may, however, be indicated.

The specific direction and coordination of all studies on this project was the joint work of Cryptanalyst Frank B. Rowlett and Assistant Cryptanalyst Robert O. Ferner. ... They were also extremely active in pushing the solution to a successful conclusion by organizing and directing the reconstruction of the developments of wirings of the switches.[32]

Friedman also called out by name Genevieve Grotjan, Sam Snyder, and Leo Rosen for their special work in the solution of PURPLE. So, the solution of the PURPLE machine, like all large, complicated problems, was a team effort, with all of the team members pulling together and working enormously long and difficult hours for a year and a half before finally achieving their goal. William Friedman's major contribution to the solution of the PURPLE machine came not during these 18 months, although he did certainly contribute then, but years before as he selected, trained, and instilled a sense of camaraderie among this remarkable group of people. The SIS of 1939–40 would be the heart of the Army cryptologic units in the coming war; that is William Friedman's greatest legacy.

---

[32] Friedman, *Preliminary Historical Report*, 8–10.

# Chapter 16
# Yardley Abroad

In May 1938, at the urging of Chiang Kai-shek's intelligence chief Dai Li,[1] Major Sin-ju Pu Hsiao, the Chinese assistant military attaché for intelligence in Washington approached Herbert Yardley with an offer to come to China to train cryptanalysts for them and to solve Japanese military cryptosystems in the Nationalist-held city of Chungking (now called Chongqing).[2] The attaché offered Yardley $10,000 per annum for a 6-month contract with an optional extension for another year. Yardley, likely in need of money as usual, accepted immediately. The arrangements took the Chinese 3 months of clandestine meetings with Yardley to complete, but on September 4, 1938, Herbert Yardley sailed from New York on board the White Star Line's *MV Britannic*, bound for Le Havre, France. From Le Havre, Yardley headed to Gibraltar and into the Mediterranean Sea, through the Suez Canal and on into the Indian Ocean. Yardley finally arrived in Hong Kong on October 12, 1938. There he met up with his Nationalist Government interpreter, Yen Shih.[3]

After his arrival in Hong Kong, Yardley had to wait once again. He was supposed to take a plane to Hangkow (modern day Hankou), but by October that city was being overrun by the Japanese, so Yen Shih had to find them alternate transport. Yardley did not waste his time, however. Using expense money provided by his new employer, he proceeded to sample the sights, sounds, food, drink, and women of Hong Kong. He bought himself a tailor-made suit and tried to get Yen Shih to sample the delights of Western women. Finally, at the end of October, they boarded a small freighter, the *SS Kiangsu*, for a hot and steamy crossing of the South China Sea to Haiphong, French Indochina. There, they took a narrow-gauge railway

---

[1] Yardley called General Dai Li, "The Hatchet Man."

[2] Major Sin-ju Pu Hsiao, "Hsiao to HOY Re: Invitation to China," May 18, 1938, Edna Yardley Papers, National Cryptologic Museum Library, Ft. Meade, MD.

[3] In his posthumously published memoir about his time in China, Yardley uses the name Ling Fan for his Chinese translator. Herbert O. Yardley, *The Chinese Black Chamber*, (Boston: Houghton Mifflin Company, 1983), xxv.

© The Author(s), under exclusive license to Springer Nature Switzerland AG 2023
J. F. Dooley, *The Gambler and the Scholars*, History of Computing, https://doi.org/10.1007/978-3-031-28318-5_16

northwest to Kunming and were then finally able to fly northeast to Chungking, arriving on November 5, just over 2 months after Yardley had left New York.

In 1938, Chungking, at the confluence of the Jialing and Yangtze rivers in west-central China, was the war-time capital of Nationalist China. It was where Chiang Kai-Shek and his army had retreated as they fell back across China during the first year and a half of the Second Sino-Japanese War. After the start of the war on July 7, 1937, Peking and Tienjin both fell to the Japanese almost immediately, followed by Shanghai on November 12 and Nanjing on December 13. The Chinese Nationalists then fell back to Wuhan but were defeated in October 1938 after a nearly 5-month battle that resulted in very heavy casualties—possibly over 1.2 million—on both sides. The Nationalists finally fell back to Chungking, where they set up their war-time capital just before Herbert Yardley arrived.

When Yardley arrived in Chungking, he was there to create a cryptologic school and cryptanalytic bureau. This was not the only cryptanalytic organization in the Nationalist government. In fact, Yardley's new organization was the fifth.[4] Yardley was employed because he had experience with Japanese codes and because Dai Li wanted to increase his own power within the Nationalist administration.

Within a week of his arrival in Chungking, Yardley was set up in a 20-room chateau on a hill overlooking the Yangtze River (Fig. 16.1). The chateau was formerly the mayor's house, but that luminary had been summarily moved out just as Yardley arrived in town. The chateau was also to be the location of Yardley's cryptologic school and his cryptanalytic bureau. Yardley's move-in wasn't an auspicious beginning, however. Yardley had two large adjoining rooms in the chateau to himself, one for his bedroom and one as a living room and office. There was no heat, no running water, and no toilet facilities or kitchen. There were also no desks or other class-room materials for the students, and Yardley had yet to create the curriculum.

Between Yardley and Yen Shih, they shortly had a newly made charcoal stove burning in his rooms for heat, a bed, a couch, carpeting, and a way to get water and bring it up to his rooms. Eventually, in addition, the Chinese government would provide a servant, a car and driver, "a modern desk, a chaise lounge, two chairs, two native rugs, and a lamp with a two-hundred-watt bulb, required because the current was so weak. It cast little light and hurt his eyes frightfully. He was not happy."[5] For much of his time there, Yardley's toilet was a bucket whose contents his servant sold every day for fertilizer. He would eventually get a bath and toilet. His servant also acquired some chickens, so Yardley had fresh eggs for breakfast. The chateau, like most other residences in Chungking, was also overrun with rodents. Yardley tried to close as many holes in the walls and floor as he could and resorted to several different types of traps, both manufactured and homemade. Nothing made much of a difference. While it does not get overly cold in the winter in Chungking, the proximity of two rivers and the mountainous terrain leads to chilly, damp weather all

---

[4]Yardley, *Chinese Black Chamber*, xv.

[5]David Kahn, *The Reader of Gentlemen's Mail: Herbert O. Yardley and the Birth of American Codebreaking* (New Haven: Yale University Press, 2004), 190.

**Fig. 16.1** Yardley in China, 1939. (National Cryptologic Museum Library)

winter, with many days that started and ended with dense fog. The climate in Chungking was one of Yardley's nearly constant complaints. Within a couple of weeks of arriving in Chungking, Yardley was sick. First, it started with a cold and then included infected sinuses, and finally, he developed iridocyclitis in his right eye, an inflammation of the iris and the ciliary body, which controls focusing of the lens in the eye. Over the course of several weeks, the sight in his right eye diminished severely to the point where he was nearly blind in that eye.[6] His only cure was to eliminate the sinus infection, which then should clear up the iridocyclitis. In the days before antibiotics, clearing up the sinus infection and regaining the sight in his right eye took many weeks, but eventually he could see again.

Yardley's cover was as a businessman in hides and leather, but no one in Chungking was fooled. He started immediately preparing materials for his

---

[6]Yardley, *Chinese Black Chamber*, 19–20.

cryptanalysis course. His day was not that of a typical businessman. He would get up around 10 or 11 a.m., eat breakfast prepared by his servant, and then work on the cryptanalysis texts until about 6 p.m. He then headed downtown to have a drink or two and order dinner at one of several restaurants that Westerners frequented. He would return to the chateau at approximately 11 p.m. and work through the night on his lessons, finally retiring around 5 a.m. He had not yet performed any cryptanalysis of Japanese military intercepts because Dai Li wanted to meet with him to discuss the organization of the cryptanalytic bureau and because he had no radio operators or radios for intercepting messages. Within a month, he had the assistance of a Chinese scholar who had just returned from Germany and who spoke and wrote better English than Yardley's interpreter. This scholar translated Yardley's cryptanalysis texts, which were then printed into brochures for the students.

The desks for Yardley's school arrived near the end of November, and his first 15 students and 15 radio operators all arrived later in December. At this point, he was now getting radio intercepts, so his students had material to work with. Yardley began holding classes and worked his students from 8 a.m. until 10 p.m. with breaks for meals. The entire day was not taken up with lectures because the students would spend time working on the newly acquired intercepts as well. Luckily for Yardley, many of the intercepted messages were low-level tactical messages that were in simple substitution and transposition systems. Some of them were also in an enciphered code, using a simple superencipherment and with most of the Japanese Army units using the same standard codebook. Yardley complained about his students in his correspondence; he "was disappointed in the students. He complained, in one of his depressed moments, that they were not worth a damn."[7] What was worse was that the Chinese did not treat prisoners of war as assets to be milked for information as all the Western powers did. This additional information gleaned from prisoners was crucial to breaking tactical and higher level cryptosystems. Mostly, the Chinese took very few prisoners, and of those that they did capture, killed nearly all of them, much to Yardley's chagrin.[8]

Mirroring many of his contemporaries, Yardley was a casual racist, and it showed in his letters and later in his memoir of his time in China, *The Chinese Black Chamber*. He often claimed that the Chinese were lazy and lacked any ambition, even going so far as to call them shiftless "monkeys."[9] He just assumed his white privilege and that he and all other Westerners were there to "be a real service to this lovely nation."[10] Despite this, Yardley also truly loathed the inequality, abject poverty, and mostly nonfunctional government at all levels that he found in China. He thought that the Chinese bureaucrats were completely failing to help their people. He also despised the casual attitude that most of the people he encountered had

---

[7] Kahn, *ROGM*, 192.

[8] Kahn, *ROGM*, 193.

[9] Kahn, *ROGM*, 191.

[10] Herbert O. Yardley to Edna Ramsier, "HOY to Edna Ramsier," October 27, 1938, David Kahn Collection, Box Y, Folder China, National Cryptologic Museum Library, Ft. Meade, MD.

toward death and suffering. Over the months that he was in China, Yardley became increasingly lonely, depressed, and restless. He interspersed bouts of heavy drinking with periods of abstinence. Despite being the acknowledged expert and in charge of his own bureau again, it was not a happy time for him.

General Dai Li finally visited Yardley's school in late December 1938, along with his chief of radio intelligence Wei Daming. After this visit, Yardley began to obtain more regular infusions of new students and radio intercept operators. By late January, he had 50 students and 100 radio operators scattered at 50 intercept posts across the front (Fig. 16.2). Yardley also made his own mark with the Chinese and cemented his credentials with General Dai.

One day in February 1939, while studying a series of kana messages transmitted every day at 6 a.m., noon, and 6 p.m., he noticed that of the forty-eight kana only ten were used, perhaps representing numerals, and that the messages were extremely repetitious in format, perhaps therefore meteorological. He arbitrarily converted the kana into figures and studied them. His team's rough direction-finding indicated that the messages were being sent from near Chungking and Yardley concluded that the first group of all the messages, 027, stood for Chungking. He further observed that all the messages sent at 6 a.m. had, as their second

**Fig. 16.2** Herbert Yardley and two of his students in Chungking, 1939. (National Cryptologic Museum Library)

group, 231, those sent at noon, 248, and those at 6 p.m. 627. The third group in nearly all
the messages was 459—except for a message of noon that day, where it was 401. Yardley
noted that the light rain of several days had cleared at noon and he concluded that 459 meant
rain and 401 fair weather. It was 1 p.m. He called in his Chinese liaison officer and told him
that he believed Chungking would be bombed that afternoon. While he was explaining his
analysis, the sirens wailed. Yardley's reputation was made.[11]

By mid-1939, Yardley and Wei Daming together had solved a Japanese Air Force
code that enabled the Chinese to predict Japanese air raids much more accurately.
Chiang Kai-Shek was delighted with his American cryptanalyst.

Once his cryptanalytic school had started graduating cryptanalysts and his radio
operators were intercepting Japanese code messages in the spring of 1939, Yardley's
cryptanalytic bureau moved into high gear. By mid-1940, Yardley had over 700
people working for him. His organization had intercepted nearly 200,000 radio messages and decrypted 20,000 of them. Of these, Yardley recognized approximately 20
different codes, all of them enciphered.[12]

A side effect of his cryptanalytic bureau's smooth working was that Yardley had,
for him, the worst thing he could have, spare time. Starting in early 1939, he began
peppering George Bye with proposals for articles for magazines such as the *Saturday
Evening Post* and *Cosmopolitan*. He wrote up drafts of several of them and sent
them off to Bye. None of them sold. Yardley then started taking pictures of the aftermath of bombing raids in Chungking—starting in early 1939, the Japanese were
bombing Chungking nearly every day—and sending them off for possible sale.
They didn't. He proposed an exclusive series of articles along with photographs for
the *Saturday Evening Post*. They declined. He even got in touch with his former
cryptanalyst from the Cipher Bureau, Victor Weiskopf, inquiring if Weiskopf wanted
Chinese stamps for his business in New York. Weiskopf never got back to him.

By the end of March 1939 and the end of his first 6-month tour, Yardley was in
good standing with his Chinese employers, and after some negotiations, they
extended his contract for a year, with the option of extending it again. Yardley
insisted on some new terms in the contract, which included lightening up the workload on his students, allowing them to visit their families periodically, the ability for
the students to get passes to leave the chateau, and the right for him to inspect the
radio operators' school. Yardley signed the new contract, figuring he could use the
money, although he was still far from adjusting to living in war-torn China and
learning the new and strange, to him, culture. Yardley was also increasingly weary
of the constant security and restrictions on his movements imposed by his Chinese
handlers. At one point he made a copy of the ignition key to his government car and
after that would sneak out early in the mornings or late in the day just so he had
some sense of freedom.[13] In April 1939, just before his 50th birthday and after a
particularly nasty air raid, Yardley moved out of the chateau and into a mud-and-
brick house a couple of miles outside of Chunking. This gave him slightly more

---

[11] Kahn, *ROGM*, 193.

[12] Kahn, *ROGM*, 195.

[13] Yardley, *Chinese Black Chamber*, 59.

freedom and allowed him to get fresher food and drink. It also let him have dinner parties away from the inquisitive eyes of his superiors. This served him well until his house was mostly destroyed by a Japanese bomb later in the year, and he had to move back into town.

Yardley started spending more time at the Chungking Hostel, a hotel, restaurant, and bar primarily for Westerners. It was here that he would eat his evening meals, have a few drinks, play pool and engage in his favorite pastime, playing poker. Yardley was an excellent poker player, conservative, consistent, and patient. He had learned to play in several of the backrooms of saloons in his hometown of Worthington and had been a quick and apt pupil. He was a cautious gambler, playing a conservative type of poker, but one that served him well. Over the course of many an evening, Yardley would come out ahead because he was patient and his opponents were not; his skill as a cryptanalyst also served him well because he could count and remember which cards had been played and to whom, thus increasing the odds of winning in his favor. At the Hostel, he met a number of Western journalists covering the war, diplomats who had followed the Chinese government's move to Chungking, and businessmen (and they were nearly all men) trying to take advantage of the turmoil to make a profit.

One of the young people he met at the Hostel was the soon-to-be famous journalist and chronicler of American presidents, Theodore White. Working first as a propagandist for the Nationalist government and then as a stringer for *Time* magazine, at the age of 23, White met Yardley at the Hostel and the two became good friends. White described Yardley as "a balding middle-aged little fellow with the attractive and happy garrulousness of a country storekeeper ... an extremely witty man."

> Osborn took a fancy to me. He was a man of broad humor and unrestrained enthusiasms, and among his enthusiasms were drink, gambling, and women. He decided after we had become friends that he should teach me poker, which he did by letting me stand over his shoulder and watch him unfold his hands and sweep up the pots. He also felt I should be taught sex, and tried to persuade me to sample that experience by inviting some of the choicest ladies he knew to a banquet in his house. I would not learn; Boston was still strong in me. But he did teach me something more important than anything I have learned since from any official American adviser or wise man; how to behave in an air raid. Yardley's theory was that if a direct hit landed on you, nothing would save you. The chief danger of an air raid, he said, was splintered glass from windows. Thus, when one hears the siren, one should get a drink, lie down on a couch and put two pillows over oneself—one pillow over the eyes and the other over the groin. Splintered glass could hurt those vital organs, and if the eyes or the groin were injured, life was not worth living. It was good advice for any groundling in the age before atom bombs; and I took it. Yardley was excessively kind to me, as were so many older men in Chiang K'ai-shek's Chungking.[14]

Not all the journalists were as smitten with Yardley as White. The American journalist Emily Hahn also met Yardley in Chungking. They didn't get along, and a decade later in her book *China to Me*, she said of Yardley as "an American with a loud

---

[14] Theodore H. White, *In Search of History: A Personal Adventure*, (New York, NY: Harper & Row, Publishers, 1978), 75–76.

manner of talking" and that his conversation was "mostly about women."[15] White also agreed that women were one of Yardley's main preoccupations. The American military attaché in Chungking reported to his superiors that "Sex is a major obsession with him and his conversation is filled with vulgar and bawdy references to women."[16] One woman to whom he was not vulgar but also not romantic was Edna Ramsier Hackenberg. The two kept up a constant correspondence while Yardley was in China. None of Edna's letters survive—either she destroyed them after his death, or he just threw them out before he came home. However, many of Yardley's letters to her still exist. They are uniformly not romantic but are filled with various requests for items Yardley couldn't get in China, bits of information, and complaints that Edna was not answering his requests quickly enough. Regardless of Yardley's tone, Edna was so much in love with him that she seems never to have complained.[17]

By the late winter of 1939–40, as the expiration of his current contract with the Nationalist government drew closer, Yardley was increasingly eager to go home. He agreed to a month-to-month extension of his contract, but as the months dragged on he grew increasingly restive. In a formal report on the work of his bureau in mid-March 1940, Yardley told Dai "he had solved seven two-figure codes, three three-figure codes, two transposition systems, three so-called tana codes, and systems called kwantung A, two-kana B, German five-letter, and fifty-indicator." All of these solutions had been documented by his students and were in the records of the bureau.[18] Yardley had also lost over 40 pounds—his hand-tailored Hong Kong suit no longer fit—and his health was deteriorating by the month. In this final memo to General Dai Li, Yardley concluded with "Though I should like to remain to complete the work I have begun, I feel that to do so may permanently injure my health … I shall remember my stay here as one of the most interesting experiences I have ever had. I came here to help this nation and I myself feel that I have done a good job."[19]

In the early part of 1940, Yardley was approached by the American military attaché in Chungking, who was interested in getting information on Japanese Army codes and ciphers. Yardley offered to give the Americans information—for a price, which included money for him and a job for Edna in Washington.[20] Part of his request was because of his growing dislike and desire to strike back at Friedman, whom he blamed for not being able to get a cryptologic position in the War Department.[21] After several meetings, Yardley was turned down. In a letter to the

---

[15] Emily Hahn, *China to Me*, (Philadelphia, PA: Blakiston Company, 1944).

[16] Kahn, *ROGM*, 195–196.

[17] Kahn, *ROGM*, 197.

[18] Herbert O. Yardley, "Progress Report to General Dai Li," Progress Report (College Park, MD: National Archives, Herbert Yardley Collection, RG 457, Box 56, Folder Memoranda and Letters Concerning H. O. Yardley, 1919–1940., March 1940); Kahn, *ROGM*, 198.

[19] Yardley, *Progress Report;* Kahn, *ROGM*, 198.

[20] Yardley apparently did not know that by this time Edna was already working as a clerk in Friedman's SIS.

[21] Kahn, *ROGM*, 197.

attaché, the Assistant Chief of Staff, G-2, who was in charge of military intelligence and military attachés, termed Yardley's offer "impossible" and warned the attaché "For your confidential information, the gentleman's past publications have seriously jeopardized national defense. War Department fears repetition upon his return. Exercise greatest discretion."[22] Yardley's past indiscretion with *The American Black Chamber* continued to haunt him.

By April 1940, General Dai Li started to avoid Yardley, and he refused to answer his calls or letters. Yardley finally threatened to talk to his newspaper friends and call the American military attaché unless Dai let him leave. Dai finally relented and Yardley flew out of Chungking in early July 1940[23] (Fig. 16.3). He landed in Manila on July 18 and in Honolulu on July 22. At each stop there were journalists waiting for him and trying to determine why he had been in China and why he was coming back. Yardley put them all off by saying that he had been researching a novel.

**Fig. 16.3** Herbert Yardley in Los Angeles, July 1940. (National Cryptologic Museum Library)

---

[22] "ACoS, G-2 to China Military Attache Re: Yardley," March 13, 1940, Herbert Yardley Collection, RG 457, Entry 9037, G-2/10039-299, National Archives and Records Administration, College Park, MD. The ACoS at this time was Colonel E. R. W. McCabe.

[23] Yardley, *Chinese Black Chamber*, 218–219.

He finally arrived in Washington late in July 1940. Yardley rented a small apartment just off Constitution Avenue. He had his reunion with Edna Ramsier, who had gotten a divorce in the interim, resumed her maiden name, and started a job with the SIS in March 1940. Then Yardley began to think about what he should do next.

A regular job in cryptanalysis with the US government was still out of the question owing to the continuing ire within the cryptologic community over *The American Black Chamber*. However, in the late 1930s, William Friedman's SIS was in the process of setting up radio listening stations in the United States, Panama, Hawaii, and the Philippines. This led them to a wealth of Japanese Army traffic that they had not yet been able to analyze or cryptanalyze. What Friedman and the SIS needed was an expert in tactical Japanese Army codes and ciphers. Unfortunately for Yardley, while he had the skills, there was no way Friedman was going to hire him on a permanent basis. However, Friedman's bosses, Colonel Spencer B. Akin, and General Joseph Mauborgne, the current Chief Signal Officer, had different plans. Mauborgne hired Yardley as a short-term contract employee with a scope of work to write a series of brochures on Japanese army and air force codes and ciphers, being as detailed as possible, and giving SIS a leg up in decrypting their Japanese military intercepts. Yardley was to get $4000 for his work.

William Friedman was extremely reluctant to be the contact person for Yardley because his dislike of Yardley had only grown in the years since the publication of *The American Black Chamber*. He also adamantly refused to have Yardley in the SIS offices in the Munitions Building. So, Akin assigned Friedman's chief cryptanalyst Frank Rowlett to be the contract officer on this project and had Rowlett go to Yardley's apartment to review the work that Yardley would be producing for SIS. Over the course of about 5 months, Rowlett visited Yardley at his apartment around twice a month. They would go over the work that Yardley had done, talk about the approaches, and decide if what Yardley was writing was what SIS really wanted. Yardley did go to Akin's office in the Munitions Building several times, most likely to be paid for his work.

Over the course of their meetings, Rowlett came to like and appreciate Yardley despite his faults, all the while keeping him at a distance because the official policy of the Department was that Yardley was not to be told anything about their work. Rowlett was aware that Edna Ramsier, who was working as a clerk in the Japanese diplomatic section of SIS, was involved with Yardley, and he was suspicious that Edna was telling Yardley about SIS's work. However, he had no proof of his suspicions, and nothing ever came out that indicated that Yardley was being given any information to which he was not entitled.[24] Overall, Rowlett thought that the work that Yardley was producing was of only marginal use to SIS. "...he sort of confirmed what we deduced ourselves and the information he brought there was some of it was new and useful, but it wasn't enough to help us master the situation. It was

---

[24] Frank R. Rowlett, "Oral History of Frank Rowlett (1976)," Oral History, Oral History Collection (Ft. George G. Meade, MD: National Security Agency, Center for Cryptologic History, 1976), 82–84. There has not been any documentary evidence found that Edna Ramsier ever told Yardley anything about the work of SIS during 1940.

a tough situation. ... Yardley illuminated information that we had developed and in some degree confirmed it."[25]

Friedman wasn't pleased with the arrangement. However, Colonel Akin told Rowlett that as far as he was concerned, "if I let Friedman go up there, I won't get this."[26] Rowlett also had his own opinions about Friedman and his relations with Yardley, "I think he enjoyed the confrontation with Yardley. Yardley you see one time was up there and Friedman was here, and now the roles were flipped. This I think was Friedman's ego that was hurt rather his judgment and I think Akin very wisely avoided the confrontation between Yardley and Friedman and I don't think it would have been pleasant because Yardley did still at that time have quite a few followers."[27]

Rowlett himself complained about Yardley's work habits—he stayed up late and woke late; he came to meetings in just his T-shirt; he also drank too much. Rowlett also thought that the senior administrators in the Signal Corps just wanted to keep Yardley out of the way and to keep all knowledge that Yardley was working for SIS as quiet as possible. However, with the exception of Friedman, he didn't think that the Signal Corps had any leftover animus toward Yardley for the publication of *The American Black Chamber.*

> ...there was no punishment context here at all. ... It was very simply that Yardley had broken faith with the cult when he published the book and he might publish another one. It was that simple. They didn't look on Yardley as a traitor. Yardley was admired but he'd done this thing and he hadn't been forgiven for it and that's I mean it was that simple. ... People who were running the SIS and responsible for its activity didn't go out on a "get rid of Yardley campaign" except where his activities impinged on our activities and there they took steps to insulate it and that was the measure of their action.[28]

Yardley finally finished and delivered his brochures in December 1940. His final product was called "Japanese Military Codes and Ciphers in Occupied China: Period 1938–1940", and he produced six brochures, a total of 224 pages.[29] One of the characteristics of these documents is that Yardley describes only manual codes and ciphers and pencil-and-paper cryptanalysis. There is no mathematics used beyond frequency analysis. This is a further indication that while American cryptology was moving forward into the machine age for both encryption (via cipher machines) and cryptanalysis (by using IBM accounting machines and statistical methods), Yardley was stuck back 20 years ago and was making no effort to update his skills.

Akin, Mauborgne, and Rowlett were satisfied with Yardley's work. Mauborgne said the brochures were "invaluable." Rowlett felt that SIS did not learn much, but Yardley confirmed work they had already done on Japanese military cryptosystems

---

[25] Rowlett, *Oral History*, 85–86.

[26] Rowlett, *Oral History*, 86.

[27] Rowlett, *Oral History*, 87.

[28] Rowlett, *Oral History*, 90.

[29] Kahn, *ROGM*, 201.

and gave them the confidence that they were on the right track with regard to Japanese Army systems going forward. Friedman wasn't satisfied at all and felt like the Army had not gotten its money's worth out of the contract, but Friedman probably wouldn't have been satisfied with anything that Yardley produced.[30]

By the summer of 1940, Canada had been at war with Nazi Germany for nearly a year. Canadian radio intercept stations in St. John, Newfoundland, and at the Canadian Army Signal Corps intercept station at Rockliffe Airport in Ottawa were picking up German U-boat transmissions, as well as transmissions from German spies in South America and, after June 1940, transmissions from the Vichy French government. The Canadians at Rockliffe were able to decrypt around 200 of these German spy messages using a simple cipher given to the Royal Canadian Mounted Police by the U.S. Federal Bureau of Investigation in September 1940.[31] By late 1940, the Canadians were also beginning to pick up Japanese transmissions at intercept stations on Vancouver Island in Western Canada.

With all these radio intercepts, the Royal Canadian Navy and Army were mostly passing the messages on to the British Army and Navy, who would then pass them on to the British Government Code and Cipher School at Bletchley Park. Using this system, the Canadians were not receiving decrypts of intercepted messages in a timely manner. Just which decrypted messages the Canadians received back was decided by the British intelligence officers at Bletchley Park and not in Ottawa, so the Canadians only received whatever decrypts the British were disposed to give them. What the Canadians needed and didn't have was their own cryptanalytic bureau. It happened that the creation of a Canadian Black Chamber was to be harder than it appeared.

The first attempt at creating a cryptanalytic bureau was in November 1940 when the head of the Rockliffe Signals station, Royal Canadian Army Captain Edward Drake, visited U.S. Army Signal Corps headquarters in Washington and had an interview with the Chief Signal Officer, General Joseph Mauborgne. Captain Drake explained Canada's problems and asked for Mauborgne's help and advice. Mauborgne laid out in general terms the organization of SIS and the Second Signal Company, which handled radio interception. He offered to give the Canadians all the training materials that Friedman and his team had put together over the course of the previous decade. Finally, he urged Drake to have the Canadians quickly create a cryptanalytic bureau.

Upon his return to Ottawa, Captain Drake proposed just such an agency to the Army, but the Royal Canadian Army Chiefs of Staff turned Drake down flat. "The Committee decided they were unable to recommend the institution of a Cryptographic Branch in Canada, and felt that we should continue to use the United Kingdom facilities for this work. In the event of these being seriously interfered with by enemy action, a similar organisation exists in the U.S.A. which would be available

---

[30] Kahn, *ROGM*, 201.

[31] Gilbert deBeauregard Robinson, "History of the Examination Unit—1941–1945" (Ottawa, Canada: National Archives, 1945), Volume 29,167, National Archives of Canada, 2.

to assist in the event of the United States' entry into the war. They also considered that the cost of such an organisation in Canada could not possibly be justified at the present time."[32] At least for a while, the Canadian cryptanalytic bureau was dead. Drake, however, was not the one to give up easily, and he was not alone.

After his rebuff by the Chiefs of Staff, Drake went looking for others who were interested in establishing a cryptographic bureau. He found Lieutenant C. H. Little of Naval Intelligence, who was equally keen on creating a codebreaking unit. The two of them then (and without permission from their superiors) called on T. A. Stone, the officer at the Department of External Affairs (DEA) charged with foreign intelligence matters. They asked Stone if DEA was interested in creating a cryptographic unit within the Department. Stone, who was already thinking along the same lines, put the suggestion to his superior, who encouraged him to pursue the idea.[33]

At about the same time, late January 1941, Lester Pearson, a Canadian diplomat serving in London,[34] passed on the news to the DEA that the British no longer wanted to be bothered with radio intercepts from the French Vichy government; they already had too much on their cryptographic plate. This was a surprise and a concern to the Canadians who were worried about Vichy infiltrators who would stir up trouble in Quebec. There was finally a meeting between officials in the Department of National Defence (DND) and the DEA on April 22, 1941. The result of that meeting was that the DND officials stood by the previous Chiefs of Staff decision and were not interested in starting a cryptographic organization. So, the DEA decided to go it alone.[35] Of course, the problem came down to money.

However, this problem, it turned out, was not insurmountable. A diplomat named Hugh L. Keenleyside was the DEA representative on the War Technical and Scientific Development Committee of the National Research Council of Canada (NRC). The NRC had been gifted with $1 million from a number of private donors with the express purpose of starting a group to explore military research topics. Keenleyside encouraged the NRC to send out a call for scientists and mathematicians interested in cryptology, which it did in late January 1941. Two mathematicians from the University of Toronto, Gilbert deBeauregard Robinson and Harold S. M. Coxeter, responded to the call. It turned out that Coxeter also knew Dr. Abraham Sinkov, then at Friedman's SIS. Coxeter and Sinkov had collaborated on a couple of articles, and Sinkov had written a chapter on cryptology for a general mathematics book that Coxeter was editing. In March 1941 at Keenleyside's urging, the NRC approved a grant of $10,000 for the establishment of a cryptologic unit reporting to the DEA. The two mathematicians met with the head of the NRC and with Lt. Little of Naval Intelligence in April 1941. The NRC arranged for Robinson and Coxeter to visit Washington and glean all the information they could about

---

[32] Robinson, *History*, 9.

[33] Kurt F. Jensen, *Cautious Beginnings: Canadian Foreign Intelligence, 1939–1951*, (Vancouver, BC, Canada: University of British Columbia Press, 2008), 39.

[34] Lester Pearson was also a future Canadian Prime Minister and recipient of the Nobel Peace Prize.

[35] Jensen, *Cautious Beginnings*, 39.

creating a cryptologic bureau and current American successes. Abe Sinkov arranged for the pair to meet with General Mauborgne.[36]

Coxeter and Robinson met with General Mauborgne and Abe Sinkov on May 2, 1941. Mauborgne was puzzled by their visit, mentioning Drake's visit back in November. Coxeter and Robinson were equally puzzled because neither of them had ever heard of Captain Drake or his previous visit to Washington. Mauborgne was also curious as to why the Canadians were not pursuing the information and resources they needed through the British.[37] Mauborgne told the two mathematicians that the United States Army Signal Corps could not spare any personnel or time to help the Canadians set up their new bureau. He also suggested that 50 people were the minimum number needed in a cryptologic unit—although Friedman's SIS had moved along with fewer than ten people for nearly all of the 1930s—and that a year of training would be necessary. Nevertheless, when Coxeter and Robinson enquired about anyone who could help the Canadians get set up with their cryptologic bureau, Mauborgne mentioned one person who was currently in Washington, unemployed, had the skill set they were looking for, and was looking for a way to help in wartime—former Major Herbert Yardley. He praised Yardley highly, revealing, but discounting Yardley's problems with the War Department and recommending him as "an expert cryptanalyst and especially as an organizer."[38] Mauborgne did admit that the Canadians "might not want him as a permanent director."[39]

The two Canadians met with Yardley at the Canadian legation that same day. Yardley, always the salesman, told a good story and they were suitably impressed. "Major Yardley impressed the Canadian group with his knowledge; perhaps more important, he made the project of a Canadian signals intelligence organization sound feasible with limited resources. Yardley spoke of a six-week training period and a small staff of ten or fifteen. The Canadian team's verdict was unanimous: 'We suggest... in view of his high recommendation by General Mauborgne and as a result of our conversation with him, that Major Yardley be invited to Ottawa as soon as possible and that he be consulted by everyone concerned on all matters pertaining to the project. In our opinion he is expert in the highest degree.'"[40] As Robinson put it after the war, "Yardley was a man who had blazed a flaming trail

---

[36] Kahn, *ROGM*, 203.; H.S.M. Coxeter would become one of the premier geometers of the twentieth century. Two of his 12 books, *Regular Polytopes* and *Non-Euclidean Geometry*, would go into multiple editions. He won the Smith Prize at Cambridge in 1931, joining the ranks of other mathematicians like Arthur Cayley, Alan Turing, and Fred Hoyle.

[37] Robinson, *History*, 12.

[38] Wesley K. Wark, "Cryptographic Innocence: The Origins of Signals Intelligence in Canada in the Second World War," *Journal of Contemporary History*, Intelligence Services during the Second World War, 22, no. 4 (October 1987): 639–65, https://www.jstor.org/stable/260814, 646.

[39] Robinson *History*, 14; Robinson later wrote in a footnote to his history of the unit: "It should be said in parenthesis here that some of our later difficulties might not have arisen had General Mauborgne remained in office. As it was, he retired almost immediately and his successor had no interest in Yardley." Mauborgne was put on leave in August 1941 over an administrative matter and officially retired in September 1941.

[40] Wark *Cryptographic Innocence*, 646.

across the cryptographic sky. ... He was a remarkable story teller and no amount of embroidery was too much for H. O. Yardley."[41]

Yardley was invited to Ottawa and met with Keenleyside from the NRC, Lt. Little from Naval Intelligence, a Colonel Murray from Military Intelligence, and several others on May 12, 1941. In this meeting, Yardley reiterated his recommendations on how the new unit should be organized, and he suitably impressed the people from the Research Council and from the Department of External Affairs. He suggested that the Canadian bureau begin with Japanese diplomatic intercepts, but the Canadians really wanted help with German spy and Vichy French messages. He was offered a 6-month contract at $500 USD per month with the possibility of an extension. Yardley also negotiated a contract for Edna Ramsier on the grounds that she had experience in cryptanalyzing Japanese diplomatic codes and ciphers and had worked with him for a decade. He was back doing what he loved once again.

The Canadians, mildly sensitive to the political turmoil that hiring Yardley might generate, asked him to use an alias—Herbert Osborn—the same one he had used in China and that, once again, fooled no one. The new cryptanalytic bureau was to be called the *Examination Unit* (XU), a name seen as appropriately vague enough to hide its true raison d'être.

Apparently no one had yet thought to notify either the British government or the US State or War Departments that Yardley would now be working for the Canadian intelligence services. This would come back to haunt them.

Yardley went back to Washington. Edna asked for a leave of absence from her job at the SIS, the two packed and were back in Ottawa in early June. The Examination Unit formally came into existence on June 9, 1941. Its first organizational meeting was on June 11 with Yardley, Ramsier, and representatives from the NRC, DEA, Naval Intelligence, Military Intelligence, the Army Signal Corps (Captain Drake finally back in the loop), and the units first cryptanalyst, Dr. Robinson, all present; Coxeter had declined a position when offered. Yardley reported to a Supervisory Committee of the NRC. Since the sponsoring organization was the Department of External Affairs, T. A. Stone, who ran the intelligence activities at the DEA, was Yardley's other supervisor and main contact with External Affairs. The Unit was housed in a few rooms at the Montreal Road Laboratories of the RNC in Ottawa, where they would stay for nearly a year until they outgrew the space.[42] Dr. Gilbert Robinson, Yardley, Ramsier, and six others were the initial staff (Fig. 16.4). All of them had taken an oath of secrecy. A week after its creation, the training materials from Mauborgne arrived, including copies of William Friedman's *Military Cryptanalysis* texts, and Yardley began his classes. He would teach cryptanalysis for a couple of hours a day, and the rest of the time his group practiced by trying to break the incoming radio intercepts. Yardley and his group received the first intercepted German messages from Rockliffe station around June 16, and

---

[41] Robinson, *History*, 13–14.

[42] Robinson, *History*, 16.

**Fig. 16.4**   Edna Ramsier in Canada, Fall 1941. (National Cryptologic Museum Library)

Yardley had broken them 11 days later.[43] Just a month later, the Examination Unit was regularly providing decrypted Vichy French and German Abwehr[44] intercepts to DEA. According to Jensen,

> Four copies of decrypted material were made: one file copy, one each to Military Intelligence and Naval Intelligence, and one to Stone at the DEA. There had been some successes against the Vichy ciphers, and German traffic between Hamburg and Rio de Janeiro was also being deciphered. Expenditures for the month had totaled just over $2,600. The Japanese diplomatic section of the Examination Unit began operating on 8 August 1941,

---

[43] John Bryden, *Best-Kept Secret: Canadian Secret Intelligence in the Second World War*, (Toronto, Canada: Lester Publishing, 1993), 55.

[44] The Abwehr was the German military intelligence service for all of the branches of the German armed forces from 1935 to 1945.

and quickly provided a satisfactory output of reports in terms of quantity and quality. By now, the staff of the Examination Unit had grown to a dozen. There had already been one notable success when SIGINT, decrypted by the Examination Unit, led to the arrest of a German agent by the FBI in June.[45]

Most of the German Abwehr traffic used a double transposition system, similar to the one that the Germans had used during World War I and with which Yardley was very familiar. Most of the Abwehr messages were from spies in South America and concerned departures, arrivals, and routes of commercial shipping up and down the South American coast. While the work of the Unit was excellent, the contents of these messages were not particularly important; for one thing, the British Admiralty already knew the schedules of commercial ships in the Atlantic. What was important was that Yardley and the Examination Unit were decrypting current German Abwehr messages, some of which might be very useful. In his report to the Supervising Committee on June 30, Yardley said, "The entire personnel has shown a most commendable eagerness to learn and a willingness to accept the drudgery necessary for success. No one could ask for a more loyal and industrious group."[46]

The Examination Unit started working informally on low-level Japanese traffic sometime in July, with Edna Ramsier providing the expertise there until the XU cryptanalysts came up to speed. Just like the Americans, one of the problems the Canadians had was in finding sufficiently experienced Japanese translators. This problem would hamper their work on Japanese intercepts for some time. Once the XU cryptanalysts were ready, Edna switched to working on the Vichy French intercepts with the help of two typists used as code clerks. By mid-September, she had broken enough of one of the Vichy systems to get recognizable French. By November, only one of the Vichy codes remained unbroken.[47]

Throughout the summer of 1941, the Canadians were very pleased with Yardley and the performance of the Examination Unit. As Dr. Robinson put it in 1945 in his history of the unit

> On the whole, our activities were crowned with early success which was largely due to Yardley's inspiration. Whatever may have been his faults, he was an excellent organizer and could inspire those with whom he worked with his own enthusiasm. Unfortunately his education and recent cryptographic experience had been limited, so it would now appear that we obtained from him about all he was in a position to impart, but I would not minimise his importance to this office.[48]

Sometime in early June 1941, the Department of External Affairs cabled to its High Commission in London to inform the British government that Herbert Yardley was now working for the Canadians, doing cryptologic work. The British were also to be told that the Canadians welcomed any British suggestions with respect to

---

[45] Jensen, *Cautious Beginnings*, 45.

[46] Kahn, *ROGM*, 206.

[47] Kahn, *ROGM*, 208.

[48] Robinson, *History*, 20.

cryptanalytic work and offered to share any information that the new unit would uncover.[49]

Unfortunately, the code clerk in Ottawa made a mistake in encrypting the telegram, and "Yardley" was transmitted instead as "Emeley." It took over a month for the High Commission to get back to the DEA and enquire if Mr. "Emeley" happened to be H. O. Yardley, as they both appeared to have worked for the Nationalist Chinese and had both published a book on American cryptography.[50] The DEA replied to Vincent Massey, the Canadian high commissioner in London, that Emeley was indeed Yardley and there had been a mistake in the transmission, but they assured the British that Yardley's rift with American intelligence was healed because of the recommendation of General Mauborgne. Once the British intelligence community discovered that Yardley was heading up the Examination Unit, however, they declined to cooperate with the Canadians at all. After all, Yardley had also exposed British intelligence secrets in his book, so he was not to be trusted.

All the while Yardley and the Examination Unit continued to decrypt Abwehr and Vichy French messages, completely unaware of the discussions happening between the DEA and the British about Yardley's status. By early August, Yardley also started adding analyses of groups of messages to his reports, identifying networks of agents, flagging messages that seemed particularly important, and linking messages to larger spy rings within South America. All this information was given to the Royal Canadian Mounted Police, who passed it on to the FBI. Yardley was in his element again and was very happy.[51] Yardley continued to please his supervisors at the National Research Council and the Department of External Affairs. "He 'has done and is doing good and useful work,' said one. Intelligence officers in Ottawa felt that Canada 'had made a good move in bringing Yardley up here.' An External Affairs official maintained that 'the Unit is producing results of high value to our Intelligence Services.' Another agreed that 'our Unit has been producing good results.' And after visiting Yardley, the National Research Council's [president] Mackenzie was 'very much impressed with what is being done. This is another project which is proving very successful.'"[52]

Yardley's good luck and happy employment were not to last, however. The British were not convinced by Pearson's message via Massey that the Canadians should be employing Yardley. Even before Pearson had sent his message on the 22nd, Alastair Denniston, the head of the Government Code and Cipher School at Bletchley Park, was in Washington, visiting General Mauborgne, William Friedman, and the American codebreakers in the War Department. During a discussion there about cooperation with other countries in cryptographic areas, Dennison reiterated that "cooperation of his organization with the cryptanalytic section recently

---

[49] Jensen, *Cautious Beginnings*, 44.

[50] The code used to encipher the message contained code words that allowed adjacent digits to be transposed, a basic mistake in code creation. The message sent was "6972 0602," which decrypted as EME-LEY, rather than the correct "6792 0602," which decrypted as YARD-LEY.

[51] Bryden, *Best-Kept Secret*, 69.

[52] Kahn, *ROGM*, 208–209.

established by the Canadian Government at Ottawa would be wholly dependent upon the elimination of Mr. Yardley from the latter organization."[53] Denniston repeated the British position when he was in Canada later in the month.

Lester Pearson, newly returned from London to Ottawa, attempted to rebut Denniston by telegramming Vincent Massey on August 22 to try to get him to soothe the British. He reiterated the argument that Yardley was now in good standing with the American intelligence community, had been recommended by Mauborgne, and was using American cryptanalytic textbooks to teach the staff in the Examination Unit. Denniston replied that Mauborgne's opinions were his own and were emphatically not shared by the rest of the American intelligence community. Denniston also promised that GC&CS would send over an experienced British cryptanalyst to run the Examination Unit after Yardley left. Pearson began to waver. As he telegrammed to Massey, "…we are very anxious to see a closer liaison and a fuller exchange of information between our Unit and the United Kingdom Cryptographers."[54] If that desire for liaison meant that Yardley would have to go, then the Canadians were willing to consider the option. In the end, the Canadians decided that their relationships with Britain and the United States were more important than Yardley, and they decided not to renew his contract, which expired on December 9. However, they weren't going to tell Yardley until the very end, in late November.

The British now went silent on the Yardley affair for over 2 months without official confirmation that they would offer full cooperation with the Canadians and a cryptanalytic expert. This did not ease the minds of the Canadians.

Throughout the fall of 1941, Yardley and the Examination Unit continued to decrypt Abwehr, Vichy French, and low-level Japanese ciphers (Fig. 16.5). They added ciphers from Columbia and a couple of other South American nations as the months wore on. The Unit expanded, adding more cryptanalysts and Japanese, Spanish, and French linguists. However, innovations began to slow later in the fall. Yardley was teaching the Examination Unit cryptanalysts pretty much exactly the same systems and techniques that he had seen in World War I and in China. These were largely low-level, relatively simple, substitution and transposition ciphers. They were learning things from Friedman's textbooks, particularly some of the mathematical techniques that Friedman had developed in the 1920s and his team of mathematicians at SIS had added to in the 1930s. However, Friedman and his SIS cryptanalysts had moved on from pencil-and-paper techniques and were designing their own cipher machines and consistently breaking foreign cipher machines. They were also using IBM accounting machines to help create new codes and to perform basic grunt work on intercepted ciphers. These cipher machines produced cipher messages that were significantly more complex and difficult to break than the systems that Yardley and the Examination Unit were working on. If the Canadians were to move up into the ranks of first-class cryptanalytic organizations such as those in

---

[53] Alaistair Denniston, "Denniston Visit to U.S. Signal Corps, August 1941," Meeting Minutes (Washington, DC: National Archives and Records Administration, RG 457, Historic Cryptologic Collection, Box 949, Folder 2714, August 16, 1941); Kahn, *ROGM*, 210.

[54] Bryden, *Best-Kept Secret*, 78.

**Fig. 16.5** Herbert Yardley and Edna Ramsier in Canada, October 1941. (National Cryptologic Museum Library)

the United States, Britain, France, and Germany, they needed more than last-generation experience. In truth, by this time Yardley was pretty much at the limit of what he could teach the Canadians. He had not kept up with many of the new advances in cryptology in the more than a decade that he had been out of the US Government cipher establishment.

Finally, the Canadians got tired of waiting for their ally across the sea to provide assurances that they would be able to continue their cryptanalytic bureau undiminished. Pearson fired off yet another telegram to the British on November 17 insisting that Ottawa wanted "to have definite assurances from the United Kingdom that a cryptographic expert of high qualifications and capable of taking charge of our unit will be made available to us" and "that the collaboration will be forthcoming." On November 20, Denniston, for the British government "vowed to lend Canada 'an experienced cryptographic expert' and assured 'closest collaboration.'"[55] They also wanted Yardley out of Canada before their expert arrived.

Not willing or able to wait any longer, Tommy Stone and Pearson arranged a meeting with Dr. Robinson and Yardley on November 21 at which time they told Yardley that they were not going to extend his contract and he would be replaced "by one of our own people." Yardley, understandably, erupted and gave the two diplomats "a most unpleasant half hour" according to Pearson.

> Yardley took the news very hard and was most insistent in his demands for a full explanation of the circumstances which gave rise to our decision to terminate our arrangement with him when, in fact, his Unit was just getting under way and was doing most excellent work. He said that there must be something more behind it than the mere desire to put a British subject in charge and he thought that he had a right to know. It was explained to him that for many reasons it was considered desirable now to have the whole organization in our hands and further than that by way of explanation it was not possible to go.[56]

Robinson, Mackenzie, the head of the RNC, and many of the members of the Examination Unit protested Yardley's removal. Stone was also uneasy about the circumstances of Yardley's removal. Therefore, on the following Monday, the Supervisory Committee of the RNC sent Pearson and now Lt. Commander C. H. Little to Washington to determine why the Americans were so opposed to working with Yardley. Arriving on November 26, Pearson and Little first talked to British Naval Intelligence Captain Edward Hastings, who assured them that the American intelligence community thought that Yardley "'was unreliable and untrustworthy' and more interested in publicity and money than in the work. He was 'technically no more than an ordinary cryptanalyst.'"[57] Hastings also repeated the British line that neither the British nor the Americans would cooperate with the Examination Unit as long as Yardley was in charge. However, he also said, "The reason was their general but strong dislike and distrust of him because of his having written *The American Black Chamber*. This was not due to professional jealousy or irritation at Yardley's having given away secrets of the craft, Hastings felt, but was an honest suspicion."[58] Pearson and Little then made the rounds of the various American intelligence heads, including naval intelligence, military intelligence, and the FBI, getting essentially the same answer from each. The two then saw the new Chief Signal Officer and Mauborgne's successor, Major General Dawson Olmstead, who said that he wouldn't hire Yardley in any capacity for any reason and insisted that if Yardley was the head of the Examination Unit, there would be no American cooperation with Canada at all.

---

[55] Kahn, *ROGM*, 210.

[56] Robinson, *History*, 20.

[57] Kahn, *ROGM*, 211.

[58] Kahn, *ROGM*, 212.

Finally, after a long day of running around Washington, Pearson and Little met with William Friedman for an informal conversation. Friedman said he thought that the entire reason that the Americans and British were against Yardley was the publication of *The American Black Chamber*. He reiterated his beliefs—neither of which were true—that *The American Black Chamber* had caused the Japanese to immediately improve their cryptosystems and caused many other countries to tighten their own cryptosecurity as well. Friedman said that while Yardley was a very good organizer and manager and was industrious with a flair for inspiring his staff, he was woefully behind the times when it came to cryptanalytic techniques. Friedman also said he felt that Yardley had no experience with machine ciphers and that the cryptanalysts in Washington and Bletchley Park were well ahead of Yardley's current skill set. In addition, while he sympathized with Yardley's plight, like all the other people Pearson and Little had talked to that day, said that Washington would not work with the Canadians as long as Yardley was there.[59]

Pearson and Little headed back to Ottawa and submitted their report to the Supervisory Committee. After asking Yardley to stay until the end of December and wrap up his current work, they confirmed their original decision that Yardley had to go.

Yardley, however, wasn't taking things lying down. Trying to pull strings through his literary agent, George Bye, he had Bye write to Eleanor Roosevelt pleading his case and asking for an interview with Mrs. Roosevelt. Unfortunately, the First Lady received Bye's letter and promptly passed it on to the President's military advisor. The date was Saturday December 6, 1941.

Yardley also wrote a long memo to the DEA outlining all the things his unit had accomplished and teased out other things that he had planned for the organization. It was of no use. However, many of the Canadians felt that Yardley and Edna had been treated poorly and the Supervisory Committee tried to help make their move back to the United States as smooth as possible. The NRC put them both on "special duty" for two and a half months at full salary and paid all their moving expenses back home. They also facilitated their passage through US and Canadian customs and wrote them letters of thanks. By the beginning of January 1942, Herbert and Edna were back in Washington.

At the age of 52, Herbert Yardley would never work as a cryptographic professional again.

---

[59] Lester Pearson and Lt. Cmdr. T. H. Little, "Memorandum on a Visit to Washington to Enquire into the Situation Regarding H. O. Osborn," Memorandum (Ottawa, Canada: National Research Council, November 26, 1941), Volume 29,166, File WWII, part 1, 0235–0243, National Archives of Canada.

# Chapter 17
# The Friedmans at War: William

The 1940s did not start off well for William Friedman. After his team's success with breaking the Japanese Purple cipher machine, Friedman had what amounted to a nervous breakdown shortly after Christmas 1940. He was voluntarily admitted to the psychiatric wing at Walter Reed Army Hospital on 4 January 1941, suffering from anxiety, exhaustion, and depression. When he appeared at Walter Reed, a psychiatrist asked him a series of questions about his mental state. "Without mentioning the Purple project, William said his work had been demanding lately. He felt a constant tension that interfered with his ability to function, and sleep provided little relief when he could manage to sleep at all."[1] In addition, Friedman was increasingly frustrated by the need to keep all of his work secret, even from his wife. Over the years, not being able to talk to Elizebeth about his work would become deeply disturbing to Friedman, even on the best of days. In an interview with the NSA with regards to William's work on the Purple machine several years after his death, Elizebeth said, "I didn't know anything about it. He didn't mention what was going on or what machines were known to be in existence or anything. And the thing that astounds me so, as I've looked back on it many times, was that the day that the first message, when they made that purple machine, … now wouldn't you have thought that any being that was human couldn't have resisted. That they would have said something on that day? Never said a word to me. I didn't know anything about it."[2]

William was assigned to a ward in the psychiatric wing at Walter Reed along with about 20 or so other patients and stayed there for the next two and a half months while he was evaluated. Finally, the army doctors decided that Friedman

---

[1] Jason Fagone, *The Woman Who Smashed Codes*, (New York, NY: William Morrow, 2017), 220.

[2] Elizebeth S. Friedman and Forrest Pogue. "Transcript of Forrest Pogue Interview with Elizebeth Smith Friedman, 1973." Oral History. Oral History Collection. Lexington, VA: George Marshall Foundation Research Library, May 16, 1973. NSA Archives, Center for Cryptologic History. http://www.marshallfoundation.org/library/wp-content/uploads/sites/16/2015/06/Friedman_Mrs-William_144.pdf, 25.

© The Author(s), under exclusive license to Springer Nature Switzerland AG 2023
J. F. Dooley, *The Gambler and the Scholars*, History of Computing, https://doi.org/10.1007/978-3-031-28318-5_17

was now recovered from his nervous exhaustion and anxiety, and he was released from the hospital on 22 March 1941. He returned to active duty on 1 April.[3] However, things were different for him after this. He was more fragile, and his depression would come and go a number of times over the coming years, forcing several more hospital stays. The Army was also more wary of his behavior and stamina. He was encouraged to work only a few hours a day, and from then on, he was not assigned to new cryptanalysis tasks and was more of a technical consultant rather than the senior technical cryptanalyst in charge of Signal Intelligence Service (SIS).[4] Near the end of April he received a letter informing him that he had been honorably discharged from the Army "by reason of physical disqualification." He was not given a hearing, nor was he allowed a defense or an appeal.[5] William protested strenuously, but in vain. It would be 5 years later before his protests and appeals would bring results and he would be reinstated in the Army Reserve at his previous rank; until then he would continue to do the same work he had done since 1921, once again as a civilian.

After the increasing German and Japanese militancy and saber-rattling of the mid-to-late 1930s, the advent of World War II in September 1939 was not a surprise to anyone in America or Europe. The United States would not be officially involved in the war for over 2 years, but both the Army and the Navy foresaw the country's involvement and began to request increased funding from Congress so they could get ready for the conflict. As part of these requests, both OP-20-G and SIS began to grow. For the first 7 years of its existence, SIS stayed static at its May 1930 level of seven employees. The Navy's OP-20-G was also relatively static in size for much of the 1930s, as was the Coast Guard Cryptanalytic Section under Elizebeth Friedman.

Starting in 1937, however, both SIS and OP-20-G began to grow. In October 1937, SIS added four more positions, for a total of 11. In 1938, Friedman's group would grow by 8 more to 19; in 1939, SIS was at 45; and by mid-1941, SIS would have 93 personnel, with 70 of them civilians. On 7 December 1941, the Signal Corps' Intelligence groups were composed of 109 civilian and 222 Army personnel. Most of the Army personnel were in the Second Signal Service Company, working in the seven radio intercept stations run by the Signal Corps. There were 50 personnel in the cryptanalytic section of SIS and 26 in the cryptographic section.[6] With the growth of the organization, SIS moved in July 1942 into a former girl's school in Arlington, Virginia, a few miles southwest of Washington. Arlington Hall (Fig. 17.1) stayed the headquarters for SIS and its follow-on agencies until the 1980s.

---

[3] Ronald Clark, *The Man Who Broke Purple* (Boston: Little, Brown and Company, 1977), 158. William Friedman had been called to active duty in October 1940 at the rank of Colonel in anticipation for a trip to the United Kingdom. He was returned to duty at his previous rank of Lt. Colonel.

[4] Friedman & Pogue, *Transcript*, 31.

[5] Fagone, *Smashed*, 221.

[6] William F. Friedman, "Expansion of the Signal Intelligence Service from 1930 to 7 December 1941 (SRH-134)," trans. U.S. Army Signal Corps (Washington, DC, December 4, 1945), NSA Archives, Center for Cryptologic History.

Comparatively, by the attack on Pearl Harbor OP-20-G had over 200 personnel, 65 Naval officers, 124 enlisted personnel, and 36 civilians. Navy organizations as a whole were much stricter about requiring Naval personnel rather than civilians, even in research and cryptologic positions. This was a direct result of two long-standing Navy traditions, first, that Naval personnel were generally discouraged from reporting to civilians, and second, that women were not allowed to manage men or generally do the same jobs as men. This latter tradition would impact Elizebeth Friedman when her Coast Guard cryptanalytic section was transferred to the Navy in 1942. It was also why Agnes Meyer Driscoll never moved up the management chain in OP-20-G. It would take decades for these traditions to change.

By the early 1940s then, when he was about 50, William Friedman was effectively not doing any more cryptanalysis. His work from this point on was largely in creating cipher machines and consulting within the ever-expanding War Department cryptologic organization. Friedman was increasingly moved aside and out of day-to-day cryptanalysis tasks and management into senior technical and consulting roles but not always into decision-making roles. Friedman's depression returned in December 1941, but this time he did not seek medical help. He and Elizebeth struggled through his depression, insomnia, and suicidal thoughts for nearly 6 months until he finally worked his way into a better mental and emotional place.

Friedman worked in Arlington Hall, as did his three senior cryptanalysts (Fig. 17.2). However, Rowlett, Sinkov, and Kullback all joined the Army and had increasingly important roles in the expanded SIS.

One of the things that William missed while incapacitated in early 1941 was the SIS's first interactions with the British Government Code and Cipher School (GCCS) at Bletchley Park. A combined Army and Navy group was supposed to go to Bletchley in January 1941 to learn more about the British work on different cipher systems, including Enigma, and to share American work on Japanese systems and deliver to the British two working replicas of the Purple machine. William was supposed to lead this group; instead, Abe Sinkov was activated in the Army Reserve as a Captain, and he and then Lieutenant Leo Rosen were the SIS

**Fig. 17.2** SIS personnel at Arlington Hall in 1944. Seated: Lt. Colonel A.J. McGrail, Chief Laboratory Branch; Col. W. Preston Corderman, Chief Signal Security Agency; William Friedman, Director of Communications Research; Standing: Mark Rhoads, Asst. Director Comm. Research; Lt. Colonel Solomon Kullback, Chief Military Cryptanalytic Branch; John Hurt, Translator; Captain Edward Vogel, Chief Special Documents; Major Frank Rowlett, Chief General Cryptanalytic Branch; Lt. Colonel Abe Sinkov, Chief Central Bureau, Brisbane. (US Army photo)

representatives who went to the United Kingdom along with two Naval officers from OP-20-G. This exchange of information and materials was the first in a long series of collaborations between the American cryptologists and their British counterparts. William wasn't totally left out of consultations with the British, however. In the spring of 1943, he would be the chief technical advisor on an American visit to Bletchley and would be one of the chief negotiators of the first formal Britain-USA (BRUSA) agreement on sharing of signals intelligence between the two allies.[7]

While William Friedman wasn't doing much in the way of cryptanalysis after 1940, he continued to be very involved in cryptography—the creation, evaluation, and approval of new ciphers and cipher machines for the Army.

Friedman's greatest cryptographic accomplishment began several years before the start of World War II, took more time than anyone might have anticipated to finally come to fruition, and made a greater impact on US military cryptography

---

[7]Colin Mackinnon, "William Friedman's Bletchley Park Diary: A New Source for the History of Anglo-American Intelligence Cooperation," *Intelligence and National Security* 20, no. 4 (December 2005): 654–69, https://doi.org/10.1080/02684520500426602; Ralph Erskine, "William Friedman's Bletchley Park Diary: A Different View," *Intelligence and National Security* 22, no. 3 (June 2007): 367–79; John Carey Sims, "The BRUSA Agreement of May 17, 1943," *Cryptologia* 21, no. 1 (January 1997): 30–38.

than could have been imagined. It was the development of the most famous American cipher machine of World War II, the SIGABA.[8]

The SIGABA has a curious history. It began life as a design by William Friedman that he created in 1932 and that was implemented in late 1933 as the Army Converter M-134[9] (Fig. 17.3). Friedman was trying to improve the security of rotor-based cipher machines by attempting to avoid the single stepping behavior of rotors in machines such as the Enigma and the British Typex.

Friedman reasoned that if the rotors advanced irregularly according to a separate key that caused different rotors to turn seemingly randomly, it would be much more difficult to predict which alphabets were being used. He implemented this idea by taking a page from Gilbert Vernam's one-time pad cipher machine that he had broken in the early 1920s and integrated a paper tape reader into the M-134. The key that was punched into the paper tape controlled the stepping of the cipher rotors in

**Fig. 17.3** The original M-134 in 1934. (NSA photo)

---

[8] During this time the Army Signal Corps assigned all its cryptographic equipment six-letter code-names. The first three letters were always SIG, which stood for "signals intelligence," and the second three letters were chosen randomly.

[9] This was U.S. Patent 2,028,772, filed in 1932 and granted in 1936.

the device. This device was known as the M-134-T1.[10] These rotor-based cipher machines also came with a set of 10 cipher rotors; the machine used five at a time (as opposed to the standard German Enigma, which used three or later, four rotors), and the rotors could be inserted into the machine in either direction, although they always turned the same way. The first M-134-T1s came off the assembly line in late 1933.

At one point in the fall of 1933 as the first production M-134s were coming off the manufacturing line, Friedman asked Frank Rowlett to create a series of key materials—paper tapes with the keys on them. He was to use a machine for generating the tapes that Friedman had designed. Rowlett had a great deal of difficulty with this chore because the procedure that Friedman had outlined was cumbersome and time-consuming; the machine that was to generate the key tapes was very delicate, difficult to use, and broke often; and the key tapes had to be very long, so that there were no repeated sequences over the course of many transmitted messages. However, Rowlett was not particularly interested in what he considered to be largely clerical work. He was also very concerned about the use of key tapes in the field—they were fragile and likely to tear or be ruined some other way, and he was concerned about the very large number of tapes that SIS would have to create if many M-134s were manufactured. Instead, he started using some of his spare time trying to think of a better way to generate the key sequences for the M-134. In a burst of inspiration, Rowlett had the idea that one could use an extra set of rotors to generate the key sequence for the cipher rotors in the machine. Rowlett then came up with a different electromechanical way to generate the key stream randomly that would be integrated into the M-134 and that did not require creating any key materials a priori.[11]

When Rowlett first brought his idea to Friedman in early 1934—an idea that replaced one of Friedman's own—Friedman dismissed it out of hand. He refused to believe that a machine using rotors would be able to generate a random sequence of key letters that could be used by another machine and create complex ciphertext.[12] He may also have been afraid to admit that he could be wrong about his paper tape idea. It took Rowlett nearly a year to convince Friedman that his electromechanical key maze, as he called it, would work better and faster than the paper tape apparatus. This was a year in which their relationship became increasingly frayed as Rowlett continued to push his new idea and Friedman continued to reject it. This conflict over technical details was just the beginning of a number of disagreements between

---

[10] U.S. Patent 6,097,812, filed July 25, 1933 and granted August 1, 2000. The patent was kept secret by the Army all that time.

[11] Frank R. Rowlett, *The Story of Magic: Memoirs of an American Cryptologic Pioneer*, Hardcover (Laguna Hills, CA: Aegean Park Press, 1998); Timothy Mucklow, "The SIGABA/ECM II Cipher Machine: 'A Beautiful Idea'" (Fort George G. Meade, MD: Center for Cryptologic History, National Security Agency, 2015), https://www.nsa.gov/about/cryptologic-heritage/historical-figures-publications/publications/assets/files/sigaba-ecm-ii/The_SIGABA_ECM_Cipher_Machine_A_Beautiful_Idea3.pdf, 8.

[12] Mucklow *Beautiful Idea*, 9; Frank R. Rowlett, "Oral History of Frank Rowlett (1974)," Oral History, NSA Oral History Collection (Ft. George G. Meade, MD: National Security Agency, Center for Cryptologic History, 1974), 45g.

the two men. Frank Rowlett was also very ambitious and increasingly confident in his technical skills. He eventually came to feel, whether erroneous or not, that Friedman wasn't giving him enough credit for his work in SIS.

Rowlett finally had to threaten to go over Friedman's head unless the two sat down and Friedman gave Rowlett and his idea a fair and considered hearing. This happened, and once Friedman was finally convinced of the efficacy of Rowlett's idea, he accepted it enthusiastically, calling it "a beautiful idea," and they reworked Friedman's patent for the M-134, removing the paper tape reader and adding Rowlett's key maze to it.[13] The two of them worked on the design of Rowlett's idea, producing drawings for an implementation in late August 1935 when they began writing their new patent application. However, because some M-134s using the old design had already been manufactured, they had to create an add-on device, called the M-229 (also called the SIGGOO), to attach to the M-134s that had already been distributed to the field. Its appearance on top of the existing M-134 was ungainly, and it was awkward to use, but it did the job on the original M-134s. Rowlett and Friedman worked on getting the army to produce a prototype of the new M-134 with a key maze and submitted their updated patent application for the device on 23 March 1936.

Unfortunately, in 1935 the Army was suffering financially just as much as the rest of the country from the Great Depression, and Friedman could not obtain the funds to develop and manufacture the integrated device that combined the M-134 and M-229. In October 1935, Friedman did, however, have a conversation with Navy Lt. Joseph Wenger, the current head of OP-20-G. During that conversation, Wenger told Friedman that the Navy was unhappy with the Hebern cipher machines that they had contracted for and were considering doing their own development. He also said that the Navy had development monies available and asked Friedman if the Army had any ideas on cipher machines. Friedman then arranged a meeting on 21 October and proceeded to tell Wenger and several of his assistants—but without Rowlett present—about the M-134 and its new integrated device and left them with a current version of his and Rowlett's drawings and description. Throughout several meetings between Friedman and OP-20-G during October and November 1935, Wenger and his assistants all seemed unenthused about the device but let Friedman continue explaining the details. Weeks passed with no further word from the Navy, and Rowlett urged Friedman to go back to the Navy and find out what their impressions of the new ideas were and whether they were going to use them. Friedman met with Wenger again and reported back, to Rowlett's dismay, that the Navy thought the new ideas were impractical and would not work. Rowlett was sure that they were wrong. "I thought the doggone thing would work and maybe they weren't as smart as they thought they were."[14] Friedman and Rowlett were then left with the impression that the Navy was not interested in pursuing the improved M-134 device,

---

[13] Rowlett, *Oral History 1974*, 45j; The two men also filed a patent application just for the wheel cage system. U.S. Patent 2,166,137 was applied for on August 19, 1935 and granted on July 18, 1939.

[14] Rowlett, *Oral History 1974*, 45n.

so they had to let it drop until the Army had development funds available. This was also during the time that the SIS team was involved first with breaking the Japanese diplomatic RED machine cipher and then the PURPLE machine, so the new version of the M-134 was definitely on the back burner.

However, it turned out that the Navy was interested in the new design and apparently just didn't want the Army to know that. In early 1936, when Wenger passed this information on to his successor as head of OP-20-G, Captain Laurence Safford, Safford was excited by the idea and the Navy proceeded to develop the device—without telling Friedman or Rowlett.[15] Safford was particularly interested in the new key maze and in the reciprocity of the cipher wheels. However, he didn't like the plugboard that Friedman had originally added to the device. Instead, what he and Lieutenant (later Commander) Donald W. Seiler of the Washington Navy Yard recommended was that a separate cage be added to the machine that housed all 15 rotor wheels, five cipher rotors, five control rotors, and five 10-element index wheels. They also constructed a way for the control rotors to manage the stepping of the cipher rotors in conjunction with the index wheels, all based on Friedman and Rowlett's original ideas. The index wheels themselves replaced the plugboard that Friedman had originally designed. The resulting rotor cage is illustrated in Fig. 17.4. It was attached to the top of the machine via four thumb screws. This made it easy to install and remove the rotor cage. A removable pin (visible on the left-hand side of the cage) provided the axis for each set of five rotors, making it easier to insert and remove them.

In early 1940, 4 years after the Navy apparently decided not to pursue the new machine, Frank Rowlett was working with Navy Lt. Ham Wright on some issues with their joint work on the Purple machine. At one point, Wright told Rowlett that one of the principles they were discussing was just like a feature of the Navy's new cipher machine. The conversation continued

> Ham sat down there and he developed the logic of the system that Friedman had revealed to Wenger and the other Navy people and clearly indicated that the key generator that was being involved in this Navy machine was exactly the one that we wanted to have involved in the Army machine that we'd been denied the opportunity to develop because the funds weren't available. ... I said "Where did you get these ideas?" and he said "Well Wenger got them somewhere." you see and I said "Well what is the status of it?" and he says "Well we're having one built." He says "It'll be down here and I'll see if I can't arrange for you to look at it." and this, well I sort of sat there and kept my cool thinking about this because I wondered my goodness what's going on here sort of. I know where Wenger got the idea but why didn't the Navy tell Friedman about it? ... [Rowlett now goes to talk to Major Reeder, the current administrative head of SIS] I said "Now it seems to me that this is exactly the information that Friedman had given Wenger ... and that the Navy had told us that they weren't going to do anything about it." and he says, "Well, what do you think about it Frank?" sort of and I said "I think it's a damn good thing. I'm glad they've done it."[16]

---

[15] Rowlett, *Story of Magic*, 101; Mucklow *Beautiful Idea*, 12–13.

[16] Frank R. Rowlett, "Oral History of Frank Rowlett (1976)," Oral History, Oral History Collection (Ft. George G. Meade, MD: National Security Agency, Center for Cryptologic History, 1976), 438–440.

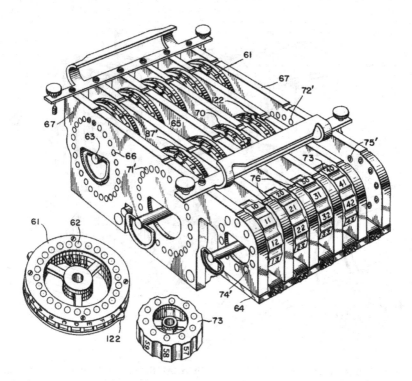

**Fig. 17.4** M-134-C (SIGABA) Rotor cage. (U.S. Patent Office)

Several weeks later on 3 February 1940, Friedman, Rowlett, Abe Sinkov, Sol Kullback, and Reeder were invited to a meeting over at the Navy department where OP-20-G would be demonstrating the first prototype of their new rotor-based cipher machine, called the Electrical Ciphering Machine (ECM) Mark II (Fig. 17.5). This was the machine that Safford and Seiler had been working on for nearly a year and that incorporated Friedman's M-134 ideas, Rowlett's cipher key maze, and the new rotor cage that the two Navy men had developed.[17] All the Navy officers knew that the basic ideas for the cipher machine and the key maze had originated with Friedman and Rowlett, and they were very enthusiastic in their praise for the ideas that they had been able to incorporate into their new machine. The longer the SIS team listened and the longer they spent examining and testing the new machine, the greater their pride and admiration of the device grew. After a time, both Friedman and Rowlett suggested some minor improvements to the new machine that the Navy agreed to.

The Army and Navy had finally gotten together on the device and completed development together. The Army called the new machine the M-134-C (also

---

[17] Laurance F. Safford and Donald W. Seiler, Control Circuits for Electric Coding Machines, U.S. Patent Office 6,175,625 (Washington, DC, filed December 15, 1944, and issued January 16, 2001), https://image-ppubs.uspto.gov/dirsearch-public/print/downloadPdf/6175625

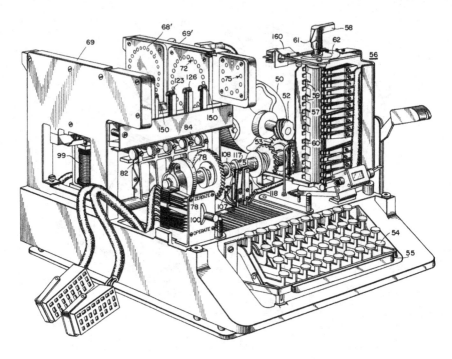

**Fig. 17.5** Safford and Seiler's version of the SIGABA/CSP-888. (U.S. Patent Office, patent #6,175,625, Figure 1)

SIGABA), and the Navy called it the CSP-888 (also Electrical Cipher Machine (ECM) Mark II).[18]

SIGABA machines began to be released to Army and Navy units in the spring of 1942. By the end of the war, more than 10,000 of them had been shipped and were in use in all theaters of the war. While the Navy put a number of SIGABA machines on board ships, the Army only used them for upper level communications, never for tactical messages. This was mostly because the SIGABA (Fig. 17.6) was very heavy at approximately 93 pounds and also fairly fragile, which made frequent moves of the machine problematic.[19] Its weight made it impractical for infantry and limited its use to only larger units with more transportation. There is no evidence that either the Japanese or the Germans ever successfully broke a SIGABA message. The machine was used for high-level cryptographic communications well into the 1950s.

Despite the fact that by the time SIGABA was delivered, both the Friedmans were actively working in cryptology, he for the Army and she for the Navy, neither talked about their work to the other. With respect to the nearly decade-long effort on

---

[18] Mucklow, *Beautiful Idea*, pp. 14–17.

[19] https://maritime.org/tech/ecm2.htm

**Fig. 17.6** A complete SIGABA machine. (National Cryptologic Museum)

SIGABA, when asked about William's work on the device, Elizebeth replied, "Never said a word to me."[20]

The next cipher machine that engaged William Friedman in the lead up to World War II was not invented by him, but he was involved in its final design and approval by the Army. The M-209 cipher machine is the military version of Boris Hagelin's C-38 cipher device. It was introduced by the US Army as a replacement for the M-94, which was considered too insecure by this time. It had, after all, been in service since 1922.

Boris Hagelin and his Swedish company, A. B. Cryptoteknik, developed the C-35, C-36, and C-38 cipher machines starting in the mid-1930s. This development was started at the request of the French, who wanted a small, lightweight, tactical cipher machine that could also print. Hagelin developed the C-35 and then the C-36 for the French, and he delivered the first machines to them in 1935. The design included elements of his previous B-21 cipher machine, as well as parts from a vending machine he had developed. He brought two C-38s to the United States from his home in Sweden in March 1940. Hagelin smuggled the two machines in his luggage as he traveled south from Sweden through Germany and into Italy. On 10 May 1940, he was able to leave from Genoa, Italy for America on the last ocean liner to depart before the Italians entered World War II. He would stay in the United States

[20] Fagone, *Smashed*, 150.

for the next 4 years before being able to return to Sweden.²¹ Once in the United States, Hagelin, who had met William Friedman in Sweden back in 1928, talked to Friedman and offered to license the C-38 to the US Army. Friedman and SIS performed a security analysis of the machine. They proposed several changes that would ruggedize the machine and make it easier to use in the field. Hagelin agreed to the changes, and the two parties agreed to a licensing contract. The machine was designated the M-209 and was approved for Army use in 1942 (Fig. 17.7). The M-209 was manufactured by the Smith-Corona Company in Syracuse, NY for $64.00 each. About 140,000 machines were built over the lifetime of the M-209. Its first general use was in the American invasion of Northern Africa in November 1942. It was used throughout World War II, the Korean War, and into the early 1960s. The machine made Boris Hagelin the first cryptologic millionaire.

The M-209 was a strictly mechanical device that used six cipher wheels and a pin-and-lug system to encrypt plaintext letters. The pin-and-lug system controlled the rotation of the cipher wheels. The machine automatically broke the ciphertext into groups of five letters separated by spaces for printing. It printed out the

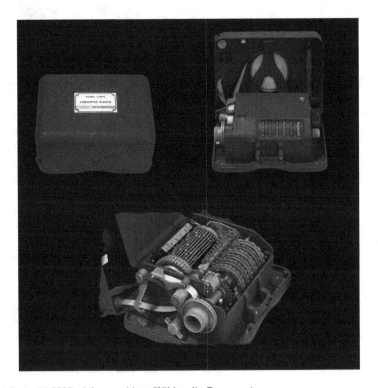

**Fig. 17.7**  An M-209B cipher machine. (Wikimedia Commons)

---

²¹ Boris Hagelin and David Kahn, "The Story of the Hagelin Cryptos," *Cryptologia* 18, no. 3 (July 1994): 204–42, https://doi.org/10.1080/0161-119491882865, 221.

ciphertext (when enciphering) or plaintext (when deciphering) on an attached printer that used a simple paper tape.

Experienced M-209 operators could encipher or decipher approximately 30 letters a minute.

Despite the fact that it had a period of more than 101 million, the M-209 was not particularly cryptographically secure. In fact, with a sufficient amount of traffic and with messages of sufficient length or two or more messages that overlapped and used the same key, it could be broken within 24 h or so. This meant that the US Army and Navy, while satisfied with its operation and short-term security, only used it for tactical messages whose value expired in a few hours. By 1943, German cryptanalysts could read between 10% and 30% of intercepted M-209 messages. However, unless they had at least two messages with overlapping plaintext or that used the same message key (called "depth" by cryptanalysts), the decryptions took them several days.[22]

Early in 1942, William Friedman was tasked by the Chief Signal Officer with developing a new and cryptographically secure teletypewriter system for use by the Army. Its most important use was to be between major Army commands to transmit logistical data, the amount of which had skyrocketed after America's entry into the war. Friedman enlisted Frank Rowlett to help with the project, and the two began to design a machine based on some ideas that Friedman had come up with. Based on both their experiences with AT&T Teletype machines and Friedman's previous experience with the Vernam cipher machine in the early 1920s, they immediately rejected the idea of a second paper tape to hold key sequences. Their ideas were based on adding a new device to existing Teletype Corporation teletype machines to generate a key stream with an extremely long period. The machine that they designed was called the M-228 (SIGCUM).

Friedman's original design for the M-228 had some fatal flaws that Rowlett picked out after Friedman explained the design. While once again, Friedman took quite some convincing, Rowlett finally got him to agree that the flaws existed and the two men then revised the design. Their new design resembled the rotor cage that they had used on the SIGABA machine.

Friedman and Rowlett's design for the M-228 was approved by the Signal Corps in the fall of 1942, and the first prototype produced by the Teletype Corporation was available before the end of the year. It passed an initial series of tests easily with no obvious signs of cryptographic errors found. Because the Army was desperate to have the machine in use, it was rushed into production in January 1943 despite the fact that SIS had not been allowed to see the final circuit diagrams of the machine and Rowlett's protests that it needed more comprehensive cryptographic testing

---

[22] Anonymous, "European Axis Signal Intelligence in World War II As Revealed by 'TICOM' Investigations and by Other Prisoner of War Interrogations and Captured Material, Principally German," TICOM (Washington, DC: Army Security Agency, May 1, 1946), National Security Agency, https://www.nsa.gov/portals/75/documents/news-features/declassified-documents/european-axis-sigint/volume_1_synopsis.pdf, 5.

before release.[23] To placate SIS, the Army agreed to monitor the M-228 traffic to and from the Pentagon and allow Rowlett to analyze the transcripts. Both Friedman and Rowlett were very happy with this idea. The first transmissions using the newly installed M-228 machines began on 9 January 1943. Within a week of its release, a machine operator in Algiers reported that parts of a message he had just received were garbled and asked for retransmission. The code clerk in the Pentagon agreed and set up his machine and proceeded with the retransmission. However, instead of changing the message key as required by the operating procedures, the clerk used the same key as before, providing anyone who was listening with two messages that were slightly offset but that had used the same key sequence. This is known as providing a message "in depth." Two messages in an additive system such as that used by the M-228 can be compared to reveal the key sequences and thus the plaintext.

Rowlett immediately realized what had happened and had the Pentagon discard the current days keys and switch to an alternative set. Rowlett then took all the transmitted messages with him back to Arlington Hall and proceeded to see if he could recover the keys and thus the transmitted messages from the ciphertext he had in hand.[24]

By 2 a.m. the following morning, Frank Rowlett not only recovered the plaintext of the transmitted messages but also had the key sequence, which allowed him to uncover the wiring diagrams for two of the M-228's five rotors, the fast rotor on the right and the medium speed rotor next to it. This was a disastrous news. However, "the weaknesses ... were not in the cryptographic logic of the system, but in the circuitry built into it by Teletype."[25] The very circuitry that Rowlett had not been allowed to examine before the machines were put into operation. It was clear that M-228 had to be replaced immediately.[26]

Rowlett immediately reported his findings to his superiors and the next day they all met. Rowlett laid out the mistake that led to the messages in depth and then described his analysis and showed his recovery of the plaintext of the messages, the key sequence, and the wiring of the two rotors. He then recommended that all M-228 machines be removed from service until they could be redesigned.

Rowlett and Friedman went back to the drawing board and, over the course of the next 3 months, redesigned the rotor cage and electrical connections for the M-228, simplifying some, securing others, and came up with a new and cryptographically secure machine. The M-228 went back into production in April 1943. When released back into the field, it was at first only allowed to send messages rated up to the CONFIDENTIAL level, but this was later increased to SECRET. The machine was used throughout the war and into the early 1950s.

---

[23] Stephen J. Kelley, "The SIGCUM Story: Cryptographic Failure, Cryptologic Success," *Cryptologia* 21, no. 4 (October 1997): 289–316, https://doi.org/10.1080/0161-119791885940, 298.

[24] Kelley, *SIGCUM Story*, 302.

[25] Kelley, *SIGCUM Story*, 309.

[26] Kelley, *SIGCUM Story*, 309.

During the rest of the war, Friedman continued to play the role of technical consultant at the SIS, the Signal Security Agency and the Army Security Agency, but his age—he was 50 in 1941, while Rowlett was 33 and Abe Sinkov and Sol Kullback were both 34—and the lingering effects of his depression were slowing him down. According to Rowlett, who continued to work with Friedman,

> Things were just happening too fast. Friedman could never keep up with them and so he finally paced himself until where he acted more in the capacity of an advisor instead of being involved in the administration and he, in this capacity he got involved in several things. ... I found that he was beginning to realize that he was going to have to turn over the reins to the rest of us because he just couldn't stand the pace. [3 lines redacted] I think he wanted to produce more. He wanted to give more than he was able to give and I think that bothered him and I think he reacted to it and finally he was put in a position of senior consultant and of course in a way was insulated from some of the greater pressures, organizational pressures and wartime pressures, and he pretty soon accepted this but it was only an overt acceptance I think.[27]

William Friedman's recovery from depression in 1941 and his good mental health did not last long, however. By December 1941, Friedman was under psychiatric care again, this time as an outpatient. After his last experience, he refused to go back to Walter Reed's psychiatric ward; William continued to see his psychiatrist, and he and Elizebeth toughed it out for the next several months until William was feeling better again.[28]

He would remain as a technical consultant and advisor, but his days as a hands-on close supervisor of cryptanalytic work were pretty much over, and his time as a full-time cryptanalyst and cryptographer was also mostly past.

As the war in Europe was winding down, William Friedman had one last, very important job to do for the US Army. By late 1944 the Americans and British were starting to worry about the postwar intentions of their other ally, the Soviet Union. In particular, the two Western nations were particularly concerned about the fate of German scientists, engineers, technicians, and all the German records relating specifically to rocketry, propulsion, cryptology, and signals intelligence. The British and Americans put together a secret project called the Target Intelligence Committee (TICOM) that was to organize teams of Allied scientists and cryptologists to go through occupied Europe, locating German intelligence assets, records, cryptanalysts, and technology of the various German intelligence agencies and recover those assets for their governments. All these materials and people were to be transported back into American- and British-occupied territories and away from the Soviets. TICOM was made up of six teams composed of frontline troops and scientists and cryptologists, each with a specific target and mission. In June 1945, William Friedman was activated in the Army at his previous rank of Lt. Colonel and assigned to an ad hoc TICOM Team on a 90-day mission, which was to search through southern Germany for German cryptologic people and assets. Friedman left Washington on 14 July 1945. Arriving in Paris, he met with Colonel George A. Bicher, the senior

---

[27] Rowlett, *Oral History 1976*, 463–464.
[28] Clark, *Purple*, 181.

US signals intelligence officer in the European Theater of Operations. Aside from a week spent visiting German SIGINT sites in southern Germany and a 3-day trip to Frankfort, Friedman spent most of his time shuttling between Bletchley Park and Alastair Denniston's civilian intelligence bureau at Berkeley Street in London. His diary for the period is littered with meetings and meals with many of the outstanding cryptologists from Bletchley Park: Denniston, John Tiltman, Peter Twinn, Gordon Welchman, and, of course, Alan Turing. He worked on TICOM data that had already been collected and wrote up sets of questions to be asked of German cryptanalytic prisoners of war. His 3-month stint was wrapped up in just 2 months, and he returned to the United States on 12 September 1945.[29] William Friedman's war was over.

---

[29] William F. Friedman, "William Friedman TICOM Diary" (Army Security Agency, 1945), archive.org, https://archive.org/details/WFFTourOfShatteredEurope

# Chapter 18
# The Friedmans at War: Elizebeth

Elizebeth Friedman's war was every bit as intense and exciting as her husbands.

Starting in 1940, Elizebeth and her Coast Guard Cryptanalytic Unit became increasingly involved in counterespionage and counterintelligence, spying on spies and decoding their messages. These were known as "clandestine" operations.

By 1940, the Army, Navy, and U.S. Federal Communications Commission (FCC) all had radio intercept stations that could pick up radio signals from South America that were intended for stations in Europe, notably Germany. This was their first indication that Nazi Germany was setting up clandestine operations in South America, with an eye toward using that continent as a jumping off point for attacks on the United States should that become necessary. These espionage groups were largely set up in Brazil, Argentina, and Chile, all of which had large German emigre populations, many of whom were sympathetic to the Fascist cause. Nearly all of the Coast Guard Unit's work from 1940 through the end of the war was interception and decryption of these German spy network's messages from South America. Elizebeth's Cryptanalytic Unit worked to decrypt these clandestine messages in complete secrecy because she knew that if any of the German spies in South America had a hint that their messages were being intercepted and decrypted that they would change their systems immediately. If anything, during the war, Elizebeth's organization was more secret than William's[1].

These South American spy networks were established by two different German intelligence organizations, the SD and the Abwehr. SD is short for Sicherheitsdienst, which was the intelligence arm of the Nazi SS. The Abwehr was the German-combined armed forces military intelligence service. The SD operatives were loyal Nazis, who were specially selected and trained for espionage work. Their aims were almost always political in nature, aimed at undermining the Allies in country, pushing the South American governments toward supporting the Fascist camp, and,

---

[1] Jason Fagone, *The Woman Who Smashed Codes*, (New York, NY: William Morrow, 2017), 189.

© The Author(s), under exclusive license to Springer Nature
Switzerland AG 2023
J. F. Dooley, *The Gambler and the Scholars*, History of Computing,
https://doi.org/10.1007/978-3-031-28318-5_18

failing that, encouraging local fascists in planning coups to install sympathetic fascist governments. The Abwehr agents were all more concerned with military operations, and it was their agents who would send messages about troop transports and other ship sailings that would be passed on to German U-Boats in the Atlantic. The Abwehr and the SD were competitors/rivals, and usually no love was lost between the two agencies and their operatives. However, in Brazil and Argentina, the two organizations often worked together.

The spies in South America used a number of different cipher systems to transmit their messages. Early on, many of them were hand-based, but later they moved onto cipher machines. The Coast Guard Unit was very successful in breaking all these systems. This includes breaking at least three different versions of the German Enigma cipher machine. Most of the hand cipher systems were transposition systems of one sort or another, book ciphers, or relatively simple substitution ciphers; for the last half of 1941, these manual systems were the same ones that Herbert Yardley was breaking up in Canada.

At first, many of the Nazi spies were using these book ciphers. Each spy circuit would usually use a different book, but not always. The most frequently used book was the German language edition of the 1938 historical novel *All This, and Heaven Too*, by American novelist Rachel Field. Elizebeth and her crew solved a number of book cipher messages using this book and finally discovered the book itself.

In January 1940, the Coast Guard began intercepting messages from a radio station in Mexico intended for a station in Nauen, Germany. The odd thing about the message was that it only contained eleven letters from the alphabet, A, C, D, E, H, K, L, N, R, U, and W. Elizebeth did a quick frequency analysis of the messages and discovered that the most frequently occurring letter was N and that it was fairly evenly spaced throughout each of the messages. She guessed that the N was used as a word separator or space, leaving ten more letters. Her next guess was that these ten letters represented the numeric digits 0 through 9. However, which letters represented which digits? If this were a book cipher, then there must be a keyword that mapped the ciphertext letters to digits to identify book pages and words within pages. So Elizebeth and her team began looking for German words using the ten remaining letters; a simple task with the internet, but very tiresome in 1940. They finally came up with the word DURCHWALKEN, which meant "to give a good beating." This gave them a probable key:

```
D U R C H W A L K E N
1 2 3 4 5 6 7 8 9 0 -
```

It turned out that this group of messages replicated several of the number pairs in many messages, giving the Coast Guard team "cribs" that allowed them to solve many of the messages without even knowing the book.

In early 1941, Elizebeth's team began seeing a large increase in Coast Guard interceptions from German spies in South America. Many of these were messages from two SD operatives in Brazil, using the code names "SARGO" for a spy named Johannes Siegfried Becker and the code name "LUNA" for one Gustav Utzinger. In addition, they were seeing messages from a couple of Abwehr agents who were also in Brazil, Albrecht Engels, known as "ALFREDO" and another, Josef Starziczny, known as "LUCAS."

Becker was recruited by the SD in the mid-1930s and was sent to Brazil in 1938. Over the next several years, he was thought to be responsible for recruiting upwards of 250 Nazi agents and for the creation of nearly 30 clandestine radio stations. Gustav Utzinger was known as the *Funkmeister* (literally "Radio Master"); he was a Ph.D. chemist who was also a radio engineering expert. Utzinger was sent to South America in 1940 to improve the set up and running of the different radio circuits there. A radio "circuit" is a pair of stations, noted by their locations (e.g., Rio and Berlin).

Albrecht Engels was a German businessman living in Brazil who was already spying for the Abwehr by the time Johannes Becker reached Rio de Janeiro. His Abwehr partner, Starziczny, was based out of Sao Paulo, some 250 miles southwest of Rio. Starziczny was described by Engels as "a jittery mechanical engineer." He lived with his Brazilian mistress near the Sao Paulo waterfront and radioed messages about ship sailings. He talked too much and made Engels nervous.[2] These four men would be instrumental in the setting up of radio circuits and recruiting for their spy networks over the following 4 years. Through their messages, Elizebeth Friedman would get to know them well.

The Coast Guard decrypts were distributed to army intelligence (G-2), navy intelligence (ONI), the State Department, and to the British in the person of William Stephenson, a Canadian industrialist who was the head of the British Security Coordination (BSC) operation at Rockefeller Center in New York. BSC was set up in May 1940 by British MI6, with the blessing of the US government to catch Germans spying against Britain in the United States.

The Coast Guard Unit also distributed decrypts in 1940 and the first half of 1941 to the FBI, but their relationship was difficult and uneasy. Elizebeth's group would send solved German cryptograms to the FBI, but they never received anything in return. The FBI's Special Intelligence Service in Washington would share the Coast Guards' decryptions with their agents in South America, despite the Coast Guard asking them to keep the existence of the messages a secret. Worse yet, on J. Edgar Hoover's orders, the FBI would take credit for Coast Guard work and "systematically obscured all traces of the Coast Guard's deep involvement in the spy hunt."[3]

In addition, in its official three-volume history of the Special Intelligence Service during the war, the FBI deliberately omitted all mention of the Coast Guard and its cryptanalytic unit, leading the reader to believe that the FBI itself accomplished all the decryptions. Something that is not true at all.

In preparation for the war that he believed was coming soon, on 1 November 1941, President Roosevelt transferred the Coast Guard from the Treasury Department to the US Navy and thus all Coast Guard personnel, including everyone in the

---

[2] Fagone, *Smashed*, 227.

[3] Fagone, *Smashed*, 231–232.

Cryptanalytic Unit, were now "subject to the authority" of Secretary of the Navy Frank Knox. However, Elizebeth pushed back on the transfer of the Cryptanalytic Unit to the Navy on the grounds that her unit was doing useful work for both the Treasury and Justice departments by decrypting smuggler's and spy's encrypted messages.[4] She also had the example of Agnes Meyer Driscoll in the Navy, a strong, capable woman who was not allowed any supervisory role because of Navy traditions. So, the transfer of the Cryptanalytic Unit was deferred for a few weeks. However, this did not mean that change was not in the air.

In early December 1941, Lt. (later Lt. Commander) Leonard Jones (USCG) was put in charge of the Coast Guard Cryptanalytic Unit, which at this time was also renamed Unit 387. Elizebeth Friedman was "demoted" from Cryptanalyst-in-Charge to Cryptanalyst (grade P-4; Elizebeth was promoted to grade P-5, Senior Cryptanalyst, in June 1943).[5] Lt. Jones had taken the War Department cryptanalytic course from William Friedman in 1935, and he was working in the Cryptanalytic Unit by the late 1930s. While she was annoyed at the change, Elizebeth was still effectively in charge of the Unit. She was more than willing to let Lt. Jones do all the administrative work and leave the cryptanalysis to her and her team. By this time, Unit 387 was up to about a dozen personnel, including the four cryptanalysts and code clerks and secretaries.

Later in December 1941, just after the Pearl Harbor attack, Elizebeth and her team were loaned to William "Wild Bill" Donovan's Office of the Coordinator Of Information organization (COI, later named the Office of Strategic Services (OSS)). This was a temporary assignment to create the COI's cryptologic section in conjunction with James Roosevelt, the President's son and the COI's liaison to the Army, Navy, FBI, and other branches of the government that dealt with intelligence. Donovan's COI was created in mid-1941 and reported not to the War, Navy, Treasury, Justice, or State Departments but directly to the President. Elizebeth created the overall cryptologic section for the COI. They would not be breaking encrypted messages, but they did need to communicate securely with their operatives in the field, and between the various COI headquarters in Washington, New York, London, Cairo, and Colombo, Ceylon. She created codes and ciphers for them to use and arranged for the code clerks to be trained. She scrounged around for cipher machines, manuals, and other machines that would be needed and requisitioned them from the Navy. She laid out a cryptologic training program for the COI operatives who would go out into the field behind enemy lines. She also interviewed potential cryptographic staff personnel and made recommendations to Donovan, which he ignored. In fact, for the entire three and a half weeks of her assignment at COI, Donovan treated Elizebeth as a servant and secretary rather than as a professional cryptanalyst. She was not amused. This assignment was finished by early

---

[4] Fagone, *Smashed*, 235.
[5] "Personnel File: Elizebeth Smith Friedman" (National Personnel Records Center, 1946), VF 148-2, National Cryptologic Museum Library.

January 1942, and to wrap things up, Elizebeth wrote a "seethingly polite" final report to Donovan and went back to her office in the Treasury Building.[6]

In March 1942, CG Unit 387 was finally and formally moved to the US Navy. For a year, Unit 387 was in the Office of Naval Intelligence but not part of the official organization as such. The unit finally became a part of OP-20-G and was designated OP-20-GU in March 1943. That same month, the Cryptanalytic Unit also moved from the Treasury Building to the new Naval Communications Annex on Nebraska Avenue in Washington. This new site had been a women's college, Mount Vernon College, until it was taken over by the Navy in December 1942. Like the Army's site at Arlington Hall, the site soon swarmed with new construction as department after department of the Navy's growing intelligence apparatus moved in. For all this time, the Coast Guard Unit was kept together and separate from the other cryptanalysts in OP-20-G with Elizebeth still as chief cryptanalyst; by 1942, the Unit was up to nearly 20 people with the addition of several cryptanalysts and more clerks. They would stay together for the rest of the war.

By 1940, Unit 387 was focused solely on clandestine German networks, nearly all of them in South America. Early on, all these networks used manual cipher systems, substitution ciphers, transposition ciphers, double transposition, and grille ciphers. None of these systems gave Elizebeth or her team much in the way of problems as long as they had enough traffic to find messages in depth and they broke all these systems in short order. However, the Germans were shortly to switch to a much more complicated system.

In late 1940, the major circuits quickly moved to using machine ciphers, with the primary machine being the Enigma. Breaking these Enigma machines would occupy most of Elizebeth's time for the next four and a half years. Both the SD and the Abwehr used similar Enigma machines, typically called the *Abwehr Enigma*. These Enigmas differed from the German armed services Enigmas in three important ways. First, the Abwehr Enigma did not have a plugboard on the front of the machine, so that when a key was typed, the value of that key went directly into the first (right-hand) rotor in the machine. Second, while the Abwehr Enigma had three rotors, like the German Army and Air Force Enigmas, there was a fourth rotor that was the Abwehr's equivalent of the reflector in the other Enigmas. The difference is that in the armed forces Enigmas, the reflector was a static rotor—it did not step the way the other three rotors did; the electric signal entered the reflector at one letter, and the output was a different letter to which that first letter was wired. This feature of the reflector meant that no letter typed into the keyboard would encrypt to itself. In the Abwehr Enigma, the reflector stepped along with the other rotors. The stepping of the Abwehr Enigma's reflector had little effect on the machine's output though, because the rotor was the last one to step and thus required very long messages to move. Finally, where in each of the armed forces Enigma rotors there was a single turnover position on each rotor that marked the point where the rotor would

---

[6] Fagone, *Smashed*, 239–241; Elizebeth S. Friedman, "ESF Letter to Wild Bill Donovan," Memorandum, December 29, 1941, archive.org, https://archive.org/details/@jason_fagone

step, on the Abwehr Enigma, there were three of them, at positions 15, 17, and 19 along the rotor. These three changes ended up making the Abwehr Enigma easier to solve than the armed services versions. The absence of the plugboard greatly simplified the number of possible alphabets used in any given message. The stepping reflector made the machine into a simple four-rotor machine, with the fourth rotor having a predictable stepping pattern. The extra turnover positions were the only feature that made the machine more difficult to cryptanalyze because, like William Friedman's SIGABA machine, it made the rotor stepping sequences more difficult to predict. Unlike SIGABA, however, the Abwehr Enigma's stepping was not irregular.[7]

To solve the Abwehr, Elizebeth Friedman and her team had to figure out two very difficult things about the machine. First, the team had to determine how the rotors worked, how they were wired internally, and how the turnover positions and the reflector worked. Once they had done that incredibly difficult thing, they could then recover the keys that were used each day using cribs and the German habit of creating messages with standardized beginnings and endings. Dilly Knox at Bletchley Park independently solved the Abwehr Enigma in 1941.

The Coast Guard Cryptanalytic Unit had acquired a couple of commercial Enigma machines during the 1930s, so they were familiar with the machine's workings and wiring.[8] However, they still needed to determine the wiring of every machine on each circuit so they could begin to work on the day keys.

The first Enigma messages intercepted by the FCC and passed onto the Coast Guard occurred in January 1940. A suspicious new circuit was transmitting five to ten messages a day, but the characteristics of the new messages did not match any of the features of the manual ciphers that the Coast Guard was used to. The team opined that the messages were created using a machine cipher. They had no luck deciphering messages even as they began to pile up. However, they finally realized that no letter was encrypting to itself and that the plain–cipher equivalences of the cipher alphabet were reciprocal, characteristics of the behavior of an Enigma machine. At this point, Elizebeth broke out the commercial Enigma the team had in storage, and they got to work trying to figure out the wiring of the new machine.[9] Many months later, they were able to determine the wiring of all the rotors and begin deciphering the incoming messages. As Elizebeth would put this achievement after the war, "...this recovery of wiring assumed to be unknown was achieved without prior knowledge of any solution or technique for the recovery of Enigma wiring

[7] Peter Twinn, "The Abwehr Enigma," in *Codebreakers : The Inside Story of Bletchley Park*, (Oxford ; New York: Oxford University Press, 1993), 123–31.

[8] David Mowry, "Cryptologic Aspects of German Intelligence Activities in South America during World War II" (Ft. George Meade, MD: Center for Cryptologic History, National Security Agency, 2011), https://www.nsa.gov/about/cryptologic-heritage/historical-figures-publications/publications/wwii/assets/files/cryptologic_aspects_of_gi.pdf, 84–88.

[9] Mowry, *German Intelligence*, 84.

and is believed to be the first instance of Enigma wiring recovery in the United States."[10]

At the same time, that Elizebeth's team was working on solving the Abwehr Enigma, the responsibilities of various American government organizations were changing as a result of America's new war stance. At the urging of J. Edgar Hoover, the FBI was given responsibility for investigating all possible spy activities against the United States in the entire Western Hemisphere. This meant that FBI agents were beginning to spread out through Central and South America, with special attention given to Brazil, Argentina, and Chile. With J. Edgar Hoover trying his best to roust and capture German spies and with Elizebeth trying her best to keep them in place, so she could intercept and decrypt their coded messages and learn of their plans, a collision was sure to happen.

Throughout January and February 1942, as the Germans were increasing their U-boat attacks against American and British ships in the North Atlantic, Elizebeth and her cryptanalysts were also decrypting increasingly strident messages from the German agents in Brazil. "Measures against member of the Axis are assuming drastic form." "Bank deposits already blocked. We are destroying all compromising documents, maintaining radio operation as long as possible." At one point, in early March 1942, Unit 387 proved their worth once again by deciphering a series of messages about the ocean liner *Queen Mary*, which was transporting more than 8000 American troops to Europe. Their quick decipherment of these messages and alerting the Navy enabled the government to warn the *Queen Mary*'s captain of U-boat danger and allowed him time to change course and avoid attack. However, their good luck was not to last. Starting around March 15, 1942 and lasting for at least 2 months, internal Brazilian police, urged on by the FBI, rounded up more than 90 members of the Nazi spy ring, including Engels and Starziczny. Utzinger, the *Funkmeister*, was able to ship one of his radio transmitters to Paraguay and resume broadcasting from there. He would later move to Buenos Aires and help rebuild a spy network there under the cover of a radio repair shop. He would finally be arrested and interrogated by American agents in August 1944 when a crackdown on German spies similar to the one in Brazil occurred in Argentina.[11] Becker was in Germany at the time of the raids and finally made his way to Argentina in February 1943 and started again to set up spy networks. These raids and arrests greatly reduced the number of messages that Elizebeth and Unit 387 were intercepting. To make matters worse, the State Department and the FBI were in possession of raw decrypts of messages that the Coast Guard had been sending them as part of an information sharing arrangement to the Brazilian Foreign Minister. State and the FBI had already sent hundreds of those raw decrypts to their counterparts in Brazil. The result of this release of secret information, as reported by the Coast Guard's Lt.

---

[10] Elizebeth S. Friedman, "History of US Coast Guard Unit #387: 1940–1945" (Washington, DC: United States Navy, 1945), https://archive.org/details/HistoryOfCoastGuardUnit387/page/n1/mode/2up, 230.

[11] Fagone, *Smashed*, 244–245; David Kahn, *Hitler's Spies: German Military Intelligence in World War II*, (New York: Macmillan, 1978), 326.

Cmdr. Jones a year later, was "…the FBI had furnished verbatim copies of all messages sent or received in Brazilian circuits known to them, including hundreds of
messages in a circuit … most of which material they had received from the Coast
Guard. Brazilian officials, in questioning German agents following the arrests in
March 1942, showed deciphered verbatim messages to the prisoners, with the result
that Germany was unmistakably informed that the systems had been solved. The
inevitable consequence was that systems on all clandestine circuits were almost
immediately thereafter completely changed."[12] The immediate result was that
Elizebeth and her team were in the dark for months as they painstakingly solved all
the newly released systems.

The first messages over a new machine circuit with a call signal of TQI2 were
intercepted by the Coast Guard on 10 October 1942. The destination was a radio
with call signal TIM2. More messages throughout November and into early
December led the radio detection experts to place these two stations in a Hamburg–
Bordeaux circuit; however, one of the endpoints of the circuit was believed to be in
South America. Once again, early on, Unit 387 had no luck with the messages, but
as more messages arrived and they had more depth to work with, patterns began to
emerge. It was noticed that a number of the messages had duplicate message numbers, enabling more work with depth. "The lessons learned from solving the commercial Enigma were applied, together with the improved techniques learned from
the British, and the machine was solved. Wheel motion patterns were similar to the
Enigmas used by German agents in Europe which had been solved by the British
prior to the appearance of TQI2. Decrypted texts showed that the circuit was
between Berlin and Argentina."[13] Their experience with the first Abwehr Enigma
solution was used to recover rotor wirings and keys used. The machine was solved
around 11 January 1943. It revealed that the new radio network out of Argentina
was really three networks in one, called Red, Green, and Blue by the Nazis. The
Abwehr Enigma just solved was the one used on the Green network. Elizebeth and
her team would see the first Red network circuit messages on 4 November 1943.
Her team was warned about the new circuit by messages over the Green network
setting up the new communications. They would solve the Red machine by
mid-December.[14]

The final Abwehr Enigma machine that Elizebeth and her team solved was
named the Berlin–Madrid machine for the end points of its circuit. On 5 May 1944,
the Berlin–Madrid circuit stopped using the double transposition system they had
always employed and began using an SS/Abwehr Enigma. Unit 387 cryptanalysts
examined the traffic from this machine and compared it to the other traffic from the
SS group. This group used three different machines, a Green machine, a Red

[12] Leonard T. Jones, "History of OP-20-GU (Coast Guard Unit of NCA)," Memorandum
(Washington, DC: United States Navy, Naval Security Group, October 16, 1943), RG 38, box 115,
5750/193, CNSG Library, https://archive.org/details/HistoryOfOP20GU, 6.

[13] Mowry, *German Intelligence*, 86.

[14] This "Red" Enigma machine is not to be confused with the Japanese diplomatic RED machine
that the SIS solved in 1935. They are completely different.

machine, and a rare Engima version called "M." After several months of effort and the capturing of a number of encrypted messages on this circuit, this last machine was finally determined to be using Red rotors and a Green reflector. The machine was then solved quickly.

Elizebeth's solutions of the German spy network's Abwehr Enigma machines paid enormous dividends during 1943 and 1944 as the Cryptanalytic Unit was able to decrypt more and more of Siegfried Becker's messages to and from Berlin about his new, bigger espionage network. As Elizebeth's knowledge of the structure of the Nazi spy network grew, she was able to attach short memos to batches of decrypted messages, giving informed intelligence analysis of the contents to her superiors. She was able to identify Becker and Utzinger and a number of their colleagues. She exposed which Argentinian, Bolivian, Chilean, and Paraguayan politicians and military people they were talking to and who was on the German's side and who was not. With all this information about Argentinian politicians and generals conspiring with the Nazis, the Allies were still hesitant to confront the government in Buenos Aires because of the risks of exposing the fact that the Americans had broken the German cipher machines. The problem was solved by a fatal mistake made by Becker and an audacious play by the British. Becker had conspired with a low-level Argentinian diplomat, Osmar Hellmuth, to go to Germany and arrange for shipments of armaments for the Argentinian military, a gross violation of Argentinian neutrality. From her decrypts, Elizebeth knew the details of this plan, and her superiors in Naval Intelligence informed their British counterparts which ship Hellmuth would travel on, what was the sailing date, and at which ports the ship would be stopping. One of those ports was at the British Crown Colony of Trinidad. It was there that the British yanked Hellmuth off his ship in the middle of the night, ignored his protests of diplomatic immunity, and put him on a British warship bound for England, arriving in Portsmouth on 12 November 1943. After nearly a month of solitary confinement and increasing threats from the British, Hellmuth caved and told them all he knew about the Nazis operations in Argentina. He told them about Becker and Utzinger and Nazi involvement in a coup in Bolivia, and he gave them names of Argentine collaborators. Meanwhile, the Argentine government was increasingly worried that they might be implicated in an arms plot that would trigger American interference in their country. Therefore, they had to make a choice. On 26 January 1944, Argentina broke diplomatic relations with Germany, and throughout February and March, they rounded up all the German spies they could find. However, they missed Becker and Utzinger. Utzinger was finally captured in August 1944. Becker continued hiding and moving frequently but was finally captured in April 1945. Both men were later released from Argentine prisons after Juan Peron was elected President in February 1946. Utzinger was deported to Germany, where he was detained and interrogated by the Americans. Becker stayed in Buenos Aires but then faded away and was never heard from again, bringing Nazi espionage in South America to a close.[15]

---

[15] Fagone, *Smashed*, 279–281, 303; Kahn, *Hitler's Spies*, 324–327.

One of the fascinating parts of Elizebeth's work on Enigma machines is that she and her team solved these Enigma variations almost entirely using manual techniques and only basic mathematical and statistical operations. This was in stark contrast to the British solutions of the armed forces Enigma machines. One can certainly argue that the Abwehr variations of commercial Enigma machines were less secure than the armed forces versions and were thus easier to solve. However, that didn't make them easy to solve. "Ease of solution" shouldn't take away the enormous technical and human challenges involved in reconstructing and then solving messages for these very complicated cipher machines. Elizebeth and her team executed both parts of the solution puzzle—reconstructing the machines wiring and then recovering all the keys day in and day out, all the while under enormous time pressure. These solutions rank with the most complicated solutions of cipher machines made during the war.

The manual techniques of solution that she used were a hallmark of Elizebeth's solutions:

> Her basic puzzle-solving style hadn't changed from the smuggling days, and it remained effective: a process of trial and error with pencil and paper, deduction and experimentation, granules of eraser dust swiped away with a flick of the palm. Her scrap papers still looked like the scrap papers of a person doing the newspaper puzzle page over Sunday-morning tea; she wrote no equations, only numbers and letters grouped and stacked in rows, columns, squares, rectangles, and more exotic shapes. This approach worked for her because over the previous twenty-five years, encountering tens of thousands of messages, Elizebeth had solved so many different kinds of puzzles that she knew how to find shortcuts, to identify patterns in fields of text that were like signatures telling her what to do next. She was a kind of human computer in this sense.[16]

Once V-E Day arrived on 8 May 1945, Elizebeth and her team were left with very little to do. Almost immediately, both the Army and the Navy started some downsizing of their cryptologic organizations. After the Japanese surrender on 14 August, the pace of downsizing accelerated rapidly. By the end of 1945, fully half of all the personnel at both Arlington Hall and the Naval Annex on Nebraska Avenue were gone. Much of Elizebeth's organization, mostly the clerks, also left. Elizebeth turned 53 on 26 August 1945, while William was in Europe on his special TICOM assignment. Her daughter Barbara was serving in Panama and would be home later in September. John Ramsay was in flight school in Texas. Lt. Cmdr Jones and his wife dropped by with gifts and flowers on her birthday, and Elizebeth made them dinner.

Elizebeth took the last few months of 1945 to write the technical history of Coast Guard Unit 387 during the war. With the help of her three remaining cryptanalysts and Lt. Cmdr. Jones, she produced a 329-page document that described all 48 of the clandestine Nazi radio circuits and their code and cipher systems. The document also described how Unit 387 had broken each system, including the three Abwehr

---

[16] Fagone, *Smashed*, 193–194.

Enigma systems.[17] She was also tasked with deciding which of the tens of thousands of decrypted messages should be saved for posterity. She marked 4000 decrypted messages to be saved and shredded the rest.

Once these documents and the preserved message decrypts were safely off to the National Archives, she left the Naval Annex for good and went back to her old desk in the Treasury Building with her old team.

---

[17] Friedman, *History of Unit #387.*

# Chapter 19
# Yardley's War

Herbert Yardley and Edna Ramsier returned to Washington from Canada in early January 1942. The Canadian government had generously, and guiltily, given them two and a half months salary, letters of thanks, and moving expenses as severance to help them get started again in the United States. Yardley immediately started trying to get work with the War, State, and Navy Departments, all of whom turned him down without a second glance. On 3 February 1942, Yardley met with three of Herbert Hoover's subordinates at the FBI with two things in mind. First, Yardley was looking for employment and hoped that a position as a code and cipher consultant was a possibility. He was blocked out of the State, Navy, and War Departments, and the FBI seemed the next best thing. Second, he hoped that failing a job, the FBI could at least get him taken off the "black list" that he was on at the State, Navy, and War Departments. He railed against Friedman for blocking all his attempts to get a job and complained about all three departments and the FBI. He also tried to convince them that the government surely needed his services during the war. The three FBI men were having none of it, and so thanked Yardley for his time and sent him on his way. In their report to Director Hoover, the agents said, "He is on a fishing expedition to find out all he can concerning his inability to secure a position with the Army, Navy, or State Department. It is also obvious that he would like to be in charge of a Cryptographic Section during the present emergency."[1] Needless to say, Yardley left the FBI without a job and with no prospects of getting a job in codes and ciphers anywhere in the government.

As was usual with Yardley, he started going through the money the Canadians had given him quickly once in Washington. Edna did not go back to her clerk position at the SIS, so they were both unemployed and living on a rapidly dwindling bank account. Yardley corresponded with George Bye, and together they tried to get some work for him writing magazine articles, but with no luck. They also tried

---

[1]David Kahn, *The Reader of Gentlemen's Mail: Herbert O. Yardley and the Birth of American Codebreaking* (New Haven: Yale University Press, 2004), 218.

J. F. Dooley, *The Gambler and the Scholars*, History of Computing, https://doi.org/10.1007/978-3-031-28318-5_19

selling the movie rights to his 1937 radio scripts to Columbia Pictures, but Yardley insisted on more money than Columbia wanted to pay, and the deal fell through.

Finally, in March 1942, Herbert and Edna bought a restaurant at 1308 H Street, NW in Washington for $10,000, all of it borrowed. The restaurant was in Edna's married name—Hackenberg, but Yardley was considered a co-owner. They renamed it the Rideau, and they lived in the apartment over the restaurant. The opening day was Sunday, 15 March. Yardley and Edna both worked in the restaurant, which had a total of 13 employees. It was open 24 hours a day, largely because there were a large contingent of customers from the *Washington Times Herald* newspaper whose offices were across the street and who would drop in at 3 a.m. every night after the paper was put to bed. The restaurant was a struggle from the beginning, and the operation never made much money. The most interest Yardley and the restaurant received was from the FBI.

At some date, probably in July or early August 1942, someone from the Military Intelligence Division (MID) of the US Army requested that the FBI investigate Herbert Yardley because he was "suspected of disaffection and harboring pro-German sympathisers" at his restaurant.[2] The FBI surveillance began on 6 August 1942 and lasted through 7 September. Special Agent Frederick A. Tehaan of the FBI Counter-Intelligence Corps was the agent in charge. FBI agents dropped by the restaurant at various hours at least 11 times during the investigation and made regular reports of each of their visits. It wasn't exactly exciting work for the agents and their daily reports reconstruct how dull it was. From 6 August, "The type of people frequenting the said restaurant were of middle class caliber. Ordinary conversation was discussed by the above people." 11 August, "There were very few customers in the place and no conversations between the customers and employees were overheard by this Agent." 21 August at 8:45 p.m., "Inside the restaurant were a waitress, two counter men, four young men occupying a booth and three customers seated at the counter. This Agent sat at the counter and proceeded to drink several glasses of beer."

They may have been bored, but they were thorough. The FBI also examined Yardley's Civil Service, State Department, and Army personnel records; obtained access to his bank records and his high school records; and interviewed several of his previous landlords and even his mechanic. They checked if he had a police record in the District of Columbia, and checked whether he had a file with the Justice Department as well. They even checked with the police in Worthington, Indiana, where Yardley was still remembered fondly; "it is recalled to this day by faculty members that Yardley was one of the most brilliant students."[3] One FBI agent (Tehaan) even read Yardley's *American Black Chamber*; his conclusion was that "Subject was employed from 1921–1929 by the Military Intelligence Division,

---

[2] Frederick A. Tehaan, "FBI Files on Herbert Yardley," Memorandum (Washington, DC: Federal Bureau of Investigation, September 7, 1942), DK 079-001, David Kahn Collection, National Cryptologic Museum Library.

[3] Kahn, *ROGM*, 221.

War Department, in a secret capacity."[4] They also went so far as to gain access to rooms across the street from the restaurant, first on the third floor of an office building, and when that didn't provide a good enough view into the apartment, rooms on the third and fifth floors of the *Washington Times Herald* newspaper offices in order to spy on Yardley and Edna in their apartment. The agents dutifully listed all the furniture in the apartment. One day, Tehaan gave a detailed report of Yardley walking into the living room of the apartment in his underwear, Edna following in a housecoat. She proceeded to set up an ironing board and started ironing shirts. Yardley went into the bedroom, came out dressed, and left the apartment. He was back a few minutes later with a pile of newspapers. He opened a beer and proceeded to read the papers and talk to Edna. Tehaan's conclusion at the end of this report is "From the above indications this Agent believes that the Subject is living in the above second floor apartment with the woman mentioned herein."[5] This was pretty much the sum total of the damming information uncovered by the FBI investigation. Tehaan wrote a report to his superiors on 7 September 1942 and recommended that the investigation be closed down. One of his final conclusions was that "This Agent did learn that Yardley is deeply interested in the successful operation of the above restaurant..."[6]

Despite all the extra business that the Rideau received from the FBI agents, Edna and Yardley weren't making any money from it. They sold the whole operation in November 1942.

On 9 November 1942, at the age of 53, Yardley started a new job with the federal government. Not in codes and ciphers this time, though. He started work as an Assistant Investigator in the legal division of the Office of Price Administration (OPA) in Washington. The OPA was the government agency charged with regulating prices on various commodities during the war and investigating charges of price gouging and manipulation. They regulated prices for things such as automobiles, tires, nylon, sugar, gasoline, coffee, meats, and different kinds of processed foods. Yardley was in the investigatory arm of the agency, investigating meat price gouging. His starting salary was $2600 per annum as an assistant investigator. However, Yardley must have been an excellent investigator because he kept getting raises and promotions all throughout the war. One case that he closed involved price gouging by a slaughterhouse that was selling meat above the OPA levels; on Yardley's evidence they were convicted and fined $200,000. He was promoted to associate investigator at $3600 in March 1943, to a District Commodity Investigator at $3800 in 1944, and to a senior investigator's position at $4400 in November 1946. That same month he moved from the Washington office to Baltimore, where he switched from meat to sugar enforcement and supervised a staff of 8 to 12.

These were happy times for both Edna and Herbert. They continued to live in the apartment above the old Rideau for a while. Edna slipped and broke her leg in early

---

[4] Tehaan, *FBI Files*, 51.

[5] Tehaan, *FBI Files*, 31–32.

[6] Tehaan, *FBI Files*, 13.

1944 and went to stay with a friend who ran a boarding house while she healed. Yardley would come and visit her every few days. They made friends with a married couple in their 20s, Frank and Layton Fordham, who also lived at the boarding house, and when Edna's leg healed sufficiently, Yardley would take them all out for drives to the beach. The young couple really got to like Edna and Herbert.

> They were impressed because they knew who he was and they were just a bunch of kids in their twenties; they thought he was great not because he was famous but because he was generous. He was friendly and talkative. He told jokes. He played cards. He drove them places. Layton thought he was articulate and refined: he never used bad language. Edna called him Hoy. He and she obviously enjoyed one another's company, but in an undemonstrative way. They seemed very much in love. Edna, with blue eyes and strawberry blonde hair, always seemed to have her head tucked in coyly. The Fordhams thought she was a very attractive woman.[7]

This all likely prompted Yardley to finally decide to get a divorce and marry Edna. He and Hazel had lived apart and been legally separated since 1937, and he hadn't even been in Worthington in several years. Yardley went to Nevada in the summer of 1944. After the required 6 weeks of residency, he went to court on Friday, August 25 and petitioned for the divorce. The following Monday morning on August 28, 1944, the divorce was granted. That afternoon Herbert and Edna drove to Reno and a judge married them. Herbert was 55, and Edna, whose birthday was 26 August, had just turned 42. Hazel received her divorce decree in the mail.

Yardley did more than just work for the OPA during the war. He also returned to writing. At George Bye's urging, he started to write a novel based on his experiences in China. He contacted his old collaborator Carl Grabo and the two of them developed the story. Grabo once again did the yeoman's work of writing. This time, however, he would get credit for it. By mid-1944, Yardley and Grabo had a finished manuscript and Bye started shopping it around. Bye was excited about the novel, saying, "It has a lot of atmosphere. It has a lot of the quality of 'American Black Chamber.' I wouldn't be surprised if you were in the money again... It's wonderful to find you in such fine writing form. I always knew that a lot of exciting melodramas lurked behind your mild eyes." Yardley was excited about Bye's reaction and in his response said, "Your letter made me so happy I didn't sleep a wink all night. Be sure to include Grabo when you write out a moving picture contract! We're the original Siamese Twins." After a couple of publishers turned it down, Putnam accepted it, and Yardley and Grabo split the $1000 advance on royalties. The book, dedicated to Edna and titled *Crows are Black Everywhere*, was published in 1945 to mixed reviews. It was not a best seller, but did reasonably well. Wisely, Yardley had not quit his job. This was Yardley's last foray into writing fiction.[8]

With the end of the war, price regulations were slowly relaxed and the OPA was finally put out of business in May 1947. Yardley was once again out of a job. He had started a small electrical appliances company "Osborn Sales" in 1946, but sales languished, and it went out of business in 1948. It was time to start over again.

---

[7] Kahn, *ROGM*, 223.

[8] Kahn, *ROGM*, 227.

# Chapter 20
# Endings

For William and Elizebeth Friedman, the end of World War II brought significant changes in their professional and personal lives. The threads of their personal and professional stories would bring them back together in their fascination with cryptology for the first time in two decades.

In August 1945, Army Chief of Staff George Marshall suggested to his Navy counterpart that the two forces combine their radio interception and cryptologic organizations. "I believe we might well ask the [Army-Navy Communications Intelligence] Board to examine and make recommendations as to the advisability of combining Army and Navy intercept and cryptanalytic activities under appropriate joint direction or if this should be impossible for any reason, to recommend procedures to insure complete integration."[1] This also led to the reorganization of the War Department's signals intelligence arm, the Signal Security Agency, into the Army Security Agency on 15 September 1945. The National Security Act, passed on 27 July 1947, placed the War and Navy Departments, along with a new service branch, the Air Force under a new Department of Defense. The Act also created the CIA and the National Security Council. Finally, the Act made the Joint Chiefs of Staff the main military advisers to the President. Subsequent recommendations for the signals departments were also made, and the cryptologic organizations were united into the Armed Forces Security Agency in May 1949 and then the National Security Agency (NSA) in November 1952.

There was also a warning in all this reorganization of what was to come in the field of cryptanalysis and one that did not bode well for cryptanalysts like Elizebeth. In a memorandum discussing the future of government cryptologic organizations,

---

[1] G. Stuart Smith, *A Life in Code: Pioneer Cryptanalyst Elizebeth Smith Friedman*, (Jefferson, NC: McFarland & Company, 2017), 161; George Marshall, "Gen. Marshall to Adm. King Re: Combining SIGINT," Memorandum, August 18, 1945, National Security Agency, https://www.nsa.gov/portals/75/documents/news-features/declassified-documents/nsa-60th-timeline/pre-nsa/19450818_PreNSA_Doc_3978305_SignalIntelligence.pdf

© The Author(s), under exclusive license to Springer Nature
Switzerland AG 2023
J. F. Dooley, *The Gambler and the Scholars*, History of Computing,
https://doi.org/10.1007/978-3-031-28318-5_20

its anonymous author states, "The days of intercept copy produced by individual radiomen following morse transmissions at hand speed on typewriters are nearly past; rapidly disappearing, too, are the fields of cryptography which can be defeated by individual cryptanalysts working with paper, pencil, and intuition on small collections of traffic. Cryptography and cryptanalysis have become big business and highly mechanized ones."[2] Since Elizebeth's preferred technique for decrypting intercepted messages was indeed "working with paper, pencil, and intuition" considerations of this type in the newly professional cryptologic organizations of the US government meant that her days as a government cryptanalyst were very likely numbered.

The new bureaucratic cryptologic organizations also had worries about the Friedmans public personas. These worries, although below the surface, had abounded in both the Army and Navy before the war, and they did not abate in the increasingly security-conscious War and Navy Departments during and after the war. A 1943 memo laid out the case. After reciting a list of over 20 separate newspaper and magazine articles about the Friedmans and their work—particularly Elizebeth's work as the Coast Guard's cryptanalyst, the memo goes on "Undoubtedly, there were many other items similar to these published throughout the country. No informed observer in Washington could escape knowing who the principal cryptanalysts of the Army and the Coast Guard were. Publicity of this nature was particularly unfortunate in that Yardley's book had provided a perfect cover for work of this nature. It will be recalled that the former head of the United States cryptographic bureau had vented his wrath on Secretary Stimson for abolishing his unit. Ostensibly then, there was no more cryptanalysis of other nation's codes going on in Washington. But revelations of the activities of the Friedmans could lead to only one conclusion on the part of espionage agents—decryption of other nation's codes was in progress behind the scenes. ... it must be remembered that incidents of this kind were certainly enough to make every potential enemy agent in Washington much more cautious about communication security."[3]

Once the war had started and Elizebeth's Coast Guard unit had transferred to the Navy, she had gone completely silent as far as her public persona was concerned. So silent, in fact, that her work during the war was not even recognized for several decades after her return to the Treasury Department after the war. Despite two decades of outstanding service in the Treasury Department, Coast Guard, and US

[2] Smith, *Life in Code*, 162; Anonymous, "Memo to Vice Chief of Naval Operations," Memorandum, August 21, 1945, National Security Agency, https://www.nsa.gov/portals/75/documents/news-features/declassified-documents/nsa-60th-timeline/pre-nsa/19450821_PreNSA_Doc_3984126_MemoRe.pdf, 2–3.

[3] Smith, *Life in Code*, 164; Anonymous, "Extract from: R.I.P. No. 98 Re: Friedmans Publicity," Memorandum, April 5, 1943, William F. Friedman Collection: Correspondence, Memoranda, and Personnel File Records, NSA/CSS DocRefID A66485, National Security Agency, https://www.nsa.gov/portals/75/documents/news-features/declassified-documents/friedman-documents/reports-research/FOLDER_377/41754199079335.pdf, 118–123.

Navy, Elizebeth received no awards or public recognition for all her work; her outstanding efforts in clandestine intelligence during the war notwithstanding.[4]

William, however, continued to be revered by his peers and rewarded by his superiors.

In 1944, he was one of the War Department's first two recipients of the Commendation for Exceptional Civilian Service, the War Department's highest civilian honor.

In 1946, he was awarded the Medal for Merit by President Truman. This award is the highest civilian honor the United States gives. Friedman was cited for "outstanding service conspicuously above the usual" and "for exceptional technical ingenuity which ranks him among the world's foremost authorities." Notably absent was any mention of cryptology.

When the Army Security Agency was created in 1945, William became the Director of Communications Research and then a technical consultant in the Armed Forces Security Agency. When the new NSA was created in 1952, William, at the age of 61, was hired on as a consultant with the title Special Assistant to the Director. He was given mostly tasks that did not play to his strengths in machine design and cryptanalysis. His new jobs were almost exclusively administrative, including at least three trips overseas to cement relations between the NSA and other cryptologic organizations. As time went on, except for special assignments to smooth relations with allies, the NSA made it clear it needed and wanted him less and less. The Agency was moving on into Cold War secrecy and the computer age, and it had no room for the past.

The first director of the NSA (DIRNSA) was U.S. Army General Ralph Canine, a friend of Friedman's who valued his advice and service. However, after Canine retired in 1956, none of the next three directors, Air Force General John A. Samford (director from 1956 to 1960), Vice Admiral Laurence Frost (director from 1960 to 1962), and Air Force General Gordon Blake (director from 1962 to 1965) were from the Army, none had much, if any, operational cryptanalytic experience, and none of them had a personal acquaintance with Friedman. His influence in the Agency waned, and he was actively pushed into the background.

The NSA also became increasingly secretive and paranoid as the 1950s moved into the 1960s, which worried and upset Friedman. "As the NSA grew larger and stronger, it began to use that strength in ways that made William uncomfortable. It scooped up enormous quantities of signals seemingly because it could, towering haystacks of intelligence that would make it difficult to find the needles, and it continued to conceal and classify more and more kinds of documents that William thought should be publicly available."[5] These new classifications increasingly included more and more of his own writings, many of which had been declassified years before but were now being reclassified for no reasons that William could

---

[4] Jason Fagone, *The Woman Who Smashed Codes*, (New York, NY: William Morrow, 2017), 300–301.

[5] Fagone, *Smashed*, 332.

fathom. Why would a paper that William had written on Edgar Allan Poe be classified? Why would his 1923 cryptanalysis text need to be reclassified after all these years?

By the late 1950s, William's relationship with the NSA was becoming more fraught as he perceived an overreach on security issues that he could do nothing about. "At other times in his life he had argued for greater secrecy, as when he objected to Herbert Yardley's book in the 1930s; now he muttered darkly to friends about a 'secrecy virus' loose in government."[6]

On a brighter note, overlapping the end of the war and the start of the peace, in 1944–1946, Friedman returned to the Voynich manuscript again. He organized a group of "young specialists in philology, paleography, ancient and medieval languages, and the various sciences which appeared to be discussed in the manuscript" into a group to examine the Voynich. The group styled as the "First Voynich Manuscript Study Group," met regularly to discuss theories about the manuscript. Their biggest result was a consistent transcription of the entire manuscript so that others could begin further analyses like frequency analysis.[7] In 1951, Friedman interested John Tiltman, the famous British cryptanalyst, in the Voynich. He continued to work on the Voynich along with Friedman for a number of years and took over the role of main contact person as Friedman's health failed in the 1960s. In 1975, after giving a lecture on the Voynich manuscript, Tiltman encouraged a very interested Mary D'Imperio, an NSA employee, to take on the mantle of Voynich research coordinator, which she did with her authorship of the definitive introduction to the manuscript.[8] Tiltman wrote the Foreword to D'Imperio's work.

William Friedman ended up thinking that the Voynich was written in an artificial or manufactured language. He announced his idea as an anagram in the footnote to a paper he published in Philological Quarterly in 1959 titled "Acrostics, Anagrams, and Chaucer."[9]

Elizabeth left the Naval Annex at the end of 1945 for good and went back to her old desk in the Treasury Building with her old team. But with no real work to do. So, she created her own last task; documenting all her unit's work during the 1920s and 1930s catching smugglers of various stripes; she archived many of the messages that her team had decrypted and saved a number of the articles written about her and her court testimonies.[10]

She also wrote a memorandum that recommended eliminating her Cryptanalytic Unit, including her own job. By 1946, it was becoming clear that all three of the armed services cryptologic organizations were going to be merged, so that the Coast

---

[6] Fagone, *Smashed*, 332.

[7] Ronald Clark, *The Man Who Broke Purple* (Boston: Little, Brown and Company, 1977), 215.

[8] Mary D. D'Imperio, "The Voynich Manuscript: An Elegant Enigma" (Ft. George Meade, MD: National Security Agency, 1978), https://www.nsa.gov/about/cryptologic-heritage/historical-figures-publications/publications/misc/assets/files/voynich_manuscript.pdf

[9] William F. Friedman and Elizabeth S. Friedman, "Acrostics, Anagrams, and Chaucer," *Philological Quarterly* 38, no. 1 (January 1959): 1–20.

[10] Fagone, *Smashed*, 320.

Guard's Cryptanalytic Unit would likely be subsumed into a larger organization. She laid out the case for this in her short memorandum and submitted it to the Coast Guard's Chief Intelligence Officer. Her recommendations were accepted.

CG Unit 387, the Cryptanalytic Unit, was disbanded on 14 August 1946.

Retired because of the subsequent reduction in force, Elizebeth's last day of work for the United States Coast Guard was 12 September 1946.

For a while after her release from government service, Elizebeth served as a consultant to other agencies and to businesses that were interested in using cryptology to protect their intellectual property and communications. She worked for the International Monetary Fund for a while in the late 1940s, but other government contracts she might have had were lost in the past. She was noticeably reticent to speak of them at all. According to Solomon Kullback, she "consulted with government agencies that wanted to establish secure communications systems,... But too much of the details of the activities we didn't know because of security, need-to-know, compartmentalization, even though it wasn't described in those terms in those days."[11]

In 1949, she treated herself to a 3-month European vacation—without William, who wasn't really interested in visiting the places she wanted to go, notably Switzerland, France, and Italy. He had either already been there or had no desire to go. So, she went by herself and by all accounts had a wonderful time.

After her consulting jobs, Elizebeth reluctantly acquiesced to several invitations and began a speaking career in 1951. She hopped around the country speaking to various women's groups, mostly about her work in the 1920s and 1930s. However, she steadfastly refused to speak about her work during World War II. She also worked for the League of Women Voters, finished her masters in archaeology, and took care of William, particularly during his depressive episodes. She shouldered the job of answering his mail, editing things he wrote, and began the job of cataloging their library.

After his major depression in early 1941, Friedman was fragile both mentally and physically and took some time to recover. He suffered another minor depressive episode starting in December 1941 that lasted into the spring of 1942 before he felt better. However, his periods of depression were getting closer together and would follow him throughout the next two decades.

While he was on his trip to Bletchley Park from April to June 1943, helping to negotiate the BRUSA agreement, Friedman again reported being depressed. This time his depression manifested itself mostly as insomnia and nighttime anxiety. He resorted to taking sleeping pills, and eventually the episode passed.

During 1947 and 1948, Friedman was again feeling depressed and anxious. At this time, he started seeing a psychiatrist, Dr. Paul Ewerhardt, fairly steadily during 1947 and as he improved, tapering off the visits through 1948.

---

[11] Smith, *Life in Code*, 166.

However, in early 1949, he was again severely depressed. So much so that he checked himself into the Veterans Hospital at Mt. Alto in Washington. He stayed in an open ward for a month but finally checked himself out, still depressed.

He was once again depressed at Christmas 1949, later admitting to suicidal thoughts. Dr. Ewerhardt thought that William needed more specific care, and he recommended that William consult Dr. Zigmond Lebensohn, an expert on depression, stress, and anxiety. Friedman went to see Dr. Lebensohn on 31 March 1950. Of that first visit, Dr. Lebensohn later wrote, "Colonel Friedman was so profoundly depressed and the possibility of suicide so real, that I recommended his entering the Psychiatric Unit of George Washington University Hospital for the purpose of receiving electroshock therapy." Friedman was admitted to the hospital that same day, and over the course of a 2-week period, he received six electroshock treatments "each without incident or complication." The electroshock treatments did what therapy and drugs had thus far been unable to do, and William's depression melted away. "He made a rapid and dramatic recovery and was discharged from the hospital on April 11. Although he had entered the hospital in a very glum, morose, deeply depressed and potentially suicidal mood, he was almost elated when he was discharged, and in a characteristically effusive way he kissed the nurses goodbye in a rather avuncular fashion. ... He appeared in excellent spirits."[12]

During the next 19 years, Friedman would continue to have occasional episodes of depression, but none ever as severe as this 1950 one; he was treated by Dr. Ewerhardt from time to time, including in 1956 and 1958.

Throughout the rest of their lives, the Friedmans would spend time investigating various cryptographic puzzles that had cropped up over the course of history. The Voynich manuscript was one. William also spent some time looking at a curious set of cryptograms rooted firmly in American soil, the mystery of the Beale Treasure.

In 1885, a 23-page pamphlet was published in Lynchburg, Virginia, that purported to tell the story of Thomas J. Beale and his adventures hunting for treasure and buffalo in the American West 65 years prior. Titled *The Beale Papers, Containing Authentic Statements Regarding the Treasure Buried in 1819 and 1821, near Bufords, in Bedford County, Virginia, and Which Has Never Been Recovered*, it was printed by a man named James B. Ward and allegedly written by an anonymous author who had contacted Ward to act as his agent and arrange the publication.

The pamphlet relates a journey from Virginia to Santa Fe, New Mexico in 1817 by Thomas Beale and 29 other men of an adventurous nature to hunt buffalo and bear in New Spain and the newly acquired Louisiana Territory. In early 1818, some of Beale's companions discovered a vein of gold and silver in what is now southern Colorado. Working for a year and a half, the 30 men were able to mine nearly one ton of gold and nearly two tons of silver. In the fall of 1819, Beale and ten of the men brought the gold back to Virginia and hid it in an "excavation or vault" somewhere near what is now Montvale, Virginia in Bedford County. The following

---

[12] Zigmond Lebensohn, "Letter to Ronald Clark from William Friedman's Psychiatrist," May 10, 1976, Box 13, File 30, George Marshall Foundation Research Library, Elizebeth Friedman Collection, 2; Clark, *Purple*, 221.

spring, Beale and his men headed back to Santa Fe. Two years later, in December 1821, Beale was back with more gold and silver, all of which he deposited with the earlier stash. The total amount was now 2921 pounds of gold, 5100 pounds of silver, and $13,000 of jewels (in 1820 dollars), all of which is worth roughly $60 million today. Beale lodged with an innkeeper named Morriss, and before he left in March 1822, Beale gave Morriss a locked metal box with information about the treasure and asked Morriss to keep the box safe until he returned. Forty years later, on his deathbed, Morriss gave the box to an anonymous friend and told him the story as he knew it. The box contained three cipher messages, all just strings of numbers. This anonymous friend worked on the cipher messages, which seemed to be book ciphers, for 20 more years with little success. He discovered that the key text to one of the ciphers, which he had labeled #2 and which is now usually known as B2, was a particular published edition of the American Declaration of Independence, albeit with several numbering mistakes. He was able to decrypt the B2 message, which further described the treasure and said that the first message (B1) contained the exact location of the treasure, while the third cipher message (B3) contained a list of the relatives of the original 30 men in Beale's party who should receive equal shares of the treasure. Try as he might, the anonymous friend was never able to decipher either message B1 or B3.[13]

When the Friedmans went back to look at them in the early 1950s, messages B1 and B3 remained unsolved. William and Elizabeth read the original pamphlets and several of the books that have been written about the Beale Treasure, but they also never came up with solutions to B1 and B3, nor did William ever posit a theory on what kind of ciphers they might be. He had discovered the Beale Treasure mystery back in the 1930s and had started looking at the problem. He had even assigned the cryptograms associated with the treasure as homework problems for his first three SIS colleagues, Rowlett, Sinkov, and Kullback. All three were convinced that the cryptograms were phony. When asked about whether he thought the cryptograms were real or a hoax, Friedman said, "On Mondays, Wednesdays, and Fridays, I think it is real. On Tuesdays, Thursdays, and Saturdays, I think it is a hoax." Elizabeth decided they couldn't be solved and that they were possibly a hoax with a "diabolical ingenuity specifically designed to lure the unwary reader ... In fruitless research ... or searching for a key book."[14]

In 1951, the Friedmans returned to their first cryptologic puzzle, Francis Bacon, and the search for ciphers in Shakespeare. They worked for 3 years on the problem, submitting their 1000-page manuscript with their conclusions—that Francis Bacon did NOT write Shakespeare's plays—on 31 December 1954.

---

[13]Anonymous, "The Beale Papers, Containing Authentic Statements Regarding the Treasure Buried in 1819 and 1821, near Bufords, in Bedford County, Virginia, and Which Has Never Been Recovered." (Virginia Printing Company, 1885), http://www.bibmath.net/crypto/ancienne/beale-textes.pdf

[14]Lucas Reilly, "The Quest to Break America's Most Mysterious Code—And Find $60 M in Buried Treasure," *Mental Floss (Online)*, June 4, 2018, http://mentalfloss.com/article/540277/beale-ciphers-buried-treasure

"The Cryptologist Looks at Shakespeare" won the $1000 Folger Shakespeare Library Literary prize in 1955. The prize was announced on 3 April 1955, a day that they would remember for another reason.

Through the 1950s, William continued to do consulting work for the NSA, including occasional trips to Britain and the Continent. During February and March 1955, Friedman was again in Europe and consulting with the British at the Government Communications Headquarters (GCHQ) in Cheltenham, the follow-on agency to the Government Code and Cipher School at Bletchley Park. He was away for 5 weeks and returned to Washington in late March. However, at the age of 64, the travel and strain of working for NSA was beginning to take its toll on him.

William Friedman had his first heart attack on the morning of 3 April 1955 as he was getting out of bed; at the hospital, his doctors said that he had also had an undetected one earlier that year. While William was recovering in the hospital he had another heart attack on 13 May 1955. Only about 2% of men survive two such heart attacks in such a short period of time, let alone three. William's recovery was very slow, and he did not leave the hospital until early July 1955. His recovery continued to be very slow throughout the rest of the year. His doctors told him to avoid walking long distances and playing golf; he ignored the advice as soon as he was able and was swinging golf clubs by the end of the year. However, he would remain physically fragile for the rest of his life.

Friedman retired from the NSA in October 1955 but was engaged on a part-time contract as a consultant to the Agency. He received the National Security Medal at his retirement ceremony. It was awarded for "distinguished achievements in national intelligence work." Friedman was only the fifth person to receive this award, and he was the only person besides J. Edgar Hoover to hold both the Medal for Merit and the National Security Medal.

After winning the Folger Shakespeare prize, the Friedmans were encouraged to turn their winning monograph into a book (Fig. 20.1). The Friedmans chose Cambridge University Press to publish the book. The Press demanded deep cuts in the length of the book, and at one point they suggested that because William was still recovering from his heart attacks that Elizebeth employ a collaborator. She firmly rejected that idea, and she did most of the editing with consultations and suggestions from William when he was well enough to engage in the work again. Over the course of 1956 and early 1957, they worked steadily on paring down the thousand-page manuscript into something that Cambridge Press would accept. They were finally able to submit a final version of the manuscript in the spring of 1957.

William was well enough for a combined business trip and vacation to Europe in August 1957. The Suez crisis of 1956–57 had not gone well for the British, and they had become suspicious that the Americans were reading their diplomatic cables. William was asked to travel to Britain and meet with the people at GCHQ in Cheltenham to assuage their concerns. The Friedmans left Washington on 18 August 1957 and spent a week in London before William had his several days of meetings at GCHQ. The couple then went off to the continent, visiting France and Switzerland and arrived back in England at the end of September for some more meetings at

**Fig. 20.1** Elizebeth and William Friedman at work in their home office, 1957. (George Marshall Foundation Research Library)

GCHQ for William and just in time for the release of their book.[15] Whittled down to 288 pages, the book was published under the new title—which the Friedmans hated—*The Shakespearean Ciphers Examined* and released on 4 October 1957 to very positive reviews; it won the fifth annual Shakespeare Festival Theater and Academy award in 1958.

To give the reader a feeling of what the Friedmans finally thought about the Bacon–Shakespeare theories, the book ends with "We suggest, that those who do wish to dispute the authorship of the Shakespeare plays should not in future resort to cryptographic evidence, unless they show themselves in some way competent to do so. They must do better than their predecessors. We urge that they should acquaint themselves at least with the basic principles of the subject, and that they conduct

---

[15] Clark, *Purple*, 238–239.

their arguments with some standards of rigour. Before they add to the very large corpus of writings on the subject, they might also consider subjecting their findings to the inspection of a professional who has no strong leanings to either side of the dispute. If all this is done, the argument will be raised to a higher plane. There is even the possibility that it would cease altogether."[16]

As far as the Friedmans were concerned, the Bacon–Shakespeare controversy was over.

The Friedman's travels were not, though. In January 1958, the couple traveled to Mexico to indulge another of their cryptographic interests—deciphering Mayan language glyphs. Elizebeth had gone back to school to obtain a Master's degree in archaeology, and both the Friedmans were fascinated with the Maya and their written language. While they never uncovered the meanings behind the Mayan's written language, their 3-month trip was a balm for both of them.

Just a month after their return to Washington, William was asked by the NSA in April to make another trip to Europe where he met with NSA officials in Germany, the British at GCHQ again, and in London to discuss matters related to computers and cryptology with engineers from the Italian firm of Ferranti.

In late 1958, William and Elizebeth planned a European trip for early 1959. Since he was still under a consulting contract with the NSA, William had some secret materials at his home, most of which were in a safe in his study. At that time, William informed the NSA of his plans to be out of the country beginning in January 1959. The NSA's Chief of Security, S. Wesley Reynolds, wrote a memorandum on 5 December 1958 saying that he had contacted William Friedman and "suggested that since he anticipates being out of the city for an extended period of time, the Agency classified documents in his possession should be maintained at NSA for safekeeping until his return." Friedman agreed to have the Agency pick up the secret materials during the week of 29 December. Reynolds also said that "Mr. Friedman voiced no objection regarding Agency classified documents in his possession. He did indicate that he has a considerable amount of material which is historical and was once classified. It has since been declassified … and subsequently classified again."[17] Reynolds went on to say that Friedman told him that some of that historical material had since been reclassified but because it was integrated into his library, would be difficult to locate. Much of this historical material was in the public domain anyway, and "He expressed extreme reluctance in having this material turned over to the Agency."

Reynolds concluded his memo with "It is felt that Mr. Friedman is probably true in his observations that much of this material is widely disseminated and in the hands of people without clearances. It is felt that no grave Security problem would result by leaving this material in the home of Mr. Friedman during his absence. Mr. Friedman is on notice that this material is classified and therefore is enjoined from

---

[16] William F. Friedman and Elizebeth S. Friedman, *The Shakespearean Ciphers Examined*, (London: Cambridge University Press, 1958), 287–288.

[17] This was due to Department of Defense Directive 5200.1, dated July 8, 1957, which moved many documents from the Restricted classification back to the Confidential classification.

using it in the preparation of any articles or books which he may desire to write. It is recommended that personnel from this Office, accompanied by personnel from the Office of Administrative Services, visit Mr. Friedman during the week of 29 December to recover Agency classified material and other material in Mr. Friedman's possession which is easily identifiable and which he agrees could be held at NSA during his absence."[18]

So, on the afternoon of 30 December 1958, three NSA men, including Reynolds and Paul Gilliam from the Attorney General's office, arrived at the Friedman's home with a truck to pick up the classified Agency material. However, there was apparently a difference between Reynold's "no grave Security problem... leaving this material in the home of Mr. Friedman during his absence" and an additional reference to "Agency classified and other material in Mr. Friedman's possession which is easily identifiable." A difference of which the NSA and the Friedmans had conflicting interpretations.

The NSA men not only took William's personal safe, which *did* contain classified material, but they also took a number of different items that William and Elizebeth were under the impression would fall under the "no grave Security problem" rubric. In fact, the NSA took more than 48 different items that the Friedmans were not prepared to have taken. Even Reynolds, in a follow-up memo a few days after their visit, figured this out. "...it was quite obvious that he felt deeply hurt and that the material was being taken for reasons other than Security. He states that this material deals with the history of cryptography and should belong to the American people. ... He feels therefore, that the material in his possession which has previously been declassified should remain that way and should not now be considered classified CONFIDENTIAL."[19] Despite the fact that Reynolds insisted that the Agency was holding these documents just while the Friedmans were out of the country, this felt like a violation to both William and Elizebeth.

The inventory, when it was produced by Paul Gilliam of the Attorney General's office, was ten pages long and included items such as "Correspondence regarding Friedmans desire to patent and market a cipher device for children," "letters of appreciation for lecturing," all of William's reports on German codes from World War I, several of William's own copies of his Riverbank publications including *The Index of Coincidence*, a table of the binomial distribution from the American Statistical Association, and William's own copies of his texts on *Military*

---

[18] S. Wesley Reynolds, "Classified Documents in Possession of William F. Friedman," Memorandum, December 5, 1958, William F. Friedman Collection: Correspondence, Memoranda, and Personnel File Records, NSA/CSS DocRefID A99778, National Security Agency, https://www.nsa.gov/portals/75/documents/news-features/declassified-documents/friedman-documents/correspondence/ACC4282/41783879082293.pdf

[19] S. Wesley Reynolds, "Retrieval of Classified Agency Documents from Home of W.F. Friedman," Memorandum, January 2, 1959, William F. Friedman Collection: Correspondence, Memoranda, and Personnel File Records, NSA/CSS DocRefID A99780, National Security Agency, https://www.nsa.gov/Portals/75/documents/news-features/declassified-documents/friedman-documents/correspondence/ACC4282/41783909082296.pdf

*Cryptography* and *Military Cryptanalysis*, which were both on the shelves at the Library of Congress. The Friedmans were furious.

All this being said, the issue with the "confiscation" of materials from the Friedman's home was not some sudden raid by the NSA on innocent American citizens as it was made out to be in both of the Friedmans biographies.[20] The Friedmans had agreed with the NSA Director of Security that some of their holdings would be taken by the NSA and stored for safe-keeping while they were on their European trip. They were expecting the NSA officials to show up at their door on that Tuesday afternoon. Additionally, they did get many of their materials back after they returned from their trip; however, the NSA insisted on keeping those 48 items they wanted classified as CONFIDENTIAL. The problem was that what Mr. Reynolds and Mr. Gilliam thought were the rules laid out in Directive 5200.1 went far beyond what the Friedmans thought was appropriate for their historical materials. Even though the Friedmans recovered many of their materials, the new classification of CONFIDENTIAL meant that William could not use much of his library as references for future research projects and publications. It also made it more difficult for the Friedmans to give their collection to the George Marshall Library a dozen years later. In fact, a number of the items taken that day in 1958 were not returned to the Friedman Collection at the Marshall Library until decades later.

This overly broad classification of his collection cemented William's growing opinion that the NSA was becoming too secretive and controlling. This was the real beginning of his disaffection with the NSA and with government in general. There was no good reason for these document seizures except that by this time, the NSA was beginning to work its way into the "secrecy for secrecy's sake" attitude it would have for the next four decades. Whether it was a reaction to the Cold War or the Soviet moles within the CIA and the NSA, the Agency was becoming more secretive and closed as the years went by.

This attitude of the NSA and its effects on the Friedmans continued until and even past William's death. For example, in 1960, the Yale University mathematician Edward G. Begle asked Friedman to contribute a monograph on cryptology to a book he was editing for high school students. William dutifully asked the NSA if he had permission to write the monograph for publication. He was turned down; the NSA forbade him from writing a monograph for high school students. In a response to Begle in February 1962, Friedman put his disgust and annoyance in words

I have delayed embarking on a project by what I can only consider to be an absurd, foolish and dangerous attitude on the part of DoD authorities in regard to the publication of any sort of material on any phase of cryptology whatever. They seem to think that this whole subject is taboo, a private preserve, and poachers thereon will do so at their peril. And they have the laws and the means to enforce their views. I have in recent months tried to inject some new thoughts with a view to changing their attitude, but I am afraid I am making only very slow

---

[20] Clark, *Purple*, 251–252; Fagone, *Smashed*, 327–329.

progress. ... I am sure that their attitude is indefensible, but I do not wish to jeopardize my liberty in proving that it is.[21]

and he was forced to recommend that Begle find someone else to write the monograph, someone who had never worked for the government.

In the 1950s and 1960s, William also continued to dabble in historical cryptology. At one point in 1960, his old World War I Army acquaintance J. Rives Childs asked him for some help examining coded messages left by the Italian adventurer Giacomo Casanova.[22] Childs' career had taken him from the Army to journalism and then to the State Department Foreign Service, where he had risen to the rank of Ambassador. Now retired, Childs had written a definitive biography of Casanova and was interested in Friedman having a look at some coded messages. Friedman discovered that Casanova, who was not shy about self-promotion, had interests in cryptography, and he had been challenged to decrypt a mysterious message. Casanova discovered that the message was written using a Vigenère cipher, and he decrypted it, one of the first such examples of someone being able to decrypt a polyalphabetic cipher. Casanova's feat was the more interesting because it came more than a hundred years before Kasiski's method for solving Vigenère ciphers made them much less secure and easily solvable in most cases. Friedman's paper on the cipher was published in 1961 and was his last publication on cryptology.

In 1962, Friedman organized another after-hours group to study the Voynich. This "Second Voynich Manuscript Study Group" thought to try to use the newer computer technology to evaluate the Voynich text, this time a new RCA computer. Two of their results include a 63-page printout of a transcription of pages 120 through 175 of the Voynich, resulting in 46,424 characters, and an enormous 692-page printout of a cross reference—a Keyword in Context tabulation—of their initial transcription.

Not to be outdone, in 1962, Elizabeth Friedman wrote a general readership article on the Voynich manuscript for the *Washington Post*.

In the latter part of 1959 and into the summer of 1960, the Friedmans were plagued by family problems that pushed him into another depressive episode. "He felt that his neurosis had become worse, that cryptology had now become abhorrent to him."

In June 1961, William saw Dr. Lebensohn again for "several sessions," and the doctor began to prescribe mild antidepressants. By mid-July, Friedman reported he was much better and "felt much more relaxed."[23]

William's depressive episodes were becoming more frequent, averaging at least one per year at this point. In January 1963, he was back to see Dr. Lebensohn "in the

---

[21] Rose Mary Sheldon, "William F. Friedman: A Very Private Cryptographer and His Collection," *Cryptologic Quarterly* 34, no. 2015–1 (January 2015): 4–29, https://www.nsa.gov/about/cryptologic-heritage/historical-figures-publications/publications/cryptologic-quarterly/, 20.

[22] Later in life, Casanova signed his missives Jacques Casanova de Seingalt after he was exiled from Venice and moved to France.

[23] Lebensohn, *Letter to Clark*, 3.

throes of a deep depression with 'no desire to go on.'" The doctor placed him back on antidepressants, but they did not seem to help as much this time. On 10 February 1963, William was again admitted to Veterans Hospital for a period of observation and treatment. After trying a variety of medications, Friedman seemed to be getting better and was discharged on 6 March 1963.

In April 1963, William and Elizebeth went to Europe again for a vacation; they stayed in various places until mid-September. William reported that aside from a few good days, he remained depressed for the entire duration of the trip. He consulted a psychiatrist in Zurich who prescribed a new antidepressant, which did not seem to help.

After their return to Washington in September 1963, Friedman got "much worse, cried fitfully, became very depressed... felt hopeless and senile." Friedman was 72 at the time. On 28 September 1963, William was readmitted to the George Washington University Hospital and was seen daily by Dr. Lebensohn until his discharge on November 4, much improved.

Dr. Lebensohn had appointments with Friedman intermittently throughout 1964. Throughout the next several years, William's depression came and went, and he continued to be distressed about how NSA had been treating him.

Elizebeth Friedman went to see Dr. Lebensohn twice in December 1966 to discuss William's mental health. During their talks, they identified his periods of depression as originally happening about once every 7 years, but that they were getting more frequent as Friedman got older. She identified many mood swings, with William being happier ("somewhat euphoric") in the spring and becoming increasingly depressed in the fall. Because of this increased focus on his treatment by the NSA, he "felt that he had been grossly hurt by the people at NSA because they distrusted him and reclassified all of his papers... and he began feeling that the people at NSA were 'out to get him.'" The two of them finally determined that William probably had Manic Depressive Illness, and his mood swings were a result of that. This was Lebensohn's last contact with the Friedmans.[24]

In a lengthy 1976 letter to Elizebeth, but intended for William's biographer, Ronald Clark, Lebensohn concludes by saying that he personally liked Friedman very much and "admired him enormously for what he had done for his country and for his highly specialized profession" and that he was very happy and full of admiration that Friedman had been able to handle his bouts of depression so well and had such a spectacular and productive career.[25]

The rest of the 1960s were mostly quiet for Elizebeth and William. They celebrated their 50th wedding anniversary in 1967. Both now in their 70s, their travels were largely over, but they maintained a lively correspondence with a number of people. Particularly moving are their letters back and forth with Boris Hagelin, who had moved his cipher machine company from Sweden to Switzerland. The

---

[24] Lebensohn, *Letter to Clark*, 6–7.
[25] Lebensohn, *Letter to Clark*, 7.

Friedmans had often visited Hagelin and his wife on their trips to Europe, and the Hagelins had come to Washington for visits over the years.

Given their increasing distrust of the NSA and of the government in general, the Friedmans decided against leaving their papers to the Library of Congress, instead agreeing to leave them to the George Marshall Foundation Library in Lexington, Virginia. They spent much of their time during this decade cataloging the collections.

Every once in a while, Elizebeth had an urge to write her memoirs. She wrote a short draft version in 1966, and later on, she sat for oral history interviews in 1973 and 1976 with NSA historians. The oral history interviews she conducted, contained very little about her most significant work during World War II. She never finished her own memoir, focusing instead on making sure that her husband's reputation and accomplishments were remembered and praised.

William had another heart attack in May 1969, but recovered remarkably quickly and was back home and working within weeks, a remarkable event for someone who had already suffered as much as he had.

Just after midnight on 2 November 1969, William had his last heart attack. Elizebeth called for an ambulance and called William's doctor, but by the time they got to their house, there was nothing to be done. William passed away at the age of 78.

William Friedman was buried 3 days later with full military honors at Arlington National Cemetery. Senior officials from the NSA and the Army were in attendance. Elizebeth received over 750 letters and sympathy cards during the month. A cryptanalyst who worked at Arlington Hall during the war wrote, "Our business now involves many more people and disciplines. ... It has become more abstract and impersonal. There are no more William Friedmans nor will there ever be."[26]

Elizebeth arranged for William's tombstone to be engraved with his motto from many years before, *Knowledge Is Power* (Fig. 20.2). Just to make sure that William went out with a remembrance of his life's work, she had the engraver use the same font for all the letters of the motto, but with some letters with serifs and some without so that the engraving was a cryptogram using Francis Bacon's biliteral cipher. The cryptogram, embedded in the motto, was "KnOwl/edGeI/spOwE" (babaa/aabab/aabab) reading when decrypted "WFF."

After William's death, Elizebeth focused like a laser on getting a biography of him written and published. After a long search, she finally chose the renowned biographer Ronald Clark to write William's story. She insisted on remaining involved in all the details of the book, which unfortunately made it not as even-handed and honest as it might have been. The book was published to favorable reviews in 1977, although Elizebeth and her children were disappointed. Elizebeth said that it did not contain "the man I knew and loved." It is a flawed biography, much more of a hagiography than a balanced treatment of William Friedman's life. Published without footnotes or references, it is difficult for the reader or researcher to grasp the parts

---

[26] Fagone, *Smashed*, 334.

**Fig. 20.2**   William and Elizebeth Friedman's headstone in Arlington Cemetery. (US Army photo)

that are fact and the parts that might be exaggeration or fiction. Even the title, "The Man Who Broke Purple: The Life of Colonel William F. Friedman, Who Deciphered the Japanese Code in World War II" is not completely correct. While Friedman recruited and trained the team that worked on breaking the PURPLE cipher machine, and while he provided general supervision, it was Frank Rowlett and his team of cryptanalysts who did the yeoman's work over the course of 18 months of breaking the cipher system and reconstructing the machine from scratch. Regardless, the book places him in the exalted position in American cryptology that he deserves.

For the remaining years of her life, Elizebeth was consumed with finishing the job of cataloging their cryptologic collection and getting both collections moved down to the Marshall Library. She started first with William's books and papers and finished that work in 1971. Elizebeth drove herself down to Lexington right behind the truck that carried William's collection. She then got to work on organizing her own papers. She was also determined to get all of William's work declassified as it should have been. She was a thorn in the NSA's side until they began to reluctantly return some of the materials that had been removed from their home those many years ago.

Elizebeth finally sold the townhouse on Capitol Hill in Washington, where they had been since the early 1950s, and lived for a time with her son, John. Eventually, she moved into a nursing home near John's house in New Jersey. She let it be known that she wanted to be cremated and her ashes scattered over William's grave.

Elizebeth Smith Friedman died on 31 October 1980 at the age of 88. Her ashes were indeed scattered over William's grave in Arlington.

After the Office of Price Administration (OPA) was dissolved and his Osborn Sales company folded, Herbert Yardley found another government job as a sales assistant in the Public Housing Administration (PHA) of the Housing and Home Finance Agency (HHFA). He stayed there from early January 1949 until the end of April 1952 when he retired from the government with a total of nearly 25 years of service. He had just turned 63 years old. While at the PHA, Yardley generally received very good performance evaluations and was once again promoted several times, ultimately to a management position with his salary going from an initial $5232 up to $6940 over the course of just 3 years. He retired "in order to devote more time to the construction business." During this time, Edna was working as a secretary in the PHA, and she kept her job after Yardley retired (Fig. 20.3).

The first house that Herbert built was at 9813 Rosensteel Avenue in Silver Spring, Maryland for he and Edna; a two-story, 1700-square-feet house on a tree-lined street.

While they lived on Rosensteel Avenue, Edna and Herbert took in a boarder, a young man in his late 20s named Grover Batts. Batts worked in the same office as Edna, and he stayed with the Yardleys for 2 years. He found Herbert fascinating and Edna strong and kind. He gave an interesting view of Herbert in his mid-60 s in an interview many years later with David Kahn:

> I really admired Herbert tremendously. I liked to listen to him talk, especially about his time in China. He had a compelling way of expressing himself. When he spoke, it wasn't your ordinary boring thing. He talked in a way that made you listen to him.
>
> … he was always an interesting person to be around. He had a brilliant mind. He was a good arguer.
>
> He really had a vocabulary when it came to cussing. … It didn't make any difference to Herbert who was there, what company he was in. He'd use that language just in general conversation. It would embarrass me to death. I think he did it almost for shock value. I have an idea that in his earlier years he was not like that.
>
> … His attitude toward life was antagonistic. He was not a very happy man (at least then—I don't know what he was like as a younger man). I can't remember him ever really bubbling over with laughter. He was kind of dour. …
>
> I can't remember people visiting Herbert. I can't remember a living soul who was a close friend. …
>
> He treated Edna well, courteously. He never was unkind to her in any way that I was aware of. Edna had such an attractive personality. A very warm, caring person. You felt that she really cared about you. It was really a sincere feeling—not put on. She had a strong personality and wouldn't have stayed around with Herbert if he wasn't worth something.[27]

While Edna and Herbert lived in Silver Spring, Herbert made most of his living as a general contractor. He built three more houses on Rosensteel Avenue and several more in the same neighborhood. He was quite successful as a contractor, his management skills serving him well. In December 1954, Herbert and Edna packed up and moved to Orlando, Florida, where they rented a house. Yardley had intended to

---

[27] David Kahn, *The Reader of Gentlemen's Mail: Herbert O. Yardley and the Birth of American Codebreaking* (New Haven: Yale University Press, 2004), 230–231.

**Fig. 20.3** Herbert and Edna Yardley in Washington, 1950s. (David Kahn Collection, National Cryptologic Museum Library)

continue his general contracting work in Florida but found duck hunting, fishing, and golf more attractive. He continued to be interested in writing and sent off a couple of ideas for movie scripts to his agent in Hollywood, but nothing ever came of them. He also gathered his letters to Edna and others from when he was in China and wrote them up into a book, but the 1933 Protection of Government Documents Act still had him wary, and he never sent the book to George Bye. Many years later, after Yardley's death, Edna would resurrect the book, polish it slightly and add a

**Fig. 20.4** Herbert Yardley at poker. (David Kahn Collection, National Cryptologic Museum Library)

short afterward. It was published in 1983 under the title *The Chinese Black Chamber.*[28]

The couple moved back to Silver Spring in April 1956. Yardley continued his retirement life, hunting, fishing, playing poker, and drinking. He got back into contracting and built several more houses. He started playing more poker. Yardley continued to be very patient, was able to count cards well, was a good observer of his fellow players' habits, and won fairly consistently, although he only played for relatively small stakes. His poker games brought back memories of learning to play poker in Worthington, of poker games in Paris and Chungking, and started him thinking about writing another book. This time about how to win at poker (Fig. 20.4).

---

[28] Kahn, *ROGM*, 230–231.

Yardley spent the better part of a year writing, and *The Education of a Poker Player* was published by Simon and Schuster in November 1957. In an homage to his first book 26 years earlier, the book was preceded by an excerpt in the *Saturday Evening Post*. Both the article and the book were smashing successes. Once again, the issue of the *Post* where the article appeared broke the *Posts* number of copies sold record with 5.6 million copies. The reviews were mixed. The *New York Times* wouldn't even review the book because it was a "how-to" book. However, the public loved it. Simon and Schuster ordered a second printing almost immediately.[29]

Where Yardley was really pretty terrible at writing fiction, he was an excellent real-life story-teller and first-person narratives were his real skill. Just like *The American Black Chamber*, *Education of a Poker Player* was full of stories about poker, poker hands, bluffs, winning and losing and was laced with memorable descriptions of the people that Yardley would sit down to play with. All the stories take place either in Yardley's hometown of Worthington and feature a young Herbert Yardley, or they take place in Chungking, China, while Yardley was in charge of the Nationalist Chinese cryptanalytic bureau. While it is these stories that make *Education of a Poker Player* a memorable read, Yardley also delivers a hard and deliberate tutorial on how to play the game, told as someone who has played thousands and thousands of hands and who is deeply intense and involved with the mechanics of play. In his introduction to the 1959 publication of the book in the United Kingdom, author and former spy Ian Fleming is effusive in his praise of the book. He spent months convincing his publisher to acquire and release the book. "I said that the book contained only a dozen pages of instruction—brilliant instruction—and that the rest was a hatful of some of the finest gambling stories I had ever read. It didn't matter that the game was poker. These were wonderful, thrilling stories about cards. The book would certainly become a gambling classic. English card players would read it and love it. The book had zest, blood, sex, and a tough, wry humour reminiscent of Raymond Chandler. It was sharply, tautly written. It would be a bestseller—well, anyway, it would look very well on the backlist."[30]

Al Alvarez, the poet, novelist, critic, and poker aficionado—who learned to play from *Education*—wrote "There are two types of poker books: the how-tos, which are more or less abstract and often contain a good deal of mathematics about probabilities and percentages, and the autobiographical, like Yardley's classic, in which examples and solid advice are sandwiched between racy stories about dramatic games."[31]

In his introduction to a reprint of Yardley's book decades later, Alvarez says:

> ... a friend lent me Herbert O. Yardley's *The Education of a Poker Player* and I began to
> understand what the game is about. Not luck but calculation, memory, patience, skill in

---

[29] Kahn, *ROGM*, 233. This author has a hardcover copy of the 1957 edition of *The Education of a Poker Player*, which is marked "Tenth Printing."

[30] Ian Fleming, "Introduction to 'The Education of a Poker Player' by Herbert O. Yardley," in *The Education of a Poker Player: Including Where and How One Learns to Win* (London, UK: Jonathan Cape, 1959).

[31] Kahn, *ROGM*, 233.

reckoning the odds and percentages and, above all, observation: the ability to recognize and interpret the small fidgets and quirks, the hesitations, the voice's faint changes in timbre which indicate tension or confidence. ...

Yardley's stories are dramatic, simple and loving, like the folk tales collected by the Brothers Grimm. And in a way, this is what they are: the mythology of America on the move, the winners winning, the losers going under. ...

This interplay between the personalities round a poker table and the combination of cynicism and insight necessary to win is where the real fascination of the game lies. Perhaps this is why Yardley's book continued to hold me, even after I had assimilated his advice and had a working knowledge of the percentages.[32]

After the first publication of *The Education of a Poker Player*, for the first time Herbert Yardley got fan mail, many of the letters with technical questions about poker. He answered as many of them as he could. However, not all of the opinions about Yardley and his book were positive. His former colleagues in MI-8, the US Army, and the Cipher Bureau were largely silent, but there were occasional outbursts. In a letter to David Kahn on his relationship with Yardley over the years, J. Rives Childs wrote, "I had one or two letters from him (from China) and then all communication between us ceased. I had already observed his gradual transformation into one of the most deeply cynical men I had ever known. From what I later learned China furthered rather than stayed this trend. On his return I believe he was up against it for a while. Then, before his death several years ago, he reappeared briefly in the news with a book, *The Education of a Poker Player*, incorporating a summary account of his Chinese experiences. It was an anti-climactic ending to a life of brilliant promise."[33]

Just before the publication of *Education of a Poker Player*, Yardley was home in Silver Spring when he had a "mild" stroke and spent some time in the hospital. He recovered fairly well and was back home with Edna in a few weeks. However, he was still partially paralyzed. Edna took care of him, wrote his letters, and helped with the *Education of a Poker Player* release. Herbert recovered very slowly. His 69th birthday was in April, and he was doing better, but on 2 August 1958, he had a second, major stroke. This time there was no recovery, and Herbert Yardley died at home 5 days later around 1 p.m. on 7 August 1958. Just like his former friend William Friedman, Yardley was buried several days later with full military honors at Arlington National Cemetery. Probably not intentionally, but in a strange symmetry, the two men are buried practically as far apart as it is possible for two graves to be at Arlington Cemetery[34] (Fig. 20.5).

Edna Yardley, just like Elizebeth Friedman, spent much of the rest of her life working to preserve and burnish the memory of her husband. Edna worked hard to

---

[32] Al Alvarez, "Introduction to 'The Education of a Poker Player' by Herbert O. Yardley," in *The Education of a Poker Player*, (Harpenden, United Kingdom: Oldcastle Books, Ltd., 1990), 160, i–iii.

[33] J. Rives Childs, "Childs to Kahn Re: Yardley," August 27, 1963, DK 55-20, David Kahn Collection, National Cryptologic Museum Library.

[34] William and Elizebeth Friedman are buried in Section 8, Grave 6379-A. Herbert and Edna Yardley are in Section 30, Grave 429-1.

**Fig. 20.5**   Edna and Herbert Yardley's Headstone in Arlington National Cemetery. (US Army photo)

find a biographer for Herbert, but had no luck. Yardley's biography was finally written by David Kahn 46 years later. Edna kept many of Yardley's papers, but not her own letters nor any of the files from the Cipher Bureau that Yardley was supposed to have made off with. She did her own oral history interviews for the NSA and her own personal papers, which include those of Herbert's that were not destroyed are in the NSA's National Cryptologic Museum Library. Yardley's will bequeathed his fishing and hunting gear to his son Jack, who would go on to become a doctor and live in Indianapolis,[35] and all the rest of his possessions were bequeathed to Edna. Edna continued to live in Silver Spring and was the last of the four to pass away, on 20 March 1990, at the age of 87. She is buried next to Herbert at Arlington.

---

[35] Hazel Yardley died in 1956, just before Herbert. Jack passed away in 1985, at the age of 60.

# Chapter 21
# Memories of Friedman and Yardley

It seems obvious that William Friedman was a brilliant cryptanalyst and cryptographer; one just needs to look at the long list of his publications on both cryptography and cryptanalysis as well as his patents—although some of his patents should have been marked as clearly derivative. Friedman was aware of all the standard techniques for solving substitution and transposition ciphers, including digraphic, polyalphabetic, running key, autokey, combinations of substitution and transposition, and so on, that were current as of the first half of the twentieth century. He helped revolutionize the creation of codes by applying solid randomizing techniques and rules for the creation of codewords. One of his patents lays out a methodology for creating secure codewords. His knowledge of cryptology was largely self-taught. He was aware of early work done by Joseph Mauborgne and Parker Hitt on various manual systems, modifications to some of which he later patented. Friedman had an excellent grasp of the history of cryptology, particularly from the late Renaissance to the twentieth century. He was also a very good self-taught electrical engineer and an exceptional inventor of cryptologic devices; for examples see the M-134 and its derivatives, his suggestions for improvements to the M-209 and the M-138A, and his many other patents. He developed his own cryptanalytic techniques that relied, probably for the first time, on statistics. He firmly believed in the application of mathematics to cryptanalysis. His thoughts on solving ciphers, his work in applying new mathematical techniques to cryptanalysis, and his work on the nascent cipher machines all predate the work of people such as Lester Hill and Claude Shannon.

By 1946, at age 55, Friedman was beginning to reminisce about his work, bemoaning the fact that parts of his discipline had moved on beyond his own work. As Fagone puts it, "You get older and want to connect to the people who understand. You try to speak with the young and find that something is wrong with your ears. They use their own slang, their own code, and you start to feel nostalgic about your

J. F. Dooley, *The Gambler and the Scholars*, History of Computing, https://doi.org/10.1007/978-3-031-28318-5_21

former enemies, who at least shared the same intense moment on earth and spoke words you could understand."[1]

He was interested in machine cryptography and did a significant amount of work in the field. He was also, to a lesser extent, interested in machine cryptanalysis, but had his limits with respect to how it would work.

Friedman also had many self-doubts, and he suffered for a large part of his life from clinical depression; he was finally diagnosed with Manic Depressive Illness. This illness, which became more pronounced and with more frequent depressive episodes as he got older, shadowed the entire last half of his career.

Finally, Friedman at times seemed resentful of Herbert Yardley, viewing him as somehow more successful, more colorful, and more popular than Friedman himself. Friedman was more introverted than Yardley, and he was envious—and at the same time enraged—that Yardley was able to break out of the government security shell and gain notoriety where he could not. Friedman ended up being more famous, more celebrated, and with a much better reputation than Yardley, but that was largely within the American cryptologic community. Friedman, not Yardley, was the person revered by the cryptologic community as the "Father" or "Dean" of modern American cryptology. However, because of his books, magazine articles, and showmanship, Yardley was better known during his lifetime and had the interest and admiration of the general public, where Friedman was not as well known in those circles. In fact, through the 1920s and 1930s, before they both went underground during World War II, Elizebeth was better known and more admired by the public than William would ever be.

Elizebeth, in her turn, was also a very talented cryptologist. She worked with her husband in the early 1920s to create new codes for the Army, organized the Coast Guard's Cryptanalytic Unit and set up Wild Bill Donovan's cryptologic organization for the Office of Strategic Services (OSS). Like William, she was almost entirely self-taught in cryptology. She taught her cryptanalysts how to break rumrunner, drug smuggler, and German spy codes and ciphers. She led the group to break three different German Abwehr Enigma machines with no help from outside. However, like Yardley, she did not apply many modern cryptanalytic techniques to her work. She was an old school pencil and paper, intuitive cryptanalyst. She did use some mathematics in her work, including her husband's Index of Coincidence, but she was much more intuitive than mathematical in her approach. Elizebeth was also one who had the facility to explain her work to a general audience, including juries and opposing attorneys. She was also quite happy to give up her work and walk away at the end of World War II. As one might guess from the fact that she had a degree in English literature, she was much more interested in researching problems in cryptology that related to language and literature, including her fascination with the Mayan language and her and William's work on Francis Bacon and Shakespeare.

Along with Genevieve Hitt, Edith Rickert, and Agnes Meyer Driscoll, Elizebeth was in the vanguard of American women entering the field of cryptology at the

---

[1] Jason Fagone, *The Woman Who Smashed Codes*, (New York, NY: William Morrow, 2017), 313.

beginning of World War I. In fact, taking into account that she started solving US Army intercepted cryptograms in the summer of 1917, she was likely the first or second woman professional cryptologist who worked (at least indirectly) for the federal government, along with Genevieve Hitt, who had been solving intercepted Mexican Army messages—unpaid—during the Punitive Expedition since August 1917 and who was officially hired by the Army to be in charge of code and cipher work for the Army's Southern Department in April 1918.[2] Edith Rickert joined MI-8 as a cryptanalyst along with John Manly in November 1917, and Agnes Meyer enlisted in the Navy in June 1918.[3]

After William's death, Elizebeth turned her energy and talents to preserving his memory. She was always the dedicated, devoted helpmate. She finished the job of cataloging her husband's papers and book collection and sent them off to the George Marshall Foundation Library, rather at the expense of her efforts to catalog her own collection. She searched for and engaged the English biographer Ronald Clark to write an authorized biography of William. It is certainly possible that without her determination to make sure everyone knew who the real "Father of modern American cryptology" was, that there would not now be a *William and Elizebeth Friedman Auditorium* at NSA headquarters in Fort Meade. Without her marvelous two decades working for the Treasury Department, Coast Guard, and US Navy, however, there would also not be the *Elizebeth Smith Friedman Auditorium* at the headquarters of the Bureau of Alcohol, Tobacco, and Firearms in Washington,[4] or the *Elizebeth Smith Friedman Intelligence Award of Excellence*, awarded by the Women in Federal Law Enforcement (WIFLE), nor would there be a Coast Guard National Security Cutter (NSC) named the *USCGC Friedman*, in her honor.[5]

In addition to William Friedman being a great cryptanalyst, it also seems obvious that Herbert Yardley was a mediocre to good cryptanalyst. Some of his contemporaries, particularly after the publication of *The American Black Chamber*, characterized his cryptanalytic abilities variously as "old-fashioned," "so-so," and "not particularly great."[6] In the sense of new cryptanalytic techniques or methodologies, Yardley did not contribute anything to the canon of cryptology, but he did quite a

---

[2] David A. Hatch, "The Punitive Expedition Military Reform and Communications Intelligence," *Cryptologia* 31, no. 1 (January 2007): 38–45, https://doi.org/10.1080/01611190600964264, 41; Betsy Rohaly Smoot, "Pioneers of U.S. Military Cryptology: Colonel Parker Hitt and His Wife Genevieve Young Hitt," *Federal History* 4 (2012): 87–100.

[3] Betsy Rohaly Smoot, "An Accidental Cryptologist: The Brief Career of Genevieve Young Hitt," *Cryptologia* 35, no. 2 (March 31, 2011): 164–75, https://doi.org/10.1080/01611194.201 1.558982, 164.

[4] Craig Bauer, "Friedman Auditorium Times Two," *Cryptologia* 39, no. 2 (April 3, 2015): 173–77, https://doi.org/10.1080/01611194.2015.1009747

[5] Anonymous, "Eleventh Coast Guard National Security Cutter Named for Elizebeth Smith Friedman," *Coast Guard News*, July 7, 2020, https://coastguardnews.com/eleventh-coast-guard-national-security-cutter-named-for-elizebeth-smith-friedman/2020/07/07/; See also https://content.govdelivery.com/accounts/USDHSCG/bulletins/293c4ec

[6] David Kahn, *The Reader of Gentlemen's Mail: Herbert O. Yardley and the Birth of American Codebreaking* (New Haven: Yale University Press, 2004), 237.

good job of using what he did know. He was a much better entrepreneur, organizer, leader, and manager than Friedman. He was a better salesman and storyteller. Yardley also had a pretty good grasp of the history of cryptology, although again, not as good as Friedman's.

Yardley did not really embrace machine cryptography and did not seem to be particularly interested in it. Early on, Yardley ignored the development of new cipher machines and he never developed any techniques for breaking cipher machine cryptograms. While he occasionally would write things in support of cipher machines, notably calling them "unbreakable," he never really learned much about them, nor did he have any desire to because cipher machines were all about creating more secure crypto systems and Yardley only had eyes for cryptanalysis. In his mind, that was where all the glory was. Yardley's clear strengths and where he really did outshine Friedman were in organization, management, and personnel. His employees for the most part admired him, and a number of them had a great deal of affection for him. Friedman's employees, on the other hand, respected him, but affection was generally not there.

Overall, Yardley had lots of talent, including as a salesman and storyteller; he could almost always get people to do what he wanted them to do. He was charming and magnetic and inspired his subordinates to do the hard work and obtain the information that his superiors in the State and War Departments needed. Overall, right up until 1931, his workers and superiors praised him and his accomplishments. However, he was also much more concerned about himself, money, and women than he was about any particular job he was doing. So, while his contributions to the creation of modern American cryptology in the early twentieth century are many, they are all very nearly overshadowed by his character flaws. However, this criticism misses Yardley's greatest contribution to American cryptology. Yardley was the one who demanded and worked hard to create America's first permanent organization to provide intelligence information to the US government. Regardless of the fact that his original organization did not survive, the idea of the Cipher Bureau did and that idea moved forward in the SIS and its follow-on agencies right up to the National Security Agency.

Where Yardley saw cryptanalysis as his key to fame and fortune in cryptology, Friedman was the opposite. Early in his career, he delved deeply into cryptanalysis and moved it decisively into the twentieth century by bringing new statistical and other mathematical tools to the table. He then spent many years designing cipher machines and improvements to existing cipher machines because for many of those years his main job was not cryptanalysis, but cryptography—making new crypto systems to protect the Army's signals. His more than 20 patents are a testimony to his long arc of designing improvements for the Army's crypto systems. Friedman loved cryptology for its own sake; it was a beautiful, complex problem to solve.

For Yardley, cryptology was the means of breaking out of the small Midwestern town where he grew up and moving into a larger, more exciting world. Yardley was much less troubled by any ethical issues regarding communications security and cryptanalysis than Friedman was. In fact, he was generally less troubled with ethics and morals in any sphere. Intercepting people's messages, decrypting government documents, and interfering with diplomatic negotiations did not bother Yardley at all. He saw all the undercover and clandestine operations of the intelligence agencies as a means to the end of providing his side with the upper hand. It was also the way that he could move up in the world of military cryptology and earn more money and get more notice. That was more important than the ethical issues of spying on other governments and people.

Yardley had quite a number of flaws; he was insecure and envious of those who were in the inner circle when he was not—no matter what inner circle it was. He was a self-promoter and occasionally took credit for things he did not do. He inflated his own accomplishments almost constantly, and in his fiction he is the hero he writes about and the hero he always wanted to be. He was almost certainly unfaithful to his first wife, he gambled and drank, possibly to excess. He seemed to be insensitive to other peoples' feelings, mostly because he was usually just thinking of himself. He was much more interested in enriching himself than his Cipher Bureau or his profession. To quote David Kahn, "While Friedman became the wave of the future, Yardley languished, and so did his agency."[7]

That said, Yardley was basically honest, and it is likely he never betrayed his country. Time after time there were people who remarked on Yardley's honesty, patriotism, and dedication to his job. This is not the personality of someone who sells his country's secrets to an enemy for a measly $7000. As David Kahn eloquently puts it, Yardley was a rotter, not a traitor.[8]

As to his most infamous book, the evidence points to the conclusion that Yardley published *The American Black Chamber* for two reasons. First, he was unemployed and needed money. He had a skill set that did not allow him to find gainful employment that would feed his family. And second, he really did believe that the closure of the Cipher Bureau was a grave mistake and would put the United States and especially the State Department in a disadvantageous position with respect to all the other major powers in the world. Here, Yardley and Friedman would agree. They both felt that the time was long past for the United States to have a professional, permanent cryptanalytic organization that would be able to provide solid and accurate information to the executive branch and help guide American policy and protect America's interests.

One can also say that Yardley was motivated by a desire for revenge on the agencies that shut down his Cipher Bureau, forced him out of his admittedly cushy job, and left him unemployed. And that is exactly what Friedman and his friends did say about Yardley, and continued to say about him through the 1930s and 1940s. It was those arguments that kept Yardley out of the American cryptologic establishment and got him kicked out of a pretty successful run for the Canadians. However, revenge just does not seem to be the major motivation behind publishing his tell-all

---

[7] Kahn, *ROGM*, 93.

[8] Kahn, *ROGM*, 241; John F. Dooley, "Was Herbert O. Yardley a Traitor?," *Cryptologia* 35, no. 1 (January 2011): 1–15.

book. Yardley himself said multiple times that he held no grudge against anyone in the intelligence community or the State Department.

And despite the fact that he could no longer obtain employment with the US government as a cryptologist, Yardley kept reinventing himself, although not always successfully. However, he was always open to new opportunities. He started two more cryptanalytical bureaus in two different countries, he wrote both fiction and nonfiction magazine articles and books, wrote radio plays, turned himself into a general contractor, ran a restaurant, was an accomplished speaker, and he became a successful bureaucrat. And as his swan song, he wrote what was the classic introduction to playing poker for at least 30 years, *The Education of a Poker Player*.

Both Yardley and Friedman reached their peaks as professionals and reached a point where they stopped moving forward as their discipline and the organizations they created passed them by. Neither Friedman nor Yardley clearly foresaw the impact that modern digital computers would have on the field of cryptology. Friedman felt the use of business machines and computers was limited to the work of creating codes and uncovering statistical patterns in messages for cryptanalysis. He found no use for computers in everyday life (in his defense, this was the early to mid-1960s), and he did not think that computers would ever replace pencil-and-paper cryptanalytic techniques. He was always of the opinion that digital computers would never replace humans in the inspirational work required for cryptanalysis. Yardley never delved deeply into cipher machines in order to understand the mathematics and theory behind them as Friedman had, and he disparaged the use of accounting and computing machines even for such chores as frequency analysis.

As to their personal relationship, it was always a delicate dance. At its beginnings during World War I, they were competitors, and Yardley clearly had the upper hand early on because he was the one who had convinced the Army to begin a cryptanalytic bureau in the first place. Friedman was hindered by being out on the Illinois prairie, working for an authoritarian boss, and not being assertive enough in this early part of his cryptologic career to push his ideas forward with vigor. After the war, there will always be the question of what might have happened if the Friedmans and Yardley had ended up working together in the Cipher Bureau. During the 1920s, both men were at the top of their game, Yardley in charge of the Cipher Bureau and Friedman becoming increasingly the "go-to" person for all things cryptologic in the War Department. During this decade, the men approached each other more as equals than at any other time in their relationship. At this point, their friendship ripened a bit and they became more cordial, sharing information, cryptanalytic tips, and discussing mysteries like the Voynich manuscript. They visited each other, dined together, and even went to baseball games. They felt more free to ask for the others' opinion and help on work matters. They shared friends, notably John Manly and Charles Mendelsohn. It is interesting to speculate on how their relationship would have evolved if the Army and Henry Stimson had not closed down Yardley's Cipher Bureau and given Friedman the upper hand both professionally and personally. Surely, there would still have been conflict, and it may be the case that Yardley's lax attitude toward his Bureau would have doomed him within a few years in any case. Friedman was clearly more ambitious than Yardley by this time, and that would likely have frayed their friendship no matter what else happened. Friedman would continue his ascent to the top of the cryptologic establishment for nearly another decade before technology and his nascent mental health problems would slow and eventually stop his rise.

Regardless, their two lives would have continued to be interesting and exciting.

Undoubtedly, Friedman was the premier cryptologist of his day, and Yardley was an excellent organizer, storyteller, and manager. Between the two of them, they raised American cryptology into a world-class endeavor. By the time the United States entered World War II, their work was nearly done, and the organizations that they had helped to create went into the war strong and came out even stronger. That work certainly lived on long after their friendship died.

# Appendix: A Few Words of Cryptology

Secret writing is known to have existed for close to 3000 years. As individual civilizations reached certain levels of literacy, the idea that some messages should be kept secret emerged, and cryptology arose. Every discipline has its own vocabulary, and cryptology is no different. This appendix does not attempt to be a comprehensive glossary of cryptology but rather gives the basic definitions and explanations of cryptologic words that appear in this book.

*Cryptology* is the study of secret writing. Governments, the military, and people in business have wanted to keep their communications secret ever since the invention of writing. Spies, lovers, and diplomats all have secrets and are desperate to keep them as such. There are typically two ways of keeping secrets in communications. *Steganography* hides the very existence of the message. Secret ink, microdots, and using different fonts on printed pages are all ways of hiding a message from prying eyes. In the computer age, messages can be hidden inside images in documents simply by encoding the message into the bits of the image. *Cryptology*, on the other hand, makes absolutely no effort to hide the presence of the secret message. Instead, it transforms the message into something unintelligible so that if the enemy intercepts the message, they will have no hope of reading it. A *cryptologic system* performs a *transformation* on a message called the *plaintext*. The transformation renders the plaintext unintelligible and produces a new version of the message—the *ciphertext*. This process is *encoding* or *enciphering* the plaintext. A message in ciphertext is typically called a *cryptogram*. To reverse the process, the system performs an inverse transformation to recover the plaintext. This is known as *decoding* or *deciphering* the ciphertext. Because cryptologic systems typically use a *key* as part of the encryption process, if a recipient does not have the key used to create a ciphertext, they must use other techniques to recover either the key or the message. This is called *decrypting* a ciphertext.

The science of cryptology can be broken down in a couple of different ways. One way to look at cryptology is that it is concerned with both the creation of cryptologic systems, called *cryptography*, and with techniques to uncover the secret message

J. F. Dooley, *The Gambler and the Scholars*, History of Computing,
https://doi.org/10.1007/978-3-031-28318-5

from the ciphertext, called *cryptanalysis*. A person who attempts to break crypto-grams is a *cryptanalyst*. A complementary way of looking at cryptology is to divide things up by the types and sizes of grammatical elements used by the transforma-tions that different cryptologic systems perform. The standard division is by the size of the element of the plaintext used in the transformation. A *code* uses variable-sized elements that have meaning in the plaintext language, such as syllables, words, or phrases. On the other hand, a *cipher* uses fixed-sized elements such as single letters or two- or three-letter groups that are divorced from meaning in the language. For example, a code will have a single *codeword* for the plaintext "stop", say 37761, while a cipher will transform each individual letter as in X=s, A=t, V=o, and W=p to produce XAVW. While ciphers have a small fixed number of substitution ele-ments—the letters of the alphabet—codes typically have thousands of words and phrases to substitute. Additionally, the cryptanalysis methods of the two types of systems are quite different.

Table A.1 provides a visual representation of the different dimensions of cryptology.

A *code* always takes the form of a book where a numerical or alphabetic *code-word* is substituted for a complete word or phrase from the plaintext. *Codebooks* can have thousands of codewords. Most codes are used to hide the contents of their messages. However, some codes are used merely for efficiency. In telegraphy, many companies use *commercial codes* that comprise lists of commonly used words or phrases. Commercial codes were popular throughout the nineteenth and early twen-tieth centuries because telegraph companies would charge for telegrams by the word. Companies that wanted to use telegraph services would encode messages into a commercial code to make them shorter and thus save on telegram charges.

There are two types of codes, 1-part and 2-part. In a *1-part code*, there is a single pair of columns used for both encoding and decoding plaintext. The columns are usually sorted so that lower numbered codewords will correspond to plaintext words or phrases that are lower in the alphabetic ordering. For example,

1234   centenary

1235   centennial

1236   centime

1237   centimeter

1238   central nervous system

**Table A.1**   The two dimensions of cryptology

|          | Cryptography                          | Cryptanalysis                                   |
|----------|---------------------------------------|-------------------------------------------------|
| Codes    | 1-part, 2-part                        | Theft, Spying, Probable word, Context           |
| Ciphers  | Substitution, Transposition, Product  | Classical, Statistical, Mathematical, Brute-Force |

Note that because both the codewords and the words they represent are in ascending order, the *cryptanalyst* will instantly know that a codeword of 0823 must begin with an alphabetic sequence before "ce," thus eliminating many possible codeword–plaintext pairs.

A *2-part code* eliminates this problem by having two separate lists, one arranged numerically by codewords and one arranged alphabetically by the words and phrases the codewords represent. Thus, one list (the one that is alphabetically sorted) is used for encoding a message, and the other list (the one that is numerically sorted by codeword) is used for decoding messages. For example, the list used for encoding might contain

| | |
|---|---|
| artillery support | 18312 |
| attack | 43110 |
| company | 13927 |
| headquarters | 71349 |
| platoon strength | 63415 |

while the decoding list would have

| | |
|---|---|
| 13927 | company |
| 18312 | artillery support |
| 43110 | attack |
| 63415 | platoon strength |
| 71349 | headquarters |

Note that not only are the lists not compiled either numerically or alphabetically, but there are also gaps in the list of codewords that further confuse the cryptanalyst.

Cryptanalyzing codes is very difficult because there is usually no logical connection between a codeword and the plaintext code or phrase it represents. With a 2-part code, there is normally no sequence of codewords that represent a similar alphabetical sequence of plaintext words. Because a code will likely have thousands of codeword–plaintext pairs, the cryptanalyst must slowly uncover each pair and over time create a dictionary that represents the code. The correspondents may make this job easier by using standard salutations or formulaic passages such as "Nothing to report" or "Weather report from ship AD2342." If the cryptanalyst has access to enough ciphertext messages, then sequences such as this can allow her to uncover plaintext. Nevertheless, this is a time-consuming endeavor. In many cases where codes are used, the encoded message is then also enciphered, so the codewords are enciphered when the message is transmitted. This is known as a *superencipherment*. The superencipherment must be removed before the original coded message can be decrypted. Superencipherments add to the difficulty of *cryptanalyzing* a coded message. Finally, most codebooks also include a number of codewords that do not mean anything. They are merely there to add extra codewords to the ciphertext and to make decryption more difficult for the cryptanalyst. These special codewords are called *nulls*.

Of course, the best way to break a code is to steal the codebook! This has happened a number of times in history, much to the dismay of the owner.

Codes have issues for users as well. Foremost among them is distributing all the codebooks to everyone who will be using the code. Everyone who uses a code must have exactly the same codebook and must use it in exactly the same way. This limits the usefulness of codes because the codebook must be available whenever a message needs to be encoded or decoded. The codebook must also be kept physically secure, ideally locked up when not in use. If one copy of a codebook is lost or stolen, then the code can no longer be used, and every copy of the codebook must be replaced. This makes it difficult to give codebooks to spies who are traveling in enemy territory, and it also makes it very difficult to use codes in battlefield situations where they could be easily lost.

This brings us to *ciphers*. Ciphers also transform plaintext into ciphertext, but unlike codes, ciphers use small, fixed-length language elements that are divorced from the meaning of the word or phrase in the message. Ciphers come in two general categories. *Substitution ciphers* will replace each letter in a message with a different letter or symbol using a mapping called a *cipher alphabet*. The second type will rearrange the letters of a message but will not substitute new letters for the existing letters in the message. These are known as *transposition ciphers*.

Substitution ciphers can use just a single cipher alphabet for the entire message; these are known as *monoalphabeticsubstitution ciphers*. Cipher systems that use more than one cipher alphabet for encryption are *polyalphabeticsubstitution ciphers*. In a polyalphabetic substitution cipher, each plaintext letter is replaced with more than one *cipher letter*, making the job significantly harder for the cryptanalyst. The cipher alphabets may be *standard alphabets* that are shifted using a simple key. For example, a shift of seven results in

```
Plain:       abcdefghijklmnopqrstuvwxyz
Cipher:      HIJKLMNOPQRSTUVWXYZABCDEFG
```

The word *attack* becomes HAAHJR. Alternatively, they may be *mixed alphabets* that are created by a random rearrangement of the standard alphabet as in

```
Plain:       abcdefghijklmnopqrstuvwxyz
Cipher:      BDOENUZIWLYVJKHMFPTCRXAQSG
```

The word *enemy* is then transformed into NKNJS.

All substitution ciphers depend on the use of a *key* to tell the user how to rearrange the standard alphabet into a cipher alphabet. If the same key is used to both encipher and decipher messages, then the system is called a *symmetric key cipher system*. In this type of system, a function Enc is used to encipher a message, and the inverse of Enc, a function we call Dec, is used to decipher the resulting cryptogram. The way a symmetric cipher system works is illustrated as follows. Suppose Alice wants to send a message to Bob. Alice encrypts the message M using Key K, which she shares with Bob. The resulting ciphertext C = Enc(M,K) is transmitted over an insecure communications channel (e.g., the postal system, the internet) and received by Bob. The enemy, in the form of Eve, may intercept the ciphertext as it is transmitted. When Bob receives the message, he deciphers it using the inverse of the enciphering algorithm and the same Key that Alice used, retrieving the original message, so M = Dec(C, K).

Similar to the security of a codebook, the security of the key is of paramount importance for cipher systems. And just like a codebook, everyone who uses a particular cipher system must also use the same key. For added security, keys are changed periodically, so while the basic substitution cipher *system* remains the same, the key is different. Distributing new keys to all the users of a cryptologic system leads to the *key management problem*. Management of the keys is a problem because a secure method must be used to transmit the keys to all users. Typically, a courier distributes a book listing all the keys for a specific time period, say a month, and each user has instructions on when and how to change keys. Just like codebooks, any loss or compromise of the key book will jeopardize the system. However, unlike codebooks, if a key is lost, the underlying cipher system is not compromised, and merely changing the key will restore the integrity of the cipher system.

While most cipher systems substitute one letter at a time, it is also possible to substitute two letters at a time, called a *digraphic* cipher system, or more than two, called a *polygraphic* cipher system. A substitution cipher that provides multiple substitutions for some letters but not others is a *homophonic cipher* system. It is also possible to avoid the use of a specific cipher alphabet and use a book to identify either individual letters or words. This is known as a *book* or *dictionary cipher* (or *code* if entire words are used). The sender specifies a particular page, column, and word in the book for each word or letter in the plaintext, and the recipient looks up the corresponding numbers to decrypt the message. For example, a codeword of 0450233 could specify page 045, column 02, and word 33 in that column. Naturally, the sender and recipient must each have a copy of exactly the same edition of the book in order for this system to work. However, carrying a published book or dictionary is significantly less suspicious than carrying a codebook.

Starting in the Middle Ages, most governments—and it was governments that had a monopoly on cryptology for most of history—used a combination of a code and a cipher called a *nomenclator*. Nomenclators were composed of a small codebook with only special words encoded. These words were normally proper names, place names, and names related to a particular topic such as commerce or diplomacy. In the enciphered message, only these words would be encoded; the rest of the message would be enciphered, normally using a monoalphabetic or homophonic cipher system.

*Transposition ciphers* transform the plaintext into ciphertext by rearranging the letters of the plaintext according to a specific rule and key. Transposition is a *permutation* of all the letters of the plaintext message performed according to a set of rules and guided by the key. Since the transposition is a permutation, there are n! different ciphertexts for an n-letter plaintext message. The simplest transposition cipher is the *columnar transposition*. This comes in two forms: *complete columnar transposition* and *incomplete columnar transposition*. In both of these systems, the plaintext is written horizontally in a rectangle that is as wide as the length of the key. As many rows as are needed to complete the message are used. In the complete columnar transposition, once the plaintext is written out, the columns are then filled with nulls until they are all the same length. For example,

```
s e c o n d
d i v i s o
n a d v a n
c i n g t o
n i g h t x
```

The ciphertext is then pulled off by columns according to the key and divided into groups of five for transmission. If the key for this cipher was 321654, then the ciphertext would be

```
cvdng eiaii sdncn donox nsatt oivgh
```

An *incomplete columnar transposition cipher* does not require complete columns and thus leaves off the null characters, resulting in columns of differing lengths and making the system harder to cryptanalyze. Another type of columnar transposition cipher is *route transposition*. In route transposition, one creates the standard rectangle of the plaintext, but then one takes off the letters using a rule that describes a route through the rectangle. For example, one could start at the upper left-hand corner and describe a spiral through the plaintext, going down one column, across a row, up a column and then back across another row. Another method is to take the message off by columns but alternate going down and up each column.

*Cryptanalysis* of ciphers falls into four different but related areas. The *classical* methods of cryptanalysis rely primarily on language analysis. The first thing the cryptanalyst must know about a cryptogram is the language in which it is written. Knowing the language is crucial because different languages have different language characteristics, notably letter and word frequencies and sentence structure. It turns out that if you look at several pieces of text that are several hundred words long and written in the same language that the frequencies of all the letters used turn out to be about the same in all of the texts. In English, the letter "e" is used approximately 13% of the time, "t" is used approximately 10% of the time, and so on, down to "z," which is used less than 1% of the time. Therefore, the cryptanalyst can count each of the letters in a cryptogram and obtain a hint of what the substitutions may have been. This is known as *frequency analysis*.

Beginning in the early twentieth century, cryptanalysts began applying *statistical* tests to messages in an effort to discern patterns in more complicated cipher systems, particularly in polyalphabetic systems. Later in the twentieth century, with the introduction of machine cipher systems, cryptanalysts began applying more *mathematical analysis* to the systems, particularly bringing to bear techniques from combinatorics, algebra, and number theory. Finally, with the advent of computers and computer cipher systems in the late twentieth century, cryptanalysts had to fall back on *brute-force*, guessing to extract the key from a cryptogram or, more likely, a large set of cryptograms.

# Photo and Illustration Credits

All images listed are in the public domain in the United States, except where cited. All images created by the US government or employees of the US government are in the public domain, as are all published images created before 1928. All images from the National Cryptologic Museum are also in the public domain.

Fig. 2.1 Herbert Yardley in the 1930s. (US government photo. From https://media. defense.gov/2018/Sep/03/2001961288/-1/-1/0/180903-D-IM742-2111.JPG)

Fig. 2.2 Parker Hitt, 1918. (US Army photo. From U.S. National Archives, 111-SC-23349)

Fig. 2.3 State Department Blue Code page. (From page 226 of "Masked Dispatches" by Ralph Weber, Published by National Security Agency)

Fig. 2.4 Ralph Van Deman. (From US Army photo. https://api.army.mil/e2/c/ images/2017/04/10/473346/original.jpg)

Fig. 3.1 William Friedman at his desk, 1924. (From Library of Congress)

Fig. 3.2 Riverbank Laboratories Garden and Windmill. (From the author's collection)

Fig. 3.3 George Fabyan in the "Hell Chair." (Courtesy of the Kane County Fabyan Villa Museum. https://www.ppfv.org/fabyan-villa-museum)

Fig. 3.4 Elizebeth Smith Friedman at Riverbank Laboratories, 1917. (Courtesy of George Marshall Foundation Library)

Fig. 3.5 Joseph Mauborgne. (U.S. Army Photo. From Wikimedia Commons)

Fig. 3.6 William and Elizebeth Friedman Wedding, 1917. (Courtesy of George Marshall Foundation Library)

Fig. 4.1 Lt. Herbert Yardley, 1917. (US Army photo. From National Archives and Records Administration)

Fig. 4.2 John Matthews Manly, 1918. (From John Manly Collection, courtesy of University of Chicago Library Special Collections)

Fig. 4.3 Edith Rickert, 1904. (Courtesy of the New York Public Library)

Fig. 4.4 William and Elizebeth Friedman, 1917. (Courtesy of the George Marshall Foundation Library)

J. F. Dooley, *The Gambler and the Scholars*, History of Computing, https://doi.org/10.1007/978-3-031-28318-5

Fig. 4.5 "Knowledge is Power" photo, 1918. (Courtesy of the George Marshall Foundation Library)

Fig. 4.6 Pletts Cipher Device. (From the Imperial War Museum, London, UK. Used with permission)

Fig. 5.1 Herbert Yardley and J. Rives Childs at the 1919 Paris Peace Conference. (US Army photo. National Cryptologic Museum VPF007-003. Also Signal Corps photo 111-SC-155490)

Fig. 7.1 Edna Ramsier, 1919. (David Kahn Collection, National Cryptologic Museum Library. Courtesy of Edna's sister Lillian Meyer)

Fig. 7.2 Universal Trade Code Title Page, 1921. (From https://archive.org/stream/universaltradeco00code#page/n691/mode/2up)

Fig. 8.1 William Friedman with AT&T cipher machine, 1920. (Courtesy of the George Marshall Foundation Library)

Fig. 8.2 Vogel Cipher Disk, 1922. (From Riverbank Publication #22, page 3, 1922)

Fig. 10.1 Folio 78r from the Voynich Manuscript. (Yale University Beinecke MS 408)

Fig. 10.2 M-94 cipher device. US Army photo)

Fig. 10.3 Enigma Rotors. (Public Domain from Wikimedia Commons)

Fig. 10.4 Hebern Single Rotor Machine 1921. (Computer History Museum, under Creative Commons License International 4.0)

Fig. 10.5 Agnes Meyer Driscoll c1925. (NSA Center for Cryptologic History Collection)

Fig. 10.6 William Friedman in his office, 1924. (Library of Congress LCCN2016848773)

Fig. 10.7 Friedman family picture, 1930s. (Courtesy of the George Marshall Foundation Library)

Fig. 11.1 Friedman Dinner Menu, 1929. (National Cryptologic Museum Collection)

Fig. 11.2 Frank Rowlett. (NSA photo, Center for Cryptologic History)

Fig. 11.3 Abraham Sinkov during World War II. (NSA photo, Center for Cryptologic History)

Fig. 11.4 Solomon Kullback. (NSA photo, Center for Cryptologic History)

Fig. 12.1 Herbert Yardley "Codes" article, first page, 1931. (National Security Agency Archives, Entry 9032, Herbert Yardley Collection, RG 457. National Archives and Records Administration, College Park, MD. Also DK-68-24 National Cryptologic Museum Library)

Fig. 12.2 American Black Chamber 1st edition cover. (From https://cryptobooks.org/api//index.php?action=getpicture&pictureid=271. Used with permission)

Fig. 12.3 American Black Chamber dust jacket, 1st edition. (From Richard Brisson, https://campx.org. Used with permission)

Fig. 12.4 American Black Chamber Ad, 1931. (The Coastal Artillery Journal, vol. 74, p. 395. Released into the public domain)

Fig. 13.1 Elizebeth Smith Friedman, 1937. (Washington Evening Star, June 5, 1937. From Library of Congress, https://chroniclingamerica.loc.gov/data/batches/dlc_1johns_ver01/data/sn83045462/00280601950/1937060501/0140.pdf.)

Fig. 13.2 Elizebeth Smith Friedman, 1934. (U.S. Department of Defense, https://media.defense.gov/2018/Sep/03/2001961221/-1/-1/0/180903-D-IM742-2028.JPG.)

Fig. 14.1 *Yardleygram* example, Liberty Magazine, July 1933. (Permission from Richard Brisson)

Fig. 14.2 *Yardleygrams* book dust jacket, 1932. (From the author's collection)

Fig. 14.3 *The Blonde Countess* dust jacket, 1933. (From the author's collection)

Fig. 14.4 Studio publicity photo of Herbert Yardley and Rosalind Russell. (David Kahn Collection, National Cryptologic Museum Library.)

Fig. 15.1 Kryha Cipher machine. (Wikimedia Commons. From 1971markus@wikimedia.de under a Creative Commons 4.0 International license)

Fig 15.2 SIS group picture, 1935. (NSA Center for Cryptologic History Collection (National Cryptologic Museum VPF001-001))

Fig. 15.3 Leo Rosen, 1930s. (NSA photo)

Fig. 15.4 Genevieve Grotjan, 1935. (Yearbook photo from SUNY-Buffalo. Courtesy of the University Archives, State University of New York at Buffalo)

Fig. 16.1 Herbert Yardley in China, 1940. (David Kahn Collection, 90-13, National Cryptologic Museum Library)

Fig. 16.2 Yardley and Students in China, 1939. (David Kahn Collection, 90-13, National Cryptologic Museum Library)

Fig. 16.3 Herbert Yardley in Los Angeles, July 1940. (David Kahn Collection, 91-14, National Cryptologic Museum Library)

Fig. 16.4 Edna Ramsier in Canada, 1941. (David Kahn Collection, 84-03, National Cryptologic Museum Library)

Fig. 16.5 Edna Ramsier in Canada, October 1941. (David Kahn Collection, 90-13, National Cryptologic Museum Library)

Fig. 17.1 Arlington Hall, 1943. (US Army photo)

Fig. 17.2 SIS members at Arlington Hall, 1944. (US Army photo)

Fig. 17.3 M-134 cipher machine, c1934. (NSA photo)

Fig. 17.4 SIGABA Rotor Cage. (U.S. Patent Office photo)

Fig. 17.5 SIGABA patent #6,175,625, Figure #1. (U.S. Patent Office photo)

Fig. 17.6 SIGABA exhibit in National Cryptologic Museum

Fig. 17.7 M-209B cipher machine. (Wikimedia Commons M209B-IMG_0553-0559-0560.jpg)

Fig. 20.1 William and Elizebeth Friedman, 1957. (Courtesy of the George Marshall Foundation Library)

Fig. 20.2 William and Elizebeth Friedman headstone in Arlington National Cemetery. (US Army photo)

Fig. 20.3 Edna and Herbert Yardley in Washington, 1950s. (David Kahn Collection, National Cryptologic Museum Library)

Fig. 20.4 Herbert Yardley playing poker, c1957. (David Kahn Collection, National Cryptologic Museum Library)

Fig. 20.5 Edna and Herbert Yardley headstone in Arlington National Cemetery. (US Army photo)

# Bibliography

Alvarez, Al. "Introduction to 'The Education of a Poker Player' by Herbert O. Yardley." In *The Education of a Poker Player*, 160. Harpenden, United Kingdom: Oldcastle Books, Ltd., 1990.

Alvarez, David. *Allied and Axis Signals Intelligence in World War II*. London, UK: Frank Cass Publishers, 1999. https://www.routledge.com/Allied-and-Axis-Signals-Intelligence-in-World-War-II-1st-Edition/Alvarez/p/book/9781315038247.

Alvarez, David J. *Secret Messages: Codebreaking and American Diplomacy, 1930–1945*. Modern War Studies. Lawrence, Kan.: University Press of Kansas, 2000.

Anonymous. An Act for the Protection of Government Records, 18 U.S. Code § 952, Diplomatic Codes and Correspondence (1933). https://www.law.cornell.edu/uscode/text/18/952.

Anonymous. An Act for the Protection of Government Records, "Basic Cryptanalysis Field Manual." Department of the Army, 1990. No. 34-40-2. U.S. Army, Washington, DC. https://irp.fas.org/doddir/army/fm34-40-2/.

Anonymous. An Act for the Protection of Government Records, "Code Expert's MS. On Japan Seized: Federal Men Impound Work by H.O. Yardley, Wartime Head of Cryptographic Bureau." *New York Times*. February 21, 1933, sec. News. https://timesmachine.nytimes.com/timesmachine/1933/02/21/105114636.html?pageNumber=3.

Anonymous. An Act for the Protection of Government Records. "Eleventh Coast Guard National Security Cutter Named for Elizebeth Smith Friedman." *Coast Guard News*, July 7, 2020. https://coastguardnews.com/eleventh-coast-guard-national-security-cutter-named-for-elizebeth-smith-friedman/2020/07/07/.

Anonymous. An Act for the Protection of Government Records. "European Axis Signal Intelligence in World War II As Revealed by 'TICOM' Investigations and by Other Prisoner of War Interrogations and Captured Material, Principally German." TICOM. Washington, DC: Army Security Agency, May 1, 1946. National Security Agency. https://www.nsa.gov/portals/75/documents/news-features/declassified-documents/european-axis-sigint/volume_1_synopsis.pdf.

Anonymous. An Act for the Protection of Government Records. Memorandum. "Extract from: R.I.P. No. 98 Re: Friedmans Publicity." Memorandum, April 5, 1943. William F. Friedman Collection: Correspondence, Memoranda, and Personnel File Records, NSA/CSS DocRefID A66485. National Security Agency. https://www.nsa.gov/portals/75/documents/news-features/declassified-documents/friedman-documents/reports-research/FOLDER_377/41754199079335.pdf.

© The Editor(s) (if applicable) and The Author(s), under exclusive license to Springer Nature Switzerland AG 2023
J. F. Dooley, *The Gambler and the Scholars*, History of Computing,
https://doi.org/10.1007/978-3-031-28318-5

Anonymous. An Act for the Protection of Government Records. "Hearings Before the Joint Committee on the Investigation of the Pearl Harbor Attack: Part 10." Transcript. Hearings Before the Joint Committee on the Investigation of the Pearl Harbor Attack. Washington, DC: United States Congress, February 1946. U.S. Archives, College Park, MD. http://www.ibiblio. org/pha/congress/Vol10.pdf.

Anonymous. An Act for the Protection of Government Records. "Manly vs. Collier's. Facts." George Marshall Foundation Research Library, 1927. William Friedman Collection.

Anonymous. An Act for the Protection of Government Records. "Ruth Wilson." Women in American Cryptology, 2021. https://nsa-demo.dod.afpims.mil/About-Us/Current-Leadership/ Article-View/Article/1620974/ruth-wilson/.

Arnold, Jonathan P. "Herbert O. Yardley: Gangbuster." *Cryptologia* 12, no. 1 (1988): 62–64.

Ayres, Leonard P. *The War With Germany: A Statistical Summary*. Washington, DC: Government Printing Office, 1919. https://archive.org/details/warwithgermanyst00ayreuoft.

Bacon, Sir Francis. *The Advancement of Learning*. Edited by Joseph Devey. New York, NY: P. F. Collier & Son Company, 1901. http://oll.libertyfund.org/titles/bacon-the-advancement-of-learning.

Bamford, James. *Body of Secrets: Anatomy of the Ultra-Secret National Security Agency*. New York, NY: Anchor Books (Random House), 2001. www.anchorbooks.com.

Bar, Lt. Robert. "SIGNAL INTELLIGENCE DISCLOSURES IN THE PEARL HARBOR INVESTIGATION: A Study Based on the Hearings before the Joint Committee on the Investigation of the Pearl Harbor Attack." Technical Report. Washington, DC: Army Security Agency, July 1, 1947. National Cryptologic Museum Library. https://drive.google.com/ drive/u/0/folders/1jQ64F-fsqBCZDV6_ErtQ4zCiVqw_VXWy.

Barker, Wayne G., ed. *The History of Codes and Ciphers in the United States during the Period Between the Wars: Part II. 1929 - 1939 (SRH-001)*. Cryptographic Series 54. Laguna Park, CA: Aegean Park Press, 1989.

———, ed. *The History of Codes and Ciphers in the United States during the Period between the World Wars, Part I. 1919–1929 (SRH-001, Part 3.)*. Cryptographic Series 22. Laguna Hills, Calif.: Aegean Park Press, 1979a.

———, ed. *The History of Codes and Ciphers in the United States during World War I, Volume 2 (SRH-001)*. Cryptographic Series 21. Laguna Beach, Calif.: Aegean Park Press, 1979b.

———, ed. *The History of Codes and Ciphers in the United States Prior to World War I (SRH-001)*. Cryptographic Series 20. Laguna Hills, Calif.: Aegean Park Press, 1978.

Barr, Thomas H. *Invitation to Cryptology*. Upper Saddle River, NJ: Prentice Hall, 2002.

Bauer, Craig P. *Secret History: The Story of Cryptology*. Boca Raton, FL: CRC Press, 2013.

Beesly, Patrick. *Room 40: British Naval Intelligence 1914–1918*. New York, NY: Harcourt, Brace, Jovanovich, 1982.

Bellovin, Steven M. "Vernam, Mauborgne, and Friedman: The One-Time Pad and the Index of Coincidence." In *The New Codebreakers*, 40–66. Lecture Notes in Computer Science 9100. Berlin, Heidelberg: Springer-Verlag, 2016. https://doi.org/10.1007/978-3-662-49301-4_4.

Bennett, LCDR Michael E. "Guardian Spies: The Story of Coast Guard Intelligence in World War II." *American Intelligence Journal* 27, no. 1 (Fall 2009): 16–23.

Boersma, Stuart. "Elizebeth Smith Friedman and One Example of a Prohibition Era Encryption System." *Cryptologia* 46, no. 1 (January 2022a): 12.

———. "Elizebeth Smith Friedman's Recovery of the Wiring of Two Rotors from an Enigma D Machine." *Cryptologia* 46, no. 5 (September 2022b): 1–25. https://doi.org/10.1080/0161119 4.2022.2109944.

Bratzel, John F., and Leslie B. Rout. "Abwehr Ciphers in Latin America." *Cryptologia* 7, no. 2 (March 1983): 132–44. https://doi.org/10.1080/0161-118391857865.

Brumley, Mary Jane. "Local Matron Decodes Cryptic Messages for Treasury Department." *The Evening Star*. June 5, 1937, sec. Women's Features. Chroniclingamerica.loc.gov. Library of Congress. https://chroniclingamerica.loc.gov/data/batches/dlc_1johns_ver01/data/sn8304546 2/00280601950/1937060501/0140.pdf.

Bryden, John. *Best-Kept Secret: Canadian Secret Intelligence in the Second World War.* Toronto, Canada: Lester Publishing, 1993.

Buckley, Thomas H. *The United States and the Washington Conference, 1921–1922.* Knoxville, TN: University of Tennessee Press, 1970.

Budiansky, Stephen. *Battle of Wits: The Complete Story of Codebreaking in World War II.* New York: Free Press, 2000a.

———. "The Difficult Beginnings of US-UK Codebreaking Cooperation." *Intelligence & National Security* 15, no. 2 (2000b): 49–73.

Burke, Colin. "Agnes Meyer Driscoll vs. the Enigma and the Bombe." *Self-Published on the Web,* 2011a, 132. https://userpages.umbc.edu/~burke/driscoll1-2011.pdf.

———. "What OSS Black Chamber? What Yardley? What 'Dr.' Friedman? Ah, Grumbach? Or Donovan's Folly," September 9, 2011b, 29. http://userpages.umbc.edu/~burke/whatoss-black.pdf.

Callimahos, Lambros D. "Q.E.D.-2 Hours, 41 Minutes." *NSA Technical Journal* XVIII, no. 4 (1973): 13–34. https://www.nsa.gov/Portals/70/documents/news-features/declassified-documents/tech-journals/qed.pdf.

Chapman, John. "No Final Solution: A Survey of the Cryptanalytical Capabilities of German Military Agencies, 1926–35." *Intelligence and National Security* 1, no. 1 (January 1986): 14–47.

Chenery, William L. Letter to John M. Manly. "Letter to John M. Manly," September 16, 1927. William Friedman Collection, Item 811. George Marshall Foundation Research Library.

Childs, J. Rives. *Before the Curtain Falls.* Indianapolis, IN: Bobbs-Merrill Company Publishers, 1932.

———. "Childs to Kahn Re: Yardley," August 27, 1963a. David Kahn Collection, National Cryptologic Museum Library. (Comments on "Education of a Poker Player")

———. "Childs to Kahn Re: Yardley," June 27, 1964. DK 55-42. David Kahn Collection, National Cryptologic Museum Library.

———. "Childs to Kahn Re: Yardley Friedman," October 12, 1963b. DK55-30. David Kahn Collection, National Cryptologic Museum Library.

———. "Childs to WFF Re: Trench Code," September 1, 1931a. Friedman Collection, George Marshall Foundation Research Library, Lexington, VA.

———. "Childs to WFF Re: Yardley & Trench Code," October 15, 1931b. Friedman Collection, George Marshall Foundation Research Library, Lexington, VA.

———. *Foreign Service Farewell: My Years in the Near East.* Ashland, VA: University Press of Virginia, 1969.

———. *Let the Credit Go: The Autobiography of J. Rives Childs.* New York, NY: K.S. Giniger Co.: Distributed by F. Fell, 1983.

Churchill, General Marlborough. "Churchill to HOY," October 4, 1920. RG457, Entry 9032, National Security Agency, Herbert Yardley Collection. National Archives, College Park, MD.

———. "Churchill to Manly," December 11, 1919a. John M. Manly Archives, University of Chicago Library.

———. "Churchill to Mauborgne," December 31, 1919b. RG457, Entry 9032, National Security Agency. National Archives, College Park, MD.

———. Memorandum. "HOY & Churchill: HOY Salary." Memorandum, July 23, 1919c. RG 457, Entry 9032, National Security Agency (also in SRH-161). National Archives, College Park, MD.

———. "Preservation of Secrecy with Regard to Code and Cipher Work." U.S. Army Military Intelligence, April 16, 1919d.

"ACoS, G-2 to China Military Attache Re: Yardley," March 13, 1940. Herbert Yardley Collection, RG 457, Entry 9032, G-2/10039-299. National Archives and Records Administration, College Park, MD.

Churchill, General Marlborough, and Herbert O. Yardley. "Churchill to Mauborgne Re: AT&T Cipher Machine," August 8, 1918. RG457, Herbert O. Yardley Collection. National Archives, College Park, MD.

Clark, Ronald. *The Man Who Broke Purple*. Boston: Little, Brown and Company, 1977.

Curtin, Tom. Interview with Tom Curtin Re: Herbert Yardley, 1959. RG 457, Entry 9032, National Security Agency. National Archives and Records Administration, Herbert Yardley Collection, College Park, MD.

Denniston, Alaistair. "Denniston Visit to U.S. Signal Corps, August 1941." Meeting Minutes. Washington, DC: National Archives and Records Administration, RG 457, Historic Cryptologic Collection, Box 949, Folder 2714, August 16, 1941.

Denniston, Robin. "Yardley's Diplomatic Secrets." *Cryptologia* 18, no. 2 (April 1994): 81–127. https://doi.org/10.1080/0161-119491882784.

Dooley, John F. "1929–1931: A Transition Period in U.S. Cryptologic History." *Cryptologia* 37, no. 1 (January 1, 2013): 84–98. https://doi.org/10.1080/01611194.2012.687432.

———.. "Another Yardley Mystery." *Cryptologia* 33, no. 3 (2009): 276. http://www.informaworld.com/10.1080/01611190902894938.

———. *Codes, Ciphers and Spies: Tales of Military Intelligence in World War I*. New York, NY: Springer Verlag, 2016. https://www.johnfdooley.com.

———. *History of Cryptography and Cryptanalysis: Codes, Ciphers, and Their Algorithms*. History of Computing. London, UK: Springer-Verlag, 2018. https://www.johnfdooley.com.

———. "John Matthews Manly and Edith Rickert: Cryptologists." In *Collaborative Humanities Research and Pedagogy: The Networks of John Matthews Manly and Edith Rickert*, edited by Ellison, Katherine and Kim, Susan., 396. New York, NY: Palgrave Macmillan, 2022. https://link.springer.com/book/10.1007/978-3-031-05592-8.

———. "The SIS and Cipher Machines: 1930–1940." Presented at the 14th Biennial NSA Center for Cryptologic History Symposium, Ft. George Meade, MD, October 2013.

———. "Was Herbert O. Yardley a Traitor?" *Cryptologia* 35, no. 1 (January 2011): 1–15.

Dooley, John F., and Elizabeth Anne King. "John Matthews Manly: The Collier's Articles." *Cryptologia* 38, no. 1 (January 2014): 77–88. https://doi.org/10.1080/01611194.2013.797049.

Dooley, John F., and Yvonne I. Ramirez. "Who Wrote The Blonde Countess? A Stylometric Analysis of Herbert O. Yardley's Fiction." *Cryptologia* 33, no. 2 (2009): 108–17. http://www.informaworld.com/smpp/title~content=t725304178~db=all, http://www.informaworld.com/smpp/content~content=a910230065~db=all~jumptype=rss.

Ensign, Eric S. "Intelligence in the Rum War at Sea, 1920–1933." Master's Thesis, Joint Military Intelligence College, 2001. https://apps.dtic.mil/docs/citations/ADA485809, https://apps.dtic.mil/dtic/tr/fulltext/u2/a485809.pdf.

Erskine, Ralph. "William Friedman's Bletchley Park Diary: A Different View." *Intelligence and National Security* 22, no. 3 (June 2007): 367–79.

Fabyan, George. "Fabyan to Churchill Re: Mauborgne&AT&T," September 2, 1919a. RG 457, Entry 9032, National Security Agency. National Archives, College Park, MD.

———. "Fabyan to Churchill Re: Mauborgne&AT&T," September 6, 1919b. RG 457, Entry 9032, National Security Agency. National Archives, College Park, MD.

———. "Fabyan to Churchill Re: WFF&HOY," August 6, 1919c. RG 457, Entry 9032, National Security Agency. National Archives, College Park, MD.

———. "Fabyan to ESF," November 2, 1918a. ESF Collection, Box 1, Folder 41. George Marshall Foundation Research Library, Lexington, VA.

———. "Fabyan to ESF," November 7, 1918b. ESF Collection, Box 1, Folder 41. George Marshall Foundation Research Library, Lexington, VA.

———. "Fabyan to ESF," December 9, 1918c. ESF Collection, Box 1, Folder 41. George Marshall Foundation Research Library, Lexington, VA.

———. "Fabyan to ESF Re: WFF," January 6, 1919d. ESF Collection, Box 2, Folder 20. George Marshall Foundation Research Library, Lexington, VA.

———. "Fabyan to MID," March 15, 1917. William Friedman Collection, Item 734. George Marshall Foundation Research Library, Lexington, VA.

———. Letter to William F. Friedman. "Fabyan to WFF," November 13, 1918d. William F. Friedman Collection, Item 840. George Marshall Foundation Research Library, Lexington, VA.

————. Letter to William F. Friedman. "Fabyan to WFF," November 14, 1918e. ESF Collection, Box 2, Folder 20. George Marshall Foundation Research Library, Lexington, VA.

————. Letter to William F. Friedman. "Fabyan to WFF," December 16, 1918f. Elizebeth Smith Friedman Collection, Box 2, Folder 20. George Marshall Research Library, Lexington, VA.

————. Letter to William F. Friedman. "Fabyan to WFF," January 6, 1919e. William Friedman Collection, Item 734. George Marshall Foundation Research Library, Lexington, VA.

————. Letter to William F. Friedman. "Fabyan to WFF," March 12, 1919f. William Friedman Collection, Item 734. George Marshall Foundation Research Library, Lexington, VA.

Fagone, Jason. *The Woman Who Smashed Codes.* New York, NY: William Morrow, 2017.

Farago, Ladislas. *The Broken Seal: The Story of "Operation Magic" and the Pearl Harbor Disaster.* New York: Random House, 1967.

Finnegan, John Patrick, and Romana Danysh. *Military Intelligence.* Army Lineage Series, CMH Pub 60-13. Washington, DC: Center of Military History, U.S. Army, 1998. https://history.army.mil/html/books/060/60-13-1/cmhPub_60-13-1.pdf.

Fleming, Ian. "Introduction to 'The Education of a Poker Player' by Herbert O. Yardley." In *The Education of a Poker Player: Including Where and How One Learns to Win.* London, UK: Jonathan Cape, 1959.

Ford, Col. Stanley H. Letter to General Gibbs. "Responsibility for the Solution of Intercepted Enemy Secret Communications in War," April 4, 1929. Herbert Yardley Collection, RG 457, also SRH-038. National Archives, College Park, MD.

Friedman, Elizebeth Smith. "Autobiography of Elizebeth Smith Friedman." Memoir. Lexington, VA, 1966. https://archive.org/details/ElizebethFriedmanPartialAutobiography.

————. *Codebreaking.* Manuscript. Washington, DC, 1925. https://ia600803.us.archive.org/8/items/ESFCodebreakingBook/ESF%20codebreaking%20book.pdf.

————. "Decoded Messages Used in 'I'm Alone' Smuggling Operations." Washington, DC: National Archives and Records Administration, 1933a. RG26, Entry 297, Box 76, File 8. National Archives and Records Administration, College Park, MD. https://cryptocellar.org/files/PURPLE_History.pdf.

————. Memorandum. "ESF Letter to Wild Bill Donovan." Memorandum, December 29, 1941. ESF Collection. George Marshall Foundation Research Library, Lexington, VA. https://archive.org/details/@jason_fagone.

————. "Memorandum upon a Proposed Central Organization at Coast Guard Headquarters for Performing Cryptanalytic Work," November 1930. Elizebeth Smith Friedman Collection, Box 5, File Folder 6. George Marshall Research Library, Lexington, VA.

————. "Personnel File: Elizebeth Smith Friedman." National Personnel Records Center, 1946. VF 148-2. National Cryptologic Museum Library.

————. "Pure Accident." *The Arrow of Pi Beta Phi,* February 1933b. ESF Collection, Box 12, Folder 9. George Marshall Research Library, Lexington, VA. https://archive.org/details/ElizebethFriedmanArticlesInTheArrow.

————. "Undated Handwritten Notes Relating to the Manly Collier's Articles (Probably by Elizebeth Friedman)." Friedman Collection, George Marshall Foundation Research Library, Lexington, VA, 1969.

Friedman, William F. "The Hindu Cipher." Signal Corps Information Bulletin. Washington, DC: Office of the Chief Signal Officer, U.S. Army, December 1, 1921. VF096-015. National Cryptologic Museum Library, Ft. Meade, MD.

————. Alphabetical Chart. U.S. Patent Office 1,608,509. Washington, DC, filed January 7, 1926, and issued November 30, 1926.

————. "Analysis of a Mechanico-Electrical Cryptograph, Part I." Washington, DC: War Department, 1934.

————. "Analysis of a Mechanico-Electrical Cryptograph, Part II." Washington, DC: War Department, 1935. https://archive.org/details/41709409074875.

———. "Analysis of a Problem in Enciphered Code." Technical Report. Washington, DC: Code and Cipher Section, Signal Corps, U.S. Army, September 1924. Item 951. William Friedman Collection, George Marshall Research Library.

———. Annotated Copy of *The American Black Chamber* (Item 604). Lexington, VA: George Marshall Foundation Research Library, 1931a.

———, ed. Articles on Cryptography and Cryptanalysis from the Signal Corps Bulletin. Washington, DC: United States Printing Office, 1942.

———. *Elements of Cryptanalysis*. Training Pamphlet No. 3. Washington, DC: Office of the Chief Signal Officer, 1923.

———. "Field Codes Used by the German Army during the World War (SRMA-012)." 209. Washington, DC: War Department, February 5, 1919. RG457, Friedman Collection. National Archives, College Park, MD.

———. Method of Electrical Signaling. U.S. Patent Office 1,694,874. Washington, DC, filed July 10, 1922, and issued December 11, 1928.

———. "Notes on a Conversation with Herbert O. Yardley," February 26, 1933. William F. Friedman Collection, Item 840. George Marshall Research Library, Lexington, VA.

———. Printing Telegraph System. U.S. Patent Office 1,530,660. Washington, DC, filed July 26, 1922, and issued March 24, 1925.

———. Secret Signaling Apparatus for Automatically Enciphering and Deciphering Messages. U.S. Patent Office 1,522,775. Washington, DC, filed April 14, 1922, and issued January 13, 1925.

———. "WFF Resignation," December 16, 1920. RG457, Entry 9032, National Security Agency. National Archives, College Park, MD.

———. Letter. "WFF to ESF Re: Fabyan." Letter, December 8, 1918. Elizabeth Smith Friedman Collection, Box 2, Folder 19. George Marshall Research Library, Lexington, VA.

———. "WFF to ESF Re: Fabyan," October 7, 1918. ESF Collection, Box 2, Folder 17. George Marshall Research Library, Lexington, VA.

———. "WFF to ESF Re: Fabyan," October 14, 1918. ESF Collection, Box 2, Folder 17. George Marshall Research Library, Lexington, VA.

———. "WFF to ESF Re: Fabyan," October 15, 1918. ESF Collection, Box 2, Folder 17. George Marshall Research Library, Lexington, VA.

———. Letter. "WFF to ESF Re: Yardley." Letter, December 16, 1918. Elizabeth Smith Friedman Collection, Box 2, Folder 19. George Marshall Research Library, Lexington, VA.

———. "WFF to ESF Re: YardleyChilds," December 29, 1918. ESF Collection, Box 2, Folder 19. George Marshall Research Library, Lexington, VA.

———. Letter. "WFF to ESF Re: Fabyan." Letter, December 11, 1918. Elizabeth Smith Friedman Collection, Box 2, Folder 19. George Marshall Research Library, Lexington, VA.

———. Letter. "WFF to Fabyan." Letter, December 9, 1918. Elizabeth Smith Friedman Collection, Box 2, Folder 19. George Marshall Research Library, Lexington, VA.

———. Letter to Herbert O. Yardley. "WFF to HOY," May 1, 1919. ESF Collection, Box 2, Folder 20. George Marshall Research Library, Lexington, VA.

———. Letter to Herbert O. Yardley. "WFF to HOY," May 18, 1919. ESF Collection, Box 2, Folder 20. George Marshall Research Library, Lexington, VA.

———. Letter to Herbert O. Yardley. "WFF to HOY," June 27, 1919. RG 457, Entry 9032, National Security Agency. National Archives, College Park, MD.

———. Letter to Herbert O. Yardley. "WFF to HOY," July 2, 1919. RG 457, Entry 9032, National Security Agency. National Archives, College Park, MD.

———. Letter to Herbert O. Yardley. "WFF to HOY," July 13, 1919. RG 457, Entry 9032, National Security Agency. National Archives, College Park, MD.

———. Letter to Herbert O. Yardley. "WFF to HOY," August 22, 1919. RG 457, Entry 9032, National Security Agency. National Archives, College Park, MD.

———. Correspondence. "WFF to Manly." Correspondence, May 2, 1924. William F. Friedman Collection. George Marshall Foundation Research Library, Lexington, VA.

———. "WFF to Manly," February 12, 1921. John Matthews Manly Collection, Series 2, Box 2, Folder 12. University of Chicago Library.

———. "WFF to Manly," June 10, 1921. John Matthews Manly Collection, Series 2, Box 2, Folder 12. University of Chicago Library.

———. "WFF to Manly," February 4, 1922. William F. Friedman Collection. George Marshall Foundation Research Library, Lexington, VA.

———. Letter to John M. Manly. "WFF to Manly," June 30, 1931. John Matthews Manly Collection. University of Chicago Library.

———. Letter to John M. Manly. "WFF to Manly," November 21, 1931. John Matthews Manly Collection. University of Chicago Library.

———. Letter to Frank Moorman and Parker Hitt. "WFF to Moorman, Hitt, & Vogel," May 16, 1931. Item 840. Friedman Collection, George Marshall Foundation Research Library, Lexington, VA.

———. Personal Letter. "WFF to Roberta Wohlstetter." Personal Letter, September 17, 1969. Box 14, Folder 12. Elizabeth Smith Friedman Collection, George Marshall Research Library, Lexington, VA.

———. "William Friedman TICOM Diary." Army Security Agency, 1945a. https://archive.org. https://archive.org/details/WFFTourOfShatteredEurope.

Friedman, William F., and Louis M. Evans. Secret Signaling System Employing Apparatus for Automatically Enciphering and Deciphering Messages. U.S. Patent Office 1,516,180. Washington, DC, filed June 5, 1922, and issued November 18, 1924.

Friedman, William F., and Elizabeth S. Friedman. *The Shakespearean Ciphers Examined*. London: Cambridge University Press, 1958.

Friedman, William F., Parker Hitt, Capt. A. J. McGrail, and Frank Moorman. "Series of Letters from Hitt, Moorman, McGrail to/from Friedman Re: Publication of ABC & SEP Articles," 1931b. RG457, NSA, Entry 9032, Herbert Yardley Collection, RG 457. National Archives, College Park, MD.

Friedman, William F., and Charles Mendelsohn. "Notes on Code Words." *American Mathematical Monthly* 39, no. 7 (September 1932): 394–409. https://www.jstor.org/stable/2300386.

Friedman, William F., and Charles J. Mendelsohn. "The Zimmermann Telegram of January 16, 1917 and Its Cryptographic Background." Washington, DC: Office of the Chief Signal Officer, 1938. https://www.nsa.gov/news-features/declassified-documents/friedman-documents/assets/files/lectures-speeches/FOLDER_198/41766889080599.pdf.

Gaines, Helen Fouche. *Elementary Cryptanalysis; a Study of Ciphers and Their Solution*. Boston: American Photographic Publishing Company, 1939.

Gilbert, James L. *World War I and the Origins of U.S. Military Intelligence*. Lanham, MD: Rowman & Littlefield Publishing Group, Ltd., 2015. https://rowman.com/ISBN/9780810884601/World-War-I-and-the-Origins-of-U.S.-Military-Intelligence.

Gilliam, Paul. "Inventory of William F. Friedman/Materials Taken From His House." Inventory. Washington, DC: National Security Agency, December 30, 1958. William F. Friedman Collection: Correspondence, Memoranda, and Personnel File Records, NSA/CSS DocRefID A99794. National Security Agency. https://www.nsa.gov/Portals/75/documents/news-features/declassified-documents/friedman-documents/correspondence/ACC4282/41783989082303.pdf.

Greenfield, Amy Butler. *The Woman All Spies Fear: Code Breaker Elizebeth Smith Friedman and Her Hidden Life*. New York, NY: Random House, 2021. rhcbooks.com.

Gylden, Yves. "The Contribution of the Cryptographic Bureaus in the World War." Washington, DC: National Security Agency, 1931. SRH-335. NSA Archives.

Hahn, Emily. *China to Me*. Philadelphia, PA: Blakiston Company, 1944.

Hamer, David H. "G-312: An Abwehr Enigma." *Cryptologia* 24, no. 1 (January 2000): 41–55.

Hannah, Theodore M. "Frank B. Rowlett – A Personal Profile." *Cryptologic Spectrum* 11, no. 2 (Spring 1981a): 4–21.

———. "The Many Lives of Herbert O. Yardley." *NSA Cryptologic Spectrum* 11, no. 4 (Fall 1981b): 5–29. http://www.nsa.gov/public_info/_files/cryptologic_spectrum/many_lives.pdf.

Harrison, Leland, and General Marlborough Churchill. "Recommendation for a Permanent Cryptologic Organization." January 29, 1919. RG59, Entry 349, Box 200, Confidential File 121. National Archives, College Park, MD.

Haswell, John H. "State Department Cipher." U. S. Government Printing Office, 1899.

"Herbert Yardley Personnel Records 1942–1952." Records. St. Louis, MO: Office of Personnel Management, February 29, 1996. DK 079-014. David Kahn Collection, National Cryptologic Museum Library.

Hilton, Stanley E. *Hitler's Secret War in South American 1939–1945*. Baton Rouge, LA: Louisiana State University Press, 1981.

Historian, Army Security Agency. "The History of Army Strip Cipher Devices." History narrative. Special Research Histories. Washington, DC: Army Security Agency, November 1948. archive.org. https://ia800509.us.archive.org/12/items/ticom/Srh-366UsArmyStripCiphers1934-1947.pdf.

Hitt, Parker. *Manual for the Solution of Military Ciphers*. SRH-004. Fort Leavenworth, KS: Press of the Army Service Schools, 1916.

Hsiao, Major Sin-ju Pu. "Hsiao to HOY Re: Invitation to China," May 18, 1938. Edna Yardley Papers. National Cryptologic Museum Library, Ft. Meade, MD.

Ingles, H. C. "U.S. Army Converter M-228." Memorandum. Washington, DC: U.S. Army Signal Corps, May 19, 1944. National Security Agency, National Cryptologic Museum.

Jennings, Christian. *The Third Reich Is Listening: Inside German Codebreaking 1939–1945*. Oxford, England, UK: Osprey Publishing, 2018. www.ospreypublishing.com.

Jensen, Kurt F. *Cautious Beginnings: Canadian Foreign Intelligence, 1939–1951*. Vancouver, BC, Canada: University of British Columbia Press, 2008.

Jones, Leonard T. "History of OP-20-GU (Coast Guard Unit of NCA)." Memorandum. Washington, DC: United States Navy, Naval Security Group, October 16, 1943. RG 38, box 115, 5750/193. CNSG Library. https://archive.org/details/HistoryOfOP20GU.

Juran, J. M. "Juran Letter Re: Friedman Dinner 1929," March 30, 1992. David Kahn Collection. National Cryptologic Museum Library.

Kahn, David. "Charles Jastrow Mendelsohn and Why I Envy Him." *Cryptologia* 28, no. 1 (January 2004a): 1–17. https://doi.org/10.1080/0161-110491892737.

———. *Hitler's Spies: German Military Intelligence in World War II*. New York: Macmillan, 1978a.

———. *How I Discovered World War II's Greatest Spy and Other Stories of Intelligence and Code*. Boca Raton, FL: CRC Press, 2014. http://www.crcpress.com.

———. *Kahn on Codes : Secrets of the New Cryptology*. New York: Macmillan, 1983.

———. "Nuggets from the Archive: Yardley Tries Again." *Cryptologia* 2, no. 2 (1978b): 139–43.

———. "The Annotated 'The American Black Chamber.'" *Cryptologia* 9, no. 1 (1985): 1–37.

———. *The Codebreakers: The Story of Secret Writing*. New York: Macmillan, 1967.

———. *The Reader of Gentlemen's Mail: Herbert O. Yardley and the Birth of American Codebreaking*. New Haven: Yale University Press, 2004b.

Kawakami, K. K. "Editorial in the 'Japanese American' Newspaper (SRH-038)." College Park, MD: NARA (Record Group 457, Entry 9037), August 5, 1931.

Kelley, Stephen J. "The SIGCUM Story: Cryptographic Failure, Cryptologic Success." *Cryptologia* 21, no. 4 (October 1997): 289–316. https://doi.org/10.1080/0161-119791885940.

Kozaczuk, Wladyslaw. *Enigma : How the German Machine Cipher Was Broken, and How It Was Read by the Allies in World War Two*. Foreign Intelligence Book Series. Frederick, MD: University Publications of America, 1984.

Kruh, Louis. "Book Review: In the Name of Intelligence: Essays in Honor of Walter Pforzheimer." *Cryptologia* 19, no. 1 (January 1995): 97–101. https://doi.org/10.1080/0161-119591883791.

———. "Cipher Equipment." *Cryptologia* 1, no. 2 (April 1977): 143–49. https://doi.org/10.1080/0161-117791832878.

———. "STIMSON, THE BLACK CHAMBER, AND THE 'GENTLEMEN'S MAIL' QUOTE." *Cryptologia* 12, no. 2 (April 1, 1988): 65–89. https://doi.org/10.1080/0161-118891862819.

———. "The Inventions of William F. Friedman." *Cryptologia* 2, no. 1 (January 1978): 38–61. https://doi.org/10.1080/0161-117891852776.

Layton, Edwin T., Roger Pineau, and John Costello. *And I Was There: Pearl Harbor and Midway - Breaking the Secrets*. New York, NY: William Morrow & Company, 1985.

Lebensohn, Zigmond. "Letter to Ronald Clark from William Friedman's Psychiatrist," May 10, 1976. Box 13, File 30. George Marshall Foundation Research Library, Elizebeth Friedman Collection.

Lyle, Katie Letcher, and David Joyner. *Divine Fire: Elizebeth Friedman, Cryptanalyst (The 1910s–1930s)*. Lexington, KY: CreateSpace Independent Publishing Platform, 2015.

Mackinnon, Colin. "William Friedman's Bletchley Park Diary: A New Source for the History of Anglo-American Intelligence Cooperation." *Intelligence and National Security* 20, no. 4 (December 2005): 654–69. https://doi.org/10.1080/02684520500426602.

Macrakis, Kristie. *Prisoners, Lovers, & Spies: The Story of Invisible Ink from Herodotus to Al-Qaeda*. New Haven, CT: Yale University Press, 2014.

Mahony, Francis A. "Interrogation of Edmund Von Thermann, German Ambassador to the Argentine 1934 to 1942." Interrogation Transcript. Washington, DC: Department of State, June 6, 1945. RG 59, Entry 188, Box 26. National Archives and Records Administration, College Park, MD. http://lawcollections.library.cornell.edu/nuremberg/catalog/nur:01190.

Mallon, Winifred. "Woman Wins Fame as Cryptanalyst." *New York Times*. February 12, 1938, sec. Society. New York Times Archive. https://www.nytimes.com/1938/02/13/archives/woman-wins-fame-as-cryptanalyst-mrs-friedman-lent-by-coast-guard-to.html.

Manly, John M. "Articles for Collier's Magazine," 1927a. Item 811. Friedman Collection, George Marshall Foundation Research Library, Lexington, VA.

———. "Manly Letter to Voynich," July 9, 1921a. John Matthews Manly Collection, Box 2, Folder 8. University of Chicago Library.

———. Letter to Herbert O. Yardley. "Manly to HOY," January 30, 1931a. John Matthews Manly Collection, Box 1, Folder 19. University of Chicago Library.

———. Correspondence. "Manly to WFF." Correspondence, April 1, 1924. University of Chicago Library.

———. "Manly to WFF," February 23, 1921b. William F. Friedman Collection, George Marshall Foundation Research Library, Lexington, VA.

———. "Manly to WFF," January 26, 1922. Friedman Collection, George Marshall Foundation Research Library, Lexington, VA.

———. Letter to William F. Friedman. "Manly to WFF," July 24, 1931b. William F. Friedman Collection, Item 840. George Marshall Foundation Research Library, Lexington, VA.

———. Letter to William F. Friedman. "Manly to WFF," August 28, 1931c. William F. Friedman Collection, Item 840. George Marshall Foundation Research Library, Lexington, VA.

———. Letter to William F. Friedman. "Manly to WFF," December 12, 1931d. Friedman Collection, George Marshall Foundation Research Library, Lexington, VA.

———. "Manly-Churchill Letters Re: SRH-030," October 19, 1932. RG457, Entry 9031, Box #1, Folder 10. National Archives, College Park, MD.

———. "Roger Bacon and the Voynich MS." *Speculum* 6, no. 3 (July 1931e): 345–91. https://doi.org/10.2307/2848508.

———. "Roger Bacon's Cipher Manuscript." *The American Review of Reviews* 64, no. 1 (July 1921c): 105–6.

———. "The Most Mysterious Manuscript in the World: Did Roger Bacon Write It and Has the Key Been Found?" *Harper's Monthly Magazine*, July 1921d.

———. "Transcript of John M. Manly Testimony in the Trial of Lothar Witzke (Aka Pablo Waberski)." United States Army, August 14, 1918. William Friedman Collection, Item 811. George Marshall Foundation Research Library.

———. "Waberski," 1927b. Item 811. Friedman Collection, George Marshall Foundation Research Library, Lexington, VA.

Manly, John M., and Edith Rickert. *The Text of The Canterbury Tales*. 10 vols. Chicago, IL: University of Chicago Press, 1940.

Manly, John M., and Herbert O. Yardley. "A History of the Code and Cipher Section during the First World War." College Park, MD: National Archives, Record Group 457, 1919.

Manly, John M., Herbert O. Yardley, and William F. Friedman. "Achievements of the Cipher Bureau (MI-8) During the First World War: Documents by Major Herbert O. Yardley," May 25, 1945. National Security Agency, Herbert Yardley Collection. https://www.nsa.gov/news-features/ declassified-documents/yardley-collection/.

Marshall, George. Memorandum. "Gen. Marshall to Adm. King Re: Combining SIGINT." Memorandum, August 18, 1945. National Security Agency. https://www.nsa.gov/portals/75/ documents/news-features/declassified-documents/nsa-60th-timeline/pre-nsa/19450818_ PreNSA_Doc_3978305_SignalIntelligence.pdf.

Mauborgne, Joseph. "Mauborgne to WFF," October 16, 1920a. RG457, Entry 9031, Box #1, Folder 10. National Archives, College Park, MD.

———. "Mauborgne to WFF," November 15, 1920b. RG457, Entry 9031, Box #1, Folder 10. National Archives, College Park, MD.

———," November 27, 1920c. Item 734, Folder 1. Friedman Collection, George Marshall Foundation Research Library, Lexington, VA.

———," December 16, 1920d. RG457, Entry 9031, Box #1, Folder 10. National Archives, College Park, MD.

Mendelsohn, Charles. "Studies in German Diplomatic Codes Used During the World War." War Department, Washington, DC: Office of the Chief Signal Officer, Government Printing Office, 1937.

Mendelsohn, Charles J. "Mendelsohn Review of 'The American Black Chamber,'" 1931. William F. Friedman Collection, Item 840. George Marshall Research Library, Lexington, VA.

Moorman, Frank. "Moorman to ACoS Re: Yardley," September 9, 1931. William Friedman Collection, George Marshall Research Library.

———. "Wireless Intelligence." Presented at the Meeting of Officers of the Military Intelligence Division, Washington, DC, February 13, 1920.

Moran, Christopher. *Company Confessions: Secrets, Memoirs, and the CIA*. New York, NY: St. Martin's Press, 2015.

Mucklow, Timothy. "The SIGABA/ECM II Cipher Machine: 'A Beautiful Idea.'" Fort George G. Meade, MD: Center for Cryptologic History, National Security Agency, 2015. https://www. nsa.gov/about/cryptologic-heritage/historical-figures-publications/publications/assets/files/ sigaba-ecm-ii/The_SIGABA_ECM_Cipher_Machine_A_Beautiful_Idea3.pdf.

Mundy, Liza. *Code Girls: The Untold Story of the American Women Code Breakers of World War II*. New York, NY: Hachette Books, 2017.

Munson, Richard. *George Fabyan*. North Charleston, SC: CreateSpace Independent Publishing Platform, 2013.

Nedved, Gregory J. "Herbert O. Yardley Revisited: What Does the New Evidence Say?" *Cryptologia* 44, no. 5 (June 25, 2020): 1–27. https://doi.org/10.1080/01611194.2020.1767706.

New York Times. "Kato's View Personal Declares Tokugawa." *New York Times*. November 30, 1921a, sec. News.

———. "Pacific Agreement Near: All Powers Represented in a Declaration of Policy." *New York Times*. December 6, 1921b, sec. News.

———. "Ratio Agreement Depends on Japan." *New York Times*. November 30, 1921c, sec. News.

O'Toole, G.J.A. *Honorable Treachery: A History of U.S. Intelligence, Espionage, and Covert Action from the American Revolution to the CIA*. New York, NY: Atlantic Monthly Press, 1991.

Ozimek, Timothy K. "Captain Charles Stevens Root." *American Intelligence Journal* 35, no. 1 (2018): 41–47. https://www.jstor.org/stable/10.2307/26497148.

Parker, 1st. Lt. Will V. "Orders, No. 35." Headquarters, Service Company No. 17, Signal Corps, October 22, 1924. Item 1809. William Friedman Collection, George Marshall Research Library.

Pforzheimer, Walter. "Herbert O. Yardley, The American Black Chamber, Japanese Diplomatic Messages." Memorandum. Washington, DC: CIA, December 12, 1967. https://www.scribd.com/doc/79284275/CIA-Herbert-Yardley-Spy-Memorandum#download.

Powell, J. A. *The Greatest Work of Sir Francis Bacon*. Geneva, IL: Riverbank Laboratories, 1916.

Reeds, James. "William F. Friedman's Transcription of the Voynich Manuscript." Murray Hill, NJ: AT&T Bell Telephone Laboratories, September 7, 1994.

———. "William F. Friedman's Transcription of the Voynich Manuscript." *Cryptologia* 19, no. 1 (January 1995): 1–23. https://doi.org/10.1080/0161-119591883737.

Reynolds, S. Wesley. "Classified Documents in Possession of William F. Friedman." Memorandum, December 5, 1958. William F. Friedman Collection: Correspondence, Memoranda, and Personnel File Records, NSA/CSS DocRefID A99778. National Security Agency. https://www.nsa.gov/portals/75/documents/news-features/declassified-documents/friedman-documents/correspondence/ACC4282/41783879082293.pdf.

———. "Retrieval of Classified Agency Documents from Home of W.F. Friedman." Memorandum, January 2, 1959. William F. Friedman Collection: Correspondence, Memoranda, and Personnel File Records, NSA/CSS DocRefID A99780. National Security Agency. https://www.nsa.gov/Portals/75/documents/news-features/declassified-documents/friedman-documents/correspondence/ACC4282/41783909082296.pdf.

Rhodes, John Kidder. "He Solves the Secrets of Cipher Writing." *The American Magazine*, January 1925. https://doi.org/catalog.hathitrust.org/Record/000598163.

Rowlett, Frank R. "Oral History of Frank Rowlett (1974)." Oral History. NSA Oral History Collection. Ft. George G. Meade, MD: National Security Agency, Center for Cryptologic History, 1974.

———. "Oral History of Frank Rowlett (1976)." Oral History. Oral History Collection. Ft. George G. Meade, MD: National Security Agency, Center for Cryptologic History, 1976.

———. "Review of 'The Man Who Broke Purple' by Ronald Clark." *Studies in Intelligence*, 1977.

———. *The Story of Magic: Memoirs of an American Cryptologic Pioneer*. Laguna Hills, CA: Aegean Park Press, 1998.

Rowlett, Frank R., Solomon Kullback, and Abraham Sinkov. "General Solution for the ADFGVX Cipher." Washington, DC: U.S. Army Signal Intelligence Service, 1934.

Sabine, Paul E., and William F. Friedman. Apparatus for and Method of Rapid Transmission of Telegraphic Messages. U.S. Patent Office 1503250. Geneva, IL, filed August 7, 1920, and issued July 29, 1924.

Safford, Captain Laurance. "A Brief History of Communications Intelligence in the United States (SRH-149)." College Park, MD: National Archives and Records Administration, RG 457 (SRH-149), March 21, 1952.

———. "History of Invention and Development of the Mark II ECM (SRH-360)." College Park, MD: National Archives and Records Administration, October 30, 1943. SRH Files. National Cryptologic Museum Library. https://drive.google.com/drive/folders/1jQ64F-fsqBCZDV6_ErtQ4zCiVqw_VXWy.

Safford, Laurance F., and Donald W. Seiler. Control Circuits for Electric Coding Machines. U.S. Patent Office 6,175,625. Washington, DC, filed December 15, 1944, and issued January 16, 2001. https://image-ppubs.uspto.gov/dirsearch-public/print/downloadPdf/6175625.

Sakuma, Shin. "Answers to Hypothetical Questions from the Diet about Yardley's Book 'The American Black Chamber.'" Microfilm. Tokyo, 1931a. UD 29, Frames 1–28. Archives of the Japanese Ministry of Foreign Affairs, Library of Congress.

———. "Sakuma to Minister and Vice Minister, 10 June 1931, Subject: A Book Written by Yardley, the Former Chief of the Cryptographic Bureau of U.S. Army Intelligence." Washington, DC: Telegraph Section, Japanese Embassy, 1931b. UD 30, Frames 157–174. Archives of the Japanese Ministry of Foreign Affairs, Library of Congress.

Schmeh, Klaus. "Alexander von Kryha and His Encryption Machines." *Cryptologia* 34, no. 4 (January 2010): 291–300. https://doi.org/10.1080/01611194.2010.485440.

Schoenfeld, Gabriel. *Necessary Secrets: National Security, the Media, and the Rule of Law*. New York, NY: W. W. Norton & Company, Inc., 2010. https://wwnorton.com/books/9780393339932.

Sharp, Alan. "'Quelqu'un Nous Écoute': French Interception of German Telegraphic and Telephonic Communications during the Paris Peace Conference, 1919: A Note." *Intelligence and National Security* 3, no. 4 (October 1, 1988): 124–27. https://doi.org/10.1080/02684528808431974.

Sheldon, Rose Mary. *The Friedman Collection: An Analytical Guide*. Electronic. Lexington, VA: George Marshall Foundation Research Library, 1999. http://marshallfoundation.org/library/wp-content/uploads/sites/16/2014/09/Friedman_Collection_Guide_September_2014.pdf.

———. "William F. Friedman: A Very Private Cryptographer and His Collection." *Cryptologic Quarterly* 34, no. 2015–1 (January 2015): 4–29. https://www.nsa.gov/about/cryptologic-heritage/historical-figures-publications/publications/cryptologic-quarterly/.

Sherman, David J. "The First Americans: The 1941 US Codebreaking Mission to Bletchley Park." National Security Agency, 2016. Special Series, Volume 12. National Security Agency, Center for Cryptologic History.

Sims, John Carey. "The BRUSA Agreement of May 17, 1943." *Cryptologia* 21, no. 1 (January 1997): 30–38.

Smith, G. Stuart. *A Life in Code: Pioneer Cryptanalyst Elizebeth Smith Friedman*. Jefferson, NC: McFarland & Company, 2017. www.mcfarlandpub.com.

Smoot, Betsy Rohaly. "Sources and Methods: Uncovering the Story of American Cryptology in World War I." *Cryptologia* 45, no. 1 (January 2021): 81–87. https://doi.org/10.1080/0161119 4.2020.1858371.

"Stories of the Black Chamber." *Stories of the Black Chamber*. New York, NY: NBC, January 21, 1935.

Tehaan, Frederick A. "FBI Files on Herbert Yardley." Memorandum. Washington, DC: Federal Bureau of Investigation, September 7, 1942. DK 079-001. David Kahn Collection, National Cryptologic Museum Library.

Tomokiyo, Satoshi. "A Specimen of Yardley's Deciphering of Japanese Diplomatic Code Jp (1921)." *Cryptiana* (blog), June 2, 2013. http://cryptiana.web.fc2.com/code/redcipherma-chine.htm.

———. "Development of the First Japanese Cipher Machine: RED." *Cryptiana* (blog), May 20, 2014. http://cryptiana.web.fc2.com/code/redciphermachine.htm.

———. "Japanese Reaction to Yardley's 'The American Black Chamber.'" *Cryptiana* (blog), February 23, 2018. http://cryptiana.web.fc2.com/code/yardley_jp.htm.

Tunney, Thomas J., and Paul Merrick Hollister. *Throttled! The Detection of the German and Anarchist Bomb Plotters*. Boston, MA: Small, Maynard and Company, 1919. https://play.google.com/books/reader?id=bNcLAAAAYAAJ&printsec=frontcover&output=reader&authuser=0&hl=en&pg=GBS.PR8.

Twinn, Peter. "The Abwehr Enigma." In *Codebreakers: The Inside Story of Bletchley Park*, 123–31. Oxford; New York: Oxford University Press, 1993.

Vernam, Gilbert S. "Cipher Printing Telegraph Systems for Secret Wire and Radio Telegraph Communications." *Journal of the American Institute of Electrical Engineers* XLV, no. 2 (February 1926): 109–15. https://www.doc.ic.ac.uk/~mrh/330tutor/vernam.pdf.

Wakeman, Jr., Frederic. *Spymaster: Dai Li and the Chinese Secret Service*. Berkeley, CA: University of California Press, 2003.

White, Theodore H. *In Search of History: A Personal Adventure*. New York, NY: Harper & Row, Publishers, 1978.

"William Friedman TICOM Diary." Army Security Agency, 1945b. archive.org. https://archive.org/details/WFFTourOfShatteredEurope.

Winslow, Lawrence L. Personal Letter. "Winslow to Leland Harrison." Personal Letter, May 2, 1919. RG 59, Entry 349, Box 3, Folder: German Codes and Ciphers. National Archives and Records Administration, College Park, MD.

Yardley, Edna. "Oral History: Interview with Edna Yardley by NSA Historians (SRH-016)." Oral History. Ft. George Meade, MD, February 3, 1977.

Yardley, Herbert O. "Are We Giving Away Our State Secrets?" *Liberty Magazine*, December 19, 1931a.

———. "Ciphers." *The Saturday Evening Post*, May 9, 1931b, National Cryptologic Museum Library, Ft. Meade, MD, David Kahn Collection, DK 68-25.

———. "Codes." *The Saturday Evening Post*, April 18, 1931c, National Cryptologic Museum Library, Ft. Meade, MD, David Kahn Collection, DK 68-24.

———. "Cryptograms and Their Solution." *The Saturday Evening Post*, November 21, 1931d.

———. "Double Crossing America." *Liberty*, October 10, 1931e.

———. "H-27, The Blonde Woman from Antwerp." *Liberty Magazine*, April 21, 1934.

———. Memorandum. "HOY Memo: Cipher Bureau Personnel List." Memorandum, July 22, 1919. RG 457, Entry 9032, National Security Agency (also in SRH-161). National Archives, College Park, MD.

———. Letter to Rosario Candela. "HOY to Candela: Gestapo Ciphers, Sample Problems," May 5, 1942. David Kahn Collection, DK 65-29. National Cryptologic Museum Library, Ft. Meade, MD.

———. Sample Problems. Letter to General Marlborough Churchill. "HOY to Churchill Re: Japanese Code Trick," December 1, 1919a. National Security Agency, Herbert Yardley Collection. https://www.nsa.gov/news-features/declassified-documents/yardley-collection/.

———. Letter to General Marlborough Churchill. "HOY to Churchill Re: Japanese Codes," December 15, 1919b. National Security Agency, Herbert Yardley Collection. https://www.nsa.gov/news-features/declassified-documents/yardley-collection/.

———. Letter to General Marlborough Churchill. "HOY to Churchill Re: Riverbank & AT&T," August 14, 1919c. National Security Agency, Herbert Yardley Collection. https://www.nsa.gov/news-features/declassified-documents/yardley-collection/.

———. Letter to General Marlborough Churchill. "HOY to Churchill Re: WFF," August 14, 1919d. National Security Agency, Herbert Yardley Collection. https://www.nsa.gov/news-features/declassified-documents/yardley-collection/.

———. Letter to Col. Stanley H. Ford. "HOY to Colonel Ford," February 26, 1929a.

———. Letter to Edna Ramsier. "HOY to Edna Ramsier," October 27, 1938. David Kahn Collection, Box Y, Folder China. National Cryptologic Museum Library.

———. Letter to Frank Moorman. "HOY to Frank Moorman," February 28, 1922a. 6647096. NSA Archives, Herbert O. Yardley Collection. https://www.nsa.gov/news-features/declassified-documents/yardley-collection/.

———. "HOY to Locke Re: AZ and Codes," March 10, 1922b. National Security Agency, Herbert Yardley Collection. https://www.nsa.gov/news-features/declassified-documents/yardley-collection/.

———. "HOY to Locke Re: AZ and Meeth," March 15, 1922c. National Security Agency, Herbert Yardley Collection. https://www.nsa.gov/news-features/declassified-documents/yardley-collection/.

———. "HOY to Locke Re: TB & Arizona," March 8, 1922d. National Security Agency, Herbert Yardley Collection. https://www.nsa.gov/news-features/declassified-documents/yardley-collection/.

———. "HOY to Locke Re: TB & Europe," March 6, 1922e. National Security Agency, Herbert Yardley Collection. https://www.nsa.gov/news-features/declassified-documents/yardley-collection/.

———. Personal Correspondence. "HOY to Manly." Personal Correspondence, March 1931a. Manly Papers, Box 3, Folder 3. John M. Manly Archives, University of Chicago Library.

———. Personal Correspondence. "HOY to Manly." Personal Correspondence, April 13, 1931b. Manly Papers, Box 3, Folder 3. John M. Manly Archives, University of Chicago Library.

———. Personal Correspondence. "HOY to Manly." Personal Correspondence, April 30, 1931c. Manly Papers, Box 3, Folder 3. John M. Manly Archives, University of Chicago Library.

———. Letter to John M. Manly. "HOY to Manly," August 29, 1930a. John Matthews Manly Collection, Series II, Box 3, Folder 2. University of Chicago Library.

———. Letter to Frank Moorman. "HOY to Moorman," May 5, 1922f. 6647162. NSA Archives, Herbert O. Yardley Collection. https://www.nsa.gov/news-features/declassified-documents/yardley-collection/.

———. Letter to Frank Moorman. "HOY to Moorman," May 22, 1922g. 6647168. NSA Archives, Herbert O. Yardley Collection. https://www.nsa.gov/news-features/declassified-documents/yardley-collection/.

———. Letter to Frank Moorman. "HOY to Moorman," June 2, 1922h. 6647210. NSA Archives, Herbert O. Yardley Collection. https://www.nsa.gov/news-features/declassified-documents/yardley-collection/.

———. Letter to Frank Moorman. "HOY to Moorman," November 22, 1922i. 6647320. NSA Archives, Herbert O. Yardley Collection. https://www.nsa.gov/news-features/declassified-documents/yardley-collection/.

———. Letter to Frank Moorman. "HOY to Moorman," April 30, 1931d. NSA Archives, Herbert O. Yardley Collection. https://www.nsa.gov/news-features/declassified-documents/yardley-collection/.

———. Letter to Frank Moorman. "HOY to Moorman Re: Codes," March 8, 1922j. 6647112. NSA Archives, Herbert O. Yardley Collection. https://www.nsa.gov/news-features/declassified-documents/yardley-collection/.

———. "HOY to Moorman Re: Illness," February 13, 1922k. National Security Agency, Herbert Yardley Collection. https://www.nsa.gov/news-features/declassified-documents/yardley-collection/.

———. "HOY to Moorman Re: TB & Arizona," March 27, 1922l. National Security Agency, Herbert Yardley Collection. https://www.nsa.gov/news-features/declassified-documents/yardley-collection/.

———. Letter to Captain M. F. Shepherd. "HOY to Shepherd," February 24, 1931e. SRH-038, p. 133. NSA Archives, Herbert O. Yardley Collection.

———. Letter. "HOY to WFF." Letter, August 20, 1919e. RG 457, Entry 9032, National Security Agency. National Archives, College Park, MD.

———. Letter to William F. Friedman. "HOY to WFF," March 5, 1928. National Security Agency, Herbert Yardley Collection. https://www.nsa.gov/news-features/declassified-documents/yardley-collection/.

———. Letter to William F. Friedman. "HOY to WFF," March 2, 1929b. Herbert Yardley Collection, RG 457, also SRH-038. NSA Archives.

———. Letter to William F. Friedman. "HOY to WFF," April 22, 1929c. Herbert Yardley Collection, RG 457, also SRH-038. NSA Archives.

———. Letter to William F. Friedman. "HOY to WFF," April 25, 1929d. Herbert Yardley Collection, RG 457, also SRH-038. NSA Archives.

———. Letter to William F. Friedman. "HOY to WFF," April 1, 1930b. William Friedman Collection. George Marshall Foundation Research Library.

———. Letter to William F. Friedman. "HOY to WFF," April 15, 1931f. Friedman Collection, Item 840. George Marshall Foundation Research Library.

———. Letter to William F. Friedman. "HOY to WFF," April 26, 1931g. Friedman Collection, Item 840. George Marshall Foundation Research Library.

———. Letter to William F. Friedman. "HOY to WFF," April 31, 1931h. Friedman Collection, Item 840. George Marshall Foundation Research Library.

———. Telegram. "HOY to WFF FormalOffer." Telegram, July 1, 1919f. RG 457, Entry 9032, National Security Agency. National Archives, College Park, MD.

———. Letter. "HOY to WFF InitialOffer." Letter, April 28, 1919g. William Friedman Collection, Item 734. George Marshall Foundation Research Library.

———. Letter. "HOY to WFF Job2." Letter, June 16, 1919h. RG 457, Entry 9032, National Security Agency. National Archives, College Park, MD.

———. Telegram. "HOY to WFF Job3." Telegram, June 30, 1919i. RG 457, Entry 9032, National Security Agency. National Archives, College Park, MD.

———. Letter. "HOY to WFF LastChance." Letter, August 14, 1919j. RG 457, Entry 9032, National Security Agency. National Archives, College Park, MD.

———. Telegram. "HOY to WFF Re: 01AugOK." Telegram, July 14, 1919k. RG 457, Entry 9032, National Security Agency. National Archives, College Park, MD.

———. Telegram. "HOY to WFF Re: NYC Location." Telegram, July 23, 1919l. RG 457, Entry 9032, National Security Agency. National Archives, College Park, MD.

———. "Lecture Delivered to Officers of the Military Intelligence Division," January 5, 1920. RG457, Entry 9032, National Security Agency, Herbert Yardley Collection. National Archives, College Park, MD.

———. Letter to Lincoln Foster. "Letter to Mr. Lincoln Foster," June 6, 1931i. 6649178. NSA Archives, Herbert O. Yardley Collection. https://www.nsa.gov/news-features/declassified-documents/yardley-collection/.

———. Letter to Secretary of War. "Letter to Secretary of War," January 31, 1931j. Herbert Yardley Collection, RG 457, SRH-038, p. 137. National Archives and Records Administration, College Park, MD.

———. Letter to William F. Friedman. "Letter to William F. Friedman," February 1, 1931k. William Friedman Collection. George Marshall Foundation Research Library.

———. "Memo to General Dai," March 11, 1940a. U.S. National Archives, College Park, MD.

———. "Memorandum for Director, M.I.D.," May 27, 1929e.

———. "Progress Report to General Dai Li." Progress Report. College Park, MD: National Archives, Herbert Yardley Collection, RG 457, Box 56, Folder Memoranda and Letters Concerning H. O. Yardley, 1919–1940, March 1940b.

———. Red Sun of Nippon. New York: A. L. Burt Company, 1934a.

———. "Secret Inks." The Saturday Evening Post, April 4, 1931l, National Cryptologic Museum Library, Ft. Meade, MD, David Kahn Collection, DK 68-23.

———. Secret Service in America; the American Black Chamber. London: Faber & Faber limited, 1940c.

———. Shadows in Washington. Unpublished manuscript. Ft. Meade, MD, 1937.

———. "Spies Inside Our Gates." Sunday Washington Star Magazine, April 8, 1934b.

———. The American Black Chamber. Indianapolis: Bobbs-Merrill, 1931m.

———. "The Beautiful Secret Agent." Liberty Magazine, December 30, 1933.

———. The Blonde Countess. New York: Longmans, Green and Company, 1934c.

———. The Chinese Black Chamber. Boston, MA: Houghton Mifflin Company, 1983.

———. "The Commissioner Turns Cryptographer." Detective Fiction Weekly, February 17, 1934d.

———. The Education of a Poker Player: Including Where and How One Learns to Win. New York, NY: Simon and Schuster, 1957.

———. Yardleygrams. Indianapolis, IN: Bobbs-Merrill Company Publishers, 1932.

Yardley, Herbert O., and General Marlborough Churchill. "Churchill to Yardley Re: Mauborgne," September 15, 1919. Folder 490. NSA Archives, Center for Cryptologic History. https://www.nsa.gov/Portals/70/documents/news-features/declassified-documents/friedman-documents/correspondence/FOLDER_490/41783109082217.pdf.

Yardley, Herbert O. "Permanent Organization for Code and Cipher Investigation and Attack: Plans for MI-8 (SRH-161)." Washington, DC: War Department, Military Intelligence Division, May 16, 1919. RG457, Entry 9032, National Security Agency, Box 777, Folder "Origin of MI-8 1919." National Archives, College Park, MD.

Yardley, Herbert O., and Carl Grabo. Crows Are Black Everywhere. New York, NY: G. P. Putnam's Sons, 1944.

Yardley, Herbert O., and Marie Stuart Klooz. Japanese Diplomatic Secrets. Unpublished edition. Washington, DC, 1933.

Yardley, Herbert O., and John M. Manly. "From the Archives: The Achievements of the Cipher Bureau (MI-8) During the First World War; Documents by Major Herbert O. Yardley, Prepared under the Direction of the Chief Signal Officer." Cryptologia 8, no. 1 (January 1984): 62–74. https://doi.org/10.1080/0161.118491858791.

Yardley, Herbert O., and Charles Mendelsohn. *Universal Trade Code*. New York, NY: Code
   Compiling Company, 1921. https://archive.org/stream/universaltradeco00code#page/n691/
   mode/2up.
Yoshida, Isaburu. "Secret Telegram No. 48." Japanese Ministry of Foreign Affairs, March 10,
   1925. Reel UD-29, frames 72–73. Library of Congress.
Zacharias, Ellis M. *Secret Missions: The Story of an Intelligence Officer*. New York, NY:
   G.P. Putnam's Sons, 1946.
Zorpette, Glenn. "The Edison of Secret Codes." *Invention and Technology*, Summer 1994. https://
   www.inventionandtech.com/content/edison-secret-codes-1?page=full.

# Index

© The Editor(s) (if applicable) and The Author(s), under exclusive license to
Springer Nature Switzerland AG 2023
J. F. Dooley, *The Gambler and the Scholars*, History of Computing,
https://doi.org/10.1007/978-3-031-28318-5

Printed in the United States
by Baker & Taylor Publisher Services

Printed in the United States
by Baker & Taylor Publisher Services